Transregional Lordship
and the Italian Renaissance

Renaissance History, Art and Culture

This series investigates the Renaissance as a complex intersection of political and cultural processes that radiated across Italian territories into wider worlds of influence, not only through Western Europe, but into the Middle East, parts of Asia and the Indian subcontinent. It will be alive to the best writing of a transnational and comparative nature and will cross canonical chronological divides of the Central Middle Ages, the Late Middle Ages and the Early Modern Period.

Renaissance History, Art and Culture intends to spark new ideas and encourage debate on the meanings, extent and influence of the Renaissance within the broader European world. It encourages engagement by scholars across disciplines – history, literature, art history, musicology, and possibly the social sciences – and focuses on ideas and collective mentalities as social, political, and cultural movements that shaped a changing world from ca 1250 to 1650.

Series editors
Christopher Celenza, Georgetown University, USA
Samuel Cohn, Jr., University of Glasgow, UK
Andrea Gamberini, University of Milan, Italy
Geraldine Johnson, Christ Church, Oxford, UK
Isabella Lazzarini, University of Molise, Italy

Transregional Lordship and the Italian Renaissance

René de Challant, 1504-1565

Matthew Vester

Amsterdam University Press

Cover illustration: René de Challant, detail from altarpiece dated 1547-1548, by an artist close to Jakob Seisenegger. Source: Archivi dell'Assessorato Turismo, Sport, Commercio, Agricoltura e Beni culturali della Regione autonoma Valle d'Aosta – fondo Catalogo beni culturali. Photograph by Cesare Diego; used with permission of the Regione Autonoma Valle d'Aosta.

Cover design: Coördesign, Leiden
Lay-out: Crius Group, Hulshout

ISBN	978 94 6372 672 6
e-ISBN	978 90 4855 067 8
DOI	10.5117/9789463726726
NUR	685

© M. Vester / Amsterdam University Press B.V., Amsterdam 2020

All rights reserved. Without limiting the rights under copyright reserved above, no part of this book may be reproduced, stored in or introduced into a retrieval system, or transmitted, in any form or by any means (electronic, mechanical, photocopying, recording or otherwise) without the written permission of both the copyright owner and the author of the book.

Every effort has been made to obtain permission to use all copyrighted illustrations reproduced in this book. Nonetheless, whosoever believes to have rights to this material is advised to contact the publisher.

Printed and bound by CPI Group (UK) Ltd, Croydon, CR0 4YY

Table of Contents

Abbreviations	9
Acknowledgments	11
1. On the edge of the Italian Renaissance	13
The Italian Renaissance	19
The Renaissance nobility	25
Spatial analysis and mobility	35
2. René's early career to 1536	53
René's early life	53
René and Sabaudo-Swiss politics prior to 1536	61
The lordship of Valangin and the counts of Neuchâtel	68
Before the storm, 1531-1534	72
3. René's growing influence during the war years, 1536-1553	77
The invasions of 1536	77
Valangin, the Reform, and relations with the Countess of Neuchâtel	83
Political leadership and mobility during a time of uncertainty	89
Struggling for the sovereignty of Valangin, 1542-1565	98
4. René and Duke Emanuel Filibert	109
René and Emanuel Filibert	109
Vercelli capture and efforts to get released	113
The twilight of a career	116
Family matters and René's last years	122
Historiographic perspectives of René's life	130
5. Kinship and noble life	139
Kin relations	143
Relations with wives and children	147
Nobles and domestic life	153
Legal issues	167

6.	**The Challant political networks**	179
	René's network	182
	The regional scope of René's ties	182
	René's ecclesiastical network	196
	René's key subordinates	198
	Mencia's network	200
	Letters and information	206
	Relations with officials	211
7.	**Finance and brokerage**	221
	Nobles and finance	221
	René as borrower and broker	224
	The financial situation inherited by René	224
	1526-1536: Finances and Swiss negotiations	226
	Finance during the war years to 1545	229
	From the 1545 'restructuring' to the second imprisonment	234
	The financial implications of ransom	237
	Financial recovery	244
8.	**Lordship**	251
	Valangin during the war years	255
	Beaufremont	265
	René and the practice of lordship	268
	Fiefs and fiscality	268
	Sample castellany accounts: Châtillon, 1559-1560	273
	Administration of the fiefs	275
9.	**The embodiment of spatial politics**	287
	About the author	309
	Index	311

Maps and Tables

Map 1	René's transregional lands.	12
Map 2	Challant fiefs in the Valle d'Aosta.	54
Map 3	The western Swiss area, with Valangin and its villages.	67
Table 1	A simplified genealogy of the Challant.	142
Table 2	Some of René's fiefs and their castellans.	269

Figures

1. The decapitation of Saint Catherine, traditionally identified as Bianca Maria. — 58
2. The castle and *bourg* of Valangin, ca. 1786. — 83
3. Coin representing René as sovereign of Valangin. — 104
4. Mencia, Philiberte, and Isabelle. — 124
5. The courtyard of the castle of Issogne. — 164
6. A receipt sealed with René's blood. — 299

Abbreviations

ADA	Archives départementales de l'Ain (Bourg-en-Bresse, France)
ADS	Archives départementales de la Savoie (Chambéry, France)
AEN	Archives d'État de Neuchâtel (Neuchâtel, Switzerland)
AHR	Archives historiques régionales (Aosta, Italy)
AHSS	*Annales. Histoire, sciences sociales*
ANA, CT	Archivio notarile d'Aosta, Tappa di Châtillon (Aosta, Italy)
APSV	Archivio parrocchiale di St. Vincent (St. Vincent, Italy)
art.	Articolo
ASMn	Archivio di Stato di Mantova (Mantua, Italy)
AST1	Archivio di Stato di Torino, prima sezione (Turin, Italy)
ASTR	Archivio di Stato di Torino, sezioni riunite (Turin, Italy)
BCT	Biblioteca civica di Trento (Trent, Italy)
Beatrice	Beatrice of Portugal
BHR	*Bibliothèque d'humanisme et Renaissance*
BNF, Mss. Fr.	Bibliothèque nationale de France, manuscrits français (Paris)
Boyvin	*Mémoires de Boyvin du Villars* in *Choix de chroniques et mémoires sur l'histoire de France*, ed. J.A.C. Buchon (Paris: Librairie Charles Delagrave, 1884)
BSBS	*Bollettino storico-bibliografico subalpino*
cat.	catégorie / categoria
Ch III	Charles III of Savoy
DBI	*Dizionario biografico degli italiani*
DHS	*Dictionnaire historique de la Suisse*
'Diverse lettere al Duca Carlo 3°'	AST1, NS, mz. 1 bis, no. 31, 'Diverse lettere al Duca Carlo 3°, ed al Maresciallo di Savoja sulli movimenti delle Truppe de Bernesi,'
EF	Emanuel Filibert of Savoy
EHR	*English Historical Review*
FC	Fonds Challant
FCC	Fonds du Conseil des Commis
FHS	*French Historical Studies*

Fornaseri	Giovanni Fornaseri, *Le lettere di Renato di Challant, governatore della Valle d'Aosta a Carlo II ed a Emanuele Filiberto* (Turin: Deputazione Subalpina di Storia Patria, 1957)
'Histoire généalogique'	AST1, Duché d'Aoste, mz. 3, Challant, no. 18, 'Histoire généalogique de la maison de Challant par l'Archevêque Madruz de Trente comte de Challant' (1638)
HJ	*The Historical Journal*
IGTDS	Inventaire générale des titres du duché de Savoie
Jeanne	Jeanne de Hochberg, Duchess of Longueville and Countess of Neuchâtel
JFH	*Journal of Family History*
JIH	*The Journal of Interdisciplinary History*
JMH	*The Journal of Modern History*
LP	Lettere di particolari
MSI	*Miscellanea di storia italiana*
mz.	Mazzo
NS	Negoziazioni cogli Svizzeri
PD	Protocolli ducali
PP	*Past and Present*
Recueil	AST1, Cité et Duché d'Aoste, mz. 1 d'addizione, no. 8, '1522 en 1657. Recueil des Matieres plus essentielles de tems en tems traittées dans le Conseil des Commis du Duché d'Aoste sous les respectifs secretariats; avec insertion de plusieurs patentes, ordres, et provisions des Ducs de Savoye en faveur du dit Duché.'
René	René de Challant
RHMC	*Revue d'histoire moderne et contemporaine*
RLC	Registri di lettere della corte
RQ	*Renaissance Quarterly*
RSI	*Rivista storica italiana*
SCJ	*The Sixteenth Century Journal*
SKB	Staatsarchiv des Kantons Bern (consulted online)
Villarsel	Charles de Challant-Fénis, Lord of Villarsel
ZHF	*Zeitschrift für Historische Forschung*

Acknowledgments

This book represents one piece of a larger project on the history of political culture in the sixteenth-century Western Alps. Over the course of many years, I have benefited from the cheerful generosity of friends, colleagues, archivists, and, of course, family.

During one of my first trips to Aosta, I met Alessandro Celi, who has not only provided invaluable suggestions to me over the years, but has also become a dear friend. At the Archives Historiques Régionales, I benefited from the advice and assistance of Maria Costa, Giuseppe Rivolin, Fausta Baudin, and Roberto Bertolin. Omar Borrettaz has offered helpful feedback and useful reminders. Claudine Rémacle has also been prompt to assist me in various aspects of this project. At the Archivio Notarile d'Aosta, I remain beholden to Antonio Santoro. I am grateful to the Académie Saint-Anselme for their invitation to present my work on two occasions, and then to become a corresponding member of the society (special thanks to Pierre-Georges Thiébat and Joseph-César Perrin). Archivists at the Archivio di Stato di Torino have also been unfailingly friendly and professional in their assistance, especially Marco Carassi, Daniela Cereia, Paola Niccoli, and Federica Paglieri. Archivists at the Archives d'État de Neuchâtel, the Archivio di Stato di Trento, and the Biblioteca Comunale di Trento have been similarly helpful.

I am grateful to Geoffrey Symcox, Jon Mathieu, Tom Cohen, and Angelo Torre for their suggestions, and to audiences at conferences (the RSA, SCSC, Western Society for French History, and the SFHS) where I have presented portions of this work. I am particularly thankful to members of the Sabaudian Studies network, especially Alice Raviola, Laurent Perrillat, Stéphane Gal, Claudio Rosso, Pier Paolo Merlin, Andrea Merlotti, and Paola Bianchi for their encouragement. Katy Ferrari read a part of this work and I thank her for her comments. Anonymous readers on behalf of Amsterdam University Press helped me to improve the text (though probably not as much as they would have liked). Erika Gaffney also helped with encouraging words at the right times.

This project has received financial support from the West Virginia University Faculty Senate, WVU's Eberly College of Arts and Sciences, the WVU History Department, the West Virginia Humanities Council, the Renaissance Society of America, and the Harvard University Center for Italian Renaissance Studies, Villa I Tatti.

As always, my deepest debt of gratitude is to my family: Annastella, Ben, Charlotte, and Gabas. Thanks to Jean-Claude, Edith, Jean-Louis, Laure, Claude, and Salvatore for assistance in various ways. Finally, I am grateful to Jürgen, Virgil, Ali, Bobby, and the rest of the 'mentality giants' for all they do.

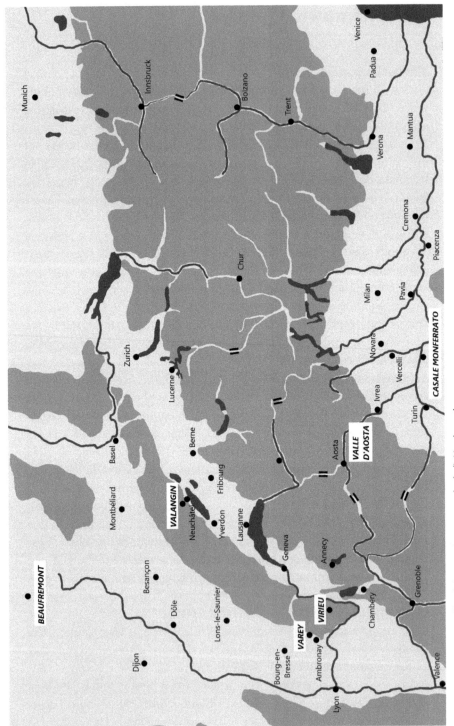

Map 1: René's transregional lands (mountainous areas shaded). Map by author.

1. On the edge of the Italian Renaissance

Abstract

This chapter situates René de Challant on the edge of Renaissance historiography in several ways. The geographic reach of his fiefs and political activities spanned from northwestern Italy across the Alps into the borderlands between France and the Empire. His service to the House of Savoy raises questions about the boundaries of scholarly work on the Italian Renaissance. His activities as a feudal lord with pretensions of sovereign status help us to reevaluate the relationship between the historiography on the European nobility and studies of Italian Renaissance elites. Biography as a genre of history is perched between contextual narrative description and comparative analysis. Recent work on the spatial dimensions of early modern history draw our attention to this material dimension of René's experiences.

Key words: Italian Renaissance, historiography, nobility, spatial history

In 1559, René de Challant seemed to be at the height of his powers. The unquestioned leader of the most powerful magnate family in the Valle d'Aosta, he held fiefs not only throughout the valley, but also in the transalpine Sabaudian lands (in what is, today, western Switzerland), in the duchy of Lorraine, and in the marquisate of Monferrato. As Marshal of Savoie, he was the chief military commander for the House of Savoy and swore allegiance to that Duke for most of his lands. The Challant family had appeared in the Valle d'Aosta by the twelfth century (when the valley accepted Sabaudian overlordship) and began acquiring fiefs and offices. François de Challant received the comital title in the fifteenth century but had no direct male heirs, so the head of another branch of the family, Jacques de Challant-Aymavilles, acquired his titles. Jacques's great-grandson René reaped the benefits, also inheriting from his mother the lordship of Valangin and the barony of Beaufremont north of the Alps. He was a transregional noble with strong service ties to a dynasty whose states themselves spanned the

---

Vester, M., *Transregional Lordship and the Italian Renaissance: René de Challant, 1504-1565.*
Amsterdam: Amsterdam University Press, 2020.
DOI 10.5117/9789463726726_CH01

Alps, embodying in his person and lands an Italian Renaissance that was itself spatially dispersed.

The force of René's influence might be one reason why the Duke of Savoy assigned him to a command that was naturally exercised from Savoie, across the Alps from his power center in the valley. Indeed, the anonymous author of a *Memoriale* presented to the Duke of Savoy in 1560 pointed out the number of strategic castles held by the Count of Challant throughout the valley, and the potential danger that these represented to the Duke's dominion there. Andrea Boldù, Venetian envoy to the court of Savoy, reported in 1561 that René had 'twenty-four castles with capital jurisdiction, and some that are fortresses; and he enjoys 30,000 *scudi* in revenues'.[1] René's influence was thus rooted in his transregional landed position, in the valley and elsewhere. His lordship over these places was directly linked to other sources of authority: his kinship relations and marriage alliances, his political networks, his roles in governance and military affairs, and his financial activities. René de Challant was a powerful Renaissance noble whose authority was tied to the spatial distribution of the places that he ruled – indeed, the fact that his patrimonial lands were located in modern-day Italy requires us to reconsider transregional lordship as a neglected element of the history of the Italian Renaissance.

The Renaissance has enjoyed a long historiographic relationship with urban life, commercial culture, and forms of artistic production associated with both, especially in the cities of northern and central Italy, whether ruled by *signori* or by republican oligarchies. Partly in response to pressures created by the academic job market (in the Anglophone world), scholars over the past couple of decades have discussed the 'Mediterranean Renaissance' or even 'global Renaissances'. Among those working on the Italian Renaissance specifically, recent historiography has begun to extend the history of the Italian Renaissance beyond well-trodden parameters – studies have examined the Venetian Empire and cultural interactions with the Ottomans, Italy's relationship with transalpine kingdoms such as Hungary, and parts of Italy that have often been left in the shadow of Renaissance studies.[2] But rural lordship has remained neglected by most historians of the Renaissance, despite the fact that chivalric culture has been seen as an inspiration for families like the Este or Gonzaga, who sought to legitimize their recently usurped authority. Feudal lords were thought to have belonged to an older

---

1   Boldù, 439.
2   See, for example, Dursteler, *Venetians in Constantinople*; O'Connell; Howard; *Italy and Hungary*; Dauverd; and Marino, *Becoming Neapolitan*.

medieval order that had been displaced by the Renaissance, especially when their lands stretched across multiple regions from northern Italy. For example, the Sabaudian lands and the areas just beyond the Western Alps, despite their location in northwestern Italy and their continual military, financial, and commercial links to the rest of the peninsula, are routinely excluded from Renaissance history and seen as extraneous to 'Italian' culture.

I argue that René de Challant, whose holdings ranged from the Monferrato northwest and over the mountains, was an Italian and transregional dynast. The spatially dispersed kind of lordship that he practiced and his lifetime of service to the House of Savoy, especially in the context of the Italian Wars, show how the Sabaudian lands, neighboring Alpine states, and even regions further afield were tied to the history of the Italian Renaissance. Even merely to situate René de Challant, his network of relations, and his experiences on the edge of the Italian Renaissance helps us to analyze several key historiographic themes with more precision. A study of René's life also draws attention to other themes connected to the spatial dimensions of transregional lordship that have been obscured due to the traditional tendencies of Renaissance studies. It uncovers an 'Italy' whose boundaries extend not just into the Mediterranean, but into regions beyond the Alps.

This book straddles traditional biography – in this case, one in which the empirical evidence has never been comprehensively compiled – and a comparative approach that situates René with respect to other Italian and European nobles. Nobles' conceptions of themselves and their place in society have been studied through analysis of the language that they used to describe these things, especially in correspondence, with an eye to the relationship between norms and practices.[3] Even in the absence of family archives and extensive sources, Edoardo Grendi has managed to write a deeply contextualized history of the Balbi family of Genoa,[4] and Joseph Morsel studied the social space of a family belonging to the lesser nobility.[5]

Historians are divided in their assessment of the utility of the biographical approach,[6] which can be conceptualized within the framework of a microanalytical global history that illuminates historical forces by focusing

---

3   Broomhall and Van Gent.
4   Grendi, xxiv (for quotation), xiv, xxiii; see Donati, 'Nobiltà e Stati,' for an appreciation of Grendi's study.
5   Morsel, discussed in Demade, 'Parenté, noblesse.'
6   Robert Rotberg viewed biography as crucial for history-writing; see Rotberg, 305. G.R. Elton was dismissive of biography (see Prestwich, 326). Prestwich argued that biographies can in fact advance new historiographic interpretations.

on the lives of 'certain unusually cosmopolitan individuals' and combining macro- and micro-analyses.[7] Whether one is writing biography or another form of history, one faces the same interpretive challenges. These might relate to the problem of understanding 'strategies',[8] the possibility that there were historically specific ways of understanding the political implications of historical evidence,[9] or assumptions about motives based on concrete actions described in the sources.[10] In biographies and other histories, sequence matters, temporality points to multiple causality, and cultural context works as a dialectic between systems of meaning and practices that constantly transform each other.[11] But both biographical and historical research are based on surviving sources and must respect the interpretive limit constituted by those sources, which creates challenges for writing broad cultural histories of groups like 'the Renaissance nobility'.

Biographers and other historians face questions about which categories of analysis to employ, especially with respect to political units. A recent move by scholars of early modern politics is to analyze small states, and the problems that they pose for uncritical assumptions about sovereignty, boundaries, and political networks.[12] By taking into account political units that were readily dismissed by nineteenth-century historians, such scholars have reacted against 'methodological nationalism', investigating instead new analytical units 'that cross borders without claiming to encompass the polities and cultural areas they slice through'.[13] Narratives situated on large spatial scales 'also tend to use large temporal scales', which can result in a disconnect 'from the time scales of human lives' and from understandings of personal experience and historic causation.[14] However, what might be called 'transnational biography'[15] permits one to recover 'actors and agency' and to

7   Aslanian et al., 1445.
8   Historians of kinship often fail to offer precise definitions of 'family strategy'; see Dolan, 292, 301. Michel Nassiet makes a similar argument in *Parenté, noblesse et États dynastiques*, 18.
9   Millstone, 84-85, 89-90.
10 Pollock, 157.
11 Sewell, 169-71. Angelo Torre has explored this relationship between cultural representations and practices, warning about a kind of history that 'sussuma le pratiche all'interno delle rappresentazioni e che rinunci all'incrocio delle fonti documentarie'. This could lead to a new kind of idealism by viewing the sources *only* according to the logic of their production (and not as signifiers of any other reality) (see Visceglia, 308-9, discussing Torre, 'Percorsi della pratica').
12 Schnettger, 639; Raviola, *L'Europa dei piccoli stati*.
13 Pomeranz, 2-3. This 'transnational' approach had been pioneered much earlier by *Annaliste* historians such as Lucien Febvre, Marc Bloch, and Fernand Braudel (see Struck et al., 573-75).
14 Pomeranz, 5.
15 This term seems to be of recent vintage; see Meneghello.

analyze 'the spatial multiplicity of individual actors' lives and experiences ranging from the local micro-scale to macro-levels including national or global scales'.[16]

This study of René de Challant takes up the challenge of showing how biography can facilitate an integration of different scales of analysis. If looked at from the perspective of only one regional history, the transregional dimension of a life such as René's is invisible. Only by reconstructing a dense context of the person's activities and relationships does the spatial significance of René's biography come to light. Close observation is what makes it possible to see the ways in which lordship, finances, diplomacy, kinship, and political networks were intertwined and spatially articulated. As we will see in the conclusion, this spatial dimension also comes to the fore in language, but only when that language can be contextualized in social and material ways. Further, as the weight of specific fields of activity is clarified, it becomes possible for the narrative to dial back the scale of analysis to a more comparative setting, and to relate René's experiences to those of other Renaissance nobles. Each of this book's two parts (Part One chronicles events while Part Two examines themes) alternates between close-up views of René's actions and relationships and wider-angle views of more macro-level events and thematic comparisons. Each part informs the other: the significance of René's experiences over time is lost if no categories for comparison are available, while comparison is meaningless if totally abstracted from a diachronic context. Close reading of all available sources relating to René's biography brings to the fore not only the importance of the transregional dimension, but also enables the identification of relevant fields of comparison.[17]

This book thus positions itself on the edge between biography and comparative history, but centrally engaged with the methodological, and particularly transregional, concerns of each. Very little has been written in English on the Sabaudian lands, not to mention the Valle d'Aosta, during the period between the late Middle Ages and early modern times, and there is no book-length biography of René de Challant in any language. A singular case like that of René is important both for its own sake and for what it shows us

---

16 Struck et al., 577; Pomeranz, 22. Historians must clarify what kind of meta-narrative is framing their research when the nation-state no longer serves as a useful category of analysis (Struck et al., 579). A biographical mode of history-writing guards against the creation of transhistorical conceptual entities that exist only as the historical products of their specific times, or were simply constituted as such by historians, untethered to any historical documentation (see Green, 552 n. 1 for the critique by Simona Cerutti and Robert Descimon of transnational studies).

17 On microanalysis and biography, see Renders.

about the limits of our broad categories of historical understanding. The fact that René's political involvement, and political imagination, does not fall within categories that are immediately recognizable in Italian Renaissance scholarship, underscores Dipesh Chakrabarty's call for a 'nontotalizing conception of the political' and a heterogeneous historical imagination.[18] In other words, the specific case that seems unimportant due to its detachment from conventional narratives is crucial precisely because it reminds us of the heterogeneity of 'the political' in past times.[19] But René's experiences can also contribute to our understanding of a number of thematic issues relating to Renaissance and early modern nobility, lordship, and politics. A close reading of an individual life can raise unexpected issues in ways that prompt one to rethink historiographic categories. In the case of René de Challant, the geographically dispersed nature of his noble tenures, his near-constant movement back and forth across the Alps throughout his life, and the peripheral location of his Italian lands with respect to the rest of Italy draw attention to the spatial dimension of Renaissance lordship and politics. Being aware of the material and spatial elements of noble power in turn sheds a different light on historiographic topics such as family relations, noble networks, information management, financial brokerage, and dynastic prestige. This book thus combines attention to a singular Renaissance life with a variety of themes in the historiography of the European nobility between 1400 and 1700. The two-part structure of the work reflects this approach, the first half focusing on the events of René's life, and the second part examining those aspects of his relationships – family connections, political networking, financial ties, and the practice of lordship – that have been studied by other historians of the European nobility. In each part, I will argue that the spatial dimension, both material and imagined, of René's experiences as a Renaissance lord was an integral part of his self-understanding and of how others perceived him. Each part will also demonstrate the degree to which, through transregional nobles like René, 'Italy' spilled over into other parts of Europe.

The remainder of this introduction will examine some of the themes in recent scholarship relating to the Italian Renaissance and the European nobility, and issues of space and mobility with respect to both topics. Just as the history of northwestern areas of the peninsula has been at the edge of Italian Renaissance studies, so has the history of lordship. René embodied both, as a 'quasi-sovereign' lord on the brink of complete political

18 Chakrabarty, 149, 178-79.
19 For a similar approach in art history, see Kaufmann.

autonomy – but also as a feudal noble who enjoyed extensive contacts with urban merchant-bankers in the Swiss cantons and was a self-declared *'bourgeois de Berne'* thanks to his fief of Valangin. Italian, but not quite; feudal lord, but a Renaissance courtier; sovereign Prince of Valangin, but loyal vassal of the Duke of Savoy (and others); landed dynast, but closely tied to Swiss burghers: in several ways, René was a liminal figure. The next several pages examine what historians have written on the themes of the peripheries of the Italian Renaissance, the place of the nobility in Renaissance historiography (discussing nobles in Italy, relations between European nobles and other social groups, and the political role of semi-sovereign nobles and small states) and the ways in which spatial analysis and mobility sheds light on these topics.

The Italian Renaissance

A transregional understanding of the Italian Renaissance can encompass a figure like René de Challant, who wrote in French and held patrimonial lands in the 'intra-mountain state' of the Valle d'Aosta. There are a number of thematic and geographic realities that have been far from the center of a traditionally urban-centered Renaissance historiography – rural areas where feudal ties remained strong, Alpine Italy, the Sabaudian states, and even transalpine zones (such as the Swiss lands) with strong links to Italy – and the question of their relation to the Renaissance remains open. Historians of France have discussed *'la France italienne'*, detailing the remarkable influence of Italian Renaissance culture at French courts and among the French nobility who felt 'the lure of Italy' during the early sixteenth century.[20] This impact created an anti-Italian backlash during the second half of the sixteenth century, and a sense that Italians had taken over French culture.[21] Just as the France of Francis I and Henry II has been included in our geography of the Italian Renaisssance, so should the border areas around northwestern Italy.

The social and cultural history of the lands formerly ruled by the House of Savoy is an in-between topic, residing comfortably neither within early

---

20   Marjorie Meiss-Even notes that 'all of the key posts in the Lorraine stables were held by Italians'; see Meiss-Even, 52.
21   Joanna Milstein cautions that historians 'tend to treat the Italian community in France as an undifferentiated whole,' rather than as representatives of specific places (Milstein, 1, 2, 5). See also H. Heller.

modern French history nor with that of the Italian Renaissance. Recent efforts to avoid the tendency to fit this history into a particular national historiography, by configuring the subject as 'Sabaudian Studies', might be usefully extended by situating the Sabaudian case within the broader Alpine arc, many parts of which face similar historiographic challenges. The question then becomes whether there was an 'Alpine Renaissance'.[22] The term 'Renaissance' seems to limit itself to a certain kind of cultural history – and a kind that we rarely associate with the Alps.[23] In part, this is because 'Renaissance' is often also linked to urban society,[24] which might seem natural: one will search in vain for scholarly works that examine the 'rural Renaissance' or the 'peasant Renaissance' – such terms sound absurd.[25] Since 1949, at least, scholars have used the term 'northern Renaissance' to describe to developments in the heavily urbanized Low Countries, juxtaposing them to the Italian (southern?) Renaissance.[26] Thereafter, more 'Renaissances' appeared, most of them national in scope – although these (including the 'Spanish Renaissance') were typically incorporated into the non-Italian catch-all category of 'northern Renaissance'.[27] The Alps seem to have played a visible role in the creation of these north-south abstractions by functioning as a boundary between Italy and the 'north' (wherever that may have been).[28] Yet, despite the heuristic visibility of the Alps in discussions of the Renaissance, they are practically invisible in concrete terms. So idealized is the function of the Alpine boundary in scholarly discourse that one finds a reference to 'one of the great Old Masters of the early Northern Renaissance, the Austrian artist Michael Pacher, [who] spent the bulk of his life as a sculptor and painter in the south Tyrol'.[29] If an artist active *south* of the Alpine watershed is a master

---

22 See *Sabaudian Studies*.
23 The hostile reaction of 'the U.S. Renaissance studies establishment' to Braudel's *Mediterranean* (at least until the early 1970s) was partly due to Braudel's total history approach; see Marino, 'The Exile and His Kingdom,' 636.
24 Guido Ruggiero's recent study of the 'Rinascimento' examines 'two [...] urban civilizations' on the peninsula before and after 1450 (Ruggiero, 286).
25 J.R. Hale recalled someone having asked him whether ice hockey was 'a part of civilization'; one could ask the same question of the Alps (Hale, xx).
26 Phillips; Telle; Préaux.
27 See Baskerville; Tilley; 'Spanish Renaissance;' Byne and Stapley; Bell; *Flemish Renaissance*; H. Cole; Whitcomb; Angyal; Miller. In 1973, a reviewer included Spain in the 'northern Renaissance' (Yost).
28 Ruggiero's history of the Renaissance invites the reader into this world along with an imaginary German pilgrim crossing the Brenner Pass on his way to Rome (Ruggiero, 23). For Hale, 'the Alps were felt to divide a northern, transalpine world from a southern, temperamentally and culturally conditioned Mediterranean one' (Hale, 62).
29 See http://www.visual-arts-cork.com/old-masters/michael-pacher.htm, 12 November 2019.

of the *northern* Renaissance, then our geographic terms need to be revised in order to attend more concretely to lived human experiences, including within that swatch of Europe that we can define as Alpine.[30]

This attention to geography has caught on in the recent past, as scholars have tried to 'globalize' the Renaissance and reexamine geographic and temporal categories that had become embedded in scholarly fields.[31] Thomas DaCosta Kaufmann discusses research fields in which 'the borders of the unified territories do not correspond to those of an atlas of political history' but can be conceptualized as 'optical zones' that shared 'stylistic peculiarities' due to 'the terrain and qualities of light'.[32] There is something to be gained from taking these cues and reshuffling the categories of Renaissance history by including the Sabaudian lands and other Alpine regions.

In terms of periodization, one can point to economic developments that began to change Alpine society beginning in the thirteenth or fourteenth centuries, followed by increasing differentiation between Alpine areas and the lowlands in the eighteenth century, both demographically and in terms of agricultural intensification.[33] One could also periodize an 'Alpine Renaissance' with reference to European political and military developments and their impact on the region. In a general sense, the Avignon papacy, the conciliar movement, and the anti-pontificate of Felix V (Amadeus VIII of Savoy), all increased ecclesiastical activity within the Alpine space and intensified through traffic toward Rome. Across the Alpine arc, a process of political consolidation was also apparent, beginning in the fourteenth and fifteenth centuries,[34] and then intensifying with the invasions of Italy in 1494 and the subsequent Franco-Imperial wars (corresponding to Guido Ruggiero's 'second Rinascimento').[35] The constant transit of armies, diplomats, and

30 It must be acknowledged that people of the time also understood the Alps as a cultural divide, referring to drunkenness as 'that "plague from beyond the Alps"' and artists who 'had no peer this side of the Alps'; see Hale, 61-62.

31 There has been at least one exhibition on the Mediterranean Renaissance (one of which included several works 'from Alpine Savoy') and the term 'maritime Renaissance' has been made to refer to artistic relations between southern Italy and Iberia; see Dombrowski.

32 Kaufmann, 9-10. *Raumstil* referred to this kind of regional style (73, 77, 97).

33 Alpine resources, including cheese, began to be exported, commercializing certain aspects of agrarian production (see Mathieu; also Pounds, 204-5). For mining and manufacturing in the Alps, see Hale, 386 and Mathieu. For other references to the Alpine economy during the Renaissance, see Appuhn and, of course, Braudel. For Alpine commerce during the sixteenth and seventeenth centuries, see Fontaine; Imboden; and Mathieu.

34 This took place in the Sabaudian lands; in Dauphiné; the Swiss cantons; Alpine Lombardy; the Tyrol and the Trentino; the archbishopric of Salzburg; Bavaria; the duchies of Carinthia, Styria, and Carniola; and the mountainous areas of Friuli and the Julian Alps.

35 Ruggiero.

political leaders across the Alpine realms undoubtedly permitted a transfer of politico-administrative ideas and practices. This ongoing structure of transit and exchange, together with the remarkable variety of political formations that characterized the Alpine space – ranging from dynastic territorial states to rural and urban republics to ecclesiastical polities to imperial fiefs, produced a distinctive political environment in this area that lasted from 1300 until 1700 or so. In some areas of the Alps, the later seventeenth century was a golden age of sorts, with the emergence of prominent court cultures in Turin, Munich, and the Austrian lands.[36]

In terms of distinguishing artistic characteristics of an Alpine Renaissance, scholars have certainly pointed to the importance of Burgundian traditions, especially in the Western Alps, and the influence of the International Gothic in mural and easel paintings.[37] The court of Savoy, midway between Burgundy and Milan, was also a musical center during the fifteenth century, while the wood sculptors of southern Germany and Austria and the stonemasons of the Ticino and northern Lombardy earned European fame. In a way, the Alps – and the very regions where René's lands were located – were where Burgundian and Italian artistic innovations collided.[38] Kaufmann's suggestion that the Swiss area occupied a 'liminal position in European geography, one that is situated between a number of worlds or regions' could be applied to the Alpine arc as a whole, and to René's transregional holdings in particular.[39]

Whether something like a shared 'Alpine identity' existed among inhabitants of this region is doubtful, even if visitors to the Alps did leave records of their impressions of the mountains.[40] We do know, however, that, by the seventeenth century, some Alpine dynasties incorporated the mountains into their representational schemes, suggesting that rulers assumed that the image of the Alps was a positive one.[41] Thinking about the Alps as a coherent historical space also requires recognition of the social and cultural diversity of the region, beginning with the variety of family structures in

36 For interactions between these courtly centers, see *Lo stato sabaudo e il sacro impero romano*.
37 See Plesch; Castelnuovo.
38 Examples to consider are the frescoes of the castles of La Manta (marquisate of Saluzzo) and Buonconsiglio (Trento), and the *Sacro Monte* of Varallo (for the latter, see Symcox).
39 Kaufmann, 98. Similar arguments could be made for a kind of religious distinctiveness of the Alpine lands, where the Theban martyrs and others provided a unique saintly tradition, and where key Reformation and Counter-Reformation events occurred. On the Alpine arc as a distinctive economic region, see *Communities and Conflicts*, which sees the region as an open zone of 'intersection between different political and institutional models' (7).
40 See Korenjak on the history of 'mountain enthusiasm'.
41 Merlotti; Pennini; Celi.

different parts of the arc.⁴² Here, we return to Braudel's classic problem of 'possibilism' – that idea that geography offered constraints to human actions but did not predetermine outcomes, leaving humans free to influence their own environments.⁴³

The general history of Renaissance historiography has been explored by many.⁴⁴ Over the last hundred years, Anglophone scholars linked the Renaissance and the theme of the birth of the modern world, republicanism, and capitalism – all of which have been tied to Italian city-states (especially Florence and Venice) – before abandoning the idea that the Renaissance was a crucial stage on a linear path of Western civilizational development. This was followed by studies of how the Italian cities were subsumed into territorial dynastic states.⁴⁵ More recent attention has been given to the reciprocal influences between Italy and other parts of Europe,⁴⁶ but a more traditional view that 'the culture of the Italian Renaissance' was permeated by humanism, and 'the energies driving that culture' were 'effectively bilingual [Italian and Latin]' has persisted.⁴⁷ This is coupled with an acknowledgment that the 'peripheral' areas of Italy (such as southern Italy, Sicily, and Sardinia) have been overlooked in Anglo-American historiography.⁴⁸ Calls for more study of the landed nobility, who have been portrayed as disrupters of Renaissance urban life, are well placed, given more recent work showing that nobles played key roles in city affairs, asserted influence through clients, and even contributed to urban expansion by facilitating agrarian growth.⁴⁹

It has been claimed that 'Renaissance political theorists spoke about politics in ways that differed from transalpine settings because the Italian context

---

42 Mathieu.
43 On Braudel's concept of 'possibilism', see Viazzo, 2-5.
44 Despite important studies by Goldthwaite and others, the term 'Renaissance' seems to pair more easily with 'culture' than with 'economics'. Although the history of objects and of consumption is changing this divergence between 'cultural' and 'material' history, 'Renaissance' as a general term of periodization most typically refers to a period of *Italian* history. For Hale, 'the word Renaissance loses much of its appropriateness when transplanted from peninsular soil' (Hale, 322).
45 From the perspective of the history of the nobility and of rural lordship, the movement away from an urban-centered Renaissance opens the door to the study of problems and regions that have been neglected in Anglophone scholarship (Muir, 1118). A recent survey found a tendency to identify the seventeenth century as the period that gave birth to capitalism (with Italy playing a peripheral or semi-peripheral role); see Visceglia, 299-300.
46 Caferro, *Contesting*, 8-9, 16.
47 *Cambridge Companion*, 1.
48 Ibid., 10-12.
49 C. Shaw, 1, 51-53, 58. Since the 1970s, Philip Jones had been revising the view that feudal institutions declined in medieval Italy and stressed instead 'the conspicuous influence of rural aristocracy on city-states' (Cengarle, 284-85).

itself was different', due to the unprecedented 'emergence of autonomous communes in medieval Italy'.[50] A transregional approach enables us to test this assertion, along with the argument that, by the early sixteenth century, 'the waning of Renaissance political thought' was underway, being replaced by 'the ideology of sacred monarchy that would dominate the political culture of early modern Europe'.[51] René's case and others show that, in many parts of Italy, small feudal principalities in fact remained vibrant for some time to come and even 'undermined the process of state formation'.[52] Renaissance Italy was a place where noble values and republican sensibilities coexisted, though perhaps not always in the same persons, and sometimes crossed regional frontiers.[53]

An older historiographic interpretation portrayed feudal institutions as having declined over the course of the Middle Ages in response to the growing power of Italian cities. More recent work has reassessed relations between cities, feudal lords, and peasants;[54] questioned distinctions between 'city', 'city-state', and 'territorial state' as political forms;[55] examined pacts and reciprocities between cities and noble families;[56] stressed cultural continuity between rural nobles and urban courtly elites;[57] and explored

50 Jurdjevic, 299.
51 Boone, 1027-28. Linda Darling, relying on Wayne te Brake, seems to agree with this assessment (Darling, 508).
52 Raviola, 'The Imperial System,' 217. While these small polities testified to the continued importance of the Holy Roman Empire in Italy, many scholars continue to identify a linear model of sixteenth-century European state development from Italian city-states to 'northern monarchies' (Caferro, *Contesting*, 157).
53 John Marino found that, in the kingdom of Naples, a 'bourgeois public sphere of civil society' emerged under viceregal rule (*Becoming Neapolitan*, 172). Angelantonio Spagnoletti argued, conversely, that 'l'amicizia, la cavalleria, il rapporto personale che lega il principe ai suoi cavalieri [...] sono qualità (virtù, si potrebbe dire) non ravvisabili nelle istituzioni repubblicane e nei loro uomini' (Spagnoletti, 100).
54 Regional princes sought to use the institution of the fief to delegate public functions, but 'a purely seigneurial logic' remained locally operative; see Cengarle, 286-87.
55 Michael Martoccio reviews the work of Gamberini and Lazzarini, who identify two historiographic views of the Italian Renaissance state. One focused on the role of cities in state development and the other ('[Federico] Chabod's model') saw the state as a creation of officials and institutions (Martoccio). In the 1970s, Giorgio Chittolini and Elena Fasano Guarini, influenced by German historiography, stressed the role of reciprocal agreements in state development, seeing the state as a mediator among constituent groups. Gamberini and Lazzarini refer to this view as 'pactist' and 'reciprocal', and find it more convincing than 'the long-lasting idea' according to which 'the trademark and cornerstone of the political history of Italy' was 'the crucial role of cities' (*The Italian Renaissance State*, 2, 4).
56 C. Shaw, 59, 60-62, 168.
57 Massimo della Misericordia shows the continued influence of noble ideals in late medieval Alpine Lombardy, where elites used castles and decorations to represent their authority, while adapting their representations to political contexts, transforming, for example, fortified castles

the variety of feudal systems in Italy,[58] which resulted in an Italian dynastic system after 1559 with important transregional elements.[59] This emerging body of work is helpful for relating René's experiences to those of other Italian nobles, even if the transregional dimension is missing from most scholarship on the Italian nobility. Feudal lordship has been depicted either as having died out with the Middle Ages or as a tool of a new absolutist dynasticism – either way, as something foreign to the Italian Renaissance. Newer scholarship is beginning to challenge some of these commonplaces, and the career of René de Challant helps to illustrate this shift.

Reciprocally, René's transregionality demands that we rethink our understanding of the Italian Renaissance and who was part of it. An unhelpful boundary between subalpine areas of Italy and the 'northern Renaissance' persists. A transregional conception of Renaissance studies can bring new problems to the fore. Already, an emerging body of scholarship on topics of transregional valence (borderlands, pilgrimage, pirates, renegades and conversion, migration, smuggling, missionary orders, political envoys and go-betweens, etc.) is beginning to destabilize traditional historiographic-geographic boundaries.[60] This transregional approach also offers ways for us to understand the nobility of the Italian Renaissance from a fresh perspective.

The Renaissance nobility

The feudal nobility has been at the edge of the concerns of most historians working on Renaissance Italy, but this is changing: few scholars would accept a thesis of noble decline beginning in the Renaissance. Rather, they would

into 'palazzi rinascimentali'. See Della Misericordia, 'Gusti cavallereschi,' 794-96; also id., 'Medioevo cavalleresco,' 7-9.
58 Spagnoletti, 14-16, 19-21.
59 This dynastic system, according to Spagnoletti, grew out of the Habsburg annexation of the state of Milan, and requires a distinction between the concepts of 'ragion di stato' and 'ragione della casa' (ibid., 28-29). For Spagnoletti, after 1559, Emanuel Filibert and other Italian rulers, 'ormai legittimati nei loro titoli e nel possesso dei loro stati,' began a state-building process by building support among elite groups in their states (ibid., 37). As has been noted, though, more recent work has complicated this state-building narrative. Spagnoletti himself seems to acknowledge this point by observing that, until the Sabaudian acquisition of the royal title in 1713, this Italian dynastic system had continued through marriage alliances between non-sovereign aristocratic families linked to the Empire and Italian territorial princes (ibid., 87).
60 *Your Humble Servant*; Rothman; Hysell; Stopani; Dursteler, *Renegade Women*; Davis; *Gated communities?*; Kwass; Armstrong; *Transregional and Transnational Families*.

focus on how nobles adjusted to changing political and economic conditions in order to maintain positions of authority, often through bureaucratic or courtly service.[61] Historians such as Franco Angiolini, Cesare Mozzarelli, and Walter Barberis have outlined these shifts and pioneered work on regional nobilities, and on how nobles interacted with princely courts.[62] Claudio Donati wrote prolifically about the Renaissance-era Italian nobility, rejecting the view that a new noble climate was created in Italy when the idea of a Renaissance Republican patriciate lost ground and a 'noble awareness' emerged.[63] Donati also emphasized the regional variation among Italian nobilities, and their relation to Spanish power.[64] He lamented the historiographic focus on how nobles were subsumed into Italian territorial states because it rendered invisible the continuation of feudal lordship after 1559, with just a few exceptions. He wondered about the houses that disappeared or were redefined (such as the Fieschi, the Pallavicino, and others – one might add the Challant –, especially 'between the Alps and the Po'), and how their 'military and knightly identity' changed so quickly.[65] He studied this question from the perspective of the Este di San Martino – a good example of a family whose transregionalism extended from northwestern to northeastern Italy.[66] The Genoese nobles studied by Céline Dauverd were

---

61 Romaniello and Lipp, 2-4; Duindam; Scott and Storrs; H. Scott, 'The Early Modern European Nobility,' 27-28.
62 This posited a new growth in noble power linked to the rise of territorial states and the investment in noble titles by wealthy financiers, contributing to economic and political decadence; Angiolini, 66-88.
63 Donati, 'Nobiltà e coscienza nobiliare,' 60, 66. Donati stressed the continued importance of an urban, communal culture, not the radical assertion of a noble-feudal one and elimination of the other; see Donati, 'Nobiltà e Stati.'
64 Donati, 'The Profession of Arms,' 300; id., 'The Italian Nobilities,' 286, 290, 306-7. John Marino would have agreed with Donati's point about regional differences, pointing to the peculiar situation in Naples (Marino, *Becoming Neapolitan*, 172, 236). Like Angiolini, Donati remarked on the divergent interpretations of northern/central and southern nobles, lamenting the fact that this historiographic division has reinforced 'the dualism between a patrician-dominated center-north and a feudal south'. See 'Nobiltà e Stati,' 70-71.
65 Id., 'The Profession of Arms,' 307-8.
66 Donati studied this cadet branch of a great family and how its members 'si vedono nel "gran Teatro del Mondo"' ('Una famiglia lombarda,' 438). Like other Italian families, the Este di San Martino constantly maneuvered between dependence on the Empire and fidelity to the main Este line and to the King of Spain. He asked how families like this exercised dominion over their own subjects in their feudal lands, which were spread across different northern Italian states. Carlo Emanuele exemplified this challenge, holding fiefs as he did from the Duke of Savoy and the King of Spain, as his overlords went from being allies to being enemies during the Monferrato wars.

tied to Liguria, the kingdom of Naples, and Spain.[67] Christine Shaw's work on the 'military nobles' of Renaissance Italy highlights their independent power,[68] while other studies have surveyed their self-fashioning of noble masculine identities.[69]

While Alessandro Barbero has depicted late medieval Piedmont as a composite entity based on contractual agreements between rulers and communities, following Chittolini's model for Lombardy,[70] most historians have emphasized differences between the Sabaudian nobility and those elsewhere.[71] The dukes of Savoy were prominent in late-Renaissance Italy due to the antiquity of their princely status and their ties to European dynasties.[72] For Walter Barberis, the uniqueness and boldness of Emanuel Filibert's political activity, his military and governing experience in the Netherlands, and his ability to mediate between nobles and power groups 'was not properly part of Italian culture and experience'.[73] This Duke was thus 'not an Italian prince' and even the physical aspect of his states 'distanced him from contemporary Italian models', given his 'Franco-Imperial state experience on the borders of Italy' that differed 'from other Italian situations'.[74] But as we have seen, situations were different all across Italy and often exhibited transregional characteristics. Furthermore, scholarship on nobilities in other parts of Europe has identified some similarities with the Italian

67 Identifying a symbiosis between Genoese mercantile and financial activity and Spanish dynastic imperialism, Dauverd shows how Genoese nobles combined government service, trade and finance, and feudal rule (Dauverd).
68 C. Shaw, 9, 10, 21, 65, 84, 100, 116, 124-25, 130-33, 148, 250, 253-54.
69 Dialeti, 14.
70 Barbero, 'The Feudal Principalities.'
71 For Claudio Donati, on the Italian side of the Alps as far as the Tiber, '"non esistono delle vere capitali [of territorial states]; e solo Torino, rimasta ai margini della grande fioritura italiana, ne presenta il carattere"' (Donati, 'Nobiltà e Stati,' 69, citing one of his earlier works). Walter Barberis likewise stressed the considerable distance between Turin and Rome in the early sixteenth century, arguing that the Sabaudian court did not have 'alcuna somiglianza con quelle che a cavaliere fra Quattro e Cinquecento avevano illuminato il tardo rinascimento padano'; see Barberis, 'Emanuele Filiberto,' 290.
72 Thalia Brero described the court of Duke Charles III as transitioning from 'une cour médiévale vers une cour d'Ancien Régime' [bypassing the Renaissance!] and reorganizing itself more opulently 'sur le modèle franco-bourguignon' (Brero, 28). Toby Osborne has analyzed the status conflict between the houses of Savoy and Medici and drawn attention to their wide-ranging dynastic ties; see Osborne, 6-7.
73 Barberis, 'Emanuele Filiberto,' 291.
74 Ibid., 295-96. Barberis's account of the Duke's various state-building actions recalls the nationalist writers who celebrated the 500th anniversary of his birth in 1928. He considers the Sabaudian case to be 'sostanzialmente eccentrica rispetto alla storia italiana' (ibid., 296-97).

context. In the Low Countries, late medieval nobles also allied themselves with cities rather than with states, even if the relationship between the city and the state was collapsed in Italian city-states.[75] But, in Genoa, links with Spain after 1528 'helped to spread [...] a European idea of nobility', which was less open.[76] Christine Shaw has noted that, although German, French, and Spanish nobles who came to Italy took on an air of superiority with respect to their Italian counterparts, they shared understandings of noble identity.[77] The literature does not seem to have clearly demonstrated how and why Italian cities, urban elites, and nobles may have been any different from Spanish, French, Swiss, German, or Low Country ones, especially since there were structural similarities in the political contexts between several of these areas.[78] The case of René de Challant permits us to examine this kind of transregional nobility in greater detail, and to assess the spatial characteristics of Renaissance lordship.

Scholars have studied the European nobility in a variety of ways, looking at individual families over time, biographies of individual nobles, regional elites, and literary evidence of the concept of 'nobility' and how it has changed.[79] Court studies have moved beyond institutional studies of power centers and ceremonial practice to consider themes such as the limits to princely power posed by religion, the role of non-court nobles, the diversity of courts, and women's activities at court.[80] Liesbeth Geevers and Mirella Marini highlight the heterogeneity of the European nobility, while stressing the utility of the dynasty or 'clusters of families' as a unit of analysis. They argue that dynasties had collective identities of their own,[81] and were 'hard to capture within a national framework'. Even when linked to a particular ruler, 'the self-fashioning of such aristocrats often occurred in a transnational context',[82] such that dynastic identity developed alongside national, confes-

---

75 Buylaert, 'Lordship, Urbanization and Social Change,' 66, 72-73.
76 Grendi, 70, 73.
77 In Shaw's telling, Italian nobles internalized this status difference, as the Italian wars 'accustomed the military nobility of Italy [...] to look to the rulers of Spain, France and the Empire' (C. Shaw, 198, 248 [for quotation]). Spagnoletti, however, believed that Italian nobles had a different sensibility from their transalpine counterparts (246).
78 For a comparative analysis of borders between and within states, see Raviola, 'Frontiere regionali,' 193-94, 196-97.
79 Scott and Storrs.
80 Smith.
81 These identities were developed through religious and political practices, negotiations between family branches, relations to rulers, and in other ways.
82 Geevers and Marini, 3-4, 5.

sional, or gendered forms of self-perception.[83] This kind of dynastic identity was perhaps stronger among transregional nobles like René de Challant who operated in multiple courts in Italy and elsewhere. Other approaches to studying the European nobility have focused on nobles' relation to the state, and the persistence of a 'chivalric ideal' among the aristocracy.[84] Here also, René's case permits examination of the way in which a transregional, spatially dispersed dimension of noble power impinged upon these issues, particularly insofar as the early sixteenth century – and especially the experience of the Italian Wars – was seen as a turning point.

Historical scholarship on nobles and other dominant social groups has catalogued their efforts to block the paths of other upwardly mobile social groups.[85] Noble families sought to identify legendary family origins, link

83   Ibid., 13-18. Brian Sandberg's work on French nobles during the wars of religion understandably focuses on the 'social and cultural practices of violence' required for military, political, and religious purposes during this period, describing such violent practices as a 'way of life' for these aristocrats (Sandberg, xvi, xxiv-xxv). Gregory Hanlon discusses Italian scholarship that has viewed 1630 as a turning point when 'warrior nobles began to return home [from military service abroad] and seek their fortunes by serving their princes' – a timeframe that seems roughly to fit Sandberg's chronology of the high tide of 'warrior pursuits' (Hanlon, 'The Decline of a Provincial Military Aristocracy,' 66 [citing Spagnoletti]).

84   Some scholars have employed the 'social collaboration' model of absolutism developed by William Beik to study how the nobility and other elites worked together with absolutist rulers to achieve various political ends in seenteenth-century France (Dee). Others have examined the relationship between nobles and territorial rulers in polities of different dimensions: Charles Lipp investigates 'small-state nobles' like the Mahuet family, who established an 'administrative dynasty' in Lorraine (Lipp, *Noble Strategies*, 1-3). But, as Eric Hassler points out, even large polities (like the Holy Roman Empire) had distinctive court cultures (Hassler, 198). According to Martin Wrede, while French historiography has traditionally depicted the Crown as the key point of reference for the nobility (although this has been changing), German scholars, who have fairly recently rediscovered the nobility, have tended to analyze them from their own (and not the ruler's) point of view (Wrede, 441, 458). Benjamin Deruelle disagrees with the consensus among scholars that chivalry died out as the early modern state grew more powerful and 'asphyxiated' noble values of equality and power-sharing. These scholars identify a decline in the value of military courage, viewing stoic self-control as its successor in response to the crisis of religious war; see Deruelle, 15-16. For Deruelle, knightly ideals remained culturally important into the early seventeenth century, forming a cultural construct that mediated the relationship between nobles and rulers; ibid., 25; see also 19-24, 27-28. Deruelle acknowledges that his distinction between what is 'knightly' and what is simply 'noble' is not always clear (354). He sees the reigns of Francis I and Henry II in particular as 'the chivalric heart' of the sixteenth century, and the French invasions of 1536 as a resurgence of dynastic conflict that spurred the publication of 21 new editions of chivalric romances between 1535 and 1540 (ibid., 62). The end of the Franco-Habsburg wars and the start of religious conflict (during the period between 1547 and 1578) saw the beginning of a shift in notions of knightly honor, though for Deruelle, different cultural forms continued to coexist (374-75).

85   Martines.

themselves to saintly figures, and (often with the ruler's help) to create 'a closed social group based on blood ties'.[86] Despite such efforts, as the meaning of nobility changed over time, so did the qualities that gave one access to it; by the late sixteenth century, 'intellectual skills and cultural dispositions' became as important as lands and titles to secure noble status.[87] This indicates a gradual shift whose impact on a transregional noble like René de Challant was unclear. Over the past couple of decades, there has been discussion about the role of the *'noblesse seconde'* within the French nobility. These were lower-level nobles who have been seen as 'key to the development of royal clientage as a network of power associated with the building of the early modern French state'.[88] Others have shown that great nobles were also able to pull lesser nobles from their areas into their own patronage systems, and that many 'second nobles' broke with the Crown during the religious wars.[89] Not only did the relationship of nobles to the ruler and to other social groups differ across Europe,[90] such relationships were further complicated for nobles like René whose geographic ties of vassalage linked them to multiple rulers in several different regions.

There has been a lively discussion among scholars of the early modern Low Countries about relationships between nobles and urban elites, helping us to think about René's relationship to patricians in Berne, Casale, Milan, and elsewhere. Jan Dumolyn claims that the elite in late medieval Flanders included both nobles and non-nobles, due to 'increased regional mobility' for princely officers, intermarriage, and new social networks.[91] Buylaert, Dumolyn, and Wim de Clercq further developed the idea of an overlap between wealthy bourgeois families and local nobles in the southern Low Countries, challenging the view that a noble lifestyle and appearance was 'an effective barrier between nobles and commoners'.[92] In Flanders,

---

86   Le Gall, 8-9 (paraphrasing André Burguière). See also Nassiet, *Parenté, noblesse et États dynastiques*, 40.
87   The nobility's 'sociocultural space' was thus transformed during the sixteenth century; see Wintroub, 389-90, 405-6.
88   Salmon, 575; see also Wintroub, 389.
89   This was the critique of Robert Descimon, who coined the term 'noblesse seconde' (Salmon, 576).
90   In Lorraine, the nobility 'never became as removed from state control as their French counterparts' (Lipp, 'Power and Politics,' 43). See O'Connell for Venetian Crete and Grendi for Genoa. In seventeenth-century England, residence in London became increasingly important for landed families, but 'the country estate and its associated ties and symbols remained the chief basis of elite identity' (Warren, 46-47, 61-62, 74).
91   Dumolyn, 433, 437.
92   Buylaert et al., 'Sumptuary Legislation,' 395-96.

nobles often resided in cities (at least seasonally) and invested in the urban economy, partly in response to urban authorities extending jurisdiction into the countryside.[93] Arie van Steensel finds confirmation of many of these findings in the evidence from Zeeland, emphasizing the tight patronage (but not marriage) connections between 'the feudal-aristocratic and urban bourgeois worlds',[94] and remarking that 'noble and civic values were not mutually exclusive', especially given the heterogeneity of the nobility.[95] These findings raise questions about interactions between urban patricians and landed nobles not only in Italy, but among transregional nobles whose lordship was exercised in different customary settings.

Increasingly, early modern nobles have been viewed not anachronistically as subjects who would inevitably be domesticated by absolute sovereigns and their new state institutions, but as autonomous political actors who continued to pursue their own agendas of aggrandizement deep into the period. This perspective helps us make sense of the goals and actions of transregional nobles like René. Such nobles were 'selfish' and 'power hungry' actors who sought authority and jealously defended their rights, but these attitudes 'derived from their conditions of existence'.[96] Many great noble families in Europe 'aspired to a semi-autonomous sovereign status', and were neither rulers nor subjects. Rather, they operated within 'a blurry pyramid of multiple forms of dynastic sovereignty', which gave way only very slowly to a definition of sovereignty as undivided.[97] Recent scholarship sees early modern sovereignty 'more in terms of territorial, personal and practical elements rather than purely philosophical notions', as 'bundles of rights which might be held to a greater or lesser extent'. This made it possible for a range of families to possess 'a measure of sovereignty' in ways that were 'fundamental to their self-identification and self-representation'.[98]

Nobles in the Low Countries pursued this autonomy in different ways, sometimes entering state service but never ceasing to press their claims.[99]

93 Buylaert, 'Lordship, Urbanization and Social Change,' 32-34, 48-50.
94 The author concludes that earlier claims made by scholars of Flanders 'that state formation and urbanisation led to the incorporation of the nobility into a new power elite in the Burgundian-Habsburg Netherlands', weakening the nobility with respect to urban groups, do not hold (Van Steensel, 'Noblemen in an Urbanised Society,' 94).
95 Ibid., 96-97.
96 Brunner, 14.
97 Duindam, 59.
98 H. Scott, '"The Line of Descent",' 231; see also Munns et al., 14.
99 In late medieval Zeeland, only a minority of nobles entered state service. Such nobles instead remained attached to their own lordships, whose concurrent rights and status 'exceeded their pure economic value' (Van Steensel, 'Noblemen in an Urbanised Society,' 86). In Holland,

Historians of the Holy Roman Empire have also stressed the continuity of the ideal of noble autonomy and the ambiguous degree to which nobles were drawn into state service.[100] In the princely states of the Empire, rulers sometimes exerted considerable influence over their nobles, but the latter were also more likely to have transregional ties.[101] The House of Nassau was 'a German line with an international scope, albeit on a more modest scale than the Habsburgs'.[102] Renaissance Italian princes like the Visconti took their cues from the feudal nobility, attempting to expand their jurisdiction when possible and occasionally overriding written norms,[103] and French nobles were deeply committed to protecting their prerogatives and sense of propriety against royal pretensions.[104] To reinforce their autonomy, nobles used violence, marriage alliances, and geographic advantages. This was true across Europe.[105] How were these attitudes affected by the transregional dispersion of noble power bases?

Reinoud van Brederode was accused of using the name and arms of the count of Holland (which belonged to Charles V) but was never accused of *lèse-majesté* and merely ordered to cease. Brederode power resulted from a generations-long 'family self-promotion policy' and made it difficult for the emperor to alienate them; see Dragstra, 22-23. Dumolyn's finding that late medieval Flanders did in fact produce 'a new "state nobility" whose political ideology was to defend the commonwealth of the Burgundian state, abandoning the traditional autonomism of the Flemish urban political elites' (431), runs against the grain of most recent scholarship.

100 Regional nobles who were creditors of the ruler of Ansbach-Kulmbach were appointed to high office and effectively controlled large parts of the state. Even the Emperor himself looked to the nobles in order to counterbalance princely power (Zmora, 1, 19-20). Megan Williams argues that '"the political" in early modern Europe' indicated an environment in which elite families and factions were as important as states and sovereigns (Williams, 372). For Charles Lipp, both nobles and princes were 'guided [...] by the autonomy principle' (*Noble Strategies*, 10-11).

101 Lipp, 'Power and Politics,' 40, 42, 44.

102 Geevers, 'Family Matters,' 469-70. William of Orange saw himself as the head of the house and imagined Habsburg power 'within a Burgundo-imperial framework, considering Ferdinand I and Maximilian II, rather than Philip II, to be Charles V's heirs, (478).

103 Black, 1.

104 Jouanna. This tradition had existed at least since the late Middle Ages when French kings sometimes saw themselves as 'one lord among many' according to Justine Firnhaber-Baker (50-51). Benjamin Deruelle has used the term 'isonomie chevaleresque' to describe the perspective that placed rulers and nobles on the same level and denied any differences 'de nature, de fonction et d'origine' (*De papier, de fer et de sang*, 312). For a similar dynamic among nobles in the Mughal Empire, see Lefèvre, 1311.

105 Historians of late medieval Ireland have tied noble factionalism to a weak central government, but feuding was not unique to Ireland (Crooks). Local warfare proliferated in southern France during the same period, as did seigniorial warfare in German-speaking lands, where it was 'a normal, necessary and licit prerogative of lordship' (Firnhaber-Baker, 41). Until the early sixteenth century, powerful noble families challenged the French king's sovereignty claims and continued to control 'vast territories' (Nassiet, *Parenté, noblesse et États dynastiques*, 23-24).

Although 'trans-regional princely families' have long been overlooked in historiographic traditions focused on nation-state development, this has started to change.[106] Henry VIII was concerned about the possibility of resistance being stirred up by Welsh Catholic nobles (in particular James ap Gruffydd) who added to their local power bases support among the English Catholic exiles in Europe.[107] Similarly, sixteenth-century nobles whose lands stretched across the area between the Low Countries and France were frequently accused of treason by rulers on each side, and risked confiscation and litigation. The transregional identities of such families sometimes resulted from placing members in the service of different rulers in order to hedge their bets. For example, Guillaume de Croÿ had lands not only in the Low Countries and France, but also in the kingdom of Naples. This gave him 'a supra-provincial "Burgundian outlook"' and an Imperial one.[108] This state of affairs was especially prevalent in the part of Europe between the Low Countries and northern Italy, along the borders of France and Germany.[109] The small states scattered throughout this region made it possible for some nobles 'to survive on the margins of the new regional configurations and to maintain their own autonomous role', entering into diplomatic relations with larger powers and offering protection to their own subjects with respect to other states.[110] Even when nobles spent most of their time in one state, where the majority of their property and patronage networks were located, 'their interests were always what historians are now calling "trans-national"', in large part due to their kinship connections.[111]

The 'military nobles' of late medieval Italy resisted the idea that they were 'subjects or vassals' and were not compelled by loyalties to princes or republics (C. Shaw, 197). Noble families also established their political independence by marrying into cadet or illegitimate lines of ruling dynasties. This could even catapult them into sovereign rank: 'a number of prominent noble lineages actually became ruling families and established themselves upon European thrones during the early modern period' (such as the Vasas, the Bourbons, the Romanovs, and the Braganzas). Such lineages set up councils, courts, patrimonial administrations, and patronized artists just as other princely rulers did (H. Scott, '"The Line of Descent",' 222-24).

106 Munns et al., 14-15.
107 Marshall
108 Soen, 89, 91-92 (where she cites Hans Cools on the 'Burgundian outlook'). In the 1550s, Nicolas de Vaudémont (head of a junior branch of the Lorraine family) complained that, in the Netherlands, 'he was considered pro-French while Paris mistrusted him as an Imperialist' (Monter, 57). The Stainville served both the King of France and the Duke of Lorraine; see Spangler, 141.
109 Munns et al., 15.
110 Cengarle, 287; on small states, see Raviola, *L'Europa dei piccoli stati*. For multiple service among the Viennese nobility, see Hassler, 176-77, 192-93. Some argue that this international outlook strengthened among European nobles during the eighteenth century (Scott and Storrs, 51).
111 Munns et al., 14.

It remains difficult, however, to compare René de Challant with other transregional lords, for a couple of reasons. First, apart from studies by Violet Soen and Laura Casella, scholarly references to the kind of lordship exercised by nobles with lands situated in multiple regions remain limited and impressionistic.[112] There are studies of sovereign rulers of composite states, and of grandees in various European kingdoms (the Guise, the Duke of Alba, etc.) but few if any of nobles operating at a lower level in transregional contexts. For example, the only biography of Antoine de Perrenot, Cardinal of Granvelle, was published over 65 years ago.[113] The sixteenth-century Nevers studied by Boltanski seem comparable to René, but her work focuses mainly on a noble's relationship with a single sovereign, rather than one operating in a properly transregional context.[114] Second, while there has been some recent attention given to 'marcher lords' in border regions like the Franche-Comté, these studies tend to examine lordship within frontier zones rather than nobles whose dispersed lands demanded constant mobility and interactions with multiple other sovereigns.[115]

Despite having been traditionally marginalized from the mainstream of historical scholarship on the Italian Renaissance, the rural nobility has attracted some attention. Scholars have focused on themes such as re-feudalization, the relationship of the nobility to regional states, and the regional specificity of the Italian nobility. The Sabaudian case has generally been regarded as an outlier, despite the acknowledgement of regional particularism throughout Italy. But, when one considers European nobles in other areas where there were both regional states and strong cities, one finds similar diversity. Dynastic behavior, attitudes related to violence and chivalry, and nobles' involvement in social collaboration with centralizing rulers have been areas of recent study. Historians of the Low Countries who study relationships between the nobility and urban elites have stressed interactions between these groups (perhaps with the exception of the great nobility). One distinguishing characteristic of Renaissance nobles that has been apparent in recent work is their ambition to act as autonomous political forces, even claiming quasi-sovereign status. They employed violence, matrimonial ties, and geopolitical leverage – especially when they inhabited border areas – to achieve these ends. René de Challant's career can be recognized at the intersection of these thematic trends.

112 Soen; Casella.
113 Van Durme.
114 Boltanski.
115 *La noblesse des marches.*

Spatial analysis and mobility

As we have seen, some historians have begun to emphasize the way in which spatial factors, whether to do with the location of family lands or the mobility of family members, affected noble power and jurisdictional claims. Some of this work has considered the relationship between spatial practices and political authority;[116] many of these findings help to understand René de Challant's experiences. Alvaro Sevilla-Buitrago sees 'territory' itself as the product of interactions in a field of power, as something that is produced from actions taken in space, such as the enclosure of common land.[117] Similarly, James Sheehan has tied the question of sovereignty to the historical development of the idea of a 'boundary'.[118] Sevilla-Buitrago's production of territory and Sheehan's new public way of thinking about space both point to a crucial early modern shift in spatial awareness but offer little specific evidence of how, why, when, or where this occurred.[119] Megan Williams makes the more concrete point that movement through space, particularly by diplomats, contributed to the construction of state territoriality and sovereignty through practices such as the use of safe-conducts, the collection of tolls, and checks at customs stations, all of which created an experiential and legal understanding of boundaries between jurisdictions.[120] Likewise, R.A. Houston usefully examines the history and geographic specificity of the relationship between boundary and law. He shows that there were 'fundamental geographical differences in configurations of law and people in space' between the English, on the one hand, and the Scots, Welsh, and Irish, on the other.[121] Different sizes of administrative units and different

---

116 See Kümin.
117 Sevilla-Buitrago, 210, 215, 217.
118 Sheehan, 5.
119 Paul Stock offers a few reflections (Stock, 7). In the afterword to Stock's volume, Beat Kümin notes that the essays tended to focus on representations of space rather than on whether there were specific early modern ways of using space. Valerie Traub sees 'spatialization' as both a cognitive process and a geopolitical phenomenon (Traub, 15, 17-19).
120 Williams.
121 He found, specifically, that the English 'attached far clearer legal meaning to territory than did peoples elsewhere in the British Isles' and considered it 'one of the elements constituting their society'. In Scotland, Wales, and Ireland, though, jurisdictional boundaries tended to be more 'person-focused' than spatial (Houston, 51-52). These variations could be identified at different spatial scales: in Scotland, domestic thresholds were porous boundaries and doors did not have locks. 'Crossing a threshold and so infringing possession troubled the English', on the other hand (ibid., 80-81). Edward Hall pointed out many years ago that 'it is possible to learn a good deal about how members of a given culture structure space at various levels of abstraction by setting up simple situations in which they manipulate objects' (Hall, 88).

kinds of residential patterns also had an impact on the relationship between space and law.[122] Many scholars have asked questions about the gendered character of early modern spaces. Some claim that, across the board, 'people divided space by gender',[123] or that all of the 'routes and spaces [through which early modern people traveled] were gendered'.[124] Other work on gender and space in early modern England has shown that particular spaces were only gendered in particular ways at particular times, given the presence or absence of other factors; some scholars have even wondered whether they were gendered at all.[125] Yet another way of thinking about space is from the perspective of an older tradition of historical geography focused on the history of European regions.[126]

Noble families, especially 'border nobles' or those whose lands were transregionally located, occupied a significant position in late-Renaissance European politics precisely due to the spatial configuration of their jurisdiction. Scott stressed the strategic importance of frontier zones between powerful monarchies, especially

> the northern sector of the Italian Peninsula, and the extended arc of territory which stretched from the Southern Netherlands through Alsace, Lorraine, [the western Swiss cantons] and Dauphiné, into Provence, Savoy and Piedmont – the 'Middle Kingdom' first created by the division of Charlemagne's inheritance in 843 and, in its northern components, subsequently the lands of the dukes of Burgundy.[127]

The geopolitically pivotal area of the Challant fiefs was marked by jurisdictional fragmentation and crisscrossed by routes between France, Germany,

---

122 Houston, 51-52.
123 Hanawalt and Kobialka, x. The authors explain that men's and women's activities occupied different spaces, but also claimed that 'the practice of space in the Middle Ages was never homogeneous, but always in flux'.
124 Wiesner-Hanks, 1. This seems more like a way of reiterating the argument that gender was always important, rather than a strategy for advancing our understanding of early modern spatial experiences.
125 See Flather; see also B. Heller.
126 Historical geographers have developed a variety of spatial theories relating to human development; a useful discussion is found in Viazzo, 1-15; see also Driver; *Deep Maps*. Maarten Prak considers definitions of 'regions' by nineteenth- and 20th-century scholars and then distinguishes between 'micro-regions' (a city and its countryside) and 'meso-regions' (southeast England-northern France-Low Countries, or Rhône valley-northern Italy). The spatial influence of political institutions or areas of cultural influence could be other ways of defining regions; see Prak.
127 H. Scott, '"The Line of Descent",' 227. For Louis XIV's attempt to rule this area during the latter half of his reign, see McCluskey.

Italy, and the Low Countries.[128] The 'border nobility', according to a recent account, 'literally operated on and around "frontiers", permitting dynastic interests to prevail over narrower political allegiance when family survival depended on it'.[129] Violet Soen has studied, through the family of Guillaume de Croÿ, 'the impact of geographical anchorage and territorial war on identity formation' for early modern nobles, whose identities were tied to their lordships.[130] Laura Casella has studied noble families in the border zone of Friuli, between Venice and the Empire, a multipolar and strongly feudal region whose nobility has frequently been portrayed as supporters of one side or the other (a view rejected by the author).[131] Marriage was the key means by which transregional or border nobles extended their spatial reach – René de Challant was a good example of this.[132]

Mobility and related actions were key spatial practices by which late-Renaissance nobles enhanced or undermined their authority. Early modern people across Europe had always been mobile, and scholars have recognized that 'mobility produces multiple allegiances', local, national, and transnational.[133] Historians of the Low Countries have linked the geographic mobility of nobles to their political influence. Such movement created 'links between different regional elites and institutions', contributing to the

---

128 Lipp, *Noble Strategies*. The author cites Johan Huizinga for the idea that these territories and inhabitants acted as mediators on a European scale; see Huizinga, 138-57. William Monter has referred to the duchies of Lorraine and Bar as a 'lost state' of early modern Europe, pointing out how its geographically in-between position has caused problems for historians trying to understand it. This is due not only to the dispersal of its archives, but also to its exceedingly complex jurisdictional status, and its numerous seigniories with multiple overlords and enclaves (Monter, 17).

129 Geevers and Marini, 5.

130 Soen, 88. Soen asks 'what happened when these lordships were located in areas where the rulers were at war', a question that has been neglected due to the historiographic tendency to study the nobility 'within one state and within the borders of that state. Yet early modern grandees often owned possessions spread across political borders' (ibid.)

131 The county of Gorizia was marked by political instability, institutional polycentrism, and variation in property structures and kinship networks. Nobles here took no account of the border with respect to their jurisdiction, property rights, commercial interests, marriage alliances, kinship ties, and clientele networks. See Casella. For similar problems in the nearby Isonzo valley, see, in the same journal volume, Panjek.

132 In the Low Countries, middling nobles from outside of a region might acquire property there through marriage, acquiring an '(intra)regional character', while great nobles might form alliances with foreign nobles or princely families (Van Steensel, 'Kinship, Property, and Identity,' 251-52). In Gorizia, marriage between local women and Venetians created a problem of property transfer to the Venetian state via dowries, so, in the seventeenth century, the Gorizian estates passed statutes prohibiting foreigners from marrying noblewomen (Casella).

133 Hesse and Sahlins, 357; see also Altman.

creation of 'a common political discourse' that bound together nobles in state service who hailed from different areas and sometimes intermarried.[134] In the Netherlands, the 'Burgundian-Habsburg personal union gave a strong impetus to geographical mobility' by elites, as they acquired cross-border feudal estates that were subject to the same lord and 'it became politically strategic to acquire properties in various principalities'.[135] French nobles often held geographically dispersed lands and moved frequently between them.[136] Rulers recognized the territorial power of their nobles and sought to appropriate this influence for themselves by consolidating ties with them.[137] On the other hand, the physical proximity of rulers to noble families in small states could give princes there greater control over social advancement than great monarchs enjoyed, since 'their subjects lacked the possibility to act in a more independent manner than geographic distance from central power afforded'.[138] Physical presence or absence affected late-Renaissance lordship in contradictory ways. Disorders often broke out when lords were absent from their lands. In Ireland, 'an absence of lords, and therefore of lordship, was far more likely to lead to crisis than "overweening" aristocratic power'.[139] But a similar principle created an incentive for lords to be away from their lands and in attendance at the Prince's court: it was '"an obvious principle of sixteenth-century political life [...] [that] political influence or political health is directly related to proximity to the prince"'.[140]

These spatial practices affected the ways in which nobles and their families thought about their own identities and relationships. Nancy Munn wrote that 'spatial and temporal forms of practices constitute a central dimension of their cultural meaning, one infused with moral value'.[141] Family honor took symbolic form in spatial property (castles, jurisdictions, etc.),

---

134 Dumolyn, 438-39. The Flemish nobility, though, 'had always been less bound to specific places of residence', since they had castles but also many urban residences (ibid.)
135 Van Steensel, 'Kinship, Property, and Identity,' 250.
136 Sandberg, 39.
137 James VI and I used networks of Scottish nobles (whom he brought to his court in London) to bind Scotland to his English realm, for example; see Groundwater.
138 Lipp, *Noble Strategies*, 14.
139 Crooks, 446.
140 Headley, 31, cited in MacKay, 776. Efforts by the Harrach family from Vienna to diversify its kin network was related to these concerns. Hassler writes that 'le polycentrisme habsbourgeois, qui impose une forte mobilité résidentielle, induit la diversification spatiale de la parentèle et la vitalité des relations entre Vienne et les autres capitales provinciales'. This made it possible to be away from court, 'sans préjudice pour le courtisan', who might even be assigned a court position without any attendance obligation; see Hassler, 188.
141 Munn cited in Bestor, 551.

while the patrimony's 'temporal duration and spatial extension elevated the name of the house and its bearers, living and dead'.[142] Julien Demade's notion of 'topo-linearity' also draws a close connection between the fief as a spatial phenomenon and family identity.[143] Although cosmopolitan and geographically mobile, the late medieval Flemish elite were also 'diligent in defending the interests of their own local communities, which served as their own power base, or as a location of their important family and patronage relationships'.[144] Spatial dynamics also animated family relationships. In early modern France, the two eldest sons of some families lived in the same house with their parents for two years after they married. Their eventual departure and 'movement across geographic space' indicated the creation of new lineages, which could then be spatially located.[145] Michel Nassiet studied heiresses uniting two geographically separate patrimonies through homogamous marriage, concluding that 'the distance across which alliances could be established depended on the wealth and influence of the lineages'.[146] One aspect of the spatial character of noble family identity that has been under-investigated is the way in which the territorial dispersion of some nobles' lands influenced their families' self-representations and political interests. Edoardo Grendi found that the topographic component of Genoese political configurations contributed to a strong ideology of kinship.[147] But how did the link between spatiality and family identity work itself out in a context in which 'vast family estates were rarely territorially consolidated or fully contiguous' and 'a territorially compact land holding of any size was difficult to create'?[148]

This question will be explored in the chapters that follow through closely examining the career and relationships of René de Challant, an Alpine lord on the edge of the Italian Renaissance whose lands spread from northwestern Italy to Lorraine. A central argument of this book is

---

142 Ibid., 551. In n. 1 on this page, Bestor describes Munn's view of time and space as a '"unitary analytic concept" – spacetime'.
143 Demade, 619. Arie van Steensel has also recognized that the late medieval move toward patrilinearity had a spatial component that tied lineage to 'the transmission of seigneurial power and feudal titles', also referred to as *topolignée*. See 'Kinship, Property, and Identity,' 259-60.
144 Dumolyn, 442. The link between specific places and dynastic identity was also operative on the level of the Empire as a whole; see Brunner, 18-19.
145 Bennini, 17, 23.
146 If the revenues of these lands could be monetized and if they could be administered by managers through correspondence, their influence could be transmitted across space (Nassiet, *Parenté, noblesse et États dynastiques*, 218 [for quotation], 222).
147 Grendi, xii-xiii.
148 Scott and Storrs, 'The Consolidation of Noble Power,' 29.

that the spatial configuration of René's fiefs was fundamental both to his identity as a Renaissance border noble of quasi-sovereign status, and to his practical political influence, positively and negatively. His status as a feudal lord made him no less a Renaissance figure, and, while the location of his county of Challant in the Valle d'Aosta might have been on Italy's edge (as perhaps the Sabaudian lands as a whole were), he epitomized the transregional reach of the sixteenth-century Italian Renaissance and was certainly at the center of the 'Alpine Renaissance'. As René shuttled between his fiefs and palaces in the Monferrato, the Valle d'Aosta, Savoie, Valangin, and Beaufremont, and from the Sabaudian court to the French and Imperial ones, he developed relationships both with other princes, nobles, and burghers – especially Swiss financiers from Berne, Fribourg, and Basel – who influenced the way that he thought about his own identity and authority. This was particularly important with respect to his claims to be both the sovereign Prince of Valangin and *bourgeois* of Berne. Due to the geographic variety of his political bases and commitments, René does not fit easily into any of the models of noble-state-city relations developed by historians of Italy or other places. He was not a 'southern Italian' rural, feudal lord, nor a 'northern Italian' urban, commercially inclined one, but a Renaissance noble whose experiences and concerns connect to those of nobles throughout sixteenth-century Italy, the Alpine region, and beyond.

This book is based on archival research carried out mainly in the Archives Historiques Régionales d'Aoste (AHR), the Archivio di Stato di Torino, prima sezione (AST1), the Archives d'État de Neuchâtel (AEN), and on a collection of René's letters housed in the *Lettere di particolari* series of the AST and published by Giovanni Fornaseri in 1957. Financial and legal records, and published sources where they exist, also support this account. Much of the correspondence at the AHR is paleographically difficult and is often missing dates or the names of authors or recipients, requiring some sleuthing and informed speculation. This is the first time that these different sources have been analyzed together in a single account of René's life, which was particularly eventful. For this reason, I am aware of the danger of crystallizing the experiences of an individual into a single historiographic caricature, since I know that such experiences can change ideas, interests, and even identities over the course of a life. This was especially true of political interests that developed between 1504 and 1565 in the Western Alps – an area and time period of significant political instability. As rulers and nobles across Europe formulated new ideas about loyalty, sovereignty, and jurisdiction, and as the events of the Reformation changed the relationship between religious authority and political claims, late-Renaissance elites caught up in the Italian wars (especially in the northwestern part of the peninsula) adjusted their views of fidelity and autonomy to fit a rapidly changing strategic context. Uncertainty was ubiquitous, and it is important to keep this in mind when trying to characterize the goals and attitudes of the actors involved.

The first part of this book is divided into three chapters that describe the key events in René's life, beginning with his early life and political leadership until 1536 (Chapter 2). The following chapter discusses the tumultuous events of 1536 – the French and Swiss invasions of the Sabaudian lands, and René's efforts to navigate this period while remaining loyal to Charles III of Savoy until the Duke's death in 1553. Key events include René's struggles with the rulers of Neuchâtel for authority over Valangin and his brief stint as Emanuel Filibert's lieutenant general in Piedmont. The last biographical chapter examines the Count's relationship with the young Duke of Savoy, his capture by the French in Vercelli and eventual release from prison, his marriage plans for his daughters, and his final years as Marshal of Savoie, concluding with a short survey of how historians have represented René's life.

The first part is narrative and descriptive, shedding light on little-known episodes and characters in the history of a transalpine Italian Renaissance. The four chapters of the book's second part take up a series of themes in more explicitly comparative fashion. The topic of Chapter 5 is René's relationship to family members and to other nobles in transregional contexts – in the Valle d'Aosta and elsewhere. These interactions sometimes took the form of legal disputes, often with kin and 'friends' scattered across Europe. The following chapter examines the transregional political networks of René and of his second wife, Mencia of Portugal-Braganza. It also shows how correspondence and informational structures affected these networks, and informed René's interactions with Sabaudian and other state officials. Chapter 7 focuses on René's role as a transregional financial creditor, broker, and borrower, highlighting his interactions with Swiss lenders and the constraints imposed by the substantial ransoms that he had to pay twice over the course of his life. The penultimate chapter draws a number of these threads together by examining René's lordship of Valangin, Beaufremont, and some of his lands in the Valle d'Aosta, exploring how the practice of spatially dispersed lordship influenced his view of personal and family identity and authority. Each chapter stresses the spatial element of René's experience, situating him variously within Renaissance Italy, the Renaissance Alps, and the 'Middle Kingdom' that stretched from the Netherlands to the Mediterranean. In some ways, his case is singular, but, in other ways, it illustrates the challenges and advantages experienced by noble families both within Italy and beyond. The conclusion argues that close examination of René's experiences and the language used to describe them shows how sixteenth-century political interactions were spatialized in a particularly embodied and material way.

Bibliography

Ida Altman, 'Review Essay: Migration and Mobility in the Sixteenth-Century Hispanic World,' *RQ* 67, 2 (2014): 544-52

Franco Angiolini, 'Les noblesses italiennes à l'époque moderne: approches et interprétations,' *RHMC* 45 (1998): 66-88

Andrew Angyal, 'Recent Hungarian Renaissance Scholarship,' *Medievalia et humanistica* 8 (1954): 72-94

Karl Appuhn, *A Forest on the Sea: Environmental Expertise in Renaissance Venice* (Baltimore: The Johns Hopkins University Press, 2010)

Megan Armstrong, 'Transatlantic Catholicism: Rethinking the Nature of the Catholic Tradition in the Early Modern Period,' *History Compass* 5, 6 (2007): 1942-66

Sebouh David Aslanian, Joyce E. Chaplin, Ann McGrath, and Kristin Mann, 'How Size Matters: The Question of Scale in History,' *AHR* 118, 5 (2013): 1431-72

Aspiration, Representation and Memory: The Guise in Europe, 1506-1688, ed. Jessica Munns, Penny Richards, and Jonathan Spangler (Farnham, UK: Ashgate, 2015)

Walter Barberis, 'Emanuele Filiberto, geopolitica e storia nazionale,' *RSI* 109, 1 (1997): 281-97

Alessandro Barbero, 'The Feudal Principalities: The West (Monferrato, Saluzzo, Savoy and Savoy-Acaia),' in *The Italian Renaissance State*, pp. 177-96

C.R. Baskerville, 'Recent Works on Phases of the English Renaissance,' *Modern Philology* 18, 9 (1921): 505-12

Aubrey Bell, *Luis de Leon. A Study of the Spanish Renaissance* (Oxford: Clarendon Press, 1925)

Martine Bennini, 'Mémoire, implantation et stratégies familiales: les Leclerc de Lesseville (XVIe-XVIIIe siècles),' *RHMC* 54, 3 (2007): 7-39

Jane Fair Bestor, 'Bastardy and Legitimacy in the Formation of a Regional State in Italy: The Estense Succession,' *Comparative Studies in Society and History* 38, 3 (1996): 549-85

Jane Black, *Absolutism in Renaissance Milan: Plenitude of Power under the Visconti and the Sforza 1329-1535* (Oxford: Oxford University Press, 2009)

Andrea Boldù, 'Relazione della Corte di Savoia' (12 December 1561), in *Relazioni degli ambasciatori veneti al Senato*, ser. 2, vol. 1, ed. Eugenio Albèri (Firenze: Tipografia all'insegna di Glio, 1839), pp. 401-70

Ariane Boltanski, *Les ducs de Nevers et l'État royal: Genèse d'un compromis (ca. 1550-ca. 1600)* (Geneva: Droz, 2006)

Rebecca Boone, 'Empire and Medieval Simulacrum: A Political Project of Mercurino di Gattinara, Grand Chancellor of Charles V,' *SCJ* 42, 4 (2011): 1027-49

Thalia Brero, *Les baptêmes princiers. Le cérémonial dans les cours de Savoie et Bourgogne (XV-XVIe s.)* (Lausanne: Université de Lausanne, 2005)

Susan Broomhall and Jacqueline van Gent, 'In the Name of the Father: Conceptualizing *Pater Familias* in the Letters of William the Silent's Children,' *RQ* 62, (2009): 1130-66.

Otto Brunner, 'Conclusion of Land and Lordship: Fundamental Questions of the Constitutional History of South-East Germany in the Middle Ages,' *Genre* 43, 1-2 (2010): 13-26

Frederik Buylaert, 'Lordship, Urbanization and Social Change in Late Medieval Flanders,' *PP* 227, 1 (2015): 31-75

Id., Wim De Clercq, and Jan Dumolyn, 'Sumptuary Legislation, Material Culture and the Semiotics of "vivre noblement" in the County of Flanders (14th–16th centuries),' *Social History* 36, 4 (2011): 393-417

Arthur Byne and Mildred Stapley, *Rejería of the Spanish Renaissance* (New York: Hispanic Society of America, 1914)

William Caferro, *Contesting the Renaissance* (Malden, MA: Wiley-Blackwell, 2011)

The Cambridge Companion to the Italian Renaissance, ed. Michael Wyatt (Cambridge: Cambridge University Press, 2014)

Laura Casella, 'Noblesse de frontière. Espace politique et relations familiales dans le Frioul à l'époque moderne,' *Mélanges de l'École française de Rome – Italie et Méditerranée modernes et contemporaines* 125, 1 (2013), https://journals.openedition.org/mefrim/1134, 12 November 2019

Enrico Castelnuovo, *Il ciclo dei mesi di Torre Aquila a Trento* (Trent: Museo Provinciale d'Arte, 1987)

Alessandro Celi, 'Une identité guerrière: les Valdôtains et la fidélité à la Maison de Savoie,' in *La Maison de Savoie et les Alpes*, pp. 211-24

Federica Cengarle, 'Lordships, Fiefs and "Small States",' in *The Italian Renaissance State*, pp. 284-303

Dipesh Chakrabarty, *Provincializing Europe: Postcolonial Thought and Historical Difference* (Princeton: Princeton University Press, 2000)

Herbert Cole, *An Introduction to the Period Styles of England & France. With a Chapter on the Dutch Renaissance* (Manchester: Sutherland, 1926)

Communities and Conflicts in the Alps from the Late Middle Ages to Early Modernity, ed. Marco Bellabarba, Hannes Obermair, and Hitomi Sato (Bologna: Il Mulino, 2015)

Contested Spaces of Nobility in Early Modern Europe, ed. Matthew Romaniello and Charles Lipp (Farnham, UK: Ashgate, 2011)

Peter Crooks, 'Factions, Feuds and Noble Power in the Lordship of Ireland, 1356-1496,' *Irish Historical Studies* 35, alt. no. 140 (2007): 425-54

Linda Darling, 'Political Change and Political Discourse in the Early Modern Mediterranean World,' *JIH* 38, 4 (2008): 505-31

Céline Dauverd, *Imperial Ambition in the Early Modern Mediterranean: Genoese Merchants and the Spanish Crown* (Cambridge: Cambridge University Press, 2014)

Natalie Zemon Davis, *Trickster Travels: A Sixteenth-Century Muslim Between Worlds* (New York: Hill and Wang, 2006)

Darryl Dee, 'Wartime Government in Franche-Comté and the Demodernization of the French State, 1704-1715,' *FHS* 30, 1 (2007): 21-47

Deep Maps and Spatial Narratives, ed. David Bodenhamer, John Corrigan, and Trevor Harris (Bloomington, IN: Indiana University Press, 2015)

Massimo della Misericordia, 'Gusti cavallereschi, stili residenziali e temi figurativi. Aspetti della cultura aristocratica nella Lombardia alpina alla fine del medioevo,' *Quaderni storici* 51, 3 (2016): 793-822

Id., 'Medioevo cavalleresco nelle memorie familiari dell'aristocrazia alpina lombarda,' *Bollettino della Società Storica Valtellinese* 68 (2015): 7-17

Julien Demade, 'Parenté, noblesse et échec de la genèse de l'état: le cas allemand,' *AHSS* 61, 3 (2006): 609-31

Benjamin Deruelle, *De papier, de fer et de sang. Chevaliers et chevalerie à l'épreuve de la modernité (ca 1460-ca 1620)* (Paris: Publications de la Sorbonne, 2015)

Androniki Dialeti, 'Defending Women, Negotiating Masculinity in Early Modern Italy,' *HJ* 54, 1 (2011): 1-23

Claire Dolan, 'Anachronisms or Failures? Family Strategies in the Sixteenth Century, as Drawn from Collective Biographies of Solicitors in Aix-en-Provence,' *JFH* 33, 3 (2008): 291-303

Damian Dombrowski, 'Eine maritime Renaissance: Neapel, das Meer und die Kunst unter Vizekönig Pedro de Toledo,' *Wallraf-Richartz-Jahrbuch* 75 (2014): 185-228

Claudio Donati, 'Una famiglia lombarda tra XVI e XVIII secolo: gli Este di San Martino e i loro feudi,' in *Archivi territori poteri in area estense* (sec. XVI-XVIII), ed. E. Fregni (Roma: Bulzoni, 1999), pp. 435-53

Id., 'The Italian Nobilities in the Seventeenth and Eighteenth Centuries,' in *The European Nobilities*, pp. 286-321

Id., 'Nobiltà e coscienza nobiliare nell'Italia del Cinquecento,' in *Per i trent'anni di 'Nobili e mercanti nella Lucca del Cinquecento'*, Conference in honor of Marino Berengo (Lucca: Comune di Lucca, 1998), pp. 51-72

Id., 'Nobiltà e Stati nell'Italia della prima età moderna (con particolare attenzione a fonti archivistiche milanesi),' in *Nobiltà e Stato in Piemonte. I Ferrero d'Ormea. Atti del convegno Torino-Mondovì 3-5 ottobre 2001*, ed. A. Merlotti (Turin: Zamorani, 2003), pp. 61-81

Id., 'The Profession of Arms and the Nobility in Spanish Italy: Some Considerations,' in *Spain in Italy. Politics, Society, and Religion 1500-1700*, ed. T.J. Dandelet and J. Marino (Leiden: Brill, 2006), pp. 299-332

Henk Dragstra, 'Heraldry and Collective Memory: A Lawsuit of Emperor Charles V against Reinoud III of Brederode,' *SCJ* 42, 1 (2011): 9-35

Felix Driver, 'The Historicity of Human Geography,' *Progress in Human Geography* 12 (1988): 497-506

Jeroen Duindam, 'Dynasty and Elites: From Early Modern Europe to Late Imperial China,' in *Dynastic Identity in Early Modern Europe*, pp. 59-85

Jan Dumolyn, 'Nobles, Patricians and Officers: The Making of a Regional Political Elite in Late Medieval Flanders,' *Journal of Social History* 40, 2 (2006): 431-52

Eric Dursteler, *Renegade Women: Gender, Identity, and Boundaries in the Early Modern Mediterranean* (Baltimore: The Johns Hopkins University Press, 2011)

Id., *Venetians in Constantinople: Nation, Identity and Coexistence in the Early Modern Mediterranean* (Baltimore: The Johns Hopkins University Press, 2006)

Dynastic Identity in Early Modern Europe, ed. Liesbeth Geevers and Mirella Marini (Farnham, UK: Ashgate, 2015)

The European Nobilities in the Seventeenth and Eighteenth Centuries, 2 vols., vol. 1, *Western and Southern Europe*, 2nd ed., ed. Hamish Scott (London and New York: Palgrave Macmillan, 2007)

Justine Firnhaber-Baker, 'Seigneurial War and Royal Power in Later Medieval Southern France,' *PP* 208 (2010): 37-76

Amanda Flather, *Gender and Space in Early Modern England* (Rochester: Boydell and Brewer, 2007)

Flemish Renaissance, Interiors and Interior Details (New York: W. Helburn, 1900)

Laurence Fontaine, *Pouvoir, identités et migrations dans les hautes vallées des Alpes occidentales (XVIIe-XVIIIe siècles)* (Grenoble: Presses universitaires de Grenoble, 2003)

Andrea Gamberini and Isabella Lazzarini, 'Introduction,' in *The Italian Renaissance State*, pp. 1-6

Gated communities? Regulating migration in early modern cities, ed. Bert De Munck and Anne Winter (Farnham: Ashgate, 2012)

Liesbeth Geevers, 'Family Matters: William of Orange and the Habsburgs after the Abdication of Charles V (1555–67),' *RQ* 63, 2 (2010): 459-90

Liesbeth Geevers and Mirella Marini, 'Aristocracy, Dynasty and Identity in Early Modern Europe, 1520-1700,' in *Dynastic Identity in Early Modern Europe*, pp. 1-23

Nancy Green, 'French History and the Transnational Turn,' *FHS* 37, 4 (2014): 551-564

Edoardo Grendi, *I Balbi: Una famiglia genovese fra Spagna e Impero* (Turin: Einaudi, 1997)

Anna Groundwater, 'From Whitehall to Jedburgh: Patronage Networks and the Government of the Scottish Borders, 1603 to 1625,' *HJ* 53, 4 (2010): 871-93

D.H., review of Phillips, *Erasmus and the Northern Renaissance*, *EHR* 65, 256 (1950): 408

J.R. Hale, *The Civilization of Europe in the Renaissance* (London: HarperCollins, 1993)

Edward Hall, 'Proxemics,' *Current Anthropology* 9 (1968): 83-109

Barbara Hanawalt and Michal Kobialka, 'Introduction,' in *Medieval Practices of Space*, ed. Barbara Hanawalt and Michal Kobialka (Minneapolis and London: University of Minnesota Press, 2000), pp. ix-xviii

Gregory Hanlon, 'The Decline of a Provincial Military Aristocracy: Siena 1560-1740,' *PP* 155 (1997): 64-108

Eric Hassler, 'Les Harrach face à la disgrâce. Les stratégies matrimoniales d'un lignage aristocratique autrichien à la fin du XVIIe siècle,' *RHMC* 61, 2 (2014): 176-201

John Headley, *The Emperor and His Chancellor* (Cambridge: Cambridge University Press, 1983)

Benjamin Heller, 'Leisure and the Use of Domestic Space in Georgian London,' *HJ* 53, 3 (2010): 623-45

Henry Heller, *Anti-Italianism in Sixteenth-Century France* (Toronto: University of Toronto Press, 2003)

Carla Hesse and Peter Sahlins, 'Introduction,' *FHS*, special issue on mobility, 29, 3 (2006): 347-357

R.A. Houston, 'People, Space, and Law in Late Medieval and Early Modern Britain and Ireland,' *PP* 230, 1 (2016): 47-89

Deborah Howard, *Venice and the East: The Impact of the Islamic World on Venetian Architecture 1100-1500* (New Haven: Yale University Press, 2000)

Johan Huizinga, 'The Netherlands as Mediator Between Western and Central Europe,' in *Dutch Civilisation in the 17th Century and Other Essays*, ed. Pieter Geyl and F.W.N. Hugenholtz (London: Fontana, 1968), pp. 138-57

Jesse Hysell, 'Contentious Coesistence: The Function of Material Exchanges in Venetian-Egyptian Relations on the Eve of the Ottoman Conquest (1480-1517),' (PhD dissertation, Syracuse University, 2017)

Gabriel Imboden, *Das Stockalperschloss in Brig* (Berne: Gesellschaft für Schweizerische Kunstgeschichte, 2005)

The Italian Renaissance State, ed. Andrea Gamberini and Isabella Lazzarini (Cambridge: Cambridge University Press, 2012)

Italy and Hungary: Humanism and Art in the Early Renaissance, ed. Péter Farbaky and Louis Waldman (Harvard: Harvard University Press, 2011)

Philip Jones, *The Italian City-State: From Commune to Signoria* (Oxford: Oxford University Press, 1997)

Arlette Jouanna, *Le devoir de Révolte. La noblesse française et la gestation de l'État moderne* (Paris: Fayard, 1989)

Mark Jurdjevic, 'Political Cultures,' in *The Cambridge Companion to the Italian Renaissance*, ed. Michael Wyatt (Cambridge: Cambridge University Press, 2014)

Thomas DaCosta Kaufmann, *Toward a Geography of Art* (Chicago and London: The University of Chicago Press, 2004), pp. 298-319

Martin Korenjak, 'Why Mountains Matter: Early Modern Roots of a Modern Notion,' *RQ* 70, 1 (Spring 2017): 179-219

Beat Kümin, *Political Space in Pre-Industrial Europe* (Farnham, UK: Ashgate, 2009)

Michael Kwass, *Contraband: Louis Mandrin and the Making of a Global Underground* (Cambridge MA: Harvard University Press, 2014)

Corinne Lefèvre, 'Pouvoir et noblesse dans l'empire Moghol: Perspectives du règne de Jahāngīr (1605-1627),' *AHSS* 62, 6 (2007): 1287-312

Jean-Marie Le Gall, 'Vieux saint et grande noblesse à l'époque moderne: Saint Denis, les Montmorency et les Guise,' *RHMC* 50, 3 (2003): 7-33

Charles Lipp, 'Power and Politics in Early Modern Lorraine: Jean-François de Mahuet and the *Grand Prévôté* de Saint-Dié,' *FHS* 26, 1 (2003): 31-53

Id., *Noble Strategies in an Early Modern Small State: The Mahuet of Lorraine* (Rochester, NY: University of Rochester Press, 2011)

Ruth MacKay, 'Governance and Empire during the Reign of Charles V: A Review Essay,' *SCJ* 40, 3 (2009): 769-79

La Maison de Savoie et les Alpes: emprise, innovation, identification XVe-XIXe siècle, ed. Stéphane Gal and Laurent Perrillat (Chambéry: Université de Savoie – Laboratoire LLS, 2015)

Mapping Gendered Routes and Spaces in the Early Modern World, ed. Merry Wiesner-Hanks (Farnham, UK: Ashgate, 2015)

John Marino, *Becoming Neapolitan: Citizen Culture in Baroque Naples* (Baltimore: The Johns Hopkins University Press, 2011)

Id., 'The Exile and His Kingdom: The Reception of Braudel's *Mediterranean*,' *JMH* 76 (September 2004): 622-52

Peter Marshall, '"The Greatest Man in Wales": James Ap Gruffydd Ap Hywel and the International Opposition to Henry VIII,' *SCJ* 39, 3 (2008): 681-704.

Lauro Martines, *Power and Imagination: City States in Renaissance Italy* (Baltimore: The Johns Hopkins University Press, 1979)

Michael Martoccio, 'Ideal Types and Negotiated Identities: A Comparative Approach to the City-State,' *JIH* 45, 2 (2014): 187-200

Jon Mathieu, *History of the Alps 1500-1900: Environment, Development, and Society*, trans. Matthew Vester (Morgantown, WV: West Virginia University Press, 2009)

Phil McCluskey, *Absolute Monarchy on the Frontiers: Louis XIV's Military Occupations of Lorraine and Savoy* (Manchester and New York: Manchester University Press, 2013)

Marjorie Meiss-Even, 'The Guise "Italianised"? The Role of Italian Merchants, Intermediaries and Experts in Ducal Consumption in the Sixteenth Century,' in *Aspiration, Representation and Memory*, pp. 47-60

Laura Meneghello, *Jacob Moleschott – A Transnational Biography: Science, Politics, and Popularization in Nineteenth-Century Europe* (Bielefeld: Transcript-Verlage, 2018).

Andrea Merlotti, 'De "re delle Alpi" à "roi des Marmottes": les Alpes dans la représentation de la Maison de Savoie (XVIIe-XVIIIe siècles),' in *La Maison de Savoie et les Alpes*, pp. 45-68

James Miller, 'The Nobility in Polish Renaissance Society, 1548-1572' (PhD dissertation, Indiana University, 1977)

Noah Millstone, 'Seeing Like a Statesman in Early Stuart England,' *PP* 223, 1 (2014): 77-127

Joanna Milstein, *The Gondi: Family Strategy and Survival in Early Modern France* (Farnham, UK: Ashgate, 2014)

E. William Monter, *A Bewitched Duchy: Lorraine and its Dukes, 1477-1736* (Geneva: Droz, 2007)

Joseph Morsel, *La noblesse contre le prince: l'espace social des Thüngen à la fin du Moyen Âge (Franconie, v. 1250-1525)* (Stuttgart: Jan Thorbecke, 2000)

Edward Muir, 'The Italian Renaissance in America,' *AHR* 100 (1995): 1095-1118

Jessica Munns, Penny Richards, and Jonathan Spangler, 'Introduction: The Context of a Dream,' in *Aspiration, Representation and Memory*, pp. 1-24

Michel Nassiet, *Parenté, noblesse et États dynastiques, XVe-XVIe siècles* (Paris: Éditions de l'EHESS, 2000)

La noblesse des marches, de Bourgogne et d'ailleurs au temps de Marguerite d'Autriche (XVe-XVIe siècle), ed. Sarah Fourcade, Dominique Le Page, and Jacques Paviot, *Annales de Bourgogne* 89, 3-4 (Dijon: Éditions universitaires de Dijon, 2017)

Monique O'Connell, *Men of Empire: Power and Negotiation in Venice's Maritime State* (Oxford: Oxford University Press, 2009)

Toby Osborne, 'The Surrogate War between the Savoys and the Medici: Sovereignty and Precedence in Early Modern Italy,' *The International History Review*, 29, 1 (2007): 1-21

Aleksander Panjek, 'I Consorti di Tolmino. Un'alleanza tra famiglie con interessi oltre confine (secoli XIV-XVII),' *Mélanges de l'École française de Rome – Italie et Méditerranée modernes et contemporaines* 125, 1 (2013), https://journals.openedition.org/mefrim/1094, 12 November 2019

Andrea Pennini, 'Attraversare le Alpi per volere del duca: percorsi e relazioni dei diplomatici sabaudi nel primo Seicento,' in *La Maison de Savoie et les Alpes*, pp. 107-18

Margaret Mann Phillips, *Erasmus and the Northern Renaissance* (London: Hodder & Stoughton, 1949)

Véronique Plesch, *Painter and Priest: Giovanni Canavesio's Visual Rhetoric and the Passion Cycle at La Brigue* (Notre Dame, IN: University of Notre Dame Press, 2006)

Linda Pollock, 'The Practice of Kindness in Early Modern Elite Society,' *PP* 211, 1 (2011): 121-158

Kenneth Pomeranz, 'Histories for a Less National Age,' *AHR* 119, 1 (2014): 1-22

N.J.G. Pounds, *An Economic History of Medieval Europe*, 2nd ed. (London and New York: Routledge, 1994)

Maarten Prak, 'Le regioni nella prima Europa moderna,' in *Regioni, culture e ancora regioni nella storia economica e sociale dell'Europa moderna*, special issue of *Proposte e ricerche* 35, 2 (1995): 7-40.

Jean Préaux, review of Phillips, *Erasmus and the Northern Renaissance*, *Latomus* 10, 2 (1951): 239-40.

Michael Prestwich, 'Medieval Biography,' *JIH* 40, 3 (2010): 325-46

Blythe Alice Raviola, *L'Europa dei piccoli stati. Dalla prima età moderna al declino dell'Antico Regime* (Rome: Carocci, 2008)

Id., 'Frontiere regionali, nazionali e storiografiche: bilancio di un progetto di ricerca e ipotesi di un suo sviluppo,' *RSI* 121, 1 (2009): 193-202

Id., 'The Imperial System in Early Modern Northern Italy: A Web of Dukedoms, Fiefs and Enclaves along the Po,' in *The Holy Roman Empire, 1495-1806: A European Perspective*, ed. R.J.W. Evans and Peter H. Wilson (Leiden: Brill, 2012), pp. 217-36

Hans Renders, 'The Limits of Representativeness: Biography, Life Writing, and Microhistory,' in *Theoretical Discussions of Biography: Approaches from History, Microhistory, and Life Writing*, ed. Hans Renders and Binne de Haan (Leiden: Brill, 2014), pp. 129-38

Matthew Romaniello and Charles Lipp, 'Introduction,' in *Contested Spaces of Nobility*, pp. 1-10

Robert Rotberg, 'Biography and Historiography: Mutual Evidentiary and Interdisciplinary Considerations,' *JIH* 40, 3 (2010): 305-24

Natalie Rothman, *Brokering Empire: Trans-Imperial Subjects Between Venice and Istanbul* (Ithaca: Cornell University Press, 2012)

Guido Ruggiero, *The Renaissance in Italy: A Social and Cultural History of the Rinascimento* (Cambridge: Cambridge University Press, 2014)

Sabaudian Studies: Political Culture, Dynasty, and Territory (1400-1700), ed. Matthew Vester (Truman State University Press, 2013)

J.H.M. Salmon, 'A Second Look at the *Noblesse Seconde*: The Key to Noble Clientage and Power in Early Modern France?' *FHS* 25, 4 (2002): 575-593

Brian Sandberg, *Warrior Pursuits: Noble Culture and Civil Conflict in Early Modern France* (Baltimore: The Johns Hopkins University Press, 2010)

Matthias Schnettger, 'Kleinstaaten in der Frühen Neuzeit: Konturen eines Forschungsfeldes,' *Historische Zeitschrift* 286, 3 (2008): 605-40

Hamish Scott, 'The Early Modern European Nobility and its Contested Historiographies, c. 1950-1980,' in *Contested Spaces of Nobility*, pp. 11-40

Id., '"The Line of Descent of Nobles is from the Blood of Kings": Reflections on Dynastic Identity,' in *Dynastic Identity in Early Modern Europe*, pp. 217-41

Hamish Scott and Christopher Storrs, 'The Consolidation of Noble Power in Europe, c. 1600-1800,' in *The European Nobilities*, pp. 1-60

Alvaro Sevilla-Buitrago, 'Territory and the Governmentalisation of Social Reproduction: Parliamentary Enclosure and Spatial Rationalities in the Transition from Feudalism to Capitalism,' *Journal of Historical Geography* 38, 3 (2012): 209-19

William Sewell, *Logics of History: Social Theory and Social Transformation* (Chicago: University of Chicago Press, 2005)

Christine Shaw, *Barons and Castellans: The Military Nobility of Renaissance Italy* (Leiden: Brill 2015)

James Sheehan, 'The Problem of Sovereignty in European History,' *AHR* 111, 1 (2006): 1-15

Hannah Smith, 'Court Studies and the Courts of Early Modern Europe,' *HJ* 49, 4 (2006): 1229-238

Violet Soen, 'The Chièvres Legacy, the Croÿ Family and Litigation in Paris. Dynastic Identities between the Low Countries and France (1519-1559),' in *Dynastic Identity in Early Modern Europe*, pp. 87-102

Jonathan Spangler, 'Points of Transferral: Mademoiselle de Guise's Will and the Transferability of Dynastic Identity,' in *Dynastic Identity in Early Modern Europe*, pp. 131-51

'Spanish Renaissance,' *The Decorator and Furnisher* 1, 3 (1882): 74

Lo stato sabaudo e il sacro impero romano, ed. Andrea Merlotti and Marco Bellabarba (Bologna: Il Mulino, 2014).

Angelantonio Spagnoletti, *Le dinastie italiane nella prima età moderna* (Bologna: Il Mulino, 2003)

Paul Stock, 'History and the Uses of Space,' in *The Uses of Space in Early Modern History*, ed. Paul Stock (New York: Palgrave Macmillan, 2015), pp. 1-18

Antonio Stopani, *La production des frontières: État et communautés en Toscane (XVIe-XVIIIe siècles)* (Rome: École française de Rome, 2008)

Bernhard Struck, Kate Ferris, and Jacques Revel, 'Introduction: Space and Scale in Transnational History,' *Size Matters: Scales and Spaces in Transnational and Comparative History*, special issue, *International History Review* 33, 4 (2011): 573-84

E.V. Telle, review of Phillips, *Erasmus and the Northern Renaissance*, BHR 12, 3 (1950): 399-401

Arthur Tilley, *The Literature of the French Renaissance: An Introductory Essay* (Cambridge: Cambridge University Press, 1885)

Angelo Torre, 'Percorsi della pratica,' *Quaderni storici* 30, 3 (1995): 799-830

Transregional and Transnational Families in Europe and Beyond: Experiences Since the Middle Ages, ed. Christopher Johnson, David Sabean, Simon Teuscher, and Francesca Trivellato (New York: Berghahn Books, 2011)

Valerie Traub, 'History in the Present Tense: Feminist Theories, Spatialized Epistemologies, and Early Modern Embodiment,' in *Mapping Gendered Routes*, pp. 15-54

Arie van Steensel, 'Kinship, Property, and Identity: Noble Family Strategies in Late-Medieval Zeeland,' *JFH* 37, 3 (2012): 247-69

Id., 'Noblemen in an Urbanised Society: Zeeland and its Nobility in the Late Middle Ages,' *Journal of Medieval History* 38, 1 (2012): 76-99

Geoffrey Symcox, *Jerusalem in the Alps: The Sacro Monte of Varallo and the Sanctuaries of North-Western Italy* (Turnhout: Brepols, 2019)

Maurice van Durme, *Antoon Perrenot, Bisschop van Atrecht, Kardinaal van Granvelle, Minister van Karel V en van Filips II (1517-1586)* (Brussels: Palaeis der Academiën, 1953)

Pier Paolo Viazzo, *Upland Communities: Environment, Population and Social Structure in the Alps since the Sixteenth Century* (Cambridge: Cambridge University Press, 1989)

Maria Antonietta Visceglia, 'L'età moderna,' *Studi storici* 53, 2 (2012): 279-316

Ian Warren, 'The English Landed Elite and the Social Environment of London c. 1580-1700: The Cradle of an Aristocratic Culture?' *EHR* 126, 518 (2011): 44-74

Merrick Whitcomb, *A Literary Source-book of the German Renaissance* (Philadelphia: University of Pennsylvania Press, 1899)

Merry Wiesner-Hanks, 'Introduction,' in *Mapping Gendered Routes*, pp. 1-14

Megan Williams, 'Dangerous Diplomacy and Dependable Kin: Transformations in Central European Statecraft, 1526-1540,' Ph.D. dissertation, Columbia University (2009)

Michael Wintroub, 'Words, Deeds, and a Womanly King,' *FHS* 28, 3 (2005): 387-413

Martin Wrede, 'Adel und Krone, Hof und Staat. Neue französische Forschungen zur französichen Frühneuzeit,' *ZHF* 37, 3 (2010): 441-62

John Yost, review of *The Northern Renaissance*, ed. Lewis Spitz, in *Church History* 42, 1 (1973): 131-32

Your Humble Servant: Agents in Early Modern Europe, ed. Hans Cools, Marika Keblusek, and Badeloch Noldus (Hilversum: Uitgeverij Verloren, 2006)

Hillay Zmora, 'The Princely State and the Noble Family: Conflict and Co-operation in the Margraviates Ansbach-Kulmbach in the Early Sixteenth Century,' *HJ* 49, 1 (2006): 1-21

2. René's early career to 1536

Abstract

Born in 1504, René de Challant inherited a sprawling array of lands stretching from Lorraine to the Swiss area, Bugey (between Chambéry and Lyon), and the Valle d'Aosta. To these, he added, by marriage, lands in the marquisate of Monferrato. His kinship connections propelled him immediately into the highest ranks of the Sabaudian nobility, and, after his first marriage to the wealthy heiress Bianca Maria Gaspardone ended tragically, he remarried Mencia of Portugal-Braganza, a kinswoman of the Duchess of Savoy and Emperor Charles V. René was named Marshal of Savoie and led Duke Charles III's diplomatic efforts with the Swiss during the early 1530s, aided in this effort by his lordship of Valangin, near Neuchâtel.

Key words: Savoy, Geneva, Swiss, Gaspardone, Mencia

René's early life

The family into which René de Challant was born (*c.* 1504) had a rich tradition of service to the House of Savoy. René's paternal grandfather, Louis, and father, Philibert, had wielded power on behalf of the dukes in the Valle d'Aosta, Piedmont, and beyond; his mother also received pensions from the Sabaudian rulers.[1] At the age of thirteen, René received his first command, replacing his recently deceased father as castellan of the Valdostano fortress of Bard. The deaths of his paternal grandfather and his mother over the next two years left him isolated, but Duke Charles III (r. 1504-1553) took a personal interest in the young count. In 1518, René was named *chevalier* of

---

1   AHR, FC 24, nos. 9-12 (patents dated 16-I-1480, 27-XI-1480, 29-XII-1480 and 14-II-1481); ibid., FC 288 no. 34, (patents dated 5-VIII-1481); ibid., FC 24, nos. 15, 19 (patents dated 10-XI-1490 and 5-IX-1498); ibid., FC 25, nos. 1, 3, 5 (patents dated 1-XI-03, 2-XII-04, and 17-XII-09); ibid., FC 209, no. 7 (patents dated 22-IX-1491); ibid., FC 24, nos. 13, 14, 17, 18 (patents dated 6-IX-83, 1485 through 1497 [various dates], 7-IX-1496, and 5-IX-1498); ibid., FC 209, no. 8 (donations dated 1497 and 1499).

Vester, M., *Transregional Lordship and the Italian Renaissance: René de Challant, 1504-1565*. Amsterdam: Amsterdam University Press, 2020.
DOI 10.5117/9789463726726_CH02

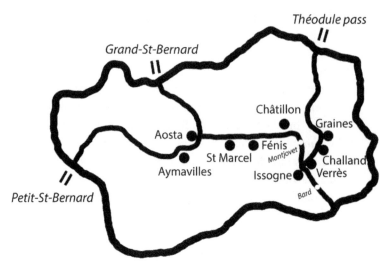

Map 2: Challant fiefs in the Valle d'Aosta. Map by author.

the Annonciade, the knightly order of the Sabaudian dynasty, was given an annual pension of 1200 florins,[2] and was appointed ducal counselor and *chambellan*. René was advised by his uncle, the cleric Charles de Challant, and his two grandmothers, Guillemette de Vergy and Marguerite de La Chambre. According to an early biographer, the Duke sent René as his envoy to Milan and to Monferrato, where he met Bianca Maria Gaspardone, the recently widowed daughter of a wealthy merchant from Casale Monferrato, who was also the treasurer of the Marquis of Monferrato.[3] They married in 1522. Bianca Maria's dowry included several farms in the Monferrato and five houses in Casale, together worth 25,000 *écus*.[4] A few weeks after his marriage, René renewed his status as a *combourgeois* of Berne through his

---

2   Ibid., FC 194, no. 12 (patents dated 12-XII-18).
3   Ibid., FC 194, no. 11 (letter of appointment dated 8-VIII-17); Vescovi, 83. The original manuscript, in French, is in 'Histoire généalogique'. There had been earlier discussions of René's marriage. An undated letter from the Sabaudian court, possibly from 1519, reports discussion of a possible marriage to a daughter of the 'grant maistre' (René de Savoie, *grand maître* of France, bastard half-brother of Duke Charles III), but it was decided that the girl was too young. Another potential match with Mademoiselle [Claudine?] de Miolans [daughter of Louis, Baron de Miolans, Marshal of Savoie], was opposed by the Duke, possibly because it would have given René control over the fortress of Miolans, the western outlet of the transalpine route across the Petit-St-Bernard pass, whose eastern endpoint through the Valle d'Aosta he already effectively dominated (AHR, FC 263, mz. 1, Sebastien Ferrero [? Bishop of Ivrea until his death in 1519] to Madame, Gaglianico? 26-I-19?).
4   Frutaz, 'Notes;' Fornaseri, ix-xxxvii.

inherited position as Lord of Valangin.⁵ If René's Valdostano inheritance and his family's tradition of Sabaudian service already located his patrimony at a transregional crossroads, the lands inherited from his mother and his wife set the pattern for a lifetime exercising spatially diffuse authority.

René's military and diplomatic career took off amid the turbulence of the early Italian wars. The armies of the Duke of Savoy's nephew, King Francis I, cut across the Alps, through the lands of Charles III, who grew weary of the damages caused by these French transits. But he failed to persuade his states' representative assemblies to fund the militia that could block the French campaigns. Francis I sensed his uncle's weakness and began to make claims on various Sabaudian territories as part of the inheritance of his mother, Louise de Savoie. As Charles III's relations with his traditional Swiss allies, the cantons of Fribourg and Berne, began to cool (due to differences over Geneva),⁶ the Duke turned to the Emperor for support, securing this alliance through his marriage to Beatrice of Portugal, the Emperor's sister-in-law (1521).⁷ When war erupted that year between Francis and Charles V, the Emperor asked Charles III to close his lands to the French army.⁸ The proxmity of French military might, however, forced Charles III not only to permit French passage, but even to organize *étapes* for the provisioning and lodging of the royal troops (doubtless in order to prevent pillaging). Another French army marched through Sabaudian territory in 1523,⁹ and then again in 1524, on its way to defeat at Pavia.

In this context of Sabaudian neutrality, the Duke's nobles and kin entered the contest on opposite sides. René borrowed 2000 *gulden* from the Swiss lender Jost Holdermeyer[10] and rode alongside King Francis (from whom he received an annual pension of 3000 florins) on the Pavia campaign, while the Duke's brother, Philippe de Savoie, commanded troops for the Emperor. Neither René nor Philippe was happy with the result, and each one eventually ended up switching allegiances. René was captured along with the King and held for ransom. Only by mortgaging his barony of Beaufremont for 3000 *écus* was he able to secure release.[11]

---

5   SKB, Stadtrecht von Bern, IV, 1, S. 174, no. 149, Renewal of 'das Burgrecht' of his predecessor lords of Valangin by René with the city of Berne, 30-VIII-22 (https://www.query.sta.be.ch/detail.aspx?ID=50500, 12 November 2019).
6   On these developments, see Mattingly; also see Naef.
7   Fornaseri, xiii.
8   Tallone, 71-76; Carutti, 270 n. 1, letter dated 19-XII-21 located in AST1 in the series LP.
9   Tallone, 76-78; citation from Ch III to Bonnivet, 13-VIII-23, cited in ibid., 78 n. 6.
10 AEN, AS-Z8, 1, 1524 loan.
11 Majolo Molinari, 44-64, 69; Fornaseri, xiv; Frutaz, 'Notes,' 250, 256.

René's capture, imprisonment, and ransom were not the only challenges faced by the 22-year-old. Not long after he was released from captivity, his wife went to prison. The saga of Bianca Maria has inspired several semi-fictionalized accounts, beginning in the sixteenth century. These are based on two sources, the fourth *novella* in Part One of Matteo Bandello's collection (published in 1554) and the chronicle of the Pavese writer Antonio Grumello (written c. 1530).[12] The story recounted by Bandello and Grumello is so sensational as to lead one to doubt its authenticity.[13] However, both seem to have encountered Bianca Maria personally, and key details of their accounts correspond despite the fact that Bandello was notoriously pro-French and Grumello equally pro-Imperial. Here is what seems to have happened.

As the French readied for the Pavia campaign, René crossed the Alps to meet them. We know that he wrote a testament in September 1523 (typically part of the preparation for going to war – in it, he referred to his '*dilectissime uxori*'), and that he was in Bugey in April 1524.[14] Perhaps he and his cohort rode through the valley on their way to Lombardy that fall. Both Bandello and Grumello place Bianca Maria in Pavia roughly during the same period (1524-1525). The former claims that, after a falling out between the lord and lady, 'she secretly fled her husband', while the latter adds that Bianca Maria brought with her 'quantities of cash, jewelry, and clothing'. Or, perhaps Bianca Maria simply accompanied her husband on the campaign: the French took control of Milan in early November 1524 and laid siege to Pavia at about the same time. Another possibility is that, following the French defeat in February 1525, she went to Lombardy to ensure that her lands in the Monferrato were not confiscated. Perhaps she even believed that her husband had been killed, as were many nobles in the service of the French King. She wrote a testament in Casale in December 1525 that did not mention her husband, and named Anne d'Alençon, the Marquise of Monferrato, as her universal heir.[15]

Both Bandello and Grumello suggest that, while in Pavia, Bianca Maria began to live 'too freely and dishonestly' (Bandello). There, she met Ardizzino

---

12   Using Bandello, François Belleforest published 'Vie desordonnée de la comtesse de Celant' in *Histoires tragiques* II, 2 (Lyon, 1564). This was followed by W. Painter, *Palace of Pleasures* II, 24 (London, 1566-1567) and J. Marston, *The Insatiate Countess* (1613). Following the publication in 1856 of Grumello's chronicle, other romanticized stories were issued; see Rosselli.

13   For Bandello's account, see Bandello; for Grumello, see *Cronaca di Antonio Grumello*, 424-28.

14   Vaccarone, 'Bianca Maria;' Fornaseri, 3, René to Ch III, Billia 3-IV-24; AST1, PD 188, ff. 274-81, will dated 10-IX-23.

15   Bianca Maria testament dated Casale 26-XII-25 in Vaccarone, 'Bianca Maria,' 326-29.

Valperga di Masino, of an illustrious Sabaudian noble house (from the Canavese, near Ivrea), who was young and handsome, although 'with a slight limp', and began a relationship that lasted over a year (Bandello). Bianca Maria then set her sights on another young gentleman, Roberto Sanseverino, Count of Caizzo, whom she considered 'a more energetic miller than her lover was' (Bandello). The accounts differ as to whether this happened when Bianca Maria was still in Pavia, or after she had moved to Milan.[16] Masino grew insanely jealous and began to 'condemn his lover in every way possible' (Grumello), to which Bianca Maria responded by calling him a 'lame cripple' (Bandello), promising to make him pay. When she asked Caiazzo to kill Masino, his ardor cooled and he left her. Caiazzo and Masino eventually became friends, shared confidences, and began circulating stories about Bianca Maria's 'villainous behavior, turning her into a popular legend' (Bandello). The insatiable Bianca Maria then met a third lover in Milan, the 22-year-old Spaniard Pietro Cardona, illegitimate son of the Count of Golisano, and successfully persuaded him to assassinate Masino. Cardona gathered a group of heavily armed men and ambushed Masino, his brother, and their servants as they returned from a dinner party at night. Cardona was immediately identified and captured, and, soon thereafter, Bianca Maria was taken into custody. Another account has Cardona confessing to a conspiracy to kill René and marry Bianca Maria. She also eventually confessed, attempted to buy her way out of prison, and was executed outside the gate of the castle of Milan on 20 October 1526. The *Liber defunctorum* of Milan notes that, on that date, 'Lady Bianca Maria, twenty-five years of age, Countess of Challant, was decapitated in the castle of Porta Giove, by public judgment'.[17]

Sometime in the midst of this drama, René was released from captivity in Spain. By August, René was at Beaugency (between Orléans and Blois), where he instructed one of his officers to collect his pensions from the French Crown.[18] The only existing evidence of René's reaction to this affair is in a letter sent to the Duke of Savoy about two weeks prior to his wife's execution. René laconically thanked Charles III for his efforts to intervene with the Milanese governor in 'the matter of the imprisoned woman'. The Duke was unable to have Bianca Maria released into her husband's custody, which would have enabled him to 'demonstrate to the world the desire that I had to show her her error and mistakes'. However, since 'God wills that

---

16 Grumello has her meet Caiazzo in Milan in mid 1526.
17 Vaccarone, 'Bianca Maria,' 329; Vescovi, 84.
18 Gachard, 76-81; AHR, FC 40, no. 15, procuration by René for Luigi di Castellamonte dated 8-VIII-26.

Fig. 1: The decapitation of Saint Catherine, traditionally identified as Bianca Maria (detail of fresco by Bernardino Luini [ca. 1530] from Besozzi Chapel in church of San Maurizio al Monastero Maggiore, Milan). Source: *Bernardino Luini e la pittura del Rinascimento a Milano: Gli affreschi di San Maurizio al Monastero Maggiore*, ed. Sandrina Bandera and Maria Teresa Fiorio (Milan: Skira/Banca Popolare di Milano, 2000), 205.

she be punished by someone other than me', he asked that the Duke cease his efforts and 'let things take their course, because I see that involvement in her business can bring no honor'.[19] The Duke offered condolences soon thereafter, reassuring him about the positive financial outcome of his wife's death, and informing him of the Emperor's goodwill toward him.[20] René spoke no more of his wife but sued to defend his rights to her inheritance against the claims of Bianca Maria's male Gaspardone relatives.[21] Relying on the legal customs of Casale, according to which 'the husband inherits from his deceased wife and children', and on the argument that Bianca Maria's testament was thereby null and void, he eventually forced the Gaspardone to cede him all of their claims to the succession in 1528.[22]

Assessing the significance of these events from the perspective of the history of the House of Challant during the sixteenth century is complicated. Had Bianca Maria fled her husband due to some sort of emotional incompatibility with him? Did she decide to take her property and return to Casale based on a rational calculation of what might happen to her and her property should her husband die and the French lose the war? Might her decision to move to Lombardy have been calculated to signal support for the Emperor, in order to diversify the couple's political investments? The fact that Bianca Maria made bequests to a host of ecclesiastical institutions suggests that she was not quite as dissolute as Bandello and Grumello indicate.[23] She perhaps viewed these donations as a kind of penance to compensate for a decadent life, but even this fits badly with Bandello's description of her as a 'stupid woman to whom no dastardly act seemed wrong'. Bandello claims that René had initiated the courtship with Bianca Maria and that the two had married secretly. We know that, on 4 August 1522, a contract was signed between the two.[24] Had there been an earlier clandestine marriage? Two entries in the accounts of the Duke of Savoy's treasurers suggest that this may have been the case. On 12 March 1522, a messenger went 'to Madame the Marquise of Monferrato for the matter of Madame de Challant'. Were René and Bianca Maria already

19 Fornaseri, 3-4. René to Ch III, Issogne 9-X-26.
20 Segre, 'Documenti di storia sabauda,' 180.
21 Act dated Casale 23-X-26 in Vaccarone, 'Bianca Maria,' 329-30. For Bianca Maria's clothing and jewelry, see ibid., and for the original, AST1, PD 188, ff. 238-39, 249-50 ('La descriptione e inventario de le zoye argenterie vestrimente et altri cosse mobile di la Illu. e Mag'ca Madama Biancha Maria comtessa di Chiallant portate da Casale in questa cita de Yverea,' dated Ivrea 29-XII-22).
22 Ibid., 319; AHR, FC 45, mz. 5, no. 2 (years 1527-1528); ibid., FC 79, mz. 2, no. 3 (years 1527-1528).
23 Bianca Maria testament dated 26-XII-25 in Vaccarone, 'Bianca Maria,' 327-28.
24 Contract dated 4-VIII-22 in ibid., 321-23.

considered married by this point, or was this a reference to René's grandmother Marguerite de La Chambre? On 9 July, another messenger was sent to 'Madame the Countess of Challant in Casale'.²⁵ It seems unlikely that this was a reference to Marguerite, who must have been over 60 and unlikely to travel in person to carry out marriage negotiations. This, together with the fact that neither René nor Bianca Maria had close male family members to guide them, suggests that the two had in fact married secretly.²⁶ René's youth, power, and influence, and Bianca Maria's experience and strategically positioned wealth likely attracted the one to the other. It is impossible to know how emotionally attached he was to his wife, and whether he thought that her inheritance was worth the dishonor of being cuckolded by a social inferior. Some accounts suggest that the Duke of Savoy was pushing for this alliance in order to strengthen his own political network in the Monferrato.²⁷ A lord like René needed to seize opportunities as they presented themselves, whether it be a marriage to a wealthy heiress, or a chance to serve in the army of a king like Francis I and establish his reputation as a warrior. In a sense, he was simply unlucky that his first wife was as passionate as she apparently was. Later events, especially his relationship to his daughters, would reveal how deeply this experience marked him. Military and financial catastrophes, which were often intertwined, increasingly undermined familial strategies during the late Renaissance. A family's transregional position both created military vulnerabilities and offered political and financial opportunities in the event of such conflict.

Charles III took the opportunity afforded by Bianca Maria's death to pull René back into the Imperial orbit by helping to arrange a new marriage with Mencia of Portugal-Braganza, a paternal cousin of Duchess Beatrice and of Empress Isabella. Mencia, daughter of Diniz of Portugal-Braganza, Count of Lemos (whose mother Isabella was the sister of King Manuel I, father of Beatrice and Isabella), and of Brites de Castro-Osorio,²⁸ was already at the Sabaudian court, serving her cousin as a lady-in-waiting. The marriage contract was signed in Chambéry on 7 January 1528.²⁹ Mencia brought a dowry of 18,000 *écus* and a grant from the Duchess of Savoy for another

25 ASTR, Camerale Savoia, Conti dei Tesorieri Generali di Savoia, entries dated 12-III-22 and 9-VII-22, cited in Vaccarone, 'Bianca Maria,' 321.
26 Claudio Donati called Bandello's *Novelle* 'a necessary reference for anyone interested in Lombard nobles or, more generally, the Italian nobility of the early Cinquecento' ('The Profession of Arms and the Nobility,' 306).
27 See Rosselli.
28 http://genealogy.euweb.cz/capet/capet61.html, 23 May 2019.
29 AHR, FC 6, no. 7 (copy of marriage contract dated 7-I-28); AST1, PD 203, ff. 8, 15, 17, 33v., 7/8-I-28 acts in favor of Mencia; Brero, 92.

10,000. Two months later, René received the fief of Varey (in Bugey, near Ambronay) from his father's brother-in-law (and third cousin) Pierre.[30] Mencia's first daughter Philiberte was born in late 1528, followed by Isabelle two years later.[31] Charles III's second son and eventual heir, Emanuel Filibert, was also born in 1528, and René was present at his baptism, initiating a long but complicated relationship between the two men.[32] The baptismal procession included several bishops and the leading Sabaudian nobility. René and three others carried the baby's blanket during the procession, while Mencia held Emanuel Filibert above the baptismal font.[33]

Following his second marriage, René served Charles III militarily and diplomatically while also attending to his own affairs in the valley, in Bugey, in Valangin and the Swiss cantons, in Beaufremont, and in the Monferrato – from northwestern Italy to Lorraine. On the very day of his wedding the Duke of Savoy named him Marshal of Savoie, the chief military-administrative official in the Sabaudian lands.[34]

René and Sabaudo-Swiss politics prior to 1536

The record is largely silent about René's activities after the Spanish released him from prison and prior to ensconcing himself in the castle of Chambéry to begin his work as Marshal (fall 1529). He refreshed his oversight of his Valdostano fiefs[35] and his litigation with the Gaspardone.[36] In 1528 and 1529, he shuttled Mencia and his infant daughter between Chambéry, the valley, and Valangin, carving out time to lead Sabaudian envoys at talks with the Bernese and other Swiss in Payerne, Berne, and Baden.[37] From this point on, René was increasingly imbricated in Swiss diplomacy, representing both the Duke's interests and his own. The next few pages explain the background to this diplomacy and then examine René's role, highlighting the kinds of transregional problems and relationships encountered as he served as the Duke's Marshal of Savoie.

The Duke of Savoy had long exercised suzerainty over towns and fiefs in the *pays de Vaud*, between the lake of Geneva, the lake of Neuchâtel,

30 AHR, FC 22, no. 14 (donation dated 14-III-28).
31 Frutaz, 'Notes,' 256-57; Fornaseri, 10, n. 3.
32 Frutaz, 'Notes,' 245, 256-57.
33 Brero, 174-75, 204, 217.
34 AHR, FC 258, no. 5 (patents dated 6-I-28).
35 Ibid., FC 172, no. 11 (receipt dated 1526).
36 Ibid., FC 79, no. 3 (litigation from 1527-1528).
37 Frutaz, 'Notes,' 246; Fornaseri, 7-8, René to Ch III, Payerne 14-IV-29? and Baden 10-VI-29?

and the cantons of Berne and Fribourg. The Sabaudian rulers also shared jurisdictional rights over the city of Geneva with the bishop of that city and the Genevan town council. The dynasty frequently managed to install one of its own (or an ally) as bishop, but conflict between bishop and duke could still erupt, with the cathedral canons asserting their own authority where possible. Vaudois towns, Lausanne chief among them, curried favor with other nobles and nearby cantons (Berne and Fribourg) in the interests of their own claims of autonomy. The *pays de Vaud* was constitutionally chaotic, as each locality embellished its own jurisdictional position.[38] Early in his reign, Charles III probably mishandled relations with the Geneva town council, which turned to Fribourg and Berne in order to balance Sabaudian power.[39] When Geneva signed a *combourgeoisie* with Fribourg in 1519, Charles III threatened violence, and the Fribourgeois seized the Vaudois town of Morges. By appealing to the other cantons, the Duke forced the Fribourgeois to withdraw.[40] The Duke of Savoy's alliance with the King of France, traditional supporter of the Swiss, created leverage here. When Charles III aligned himself with the Emperor in 1525, this leverage disappeared, freeing Berne and Fribourg to play hardball with the Duke. Thus, in December 1525, the town of Lausanne signed a *combourgeoisie* with both Fribourg and Berne, and, three months later, Geneva did the same.[41] René's unenviable task was to maintain Sabaudian authority over the Duke's subjects north of the lake, in an atmosphere of burgeoning Swiss dominion.

Proponents of religious reform had begun trickling into Geneva by 1523. In 1527, conflict between the town council and the Duke (with noble support) forced the Bishop, Pierre de La Baume, to flee the city. Geneva officially adopted the Reform in January 1528, days after Berne had. The political and diplomatic struggle was now also confessional. In 1529, when René's new office focused his attention on Swiss politics, the Bishop of Geneva was faced with a cathedral chapter divided in its loyalties between Charles III and the town council. To make matters worse, the Bishop's own political independence had cost him the Duke's confidence and support.[42] A group of pro-Sabaudian nobles formed an association, *La Cuiller*, to win Geneva back for the Catholic faith and the House of Savoy, chiefly supported by a member of the council named Michel Guillet (co-Lord of Monthoux, wealthy banker,

38 Gilliard; Bruening.
39 Mattingly; Naef; Gilliard.
40 Gilliard, 21.
41 Gilliard, 22-23.
42 Naef, 2: 34-44, 43 n. 3, 247 n. 2.

and administrator of the lakeside community of Crans for the episcopal chapter of Lausanne).[43] In the summer of 1529, Sabaudian, Bernese, and Fribourgeois envoys met at Payerne to ease tensions, and submitted the matter to an arbiter: Jean II, Count of Gruyère (vassal of both the Duke and the cantons).[44] This was the situation that René inherited upon his arrival in Chambéry as Marshal, assisted by Luigi di Castellamonte (from the Canavese), Claude de Bellegarde (Lieutenant at Valangin), and Bernardin de Granier (*maître d'hôtel* of Philippe de Savoie-Nemours).[45]

René recruited his cousin, Charles de Challant-Fénis, Lord of Villarsel – a regionally prominent lord of several fiefs in Vaud – into his mission.[46] While René was still in Valangin, he learned that Gruyère had issued a ruling in favor of Charles III.[47] His council in Chambéry urged him to stay put as they awaited the Swiss reaction, since 'your presence and neighborliness [*voysinage*] will be very useful', even as the situation remained tense in Geneva, where many persisted in the traditional faith.[48] René apprised Charles III of the progress of the Reform in various places, urging him to attend 'quickly to this Lutheran matter', or else risk 'great damage to your state'.[49] A key complicating factor was financial. The Duke of Savoy owed large sums of money to lenders in Fribourg; payments on these sums had been due in August but were just being delivered in November. Jean Guillet (brother of Michel) was involved either as a broker or a creditor (or perhaps both) in financial litigation.[50] The Governor of Vaud (Aymon de Genève-Lullin) warned of the consequences should Sabaudian officials be found guilty of financial malfeasance in Swiss courts.[51] René met with Jean Guillet, a Fribourgeois banker named Christophe Pavillard, and others to try to resolve the dispute. The Marshal viewed the real danger

---

43 Guillet, together with the Bishop of Aosta, was invested in collecting diocesan revenues; see Naef, 2: 201 n. 2, 202 n. 2, 234-35, 235 n. 2, 235-26.
44 Segre, 'Documenti di storia sabauda,' 51-52.
45 AEN, AS-K16, 8, Granyer to René, Chambéry 5-X-29.
46 Ibid., AS-F16, 10, Bellegarde and ? to René, Payerne 1-X-29.
47 Ibid., AS-K16, 8, Granyer to René, Chambéry 5-X-29; Segre, 'Documenti di storia sabauda,' 53.
48 AEN, AS-H16, 22, Bellegarde to René, Chambéry 5-X-29.
49 Fornaseri, 11-12, René to Ch III, Chambéry 12-XI-29; ibid., 18-21, same to same, Chambéry 4-XII-29.
50 Ibid., 9-11, René to Ch III, Chambéry 9-XI-29; also ibid., 14-15, same to same, Chambéry 18-XI-29; ibid., 16-17, same to same, Chambéry 27-XI-29; ibid., 18-21, same to same, Chambéry 4-XII-29; Herminjard, 8: 483.
51 A concern was that the financial dimension of the dispute would give others 'iurisdicion sur les biens qu'ilz acquierent en voz pays' (Fornaseri, 18-21, René to Ch III, Chambéry 4-XII-29). See also ibid., 9-11, same to same, Chambéry 9-XI-29.

as a weakening of the Duke's territorial jurisdiction and urged Charles III to defend 'your property and authority', even if costly.[52] For example, forgiving a debt that Guillet owed to the Duke seemed necessary to settle a dispute with another crucial player.[53] Exposure to this complicated business showed René how finance, property, jusrisdiction, and diplomacy overlapped in concrete ways relating to the spatial configuration of the interests involved.[54]

René went straight to work in early 1530, organizing meetings with the estates of Vaud and the Bishop of Lausanne. He advised the Vaudois nobles to tread carefully with the Bernese and the common people to prevent more defections to the new religion and subsequent loss of property and jurisdiction.[55] Responding to rumors of a Franco-Bernese invasion of the Franche-Comté, René counseled the Duke to communicate patiently with the other cantons, and to defuse tensions with gifts and pensions to key Swiss figures. Although only 26 years old, René already understood the subtle dynamics of inter-cantonal relations – and their spatial import.[56] By late April, René had already completed a mission to the French court (perhaps to address the Franche-Comté issue, among other things) and one to the German-speaking cantons. He then rode to Geneva, Lausanne, Moudon (where the Vaudois estates met), and Berne. The Bernese pledged their desire to 'live peacefully alongside' the Duke of Savoy, but their town council extricated itself and individual Bernese bankers from loan guarantees to Charles III, while threatening to seize the Duke's mortgaged property, including Romont and Yverdon. They also condemned the Duke for persecuting his Reformed subjects, demanding that he recognize the freedom of Geneva and Lausanne to choose their own faith. Finally, they renounced all their alliances with Charles III. René saw these acts as 'disordered' and suggested that the Duke not even bother to respond.[57] He informed the Bernese that he lacked authority to reply and then began discussions with

---

52 Ibid., 38, René to Ch III, Chambéry 28-I-30; ibid., 23-24, same to same, Chambéry 8-XII-29.
53 Ibid., 26-28, René to Ch III, Chambéry 27-XII-29.
54 For a problem involving the Count of Gruyère, see Hisely, 2: 280-83 and Fornaseri, 29-30, René to Ch III, Chambéry 5-I-30.
55 Ibid., 34-35, René to Ch III, Chambéry 14-I-30; ibid., 35-37, same to same, Chambéry 26-I-30.
56 Ibid., 38-42, René to Ch III, Chambéry 29-I-30. Several places in the *pays de Vaud* had been occupied by the Bernese and Fribourgeois since the Burgundian wars, and René still hoped that these could be recuperated; see Andenmatten; Fornaseri 38-44, René to Ch III, Chambéry 29-I-30 and s.l., ?-I-30.
57 Ibid., 44-45, René to Ch III, Chambéry 30-III-30; ibid., 46-48, same to same, Chambéry 9-IV-30; ibid., 49-53, same to same, Romont 4-V-30; ibid., 48-49, same to same, Berne 28-IV-30; ibid., 49-53, same to same, Romont, 4-V-30.

the Fribourgeois. He did, however, warn the Duke about the spread of the Reform in the Chablais, south of Lake Geneva.[58]

During a lull in the Fribourg talks, René dashed to Valangin to meet with two of the Duke's creditors whose loans were guaranteed on a specific fief. Since the Duke was not paying the rents, his two underwriters were planning to take hostages – 36 of them, each paid one gold florin per day for their expenses, to be added to the Duke's debt. If, after six weeks, the rents weren't paid, they would proceed to confiscate the property. René warned that, once such things started to happen, 'others would emulate them', and creditors everywhere would move on the Duke's mortgaged lands.[59] René saw clearly the link between specific places, ducal debt, and the loss of Charles III's territorial position, but the Duke seemed to be financially underwater and perhaps in denial about it.[60] After wrapping up the talks with the Fribourgeois, René wrote to the Duke from Chambéry, requesting that other diplomats be tasked with future trips to the Swiss Germans. When he ran these missions personally, he was forced to spend exorbitantly, in order to maintain his stature (and ducal prestige), without satisfactory returns. He also explained apologetically to Charles III that he could no longer borrow money for him, though he offered to broker loans where possible.[61] Finally, he pleaded with Charles III, for the sake of his own honor, to give fair treatment to François Bonivard, whose family had long served the House of Savoy, but whose opposition to ducal control over Geneva had landed him in prison at Chillon.[62] In another case, the Genevans had imprisoned a ducal supporter named François de Mandallaz; René sought

---

58 Ibid., 48-49, René to Ch III, Berne, 28-IV-30; ibid., 49-53, same to same, Romont, 4-V-30. For other issues discussed, including the case of Michel Mangerod, Baron de La Sarraz, see ibid., 53-54, René to Ch III, Romont, 4 to 7-V-30; ibid., 55 [first of two letters], same to same, Romont 7-V-30; ibid, 49-53, same to same, Romont, 4-V-30; Monbaron; De Charrière, 'Les dynastes,' 489; Fornaseri, 54, René to Ch III, Romont, 4 to 7-V-30; ibid., 69-71, same to same, Chambéry 1-VII-30.
59 For René's energetic efforts to forestall this, see Fornaseri, 56, René to Ch III, Valangin 12-V-30; ibid., 60, same to same, Chambéry 1-VI-30.
60 The creditors were the Lord of Colombier and Kaspar von Mülinen; on the latter, a Bernese Catholic diplomat, see Hüssy, 'Kaspar von Mülinen;' Segre, 'Documenti di storia sabauda,' 289.
61 Fornaseri, 60, René to Ch III, Moudon 28-V-30; for relations with the Fribourgeois, see ibid., 60, René to Ch III, Chambéry 1-VI-30; ibid., 63-64, same to same, Chambéry 3-VI-30; ibid., 64-65, same to same, Chambéry 4-VI-30; ibid., 65-66, same to same, Chambéry 10-VI-30; ibid., 66, same to same, Chambéry 11-VI-30; ibid., 67-68, same to same, Chambéry 17-VI-30; ibid., 69-71, same to same, Chambéry 1-VII-30; ibid., 71-72, same to same, Chambéry 4-VII-30. Brokerage involved working with creditors from Lucerne and Basel, such as the Meltinger family; see Burckhardt.
62 Fornaseri, 72-73, René to Ch III, Chambéry 10-VII-30. See also Tripet; Naef, 2: 147-48; Chaponnière.

Swiss help to free him. 'Your presence will resolve every problem', wrote René to the Duke, who was thus persuaded to come to Chambéry, freeing up René to spend some time at Virieu in August.[63] Here and elsewhere, we see how René's geographically dispersed fiefs supported his missions at various points in his career.

In late September, the security situation around Geneva deteriorated as Sabaudian soldiers crisscrossed the countryside. As the town council urgently appealed to Berne and Fribourg, the nobles of *La Cuiller*, led by Baron Michel de La Sarraz and supported by the Bishop, began burning farms and preparing to attack. The arrival of Swiss troops from several cantons caused them to retreat and they were ultimately defeated by the Genevan militia at Meyrin on 8 October 1530. 14,000 troops commanded by Hans von Erlach of Berne took up quarters on Sabaudian territory while churches and monasteries were pillaged. René did not participate in the peace talks at St. Julien, which mortgaged the *pays de Vaud* to Berne and Fribourg and constituted them as a security deposit should the Duke threaten Geneva again. He explained to Charles III that, since he represented 'your person on this side of the mountains, it is crucial that I not be present when our position is not accepted', as was the case at St. Julien.[64] Mortgaging Vaud was a huge mistake, according to René, since it forced the Duke to accede to the Swiss demands, facilitating their plan to 'invade and seize your said country, which would be difficult to recover, given their long-standing desire to establish a foothold there'.[65] He counseled the rebuilding of the alliance with Berne, which would enhance their ability to locate new lenders. For this reason, it was crucial to resolve a dispute with Wolfgang von Wingarten, a politically connected Bernese creditor who was demanding repayment. René urged the Duke to send 'someone wise and influential' for discussions with Berne, someone who would 'know what kind of language to use with them, since, as you know, it is not easy to deal with them, given their lack of reason [*le peu de raison qu'ilz usent*]'.[66] In the meantime, René attacked the

---

63 Naef, 2: 248-49; for other conflicts, see ibid., 247-48 n. 2; Fornaseri, 72-73, René to Ch III, Chambéry 10-VII-30; 74-75, same to same, Virieu 11-VIII-30; for developments with Mandallaz, see Naef, 2: 250-53.

64 For the quotation see Fornaseri, 77-78, René to Ch III, Chambéry 19-X-30; also ibid., 76-77, René to Ch III, Cruseilles 11-X-30; ibid., 78-81, same to same, Chambéry 20-X-30; and Naef, 2: 253-61. René also pointed out that 'l'affere de Vingard [...] c'est celluy qui donne plus d'empesche à voz afferez' (Fornaseri, 77-78, René to Ch III, Chambéry 19-X-30); see Annelies Hüssy, 'Wolfgang von Wingarten.'

65 Fornaseri, 78-81, René to Ch III, Chambéry 20-X-30.

66 Ibid.

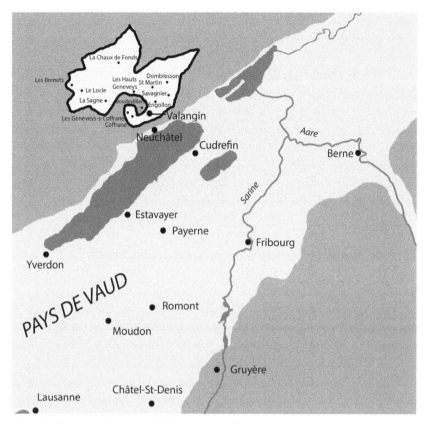

Map 3: The Western Swiss area, with Valangin and its villages (mountainous areas shaded). Map by author.

financial problem from the other end, gathering information about harvests and grain provisioning in the territories of his jurisdiction.[67]

Amid Bernese threats to seize Vaud if the Duke failed to pay his debts, René prepared for a new conference at Payerne designed to confirm the St. Julien accord. René was in Valangin in mid November, and it is not clear whether he attended the Payerne meeting. Later accounts would hold him responsible for the agreement signed there on 31 December 1530 despite his clear opposition to the deal that required a war indemnity of 21,000 *écus* from the Duke of Savoy – a third of which was to be returned to Geneva.[68] René was also scandalized by Bernese proselytizing in Lausanne,

---

67 Ibid., 9-11, René to Ch III, Chambéry 9-XI-29; ibid., 82, same to same, Chambéry 26-X-30.
68 Ibid., 83-84, René to Ch III, Chambéry 30-X-30. René again urged Charles III to 'donner ordre' to 'Vingard,' since he was the one 'qui mest en ruyne tous les aultres' (ibid.) Also AHR, FC 26, no. 28, instructions dated 20-XI-30; also in ibid., FC 247, no. 15 and in Frutaz, 'Notes,' 246; AEN,

exhorting Charles III to respond 'as the one who holds the high lordship and *souveraynité* of Lausanne' and 'the villages in Lausanne's district'.[69] Emboldened by their Swiss guarantors, Geneva then sold the episcopal property that it had seized in October, usurped the Duke's fiscal authority in the city, and rejected ducal jurisdiction over criminal affairs. René again sounded the alarm to the Duke, as matters that '[concern] your property and *estat*'.[70] Having done what he could for the time being, he crossed the Alps in April to meet Charles III in Piedmont and attend to his property in the Monferrato.[71] His negotiations with the Swiss would continue throughout his life, though, both as an envoy for the dukes of Savoy and on his own behalf in relation to his lordship of Valangin.

The lordship of Valangin and the counts of Neuchâtel

René's lordship of Valangin was a crucial element of his transregional position. Situated about halfway between his lands in Lorraine and the Valle d'Aosta, it cemented his financial and political relations with the powerful western Swiss cantons and offered him the opportunity to develop claims of sovereignty. Located in what is now the canton of Neuchâtel, the seigniory of Valangin included a castle in the *bourg* of Valangin along with lands and villages covering about a third of the present-day canton, including the communities of Le Locle and La Chaux de Fonds. In the mid-sixteenth century, the lordship counted around 3,100 inhabitants and produced annual revenues of about 2000 *écus*.[72] As Lord of Valangin, René owed fidelity to the counts of Neuchâtel. The family of Orléans-Longueville had acquired the county of Neuchâtel through Duke Louis's wife, Jeanne de Hochberg (1485-1543, granddaughter of Duke Amadeus IX of Savoy, by his daughter Marie). But the county was 'too far away and too modest to affect the base of a dynasty whose place was to be alongside the king, serving him in high military and administrative positions'. As a result,

---

AS-R5.10, uuu, René to Castellan of Landeron, 9-XI-30; ibid., ttt, René to Castellan of Boudry, 9-XI-30; ibid., sss, René to Canon Jehan de Cortonay, curé of St. Blaise, 10-XI-30 (in each of these three documents, the year was written in pencil by a later hand); Naef, 2: 264. According to Pierre Lambert de La Croix, president of the *Chambre des comptes* and author of a set of memoirs about the 1530s, Charles III was furious with the Sabaudian envoys for 'approving' the Payerne decision (*Mémoires de Pierre Lambert*, 502-3).

69   Fornaseri, 28-29, René to Ch III, Chambéry ?-XII-30.
70   Naef, 2: 265-66; Fornaseri, 85-86, René to Ch III, Chambéry 29-I-31.
71   ASMn, Archivio Gonzaga, b. 747, cart. 15, René to Federico II Gonzaga, Casale 16-IV-31.
72   Matile, 264-65; see also Faverges.

the family only made brief visits to Neuchâtel.[73] After her husband died in 1516, Jeanne was left with three sons, two of whom died early. Her grandson by her son Louis II ruled Neuchâtel for eight years (until his death in 1551) under the tutelage of his grandfather, Claude de Guise. Jeanne's third son was the Marquis of Rothelin, who died in 1548 but left a son named Léonor who married Marie de Bourbon. Léonor died nine years later, and Marie served as regent for their young son Henri (who died in 1595).[74]

When Jeanne de Hochberg married Louis d'Orléans-Longueville, the Swiss cantons became wary of such an influential neighbor and seized control of the county of Neuchâtel themselves, governing it through bailiffs from 1512 to 1529.[75] Thus, René swore fealty to the Swiss cantons for Valangin on 4 June 1523, before the gate of the castle of Neuchâtel.[76]

René's experience as Lord of Valangin has been overlooked in most accounts of his life. Conversely, George-Auguste Matile, a historian and attorney from the canton of Neuchâtel, was interested in René due exclusively to Valangin.[77] Matile's history, published in 1852, focused on René's interactions with the Bernese, the bishops of Basel, the counts of Neuchâtel, the town of Neuchâtel, and other local lords. Matile interpreted René's jurisdictional struggles with Jeanne de Hochberg and her Orléans-Longueville heirs as the result of his desire to 'act as much as he could as a true sovereign'.[78] In fact, for at least 100 years, such struggles had been the recurrent theme of the relationship between the lords of Valangin and the counts of Neuchâtel, whose lands were contiguous. During René's life, a first period of conflict was characterized by a slow process of local dispute resolution, culminating in René's oath of homage to Jeanne's son, the Duke of Longueville, in 1535. A second period was marked by an effort to clarify further René's relationship to Jeanne, ultimately resulting in his purchase of sovereignty over Valangin from her in 1542, her sons' rejection of this transaction, and their mother's death in 1543. The battle lines were drawn more clearly in 1543, and, from then until René's death, the conflict over René's claim to be sovereign Lord of Valangin continued unabated. These second two periods will be discussed in the next chapter.

In 1531, Guillemette de Vergy complained to Georges de Rive, Lord of Prangins, the Governor of Neuchâtel for the Orléans-Longueville,[79] about

73 Scheurer, 22.
74 Scheurer, 23, 33.
75 Morerod and Scheurer.
76 Matile, 245, 247.
77 Gigandet.
78 Matile, 252-53.
79 Daguet, 57-64, 100-4, 124-28.

the *maire* of the town of Neuchâtel. The town collected revenues for the counts of Neuchâtel, and the *maire* disputed Guillemette's collection of dues from the parish of St. Martin. This dispute coincided with the introduction of the Reform into the region, but it clearly related to political authority.[80] Other conflicts concerned the collection of tithes 'during the *Benisson* of Sauvagniez [*Savagnier*]', resulting in 'many of our subjects [on both sides] being banned'.[81] Such frictions were routine, and probably accentuated by the Reform, as the next chapter will show. In 1533, Jeanne apologized to René for the Neuchâtelois who 'engage[d] in insulting behavior every day in your seigniory of Valangin'.[82] As René demonstrated his resolution to defend his prerogatives as Lord of Valangin, the conflict with Jeanne intensified.[83]

One dispute involved René's request that the countess provide legal officials for his judicial quarter sessions, the '*audiances*, as should be done according to custom'. The countess's council declined to cooperate, noting that, four years earlier, René had been found guilty of having 'pardoned and forgiven a murderer who had been convicted and sentenced to death, of having built gallows of four pillars, and of having established markets and fairs in your seigniory other than the ones that you hold from [the countess] in fief'. Jeanne's officer in charge declared that 'this was to usurp too much from her', threatened René with judicial proceedings, and demanded correction and 'reparation in the hands of my said Lady' before the countess would furnish judges for the *audiances*.[84]

In April 1534, René instructed Bellegarde to schedule a meeting to settle these disputes,[85] while accumulating advice from trusted associates and devising a strategy. He would begin by consulting friends at the French court and meeting Jeanne there personally. Bellegarde would meet with jurisdictional experts in Basel and Besançon.[86] From the Longueville perspective, the conflict concerned 'the *souveraynnité* belonging to my said Lady' over Valangin, due to René's pardon of the murderer, 'which is

---

80   AEN, AS-R5.10, yyy, Guillemette to Prangins, Valangin 4-VII-31 [year penciled in]).
81   Ibid., AS-R5.10, yy, Bellegarde to Prangins, Valangin 26-VII-? 'Benisson' referred perhaps to the *bénichon*, a harvest festival typically held in the fall.
82   Ibid., AS-C4.2, a, Jeanne to René, Neuchâtel 31-III-33.
83   René wondered angrily why Jeanne's council 'me tyennent a si petitte extime et reputacion de me user de telle rigueur, ce que l'on ne feroyt au plus estrange du monde' (ibid., AS-R5.10, bb, René to Prangins, Valangin 21-XI-33).
84   Ibid., AS-R5.10, iiii, undated draft letter to René.
85   Bellegarde was to speak with Prangins, the 'doyen de Montbelliard,' the Bishop of Basel, the *doyen* of Besançon, the 'advocat de Chambéry', and others (ibid., AS-C4.2, b, René to Bellegarde, Beaufremont 5-IV-34 [?]).
86   Ibid., AS-C4.2, c, René to Bellegarde, Beaufremont 8 [or 11]-IV-34 [?].

an acte of *souveraynité* and a usurpation of authority'.[87] The matter was so important to René that he deflected a summons from Charles III while he tried to resolve the problem. Jeanne would be at the French court for the wedding of her son Louis II d'Orléans and Marie de Guise[88] and René hoped to meet her there at the end of June, and then return for negotiations with the Neuchâtelois by 6 July 1534.[89] These meetings were all delayed until the fall, when the Neuchâtel estates were on the cusp of facilitating an agreement that ultimately fell through.[90] About ten days later, the Baron de La Sarraz swore that, when he had been a page of René's grandfather Claude d'Arberg 20 years earlier, he had seen him release a prisoner who had been condemned to death. He also saw the Lord of Valangin

> judge a criminal who had been placed on the wheel as a brigand and murderer, and the said Lord of Valangin sent a gentleman who told the judge that the said Lord of Valangin had privileged him and was privileging him with the *grace de la teste*, and had the said criminal decapitated according to justice.[91]

While it is unclear whether the meeting that René had tried to organize was ever held and, if so, what the outcome was, sometime in 1535, René asked Jeanne d'Hochberg to receive his 'oath and homage for said Valangin'. In exchange, he requested permission to erect a 'gallows with four pillars', to confirm his right to hold fairs twice a year, and to verify that his judicial decisions could not be appealed to the Neuchâtel estates, but only heard by the Countess herself.[92] Later that year, René's homage was received by Louis II d'Orléans-Longueville. The attestation of this reception mentions that the Swiss cantons had recently also received homage from René, enumerated his rights (including the gallows of three pillars), and given a specific territorial description of the boundaries of his seigniory.[93]

---

87 Ibid., AS-B4.9, m, Longueville (Louis or François?) to Guillemette de Vergy, Neuchâtel 15-IV-? (appears to be 1534).
88 They did not marry until 4 August 1534.
89 René had little faith that Neuchâtel officials would treat him fairly (ibid., AS-C4.2, d, René to Bellegarde, Beaufremont 15-V-34).
90 Ibid., e, copy of Collier to Bellegarde, Valangin 11-X-34.
91 Ibid., f, deposition dated 21-X-34. Soon thereafter, Prangins expressed his desire to 'viv[re] en paix et en bonne voysinance' (ibid., g, Prangins to Bellegarde, Neuchâtel 2-XI-34).
92 Ibid., AS-B4.9, a, copy of 1535 request by René to Jeanne d'Hochberg. Matile claims that Jeanne refused to grant the confirmations requested by René and declined to receive his oath (247).
93 AEN, AS-B4.9, b, copy of 1535 reception of René's homage to Louis de Longueville. The rights included 'toute la forteresse bourg & chastel de Vallangin'; yearly judicial sessions in the Valderuz;

Before the storm, 1531-1534

Following his trip to Piedmont and Monferrato in spring 1531, René crossed the mountains again, dividing his time between Valangin and Chambéry. May 1533 found him in Crescentino, on the border of the Monferrato, whose last Paleologue marquis had died on 30 April 1533. Charles III had sent René to generate support among the Monferrato nobility for Sabaudian claims over the marquisate.[94] René huddled with 'a few individual friends' in the town of Trino, whose council was persuaded to hear René's presentation and to declare its support for the Duke of Savoy. 'They do not want the lord Duke of Mantua [the competing claimant]', René wrote; 'they would rather eat their children.' They did, however, seek guidance from Emperor Charles V. René advised Charles III to send an envoy to the Imperial commander and represent his intentions as an effort to protect the marquisate by holding its territory north of the Po 'in His Majesty's name'.[95] Despite these efforts, the Emperor awarded the Monferrato to the House of Gonzaga, and Sabaudian control would not be secured for more than a century.[96]

While Castellamonte and Aymon de Genève-Lullin served as René's lieutenants in Savoie and continued to seek out Swiss underwriters for ducal loans,[97] the Count of Challant returned to the Valle d'Aosta in fall 1533. He took up the cause of the inhabitants of Bard, where a ducal fortress was located 'at the strongest and best passage in the valley', against a ducal revenue collector, pointing out to Charles III that, since these inhabitants were already helping to pay the fort's expenses, they should not also be asked to pay feudal dues. René pleaded with the Duke to show those of Bard 'that I sometimes hold some credit in your eyes' by transferring these feudal

jurisdiction over subjects of the Valderuz even if they left to live somewhere else, until they were 'absoubz & quictes'; 'la jurisdicion & plaict des fourches du Valderue estant a trois pilliers', with high justice for half of the Valderuz and other lands belonging to the Bishop of Basel, including Le Locle and La Saigne '& toute la seigneurie dessusd' par les Raiz des Joux devers Bize entre les limites icy escriptes'; and exemption from the toll of Le Locle for the subjects of Valderuz, La Saigne, and Le Locle.

94 Fornaseri, 87-89, René and 'Jo. Jacobo de Medyo' to Ch III, Crescentino 1-V-33. Rumors were that soldiers were being raised under the Marquis of Saluzzo to send to the Monferrato (ibid., 86, René to Ch III, Casale 15-IV-33?)

95 Ibid., 87-89, René and 'Jo. Jacobo de Medyo' to Ch III, Crescentino 1-V-33.

96 René and the Duke of Savoy continued to maintain friendly relationships with Monferrato towns, waiting for opportunities to strike alliances with them (ibid., 92-93, René to Ch III, Mont Cenis 6-V-35).

97 ASTı, NS, mz. 1 bis, no. 29, 'S'ensuyt ce que Mons'r de Castellamont a deslivré en Allemaigne [...].' In Fribourg, René's negotiators were confronted with several days of meals 'en plusieurs hostelleries', at the Duke's expense, according to Swiss custom (ibid.).

rights to him so that he could gift them to the locals.[98] The Bard case again shows how spatially specific revenue production overlapped with strategic territorial authority.

Before winter set in, René was back in Chambéry and then in Valangin, where he heard that the Duke's brother, Philippe de Savoie-Nemours, had died. 'In every situation one must conform to God's will, who disposes of our lives as He wishes', René stoically observed. He regretted having learned of Nemours's passing too late to be able to accompany his body to Annecy, as Charles III had asked him. In Valangin, 'the faith of my neighbors, the source of daily troubles', compounded his sorrow. 'You know the nature of said neighbors', he told the Duke, who, some months later, scheduled talks with the Bernese at Thonon, dispatching the Count as his envoy. Berne demanded freedom of conscience for the Duke's subjects, while Charles III sought the reintegration of the Bishop of Geneva. Unsurprisingly, neither side budged.[99]

Bibliography

Bernard Andenmatten, 'La fin du Pays de Vaud savoyard et de l'État épiscopal,' in 'Vaud,' *DHS* (2017)

Matteo Bandello, *Novelle*, pt. 1, no. 4, 'La contessa di Cellant fa ammazzare il conte di Masino e a lei è mózzo il capo,' in *Tutte le opere di Matteo Bandello* (Milan: Mondadori, 1943)

François Belleforest, 'Vie desordonnée de la comtesse de Celant' in *Histoires tragiques* II, 2 (Lyon, 1564)

Thalia Brero, *Les baptêmes princiers. Le cérémonial dans les cours de Savoie et Bourgogne (XV-XVIe s.)* (Lausanne: Université de Lausanne, 2005)

Michael Bruening, *Calvinism's First Battleground: Conflict and Reform in the Pays de Vaud, 1528-1559* (Dordrecht: Springer, 2005).

August Burckhardt, 'Die Basler Bürgermeister von 1252 bis zur Reformation,' *Basler Zeitschrift für Geschichte und Altertumskunde* 23 (1925): 1-29

Domenico Carutti, *Storia della diplomazia della corte di Savoia*, vol. 1 (Rome: Fratelli Bocca, 1875)

---

98   Fornaseri, 89-90, René to Ch III, Issogne 28-IX-33?.
99   Ibid., 90-92, René to Ch III, Valangin 30-XI-33 and Valangin 6-XII-33; ibid., 91-92, same to same, Valangin 6-XII-33. In early 1534, Berne helped mediate a dispute between René and Jacques Nicollet de Lenseigne (AEN, AS-F16, 6, *Advoyer* and city of Berne to René, Berne 20-V-34); Gilliard, 31; AST1, PD 166, f. 42, patent dated 12-XI-34.

Jean-Jacques Chaponnière, 'Notice sur François Bonivard, prieur de Saint-Victor, et sur ses écrits,' *Mémoires et documents publiés par la Société d'histoire et d'archéologie de Genève* 4, 137 (1846): 137-304

A. Daguet, 'Essai sur Georges de Rive,' *Musée Neuchâtelois* (1882): 57-64

M.L. de Charrière, 'Les dynastes de La-Sarra, maison de Grandson,' *Mémoires et documents publiés par la société d'histoire de la Suisse romande* 28 (1873): 342-522

Benjamin Deruelle, *De papier, de fer et de sang. Chevaliers et chevalerie à l'épreuve de la modernité (ca 1460-ca 1620)* (Paris: Publications de la Sorbonne, 2015)

Claudio Donati, 'The Profession of Arms and the Nobility in Spanish Italy: Some Considerations,' in *Spain in Italy. Politics, Society, and Religion 1500-1700*, ed. T.J. Dandelet and J. Marino (Leiden: Brill, 2006), pp. 299-332

D. Faverges, 'Deux fiefs des Challant: la baronnie de Beaufremont et la seigneurie de Valangin,' *Publications du Centre d'Etudes Burgondo-Médianes* 15 (1973): 77-83.

Giovanni Fornaseri, *Le lettere di Renato di Challant, governatore della Valle d'Aosta a Carlo II ed a Emanuele Filiberto* (Turin: Deputazione subalpina di storia patria, 1957)

François-Gabriel Frutaz, 'Notes sur René de Challant et sur le passage de Calvin dans la Vallée d'Aoste,' *Musée neuchâtelois* 41 (1904): 242-67

Louis Prosper Gachard, *La captivité de François Ier et le traité de Madrid* (Brussels: C. Muquardt, 1860)

Cyrille Gigandet, 'Georges-Auguste Matile,' *DHS* (2012)

Charles Gilliard, *La conquête du Pays de Vaud per les Bernois* (Lausanne: Editions La Concorde, 1935)

Antonio Grumello, *Cronaca*, ed. Giuseppe Müller, *Raccolta di cronisti e documenti storici lombardi inediti* 1 (Milan: Francesco Colombo, 1856)

Aimé Louis Herminjard, *Correspondance des réformateurs dans les pays de langue française*, vol. 8 (Paris: M. Levy and G. Fischbacher, 1866-1897)

J.J. Hisely, *Histoire du comté de Gruyère*, vol. 2 (Lausanne: Georges Bridel, 1857)

Annelies Hüssy, 'Kaspar von Mülinen,' *DHS* (2009)

Id., 'Wolfgang von Wingarten,' *DHS* (2013)

Pierre Lambert de la Croix, *Mémoires de Pierre Lambert*, in *Monumenta Historiae Patriae edita iussu Regis Caroli Alberti Scriptorum*, vol. 1 (Turin: Regio Tipographeo, 1840)

Garrett Mattingly, 'Eustache Chapuys and Spanish Diplomacy in England (1488-1536): A Study in the Development of Resident Embassies,' PhD dissertation, Harvard University (1935)

Olga Majolo Molinari, *Filippo di Savoia duca di Nemours (1490-1533)* (Turin: Paravia, 1938)

J. Marston, *The Insatiate Countess* (1613)

Georges-Auguste Matile, *Histoire de la seigneurie de Valangin jusqu'à sa réunion à la directe en 1592* (Neuchâtel, James Attinger, 1852)

P.-R. Monbaron, 'La baronnie de La Sarraz et la Maison de Gingins sous l'Ancien Régime bernois (1536-1798),' in *Château de La Sarraz* (1983): 7-17

Jean-Daniel Morerod and Rémy Scheurer, 'Formation de l'État et gouvernement sous les Orléans-Longueville,' in 'Neuchâtel (canton),' *DHS* (2017)

Henri Naef, *Les origines de la réforme à Genève*, 2 vols. (Geneva: Droz, 1968 [1936])

W. Painter, *Palace of Pleasures* II, 24 (London, 1566-1567)

Donatella Rosselli, 'Bianca Maria Gaspardone,' *DBI* 52 (1999)

Rémy Scheurer, 'L'évolution politique de la Réforme à 1707,' *Histoire du Pays de Neuchâtel*, vol. 2, pt. 2 (Hauterive, Switzerland: Editions Gilles Attinger, 1991)

Arturo Segre, 'Documenti di storia sabauda dal 1510 al 1536,' *MSI* 39 (1903): 3-296

Armando Tallone, 'Ivrea e il Piemonte al tempo della prima dominazione francese (1536-1559),' in *Studi eporediesi* (Pinerolo: Tipografia Chiantore-Mascarelli, 1900): 67-200

Micheline Tripet, 'François Bonivard,' *DHS* (2008)

Luigi Vaccarone, 'Bianca Maria di Challant e il suo corredo,' *MSI* 35 (1898): 305-32

Vigilio Vescovi, 'Historia della casa di Challant e di Madruzzo,' ed. Lin Colliard, *Archivum Augustanum* 2 (1969): 1-118

3. René's growing influence during the war years, 1536-1553

Abstract

In 1536, the Sabaudian lands were invaded by the Bernese and the French. René de Challant, as Marshal of Savoie, struggled to learn what was happening and how the Duke of Savoy wished him to respond. He eventually fell back to the Valle d'Aosta and oversaw its defensive efforts. Together with the Bishop of Aosta and an executive committee of the valley estates assembly (the *Conseil des Commis*), he preserved the valley's devotion to the House of Savoy throughout the Franco-Swiss occupation of most of the Sabaudian lands. He continued to serve Charles III diplomatically over the course of the wars, while fighting with the Orléans-Longueville family over the sovereign status of Valangin.

Key words: Berne, Francis I, Charles III, *Commis*, Valangin

The invasions of 1536

In the mid 1530s, the Sabaudian lands were almost eliminated from the European map as a result of multipronged invasions and occupations. These events transformed the political-geographic context of René's position as a transregional lord and political agent acting on behalf of himself and others (especially the House of Savoy). In 1535, the Duke of Savoy initiated a blockade of Geneva, whose authorities appealed to Berne. The Bernese did not wish to act alone to protect the city, which, in August 1535, prohibited the celebration of the Mass. Various Bernese had pledged themselves as security for Sabaudian loans and were also afraid that they would lose their credit if the Duke were ruined by an invasion. But the calculus of Bernese leaders began to change when they learned that Charles V's army, which might have intervened on behalf of the Duke of Savoy, had embarked for Africa. In September, the Swiss Diet renounced its previous efforts to mediate between

---

Vester, M., *Transregional Lordship and the Italian Renaissance: René de Challant, 1504-1565*. Amsterdam: Amsterdam University Press, 2020.
DOI 10.5117/9789463726726_CH03

Berne and the Duke; in October, mercenaries were raised in the county of Neuchâtel (including Valangin) and defeated a contingent of Savoyards before being persuaded by Bernese envoys to go home. Meanwhile, Berne gave Charles III an ultimatum: lift the blockade or their alliance would be broken.[1]

The Duke stalled for time, a hastily organized conference in Aosta produced nothing, and the Duke 'returned to Piedmont, consigning his affairs to God's will and protection'.[2] The fact that a Spanish army had been readied in Lombardy did not prevent Francis I from declaring his own intention to take possession of Geneva.[3] This news forced the hand of Berne, which feared French control of Geneva more than ducal control. On 27 December 1535, they notified Jean d'Estavayer, the ducal envoy, of their decision to wage war against Charles III in support of Geneva. Charles III, suspecting that this was an empty threat and more preoccupied with the actions of Francis I, dispatched René to the French court. Meanwhile, the Emperor sent envoys to the Swiss to persuade them to hold Berne back, but, before the talks (scheduled for 30 January) could begin, the damage had been done.[4] As Bernese preparations accelerated,[5] the Governor of Vaud and the Captain of Yverdon threw themselves into repairing fortifications, while the Bishop of Lausanne attempted to raise troops in vain. It was 'a country that was three-fourths unarmed and barely defended by its masters that the Bernese were about to penetrate'.[6] A Bernese army of 6000 marched on 22 January 1536 and the Vaudois communities that did not surrender immediately were given 24 hours to submit. In Cudrefin, for example, the Bernese commander Hans Franz Naegli ordered the inhabitants to gather 'all of their property, whether in wheat or other things' and to deliver it to him, along with 'the duties that hitherto had been paid [to the Duke of Savoy]'.[7] The three town council members who asked Naegli for time to consult with the Duke were imprisoned, and the community was threatened with being sacked. When the Castellan refused to give the Bernese the keys to

1   Gilliard, 33-45.
2   For the demands made by the Bernese, see *Mémoires de Pierre Lambert*, 507. The Bernese request and the Duke's response are in AST1, Genève, cat. 1, mz. 4, no. 5, and published in Segre, 'Documenti di storia sabauda,' 248-49.
3   Gilliard, 33-45.
4   Ibid., 46-66.
5   In order to manage potential conflict with Fribourg, Berne asked them to identify their allies in the *pays de Vaud* (ibid., 67).
6   Ibid., 75; also 67-74.
7   'Diverse lettere al Duca Carlo 3°,' copy of letter from Naegli to the Castellan and inhabitants of Cudrefin, Morat 22-I-36.

the community's granaries, they broke them open and seized the grain.[8] Over the next two weeks, most of the *pays de Vaud* surrendered, and, on 2 February, the Bernese army entered Geneva.[9]

The Duke's reaction to these events was bewildering – he waited a week after the invasion to send envoys to the Swiss. His efforts to raise soldiers in the Valle d'Aosta and march them over the mountains failed, with René in France and valley communities 'claim[ing] impoverishment and quarrell[ing] about the number of soldiers'.[10] The Catholic Valaisans and Fribourgeois promptly occupied the Sabaudian lands near them, ostensibly to prevent their takeover by Berne, but also covering for them by keeping the invasion of Vaud from turning into a religious conflict. A rump Swiss Diet (in the absence of six Catholic cantons) met in Berne on 2 February 1536 to select mediators who arrived in Geneva two weeks later. On 16 February, the Diet sent a message for the Duke to René in Chambéry.[11] One reason for the Duke's apparently somnolent response was his preoccupation with the French forces that had been assembling on his western borders since late 1535. As soon as the Bernese marched, the French approached Bresse, and, rather than request safe passage (which Charles III had anticipated and for which he had prepared *étapes*),[12] they demanded territory based on Louise de Savoie's inheritance. As the Duke refused, word arrived of the Bernese invasion.[13] By this time, the King's heralds were blanketing 'Bresse, Savoie, and Bugey to command all of the subjects to submit to him and swear oaths of loyalty, otherwise threatening fire and blood'. Most of these places had already been taken 'under the guise of' the troop passage that the Duke had granted, such that resistance 'was practically impossible'.[14] Not until 12 February were Imperial troops from Milan authorized to support the Duke.[15]

By early February 1536, René was back in Chambéry, where he forestalled a Bernese advance on that town by offering a peace agreement. As the Bernese ruminated, a French envoy claiming to be a mediator for Francis I on behalf of Charles III arrived at their camp in St. Julien. He maintained

---

8   Ibid., Demolendino [?] to Ch III, Estavayer 17-II-36 (describing what had happened over three weeks earlier).
9   Gilliard, 76-97.
10 Ibid., 134.
11 Ibid., 108-20; for the Emperor's response, see ibid., 121-23, 184-85 and n. 4 – the author cites Segre, 'Documenti di storia sabauda,' 119 n. 7 for this information.
12 *Mémoires de Pierre Lambert*, 507-8.
13 Gilliard, 126-33 (see 130 n. 4 for René's reaction).
14 *Mémoires de Pierre Lambert*, 507-8.
15 Gilliard, 126-33.

this charade for two weeks; by the time the Bernese were aware of the King's true intentions, his troops had already occupied Bresse.[16] Confusion among the Duke's own officers was also widespread. For example, on 17 February, the Lord of Estavayer wrote to the Duke in despair about 'the saddest and most unpleasant things that could have ever happened', wondering what the Duke wanted him and his subjects to do and pledging obedience.[17] On the same day, the Castellan of Cudrefin resent a packet of letters to the Duke that had been dispatched over three weeks earlier to the Governor of Vaud without reaching their destination. Only then, almost a month after the fact, did Charles III learn what had happened on the first day of the invasion.[18]

By this point, the Bernese enterprise was beginning to lose its internal momentum as nearby lords made peaceful arrangements with the invaders – despite some desperate pleas to the Duke for assistance by Sabaudian subjects in Vaud.[19] The Bishop of Lausanne, Sebastien de Montfalcon, admitted to René on 20 February that 'I do not know what to tell myself about these developments [...] and I doubt whether repairing the harm done will be as easy as if we had been able to prevent it from happening'.[20] A similar sense of hopelessness reigned along the French 'front' in Savoie, where an attack on Chambéry was expected on 23 February.[21] René and other lords withdrew from Rumilly, about halfway between Chambéry and Geneva. A Savoyard noble (Michel de Viry?) had written multiple letters to the Duke several times without reply, declaring his goodwill and desire to serve Charles III, as René could confirm. The noble advised the Duke to arrange some kind of 'neutrality' with the King of France (offering himself as a negotiator) and seconded René's opinion that 'the five cantons' be involved in 'mediat[ing]' the dispute between Your Excellency and the Bernese'.[22]

René prepared to pull out of Chambéry since neither he nor the Swiss mediators could do anything to stop the Bernese advance without instructions from the Duke; the Swiss would not even issue René a safe-conduct without

16   Ibid., 148-49.
17   The subjects lamented that, without the Duke's help, 'sommes comme povres brebis sans pasteurs, voien ausi que tous aultres vous subiets de ce pais plus puissant a resister que nous en sont en tel cas et semblable dangier' ('Diverse lettere al Duca Carlo 3°,' Estavayer to Ch III, Estavayer 17-II-36).
18   Ibid., De Molendino [?] to Ch III, Estavayer 17-II-36.
19   Gilliard, 134-41, 148-49.
20   'Diverse lettere al Duca Carlo 3°,' Bishop of Lausanne [Sebastien de Montfalcon] to René, Lausanne 20-II-36.
21   Ibid., Aymé de Piobesi to Ch III, Chambéry 22-II-36.
22   Ibid., ? to Ch III, Remollier [Rumilly?] 22-II-36. The five cantons were Uri, Schwyz, Unterwald, Lucerne, and Zug.

Charles III's commitment to negotiate.²³ Michel de Viry's predicament was typical. On 24 February, he wrote desperately to René for help with his creditors in Flanders and Basel.²⁴ While his timing might seem strange, another correspondent clarified that Viry sought a document that would secure him an extension to repay his creditors – this would enable him at least to mortgage a part of his property, since the Bernese had burned all of his houses and seized his other property when he had refused to acknowledge their overlordship.²⁵ As weeks-old reports finally arrived from Vaud (via Fribourg), René wrote to Charles III of the 'irreparable damage' that would result from failure to act.²⁶ René's secretary Cavet offered to carry out a last-ditch defense of Pierre Lambert's (President of the *Chambre des comptes*) castle of La Croix, near Chambéry. But, before committing 'to die there before surrendering the place', they sought ducal guidance.²⁷ By this point, the Bernese army had returned to Vaud to consolidate their gains and the main continued threat came from the French, as local officials frantically sought instructions from Turin about how to respond.²⁸ Town councillors in Bourg-en-Bresse bought time by negotiating the particular form of the loyalty oath that the French commander demanded of them – the commander eventually advanced from the area before the oath was sworn. The Duke's Governor of Bresse informed René that 'we have done that which seemed right and possible, according to our honor and conscience', after having sought advice from everyone available.²⁹

Chambéry was evacuated by Sabaudian forces by 23 February and René withdrew to attend to the defense of the Valle d'Aosta. The French army pushed across the Alps in March, while Imperial forces marched west from Milan and René vainly sought ducal instructions. On 1 April 1536, as the French approached the gates of Turin, Sabaudian envoys finally sat down in Lausanne with the Bernese, whose negotiating position had changed due to the massively reconfigured military situation, complicating things for the Duke's diplomats. The last Sabaudian holdouts north of the lake had already fallen,³⁰ and truce talks between French and Imperial forces began

---

23 Ibid., Swiss ambassadors to René, Geneva 22-II-36.
24 Ibid., Michel de Viry to René 'mon cusin,' Nuysz [?] 22-II-?.
25 Ibid., ? [Cavet?] to Ch III, s.d., s.l.
26 Ibid., René to Ch III, Chambéry 24-II-36.
27 Ibid., Cavet to Ch III, Chambéry 24-II-36.
28 Gilliard, 150-64, 169-83.
29 AHR, FC 264, mz. 1, Philibert de La Baume to René, Bourg 28-II-36.
30 Gilliard, 187-97, 210, 219. For the Duke's memoir, see AST1, Genève, cat. 12, mz. 2, printed in Segre, 'Documenti di storia sabauda,' 253-54 (where it is dated 19 February, not 18 February).

in Piedmont, where the French vacated several of their conquests. Local communities and officials puzzled how to balance the demands of necessity with their political and moral commitments.[31] The Bernese brushed aside the Duke's concerns and appointed a commission to administer the *pays de Vaud*, which it divided into six bailiwicks.[32]

René's biographer would later write that, as his conquest unfolded, Francis I tried to seduce René with the offer of making him 'absolute lord' of the Valle d'Aosta, as the King 'understood that his predecessors had been. René pretended not to understand such promises [...] and while he was very perplexed as he saw the ruin being caused around him', he persisted in his loyalty to the Duke.[33] In fact, in early April, Charles III wrote to his secretary in Aosta, Nicolas La Creste, about the suspected loyalties of a person whose name was written in code. La Creste declared the person to be 'so virtuous and of such a good nature that, in my view, he is beyond suspicion'. Still, he suggested placing a strong guard at Bard; he and the Bailiff would do nothing more without explicit instructions.[34] Thus, much was unclear about the military-administrative situation in the Sabaudian lands in spring 1536. Charles V arrived in Piedmont, but, rather than force a French retreat, he decided to counterattack in Provence. The 'blind and presumptuous' Imperial commander Antonio de Leyva declined to support Tarentaise and Valdostano resistance fighters who still managed a temporary advance all the way to Chambéry. A negotiated French withdrawal seemed possible, but nothing was certain, except that the Valle d'Aosta was one of the few territories not occupied by foreign forces.[35]

Valangin, the Reform, and relations with the Countess of Neuchâtel

It may seem remarkable that, in late March 1536, as French and Swiss armies overran the Sabaudian lands for which René served as Marshal,

31 Tallone, 107-16.
32 The commission members included Wolfgang von Wingarten, and Rudolf d'Erlach was appointed Bailiff of Gex. Some Sabaudian nobles renounced their fidelity to the Duke; exceptions were Louis de Bonvillars-Mézières (defender of Romont, and later Governor of Vercelli and a ducal diplomat); Michel Mangerod, Baron of La Sarraz; and Aymon de Genève-Lullin (Gilliard, 221-46).
33 'Histoire généalogique,' 50v.
34 AST1, LP, C.112, La Creste to Ch III, Aosta, 8-IV-?.
35 *Mémoires de Pierre Lambert*, 510-11; Gilliard, 256.

Fig. 2: The castle and *bourg* of Valangin (detail from eighteenth-century print [ca. 1786], original at Museum of the Castle of Valangin). Photograph by author.

the Count of Challant sought the Duke's permission to meet the Duke of Longueville in Valangin and settle 'as friends' their remaining disagreements.[36] But transregional lords like René constantly faced challenges in multiple places, and he was right to be concerned about the status of his seigniory: his disputes with the Counts of Neuchâtel and their subjects were intersected by the religious conflict that had divided the region for over a decade. After Berne and Basel accepted the Reform in 1528-1529, René could have expected that traditional Christianity would come under attack in Valangin as well, and that a change in faith might spark a political upheaval.

Over the past 20 years, scholars of sixteenth-century religion have asked practical questions about how reforms were instituted, what kinds of reactions they engendered, what bi-confessionalism looked like, and what it meant to live as a Catholic, Reformed, or Lutheran Christian. Many studies have identified interactions across confessional lines. In southern Germany and the Swiss area, calls for disputations concerning the Reform (1520s) were met by imperial prohibitions of such public discussions (1524).[37] Towns held disputations anyway, and, while many adopted the Reform, the question of how 'religious choice was influenced and manifested in rural settings' has not yet been widely studied. James Blakeley has looked at this question in the village of Goumoëns (*pays de Vaud*), and found that there, a few inhabitants pushed for change and used their social networks to secure the support of outside authorities. The villagers, however, displayed

---

36 The Duke denied the request 'due to current developments' (AEN, AS-R5.10, s, René to Prangins, Aymavilles 26-III-36).
37 Flückiger, 283.

'gradations of religious sentiment' and resisted the simple dichotomy 'Catholic vs. Reformed'.[38]

As the years passed, even as the Council of Trent clarified the dichotomy that Swiss peasants preferred to avoid, Christians in Europe interacted across confessional boundaries.[39] Edwin Bezzina has uncovered a similar sensibility among lesser Protestant nobles in western France, distinguishing between the *prudent* and *ferme* positions among these elites during the reign of Louis XIII. 'A *prudent* could retain strong anti-Catholic sentiments while advocating nonviolent methods' of interacting with Catholics, including family members or business associates.[40] Greg Monahan's discussion of the pressures leading Protestant nobles to convert after 1683 reinforces the point that a variety of factors (including the appurtenances of rank) were as important a part of noble identity as religious confession.[41]

Bi-confessional environments posed a problem for traditional sacralized understandings of political power. It seems that, over time, and before political theorists articulated such arguments, Europeans gradually (or even abruptly) mentally quarantined religious difference from other aspects of their social, economic, and political relationships.[42] 'Irenic patriotism' combined utilitarian and religious arguments for peaceful arrangements during religious conflict.[43] One view is that religious peace agreements sought to transform problems of belief and truth into legal problems over which the state had jurisdiction. After the second war of Kappel (1531) between Swiss Reformed and Catholic cantons, Catholic minorities in Protestant areas enjoyed freedom of worship and a proportional claim to church property.[44]

---

38   Blakeley, 346, 365.
39   In 1553, Nicolas de Vaudémont (head of a cadet branch of the Lorraine) arranged a twelve-year monopoly of glass exports from Lorraine for Gian Angelo Calderini, 'an Italian Protestant merchant based in Basel' (Monter, 57). Richard Ninness has reported on the fascinating situation in late sixteenth-century Bamberg, where even Protestant nobles were appointed to serve the Prince-Bishop, and, in their capacity as state officials, even engaged in efforts to convert other Protestants to Catholicism. He notes that studies of confessionalization 'have thus far done a poor job of considering the role of officials and nobles', arguing that 'confession was only one of several important competing loyalties motivating these nobles' (Ninness, 700-1, 703, 719).
40   Bezzina, 341, 350, 354. Sandberg, however, found that seventeenth-century religious divisions 'severely disrupted seigneurial relationships by breaking down seigneurial bonds and dividing families' (95).
41   Monahan, 539.
42   In the United Provinces during the 1600s, there were 'private' churches where Catholics practiced, although the public-private distinction 'was as much a cultural fiction as it was social reality' (Kaplan, 1036, 1040).
43   Schmidt.
44   Wolgast.

For Maurice Barbier, spiritual and political power were linked in the early sixteenth century, and Bodin's contribution was not to separate them, but to ground the state in a kind of natural religion. Later, Grotius and Hobbes merely subordinated religion to the state, and it was not until Locke that the two were really separated.[45] As we will see, the Valangin example combined several themes discussed in recent scholarship: the ambiguity of religious confession (especially prior to the Council of Trent), a form of noble identity that saw religious fidelity as one element among others orienting noble behavior, and a kind of political understanding that privileged public order while holding religious contradictions in temporary abeyance.

As pressures for religious reform began to roil Neuchâtel in 1530, Guillemette asked the Marquis of Rothelin, one of Jeanne de Hochberg's sons, to 'send her men to protect her, if necessary', but Rothelin failed to act.[46] On 15 August 1530, Guillaume Farel began preaching the Reform at Boudevilliers, a community contiguous to the seigniory of Valangin. The immediate reaction to his provocative act[47] was mixed: some in the crowd listened to Farel talk, and others threw rocks at him and his companions and beat them with sticks as they tried to pass through Valangin on their way back to Neuchâtel. Guillemette de Vergy had them seized and thrown into the castle dungeon, threatening to drown them in the Seyon. Following their release, Farel and his companions ('some young men from Neuchâtel' – bodyguards, it seems) persisted and, before long, people from different communities in the seigniory had accepted the Reform. Guillemette tried to punish the new believers among her subjects, but the Bernese successfully pressured her to grant them freedom of worship.[48] In 1531, Engollon, Boudevilliers, and Valangin all joined the Reform; an assembly at Dombresson chose to accept the Reform, and, when Guillemette and Bellegarde had Mass celebrated in the church by force, Berne and Bienne (a town near Neuchâtel that had accepted the Reform in 1528) forced her to back down.[49] Altercations continued unabated in 1532.[50] Little evidence of René's reactions to these events remains. He ordered 'that the Mass and

45 Barbier, 'Les rapports du pouvoir spirituel,' 310.
46 Matile, 272. For a discussion of the long-term impact of the Reform on popular culture in Valangin, see Watt.
47 Farel planned his message to start as the priest was singing Mass on the Feast of the Assumption, and his companion seized the Host from the priest at the moment of the elevation.
48 Matile, 274-78 n. 3; see also Bartolini, 105-6.
49 Matile, 274-79, 278 n. 3.
50 Berne pressed René not to block the Reform and extracted a promise to 'tolérer ceux qui voudraient se ranger du côté de l'Evangile' (ibid., 280-81).

other holy services be continued' in Coffranes,[51] but Les Brenets accepted the Reform in 1534, and Le Locle did so two years later.[52] A contingent from Valangin accompanied Swiss Reformed forces that defeated a larger Savoyard army at Gingins in 1535, as René's subjects battled the troops over which René held high command.[53]

By 1536, the entire seigniory of Valangin had accepted the Reform, and arrangements were made for preachers in different villages who were confirmed in the rights that had formerly belonged to the *curés* (collecting grain, hemp, rents, tithes, etc.)[54] In 1540, René accorded a pastor to the subjects of the *bourg*. Bienne, which had rights of appointment to the churches of Dombresson and Savagnier, installed Reformed pastors there.[55] The nave of the collegial church at Valangin began to be used for Reformed services, and, over time, 'the Reform quickly invaded the choir and the transepts, and part of the nave was turned into a granary'. By 1556, the church was used neither for Mass nor for Reformed preaching (in 1567, there was still no pastor).[56] Mass continued to be said in Valangin's castle chapel, though, whose sacristy included several valuable items.[57]

The development of the Reform in Valangin obviously left René in an unusual position. Forced to accept that most of his subjects there had embraced heresy, he also saw them collect funds in 1560 to support the inhabitants of the Waldensian valleys of Piedmont in their war against the Duke of Savoy – by some accounts, the sums donated dwarfed those usually collected by René himself.[58] Still, the secular authority which he retained over his Reformed subjects gave him the right to appoint their pastors and to resolve their disputes.[59] On one occasion, René's officers had to convince his Reformed subjects of Dombresson to accept a minister whom they had rejected, and to agree to be reconciled.[60] At other times, René had to work with local pastors and communities to provide for revenues to ensure

51 AEN, AS-R5.10, ddd, Bellegarde to Prangins, just before Christmas, s.d.
52 Matile, 274-78 n. 3.
53 Ibid., 273.
54 Ibid., 282-83.
55 Ibid., 277-78 n. 3.
56 Ibid., 284-85.
57 See the inventory in AHR, FC 290, no. 41, inventory dated 26-I-58.
58 Matile, 285-86.
59 For an example of René's officers Junod and Vulpe resolving a conflict involving a minister of Le Locle, see AEN, AS-G16, 17, Blaise Junod and Jehan Vulpe 'voz admoditateurs' to René, Valangin 7-I-47; ibid., 20, Martine to René, Valangin 19-II-48.
60 The case also involved the Bishop of Basel; see ibid., AS-K16, 19, Valangin official to René, s.d. [I-48?].

ministers' livelihoods[61] or to mediate between neighboring lords and his Reformed subjects over tithe disputes.[62] During the sixteenth century, transregional lordship was likely to be multi-confessional lordship.

Relations between René (or his officers) and the counts of Neuchâtel (or their governors) varied over time but were usually marked by René's deference toward his suzerains. René exchanged courtesies with the Countess of Neuchâtel, sending her presents and facilitating information exchanges between her, the Duke of Savoy, and the French court.[63] Her governor Prangins frequently visited René, offering advice when asked; René assured him that 'I hold you among my most important friends, in whom I have perfect confidence'.[64] The officers of René and Jeanne tended to be cooperative, despite the religiously divided environment. They worked together on maintaining roads,[65] assisting financially burdened subjects,[66] and in matters involving escaped prisoners in their respective territories, since 'one seigniory should assist another'.[67]

In 1536, the Duke required René to remain in the Valle d'Aosta and organize its defense. The Count regretted that 'the responsibility that I have in this country [the valley]' prevented him from resolving his dispute with Jeanne de Hochberg but could not 'abandon' his post 'because of the dangers that could follow', especially given the Duke's withdrawal to Nice. He requested that 'our business be postponed', promising Prangins that he would remember the favor.[68] René finally visited Valangin and Beaufremont in spring 1537. Now on the table was whether René needed to swear a new oath of homage to Jeanne herself (having already sworn one to her son). A *journée* was fixed in July which René would attend if Prangins would be there. Otherwise he would go hunting and send Monsieur d'Aubonne in his stead – but he invited Prangins to stop by Valangin to share a drink and discuss these matters.[69]

---

61   In 1548, peasants and the ministers from La Chaux de Fonds, Le Locle, and elsewhere met René's fiscal officer Martine about the ministers' financial support. The Lord of Colombier (Jean-Jacques de Watteville, *avoyer* of Berne), helped René and his officers find a solution (ibid., AS-G16, 20, Martine to René, Valangin 19-II-48).
62   Matile, 266.
63   AEN, AS-H16, 11, Jeanne de Hochberg to René, 19-VI-?.
64   Ibid., AS-R5.10, c, René to Prangins, 21-I-39; ibid., rr, René to Prangins, 7-II-39; ibid., b, René to Prangins, Beaufremont 15-VII-? [1545?].
65   Ibid., xx, Bellegarde to Prangins, Quasimodo Sunday 1532 (date penciled in).
66   Ibid., qq, René to Prangins, 6-III-39.
67   Ibid., l, René to Prangins, 19-V-?.
68   Ibid., ff, René to Prangins, Issogne 7-XII-?.
69   Ibid., p, René to Prangins, 1-VII-37.

The strategic situation prevented René from meeting Jeanne at the French court that summer, so he instructed his officer, the Fribourgeois Claude Collier, to treat with her on his behalf. While he agreed to arbitration, he rejected the claim that the Neuchâtel estates had jurisdiction over their disagreement. René strongly desired a resolution since 'in these times lords and seigniories should not be in conflict with each other' but warned that Jeanne would have 'great regrets' if they could not come to terms.[70] Strangely, Jeanne also made out a procuration for Claude Collier in 1537, empowering him to sell property in her name,[71] while René continued his informal discussions with Prangins.[72] In the fall, René was back in the Valle d'Aosta and then, in early 1538, was in Nice and in Spain serving Charles III. A projected May 1538 meeting between René and Jeanne appears not to have taken place, but the two saw each other that summer in Nice, where they agreed to resolve their dispute.[73]

Jeanne and René kept trying to meet, while their officers and subjects kept fighting. The Valanginois complained of being 'molested' by the Mayor of Boudevilliers.[74] They rejected new tax assessments based on earlier agreements with Berne and revisions by the Neuchâtel estates – a 'matter of honor, with consequences', according to René.[75] Bellegarde reported the 'very strange novelty' of the Mayor of Boudevilliers demanding payments from jury members from Valangin,[76] and the Mayor's fellow villagers began trespassing on René's lands, cutting wood in his forest.[77] Neuchâtel patricians began trying to make *gaigements* (assessments of mortgaged property) on René's land, sparking a sharp dispute punctuated by an 'abundance of [accusatory] words'.[78] René personally intervened with Prangins, inviting

70 Ibid., AS-B4.9, h, 18-VII-37 procuration draft [or copy] for Collier by René, witnessed by Castellamonte, Baron Michel de Chevron, and Bellegarde. René's 'desexpoyr' would only increase if he were to 'vehoyr & entendre fere largesses & gratuyttes au grans prejudice de madicte dame a gens de moendre qualite que luy' (ibid., i, draft talking points dated 18-VII-37 [date of 8-VII written on back seems incorrect]).
71 Scheurer, 28-29.
72 AEN, AS-R5.10, y, René to Prangins, 20-VII-37.
73 Ibid., r, René to Prangins, 10-VIII-38.
74 Ibid., h, René to Prangins, 29-XI-? (1538 penciled in).
75 When the subjects were shown the assessments, 'soubdain lesd' subgectz se sont clammez', saying only that the letter and decision were 'faulce et meschant' (ibid., aa, René to Prangins, 26-III-39).
76 Ibid., ppp, Bellegarde to Prangins, 27-IV-?.
77 The mayor of Boudevilliers was also accused of having taken other unilateral actions (ibid., m, René to Prangins, 1-VI-39).
78 Ibid., mm, René to Prangins, 1-VI-39 (two letters, same date); ibid., tt, René to Prangins, 2-VI-39.

him and his assistants to come 'dine with me' and (if necessary) to visit 'the disputed sites' and reach an agreement.[79] Eventually, Prangins offered to 'turn over the *gaiges* without compromising any legal claims' until they could have 'a friendly summit' but the problem continued into the fall.[80] René continued to hope that he and Prangins could 'clear everything up through friendship'.[81] He then left for Flanders in the spring of 1540 but was kept informed of the Valangin situation, which he was able to discuss with Jeanne and the Duke of Guise.[82] Francis I then abruptly prohibited Jeanne from alienating any more property in France – property losses in her Germanic lands and in Neuchâtel had prompted her to sell fiefs in order to maintain her extravagant lifestyle at court, to the detriment of her heirs. On the day this order was issued, 21 April 1540, Jeanne borrowed 6000 *francs* from René, securing this loan on her rights over Valangin and Boudevilliers; if she were not to repay the loan within three years, René would acquire those rights.[83]

Political leadership and mobility during a time of uncertainty

During these years, René's attention was also devoted to defending the Valle d'Aosta against threats from the French and the Swiss. On 24 March 1536, the valley estates reached agreement concerning financial contributions for the war effort from the clergy. René described this as a kind of insurance policy, given that the dissatisfaction of 'the people' toward the Church, 'could have had dangerous consequences'. The estates also established an executive committee – the *Conseil des Commis*, led by the Bishop, the Bailiff, René, and deputies from each of the three estates – to oversee valley affairs during the crisis. Envoys were sent to the Bishop of Sion and the Valais to express desire for 'a good friendship and neighborhood' while also sounding out whether 'they intend to give passage to [the Duke's] enemies'. René knew

---

79 Ibid., oo, René to Prangins, 17-VII-? (internal evidence suggests 1539).
80 By this point, the Castellan of Val de Travers and his son had gotten involved, and were causing problems for René (ibid., x, René to Prangins, Virieu 20-IX-39); ibid., zz, Bellegarde to Prangins, 21-XI-39.
81 The letter also presented new complaints from his subjects of Le Locle and La Sagne about 'Monsieur de Travers mon cousin [either Lancelot de Neuchâtel-Vaumarcus, Lord of Travers or his son Jean III, who with his brother André was Co-Lord of Travers]' (ibid., dd, René to Prangins 24-XI-? [internal evidence suggests 1539]).
82 Ibid., pp, René to Prangins, Ghent 8-IV-40.
83 Scheurer, 28-32. A cousin of the House of Zähringen, Christopher I, Margrave of Baden, acquired Jeanne's Germanic lands by family agreement.

that the French envoy to the Swiss (Louis Daugerant, Lord of Boisrigaut) was trying to raise troops among them; an imminent Franco-Swiss invasion of the valley by the two St. Bernard passes was feared. The valley needed 2000-3000 well-paid troops who would not pillage the subjects and thereby 'cost [Charles III] the country's heart and devotion'. Sensitive to popular sentiment, the estates took measures to block any French herald from entering the valley, 'to prevent [ducal] subjects from here from being terrified by his arrival'. Militia captains were appointed, and, since the 'nobles of this country for the most part lack any military experience', René asked Charles III to send a dozen officers 'who have fought in wars [...] and if possible send those of *la longue d'aouy* [*langue d'oeiul*, Francophone]'. He urged the Duke to reinforce the forts of Bard and Montjovet, 'for [the preservation of] *l'estat* and to guard the things that you have placed there'.[84] René then strengthened the fortifications at Verrès and Ivrea and continued to request reinforcements despite the French invasion having stalled.[85] In late August (while the Duke was in Nice), Duchess Beatrice named René lieutenant general for Aosta, Faucigny, and Tarentaise.[86] While thanking Beatrice for the honor, René observed that such letters 'undermine my reputation by having to use them', since his office of marshal carried greater authority. He thus did not want people to think that he had been demoted from marshal to lieutenant 'due to a lack of trust in me'. He did, however, asked to be appointed governor of Aosta – the Valdostani were already murmuring that 'they did not have to obey me, seeing that I did not enjoy the preeminence that my father [formerly governor] had'. Being governor would enable him to confront 'these cells and meetings' that were generating disobedience toward the dynasty.[87]

After an initial period of confusion concerning Franco-Swiss intentions and the possibility of a Franco-Imperial peace,[88] René settled into his leadership role in the Valle d'Aosta and other Sabaudian lands, while continuing to govern his own strategic and territorially dispersed domains. For the next 25 years, he traveled constantly between them, with periods

---

84   Fornaseri, 93-95, René to Ch III, Aosta 24-III-36. The ducal archives had been sent to Montjovet for safekeeping. In October 1536, René pleaded with the Duchess from Vercelli to send soldiers quickly since 'les ennemys ne dorment point et que leur desir c'est de gaigner les passaiges' and to ensure that the soldiers are well-paid 'car aultrement cella inciteroit le pays de revolter et leur hosteroyt le bon vouloir qu'ilz vous portent' (ibid., 97-98, René to Beatrice, Vercelli 10-X-36).
85   Frutaz, 'Notes,' 248-50; Fornaseri, 95-96, René to Beatrice, Aosta 18-VII-36.
86   AHR, FC 25, no. 6, patents dated 31-VIII-36.
87   Fornaseri, 96-97, René to Beatrice, Issogne 6-IX-37 [sic, should be 1536].
88   See Tallone.

in Nice, Piedmont (Vercelli and then, for a time, Turin), Lorraine, and the Low Countries. In early 1537, he left the valley to attend to matters in Beaufremont and Valangin, but continued to receive military updates from Ivrea and surrounding areas.[89] The Duke and Duchess reported from Nice their approval of valley leaders' actions[90] and hopes were raised in March 1537 that Charles V would send reinforcements to Italy.[91] In April, René, the Bishop of Aosta, and the estates took a crucial step in preserving the valley's integrity by negotiating a neutrality accord with French envoys in Lyon, ending the war within the duchy of Aosta.[92] Soon thereafter, René held talks with the French ambassador to the Swiss (with Prangins's help) about his own 'affairs'.[93] This effectively illustrates the ambiguity of René's political position as a trusted ducal servant and also a lord with his own interests, which were frequently determined by the spatial configuration of his own jurisdictions.

In fall 1538, René was summoned by Charles III to a meeting in Nice and then returned to Ivrea to assist Imperial commanders arriving with a small force.[94] He then turned around and headed back to the coast and thence to Barcelona and Narbonne, where he represented the Duke in Franco-Imperial peace talks, along with the Piedmontese Lord Amedeo Valperga di Masino.[95] That initiative was followed up by discussions in Nice, where the Pope, the French King, and the Emperor planned to meet personally.[96] Charles V's arrival on 9 May 1539 initiated a dispute about

89   AHR, FC 260, Paolo Vagnone to René, 7-II-37; ibid., Antonio Guascho to René, 29-III-37.
90   AHR, FC 264, mz. 1, Lambert [?] to René, Nice 10-II-? [internal evidence suggests 1537]; Lambert was with Charles III at Nice in 1537-1538; see *Mémoires de Pierre Lambert*, 489.
91   AEN, AS-R5.10, w, René to Prangins, 5-III-37.
92   The valley's envoys were Castellamonte, Jean d'Avise, and Nicolas de la Creste, and they reached an agreement with Francis, Cardinal of Tournon on behalf of the King (AST1, Cité et Duché d'Aoste, mz. 4, no. 14, agreement dated 19-IV-37).
93   This related presumably to René's dispute with the Countess of Neuchâtel (AEN, AS-R5.10, z, René to Beaurigault [French ambassador to the Swiss], 20-VII-37); see also ibid., y, René to Prangins, 20-VII-37.
94   AHR, FC 260, Ch III to René, Nice 7-X-37?. René seems to have assisted in organizing the delivery of funds to pay for the reinforcements (ibid., Cesare di Napoli to René, 22-XI-37; ibid., FC 263, mz. 1, ? to ?, s.d.).
95   AST1, PD 166, f. 132, 2-I-38 patents naming René and Masino as envoys for restitution negotiations; AHR, FC 247, no. 17, 2-I-38 ducal instructions for René and Masino; Frutaz, 'Notes,' 250; Tallone, 115 n. 5. On 11 April 1538, René and Masino returned to the Sabaudian court at Nice, which was mourning the recent death of Duchess Beatrice; *Mémoires de Pierre Lambert*, 513.
96   Expecting an end to the occupation, many Sabaudian elites 'vindrent a Nyce tant pour veoir leur prince et naturel seigneur, que soubz expoir le veoir en lentiere reintegration en son estat' (ibid., 514).

where each ruler would lodge, embarrassing the Duke of Savoy.[97] Hearing that the Emperor would stay there, Sabaudian soldiers in the castle of Nice mutinied in defense of the young Prince Emanuel Filibert, fearing that the Emperor would seize the castle and take the Prince hostage. René stepped in to mediate, and, in response to Charles V's 'rude words [...] virtuously sought to pacify him, as testified all who were there, holding him in great esteem'.[98] Consulting with Charles III, René then assembled all of the Sabaudian lords and officials at his own residence. The group elected René, 'in the name of the entire company', to 'go before Their Holiness and Majesty with a reasonable message of apology to excuse my said lord [the Duke] as dutifully as possible'. The following day, the Emperor instructed Charles III to send him the castle officers who had been part of the mutiny, or to punish them himself.[99]

Following this rocky start, the Duke met with the King, while the Emperor held dicussions with the Pope. Charles III sent René to inform Charles V about the offers made by the French. By this point (7 June 1538), the Emperor's anger had subsided,[100] a truce was signed on 18 June, and, a couple of weeks later, the King and the Emperor revived their discussions at Aigues Mortes, with an eye to a permanent settlement. Charles III remained in Nice,[101] while René returned to the valley and thence to Valangin.[102] By early 1539, it appeared that a lasting peace might be reached, as French discussions with Charles V intensified. Some ducal officials complained about Imperial counterparts using their influence to plunder the Duke's treasury and hoped that the Emperor would appoint 'capable administrators and not military people' in their place once a peace was established.[103]

Within a month (February 1539), this optimism was dashed. René learned of a failed effort by Sabaudian partisans to recapture Turin by force, led

---

97 Ibid., 514-15. Charles III offered to Charles V to explain matters to the Pope, who was then at Monaco, and the Emperor lent him some galleys to do so. He then proposed the Nice castle as the Emperor's temporary residence (ibid., 515).
98 Ibid., 515-16.
99 Ibid., 516.
100 Ibid., 516-17.
101 Ibid., 517, 519. Charles V issued letters in favor of the Duke and the Count of Gruyère in late June and early July (AHR, FC 25, no. 7, patents dated 30-VI-38; ibid., FC 289, no. 46, declaration of 2-VII-38).
102 AHR, FC 264 mz. 1, Lullin to René, Nice 23-VII-38?.
103 One reason for this optimism described in AEN, AS-G16, 30, Lullin to René, Vercelli 6-I-39 was the news that Antoine Prat would replace the Marquis del Vasto as Governor of Milan. Antoine du Prat, Lord of Nantouillet, was a typical border noble whose lands were held from both the King of France and the Emperor; see Du Prat, 46-57.

by a certain Captain César Duc, who was captured and killed in prison.[104] The French Governor, René de Montjean, Lord of Beaupréau, wrote to the Constable of France about the imprisonment of Duc, who was suspected to have acted with Charles III's knowledge and approval.[105] Perhaps preparing for new hostilities, René began to arrange for a number of loans from lenders in Aarau, Lucerne, and elsewhere, while gathering updates from valley officials like Mathieu Lostan and Jean Vuillet about Sabaudian matters.[106] From Nice, Vuillet confirmed reception of the extension of a loan repayment that René had arranged on behalf of the Duke.[107] Castellamonte brought word that the César Duc plot had generated fears of a French attack. He met in Turin with René's old friend the French Governor Montjean,[108] who reported that, while René was not suspected of involvement in the plot, Charles III was,[109] and Francis I thus asked the Emperor to dispense justice to Duc and his accomplices. The ducal court was gripped by the fear that, if justice were not carried out, the truce would be broken.[110] The episode had caused 'much damage, all to our disadvantage', and René was alienated by the court intrigue described by Castellamonte: 'This poor prince is so lost and is being led by the nose by many people with neither honor nor understanding but only greed.'[111] Castellamonte also forwarded the good news that the Imperial ambassador Marnoz, who was arbitrating a dispute

---

104 AEN, AS-F16, 19, Manfredo d'Azeglio to René, 14-II-39; also ibid., AS-G16, 29, Lostan to René, 11-II-39.

105 Ribier, 367-68, Montjean to Constable, Turin 2-II-39, and ibid., 444-45, same to same, Turin 23-IV-39.

106 He borrowed 1,300 florins from the Aarau banker Jeronimus Schmitziger, 380 florins from Schmitziger's colleague Baltasar Sagisser, 1,300 *écus* from one of the Pfyffer in Lucerne, and 700 *écus* from Hentzman Schleiff; see AEN, AS-Z8, 2, 4, 3, 9, letters dated 1539; ibid., AS-G16, 29, Lostan to René, 11-II-39.

107 Ibid., 10, Vulliet to René, 29-III-39. Jean Vulliet had inherited the fief of St. Pierre from his father-in-law in 1529.

108 The two had been captured together at Pavia in 1525; see Ribier, 367-68, Montjean to Constable, Turin 2-II-39, and ibid., 444-45, same to same, Turin 23-IV-39.

109 Montjean and his companions professed their devotion to René and assured Castellamonte that no one had implicated René 'en ceste conspiration qu'avoit faict Cesar Ducz' (AEN, AS-K16, 20, Castellamonte to René, 8-V-39 [year based on internal evidence]). Duc was executed on 23 April 1539; see Ribier, Montjean to Constable, Turin 2-II-39, and ibid., 444-45, same to same, Turin 23-IV-39. Montjean died in Turin in September, five months later.

110 In other news from Nice, rumor had it that Francis I was conceding Italy to the Emperor, who was compensating the former 'della les montz'. The Pope was said to be plotting to have his daughter marry the French Dauphin and the two placed on the English throne in lieu of Henry VIII (AEN, AS-K16, 20, Castellamonte to René, 8-V-39 [year based on internal evidence]).

111 Castellamonte's version of Duc's resilience under torture differed from Lostan's account, who had written that Duc had implicated the Governor of Ivrea (Paul Vagnon) and the Sabaudian

between nobles from Settimo Vittone and René's subjects, was a 'gallant man' who desired to serve René – Valangin was not too far from Marnoz's fief of Franquemont in the Franche-Comté, and the two had overlapping transregional interests.[112]

Roz Favre, ducal Bailiff of Aosta, kept René informed about valley affairs on almost a daily basis, often via letters carried by Castellamonte that described conflicts with nearby Imperial commanders,[113] military equipment purchases in Milan, or the state of valley fortifications.[114] In fall 1539, René and the Lord De Riddes met at the former's fief of Virieu (in French-occupied Bugey). De Riddes had been soliciting René's overdue pension payments at the French court. His failure to secure payment meant that René had to pay interest on sums that he had borrowed from Swiss lenders, based on the pensions, further constricting his credit. From Virieu, René continued to Beaufremont, where he spent the fall,[115] arriving in Flanders in January as Charles III's ambassador to the Imperial court. The Duke himself was in Speyer in April, and asked René to meet him in Cologne.[116] Later that year, René was at the French court, and then back in Beaufremont, recovering from an illness. In January 1541, he expressed his disappointment to the Duke of Savoy for having been unable to carry out an unspecified task due to a (financial?) 'summit' that he had scheduled. Missing it 'would have been an irreparable loss for

official Cassiano Dal Pozzo. Vagnon's property was confiscated and Dal Pozzo fled, while his brother intervened on his behalf with the Duke at Nice (ibid.)
112 Marnoz had recently purchased the fief of Franquemont and gave Castellamonte some papers to deliver there. Castellamonte advised writing to Marnoz, since 'ung peu de papier entretient tousjours l'amistié de ceulx personages qui redondet a honeur et profit' (ibid.). Nicolas de Gilley, 'baron souverain de Franquemont', Baron of Marnoz, etc., was a Franc-Comtois who served as an Imperial ambassador in 1537-1542. A protegé of Margaret of Austria, he served at the Sabaudian court in 1540. He purchased Franquemont in 1537, a fief for which he pledged homage to the Prince-Bishop of Basel in 1538; that November, Charles V elevated Franquemont to a 'baronnie souveraine d'Empire', detaching it from episcopal authority. Gilley declared that subjects could no longer appeal judicial decisions to the Bishop of Basel and began to strike coins. After his death in 1563, his three sons co-inherited Franquemont and refused to recognize the Bishop's authority until 1577, when Jean III gave homage; see https://fr.wikipedia.org/wiki/Nicolas_de_Gilley, 12 November 2019. Gilley's case represents remarkable similarities to René's as Lord of Valangin.
113 The Bishop of Aosta acted to circumvent Del Vasto's efforts to come take command of the valley (AEN, AS-H16, 20, Roz Favre to René, ?-VI-39). In subsequent years, Del Vasto (Governor of Milan) tried to assert control over Bard and Montjovet, attempting to bypass René and issue orders to the Bailiff and the Bishop of Aosta (AHR, FC 260, Ludovico de Vallesa to Grandis, Ivrea 1-IV-40; ibid., Del Vasto to Gazino, Milan 15-VI-42).
114 AEN, AS-G16, 21, Vallesa to René, 17-V-39.
115 Fornaseri, 98-99, René to Ch III, Virieu 9-IX-39; ibid., AHR, FC 264 mz. 1, François de Riddes to René, Chambéry 10-X-? [internal evidence suggests 1539].
116 Ibid., FC 260, Ch III to René, Speyer 9-IV-40.

me', while its outcome would 'effect a good resolution to all of the matters from here, including Valangin'.[117] René seems to have remained northwest of the Alps for most of that year. There was some discussion of trying to meet Nicolas Perrenot de Granvelle (Imperial chancellor) in Milan that fall;[118] in December or January, he returned to the Valle d'Aosta.[119] Over the course of 1542, he corresponded with a lawyer at the *parlement* of Chambéry about a truce that would include most of the Sabaudian lands, the Bernese, and other Swiss,[120] and traveled several times back and forth from Valangin, where he negotiated intensively with the Countess of Neuchâtel (see below). Renewed fighting in Piedmont and Monferrato pulled him back to the valley; the abundant rainfall that limited hostilities[121] did not prevent René's agents from scouring northern Italy for willing lenders on his behalf.[122]

René's travel schedule for the next several years was brutal: he was in Aosta in late spring 1543, then he was with Charles III in Vercelli and Milan that summer and fall,[123] he was in Valangin the following February, and then he was back in the valley in October 1544. He met Mencia in Aymavilles on the sixteenth of that month (having just crossed the Alps 'already loaded with snow'), attended to the disrepair of the castle of Montjovet, and recommended his subjects of Settimo Vittone and Quincinetto to the Duke.[124] Within days, he traversed the mountains again as the Duke's

117 Ibid., draft of René to Ch III [?], Beaufremont 16/17-I-41.
118 Granvelle was traveling to Rome via Orvieto and would then return to Milan (ibid., FC 263, mz. 1, Hieronimo da Fagnano to René, Casale 21-X-42 [?]). For the movements of Charles V and Granvelle in late summer 1541, see Marchal, 600-01.
119 This was roughly the time period when Duke Antoine of Lorraine's brother, Cardinal Jean de Lorraine, had become malcontent following the disgrace of Anne de Montmorency in 1541, according to some historians. Already for a few years, the Duke of Lorraine had begun to distance himself from the King of France, strengthening his Imperial ties through the marriage of his eldest son François to Charles V's niece Christine of Denmark (July 1540). One wonders whether René had communicated with the ruling line of Lorraine about these issues; see Michon, 56. Two texts were published in 1542 to defend French actions and policies in Europe, one complaining about the mistreatment of French prisoners that had taken place after the battle of Pavia, and the other written by Guillaume du Bellay (in 1536) in defense of French policy in Italy; see Astier.
120 AHR, FC 260, copy of René to 'Mons l'advocat [Claude de Veigie] mon honoré filz,' 13-VII-42.
121 AEN, AS-R5.10, ll, René to Prangins, Issogne 26-X-42.
122 They met with Del Vasto, the Fornari and Giovanni Battista Speciano in Milan, and transferred cash from the Governor of Vercelli to other Sabaudian officers in Piedmont and in the valley (AHR, FC 264, mz. 1, Gichar [?] to René, Milan 20-XII-42 [?]). On Speciano see Chabod, 486-87.
123 In mid August, the Ottoman fleet attacked Nice with French assistance (Isom-Verhaaren, 407, 411-12, 410).
124 These subjects sought ducal support in a particular matter; René recommended them, since 'j'y aye interest pour la iurisdiction qui m'attouche' and wanted to avoid 'que j'en demour interessé de mon droit et qu'il soit saulvé' (Fornaseri, 102, René to Ch III, Aymavilles 17-X-44).

envoy to Berne,[125] and thence to the Imperial court, where there was hope for a Sabaudian restitution but need of 'an important person' to advance the cause.[126] René urged the young Prince Emanuel Filibert, who was also preparing his departure for Charles V's court, to make haste, since 'the good of his and your affairs demand it'.[127] Only the following spring did the Prince leave Vercelli to cross the Alps (via Trent), meeting the Emperor at Worms in late July.[128] The Imperial court arrived in Brussels in late August, and René seems to have met Emanuel Filibert there, since he was in Flanders from May until August or so. Following Charles V's demand that the Prince reduce the size of his suite,[129] René returned to the Sabaudian lands, met the Duke in Ivrea in September, and then fell seriously ill for two weeks. He remained in the valley until early 1546 but apparently returned to the Imperial court after that. Soon thereafter, reports arrived to him from the valley of a 'great fear amongst all the neighbors in this area', who urgently sought René's presence.[130] But René was having discussions with the Emperor concerning Sabaudian relations with Berne and possible mediation by Franc-Comtois officials – perhaps in Valangin.[131] The Bernese would be approached secretly, and René would need to be ready to meet on short notice, since, if the French found out, they would surely try to block the project. Sabaudian envoys at the Imperial court saw this plan as the best way to provide for 'the complete reintegration of Your Excellency'. But it would require flexibility 'concerning religion' and territory.[132] Charles V's interest in this initiative was keeping the Bernese neutral in the Schmalkaldic War, which was about to break out. The Emperor was successful, but Charles

---

125 Biel, 18 n. 65.
126 Fornaseri, 103, René to Ch III, Orsières 22-X-44.
127 Ibid., 104, René to EF, Orsières 22-X-44.
128 Frutaz mistakenly counted René among those who accompanied Emanuel Filibert to Germany; compare Frutaz, 'Notes,' 250-51 to Vaccarone, 'Emanuele Filiberto,' 277, 284. For Sabaudian engagement in Imperial court politics in the 1540s-1550s, see Zwierlein, 615-17.
129 Vaccarone, 'Emanuele Filiberto,' 285.
130 The Duke of Savoy sent Jean François Vaudan to convoke the estates and discuss the situation; Lullin broke to René the news that his secretary Grandis had been murdered on the road to Milan (AHR, FC 264, mz. 1, Lullin to René, 'Damsprug' [Innsbruck?] 25-III-46?). See Frey and Frey, 10-15, for a similar case of diplomats being murdered in northern Italy.
131 The officials were 'Mons'r de Thorreses cavalliero del Conseglio di Dola genero di Granvella' and the treasurer of Burgundy. The former was Jean d'Achey, Baron de Thoraise, a former page of Charles V who married Marguerite Perrenot de Granvelle; see Dunod de Charnage, 209.
132 For French interference see AEN, AS-I16, 30, Lullin & Stroppiana to Ch III, Regensburg 24-V-46. Lullin and Stroppiana also urged Charles III to table his concerns about Ferrante Gonzaga being appointed Imperial commander in Italy and to trust Granvelle's leadership.

III's frustrations continued.[133] King Henry II of France, who succeeded his father on 31 March 1547, seems to have sensed the Duke's impatience. He offered the hand of his sister Marguerite to Emanuel Filibert, along with lands in France to compensate the Duke of Savoy for his patrimonial states. When this news reached the Emperor's ears, he wrote to Charles III and had Emanuel Filibert (who, the Emperor noted, was always accompanied by 'the Lords of Challant and Lullin') deliver the message.[134]

Charles III eventually rebuffed the French offer. He also saw fit to reward René for his good service at court, naming him Baron of Fénis and Governor of Aosta and Ivrea in early 1548.[135] René's missions throughout Europe, facilitated by his lands between Italy, transalpine Sabaudia, Valangin, and Lorraine, had rendered him an indispensable servant. When rumors of a possible military conflict arrived from Valangin, the Bernese were happy to learn that René's subjects 'were armed and equipped' and ready to confront any contingency.[136] Perhaps in order to reassure the Duke of Savoy, Charles V soon thereafter sent an envoy to Berne, Fribourg, and Valais to demand that they submit to his authority and cease their occupation of Sabaudian lands.[137] During these events, in early 1548, René's wife Mencia and their two daughters Philiberte and Isabelle were also in Valangin and then in France, and, presumably, with René in Beaufremont from February through July 1548 and again in the summer of 1549.

From June 1550 through late 1553, René was mainly in Piedmont and in the valley, though he does appear to have traveled to Flanders or to Germany at some point in spring 1551. During this period, René maintained regular contact with Emanuel Filibert, congratulating him on military successes and sending

---

133 Ibid., AS-K16, 2, Ch III to René, Vercelli 10-VI-46?; ibid., AS-I16, 28, Claude-Louis Alardet (Abbot of Filly) to René, 11-VI-46?.

134 Marchand, 581-82, transcription of Charles V to Ch III, Augsburg 11-IX-47 (original in Archives nationales K 1487, B.6, pièce 83). René presumably assisted with the Bernese project from his residences in Valangin and Beaufremont, and likely facilitated negotiations between the Count of Gruyère (René's second cousin) and Fribourg for the purchase of Gruyère (with repurchase rights; essentially a loan) for 5000 écus (AHR, FC 215, no. 16, acted dated 7-V-47). In January 1548, René learned that the Swiss Diet had adjudicated a dispute between the Count of Gruyère and the French King, ruling in favor of the former (AEN, AS-K16, 19, Valangin official to René, s.d. [I-48?]).

135 AHR, FC 26, no. 30, patents dated 1-I-48.

136 AEN, AS-G16, 20, Martine to René (in Beaufremont), Valangin 19-II-48.

137 While this episode did not directly concern René, it provides a good sense of the Swiss and Imperial ceremonial political culture within with René often had to operate. For the complete account, including the herald's arrival and summons, a discussion of the herald's interactions with the Bernese, his lodging, banquets, gift exchanges, ceremonial appearances before the Bernese councils, etc., see AST1, NS, mz. 1 bis, no. 32, '14-IV-48 Ordine dell'Imperatore colla Relazione dell'Intimazione fattane dall'Eraldo, alle Lighe di Berna, Fribourg, e Valley [...].'

him news from Piedmont, such as the arrival of Ferrante Gonzaga's wife, who came 'to see the Holy Shroud' in Vercelli.[138] Emanuel Filibert and Prince Philip of Spain crossed the Brenner in June 1551 and embarked from Genoa for Spain on 3 July, the former returning to Piedmont in November on his way back to Flanders.[139] While traveling to Spain, Emanuel Filibert confirmed earlier patents naming René lieutenant general, with military command over all Sabaudian lands.[140] René seemed optimistic about Emanuel Filibert's influence at the Imperial court. Already by June 1550, René had been sending political memoirs and well-informed envoys to the Prince in Flanders.[141] Meanwhile, René remained engaged in the valley's efforts to maintain its neutrality – the *Commis* asked him, as 'the chief of this country after my lord the Duke of Savoy, their Prince' to persuade the new French commander Charles de Cossé, Marshal of Brissac, to honor their agreement.[142] René had much to offer to Emanuel Filibert. He was trusted by the Duke, his father; had a quarter century's experience in European military, diplomatic, and financial affairs; and commanded significant influence in the Sabaudian lands. He also had his own network of relations with other European leaders. For example, in October 1550, René sent an envoy to mediate with the Swiss Diet in Baden concerning new taxes created by Ferrante Gonzaga in Milan that would have affected Swiss merchants.[143] René's domains of Valangin and Beaufremont also placed him in contact not only with Swiss authorities, but with the Orléans-Longueville, the Guise, and the elder branch of the Lorraine.[144] For Emanuel Filibert, he was both a future subject and an ally – but also a potential competitor, given the transregional reach of his lands and networks.

Struggling for the sovereignty of Valangin, 1542-1565

As René's political and military duties dragged him back and forth from northwestern Italy to Flanders and points in between, he was able to check

138 Fornaseri, 107-8, René to EF, Vercelli 26-II-51. In April, René updated the Prince on his father's good health (Fornaseri, 108-9, same to same, Vercelli 4-IV-51).
139 Fornaseri 109-10, René and Giovanni [Francesco?] Costa to EF, Vercelli 8-IV-51; Vaccarone, 'Emanuele Filiberto,' 298.
140 AHR, FC 194, no. 14, patents issued 20-II-50 and confirmed on 5-VII-51.
141 Fornaseri, 106-7, René to EF, Vercelli 16-VI-50.
142 AST1, Paesi per A e B, A.22, no. 18, 'X-52 Memoria o Minuta di quello che il secretario Vautier [should be Gautier] dovrà dire, da parte del conte di Challant al Maresciallo di Brissac.'
143 AEN, AS-F16, 2, Hugues Clerc to René, 26-X-50.
144 Ibid., AS-G16, 4, Claude d'Aumâle to René, 5-III-51.

in frequently at Valangin, where various hot spots with the Countess of Neuchâtel and her subjects had been simmering. Bellegarde and Prangins continued to exchange letters about the disputes involving Boudevilliers;[145] despite this, there were also signs of goodwill,[146] such as mistakenly collected tithes being returned to their rightful owners.[147] Then, on the last day of November, came an astounding agreement by which Jeanne sold to René (through her procurator Claude Collier) all her sovereignty rights over Valangin for the sum of 9000 *francs*.[148] At around the same time, Collier proposed to Fribourg, on behalf of Jeanne, a sale of the entire county of Neuchâtel (except for Valangin and Boudevilliers) for the price of 60,000 *écus*, with the county's debts as part of the sale price.[149] This would have radically reshaped the territorial politics of the western Swiss area, giving René sovereign authority between the Franche-Comté and the Confederation.

In a copy of the Valangin sale agreement, we find that, when Jeanne had previously asked René to swear loyalty to her for Valangin, René had replied that neither he nor his ancestors were required to do so 'by right'. Negotiations between Collier (Prevost of the Valangin church and Canon of the cathedral of St. Nicolas of Fribourg, acting for Jeanne) and François Martine (René's *maître d'hôtel*) resulted in Jeanne's cession of

> all rights, titles, disputes, claims, and actions that the predecessors of the said Lady had and continue to have, which she asserts and affirms accrue and belong to her by means of the sovereignty over the said seigniory of Valangin, including the duty and jurisdiction of homage, fief, sub-fiefs, devolutions, and otherwise.

For his part, René agreed to pay her 1000 French *francs*; both would cease litigation. The accord, notarized by Trolliet, was signed 'in the castle of Valangin, in the accounting room' and was witnessed by (among others) 'Lord Claude bastard of Valangin'.[150] On the same day, Jeanne made a separate sale to René of all her revenues in Valangin and Boudevilliers for 9000 *francs*. Of this sum, 6000 were considered to have been paid in the form of forgiveness

---

145 Ibid., AS-R5.10, aaa, Bellegarde to Prangins, 25-IV-42.
146 For example, Jeanne instructed the Neuchâtel estates to 'administrer et faire bonne et briefve justice' in an unspecified case involving Valangin (ibid., AS-B4.9, 1, Jeanne to Neuchâtel estates, 22-VI-42 [?]).
147 Ibid., AS-R5.10, bbbb, Guillemette to Pierre Chambrier, 7-X-42.
148 AHR, FC 74, no. 8, sale dated 30-XI-1542.
149 Scheurer, 28-29.
150 AEN, AS-C4.11, a, copy of agreement dated 30-XI-42.

of the debt contracted by Jeanne in 1540, and another 700 in the form of interest due on that loan, leaving a balance of 2,300 owed by René.[151]

Alongside these documents in the Neuchâtel state archives is a copy of a letter dated 8 April 1543, in which Jeanne informed Collier that she had recently made a new seal and empowered a new procurator, revoking the old seal and the powers that she had given to him. She hints that others had forced her to make these changes but confirms her desire that he continue to attend to her affairs, and that past actions taken for her 'remain in full power and validity'. The letter states that 'I am very happy about the deal that you reached with Monsieur de Challant', while praising the accord with the Fribourgeois, 'truly faithful and good Christians'.[152] The next month, Fribourg accepted Collier's offer but also proposed to Berne and Lucerne that they make the purchase together. When Berne communicated with the council of Neuchâtel about this, the latter denounced Collier's actions, causing both the Bernese and the Fribourgeois to back out of the sale. Under pressure from her family, Jeanne eventually renounced the deal herself.[153] A position paper later drawn up by Jeanne and her officers claimed that Jeanne had learned about Collier's two sales on 6 June, and that she immediately sent a commissioner to nullify them, asking others to spread the word. The paper declared that 'the *souveraineté* of the seigniory of Valangin' was sold to René illegitimately and fraudulently, since Collier had acted by means of 'a forged procuration'.[154] The Duchess of Guise now took up the cause of her grandson, arguing that, since Jeanne had already donated all of her property to her sons in 1519, the sale of Valangin was invalid.[155]

René followed these developments as best he could from afar, having left Valangin in May to travel to the valley and then to Vercelli. This is an example of how transregional commitments could hinder as well as advance one's affairs. He wrote to Bellegarde in August about the 'thin threats' made against him, instructing his officer to do nothing 'that might prejudice my case' but to 'consult with our particular friends about what kind of tacit action could establish possession for the future, since for the time being nothing open can be carried out'. He hoped to 'visit the place in person' soon.[156] Jeanne died about five weeks later, on 21 September 1543,

---

151 Ibid., copy of separate agreement also dated 30-XI-42.
152 Ibid., copy of Jeanne to Collier, 8-IV-43.
153 Scheurer, 28-29; Matile, 251. According to Matile, the Longueville sons only learned about the sale after Jeanne's death (on 21-IX-43).
154 AEN, AS-B4.9, n, undated documents written after 6-VI-43.
155 Matile, 252.
156 AEN, AS-H16, 2, René to Bellegarde, Vercelli 14-VIII-43.

and, on 12 December, Claude and Charles de Guise, tutors of the Duke of Longueville (the eight-year-old François III d'Orléans, who inherited the county from his grandmother Jeanne), together with the Marquis of Rothelin (François d'Orléans, Jeanne's third son), assembled a delegation that traveled to Valangin to declare the sale illicit. Neither René nor Bellegarde was there, so they addressed Trolliet, who refused to receive the declaration on René's behalf.[157]

In February 1544, René sent a delegation (Bellegarde, the secretary Hugues Richard, Jehan Vulpez, Martine, and others) to meet with Prangins about the disputed sale. They summarized the discussion as follows.[158] When the Dukes of Longueville learned that Jeanne had sold 'the *souveraineté*' of Valangin together with her property and revenues there and in the Val de Ruz, including Boudevilliers and other places, they were 'astonished'. They argued that the sale was invalid, since their mother had 'long before' given them all of her property. René claimed that Jeanne had often asked him for loans, and that he finally gave in, hoping thereby to end the history of conflict between the counts of Neuchâtel and the lords of Valangin. So, he sold his barony of Coligny to the '*mareschalle*' of Châtillon',[159] lending to Jeanne from the proceeds. Jeanne promised to repay within three years, or else sell René her sovereignty over Valangin. She did not repay, so she made the sale. Once it was finalized (apparently, in April 1543), René proceeded to 'publish and discuss [it] in the presence of many important people in this county of Neuchâtel who were counselors and officials of the deceased said Lady, without them ever having said or done anything about it in an untoward way'. He was shocked that the Dukes of Longueville denied the validity of the sale, which was legitimate, sealed, and in proper form. According to René, Jeanne had had the power to do as she wished, given her status as 'sovereign Lady and proprietary Princess' of Neuchâtel. He was unable to comprehend her sons' claim that, as heirs, they had the right to approve or veto such an act. But René stressed his wish to have 'friendship and good neighborliness' with them and to enter arbitration rather than litigate.[160] Valangin's sovereignty was contested for decades to come between René and his heirs and Jeanne's successors. From this point on, René acted as a sovereign, establishing fairs, holding *audiences* without the permission of authorities in Neuchâtel, erecting

---

157 Scheurer, 28-29.
158 Citations in this paragraph are from AEN, AS-C4.11, b, 7-II-44 response by René's envoys to Orléans-Longueville repudiation of sale of sovereignty and property.
159 Louise de Montmorency, sister of Anne, mother of the three Châtillon brothers.
160 AEN, AS-C4.11, b, 7-II-44 response by René's envoys to Orléans-Longueville repudiation of sale of sovereignty and property.

a *gibet* with four pillars, practicing the *droit de grâce*, etc. In a letter written to Bonstetten (Governor of Neuchâtel after Prangins), the Bishop of Basel (Lancelot de Neuchâtel, Lord of Travers) referred to René as a sovereign lord.[161]

René seemed to continue on good terms with Prangins, cooperating with him in matters of local governance and seeking his assistance in setting up a meeting with the Duke of Longueville to 'resolve our dispute'.[162] He sent Martine to France 'to pursue my affair, which I want him to monitor while matters are on good terms', despite the death of the Duke of Orléans, who had been supporting René.[163] Jockeying among the various Longueville heirs complicated efforts to find a resolution. In 1550, Claude de Guise, tutor of Jeanne's grandson, tried to sell Neuchâtel and began negotiating, unsuccessfully, with various cantons.[164] The Count of Neuchâtel, François III d'Orléans-Longueville, died in September 1551 and was succeeded by Léonor, son of Jeanne's third son François d'Orléans, Marquis de Rothelin, who had died in 1548. Léonor's mother was Jacqueline de Rohan-Gié, who represented him both in the contested succession and in the ongoing disputes with René.[165] When René learned about the death of François III, he sent a secretary to France to express condolences and his desire to 'have good neighborhood with [Léonor].'[166] In 1552, René again sought negotiations, sending his secretary Pierre Gautier to Neuchâtel for talks that he hoped Prangins would help arrange.[167] Meanwhile, René referred to himself as 'sovereign Lord' and accused the other side of refusing to settle the matter amicably. The audience for these complaints seemed to be the Bernese and other Swiss facilitators.[168] A draft version of a letter from April 1553 described René as 'souverain Lord of Valangin', an edit suggesting that

---

161 Matile, 252-53.
162 AEN, AS-R5.10, a, René to Prangins, Beaufremont 8-III-45 [?]; AS-F16, 5, Martine to René, ?-I-48 (date penciled in).
163 Ibid., AS-H16, 17, 17a, René to Bellegarde, Ivrea 26-IX-45.
164 Scheurer, 29-30.
165 The Marquise appointed procurators to carry on negotiations with René, 'ce que ne pouvons faire sans vous pour le peu de cognoissance qu'avons au pays' (AEN, AS-B4.9, o, Jacqueline de Rothelin to Prangins, 1-IV-51).
166 Ibid., AS-C4.2, p, René to Prangins, 6-XI-51.
167 Ibid., q, René to Prangins, 11-IV-52. In these negotiations, René was represented by Villarsel and Bellegarde (ibid., AS-B4.9, c, 1551-1552 negotiations in Berne).
168 On the assigned day for negotiations the year before, René was present, at great expense and despite other pressing business, while his adversary was unprepared for talks (ibid., AS-B4.9, e, 1553 memoir). René called the Swiss as 'observateurs de toute équité, anciens protecteurs des seigneurs et seigneurie de Vallangin, en vertu de la bourgeoisie que lesd' s'rs de Vallangin ont avec leurs excellence' and claimed that 'quant a la souverannité de Vallangin,' he 'tousiours en demeure suffisamment saysie legitime poccesseur'.

some of his advisers supported a restrained rhetorical strategy.[169] Still, this festering conflict exacerbated the other long-standing territorial disputes concerning Valangin. The Lord of Vaumarcus tried to make some of René's subjects swear loyalty oaths to him in the early 1550s,[170] framing the matter as a dispute within his own jurisdiction. He lamented to the new Governor of Neuchâtel, Bonstetten, that 'one must not have so many sovereigns in the same county [*il ne fault point tant de souvrains en une conté*]. Otherwise the authority of his lord and master [the Count of Neuchâtel] will be dissipated'.[171] René's officer Martine urged Bonstetten to 'silence [Vaumarcus] and keep the poor people at peace until you and the estates have judged' the matter.[172]

In late 1555, René's service to the House of Savoy landed him in Brussels, where Duke Emanuel Filibert was serving as Imperial commander and Governor of the Low Countries. There, he also discussed Valangin with the Dukes of Lorraine and Guise, sensing 'the times disposed and convenient for this, knowing the good will of the lords of Berne toward me'. He instructed Martine to gather the Valangin documentation and meet him in Beaufremont to plan subsequent steps.[173] The *Conseil* and *Chambre des comptes* of the Genevois weighed in on the dispute without definitively supporting one side or the other.[174] This remained the state of the problem until the end of René's life, although the dispute renewed itself following René's death and the succession dispute between his daughters. René's officer Granyer discussed in mid 1559 or so his lord's meeting with Longueville about Valangin, dismissing a local noble's opinion that René would eventually have to 'come before the estates at Neuchâtel'. Granyer countered that, not only had René's 'predecessors […] never done it', René was to be commended for having refrained from enacting 'the remedy that [he] should have employed'

---

169 Villarsel and Gautier represented René, assisted by La Fontaine. One of the procurators of the two Neuchâtel claimants was Johann Jakob von Bonstetten, the new governor of Neuchâtel (Prangins had died in 1552). According to La Fontaine, a compromise agreement had been reached at Berne in late July 1551, but the death of François III occasioned continued discussions and René's adversaries tried to delay a resolution 'pour frustrer mond' seigneur le conte de son droict' (ibid., e2, draft letter dated 25-IV-53). Bonstetten had close ties to Berne and to the Orléans-Longueville and was the only Protestant to have served as their governor of Neuchâtel; he died in office in 1574 (see Quadroni).

170 René, then detained in Italy, was unable to defend his claims in person (see Chapter 4) (AEN, AS-B4.9, f, letter to Bonstetten, 5-VI-55).

171 Ibid., AS-C4.2, r, Vaumarcus [?] to Bonstetten, 5-VI-55.

172 Martine also pointed out that, although Vaumarcus had claimed that he was unable to meet because he had to go to Geneva, the 'paisans presents pourteurs' could testify to the fact that, the day before, he had still been in Travers (ibid., s, Martine to Bonstetten, 10-VI-55).

173 Ibid., AS-G16, l, René to Bellegarde, 4-II-56.

174 Ibid., AS-F16, l, Chevron to René, 11-V-56.

Fig. 3: Coin representing René as sovereign of Valangin (RENE · CO · CHALLAN · & · VALLENGIN · SUPR · D // & BARO · BOFFR · MONT · & · MAVILE · ET · D · CAST · & · VERRECY · C). Source: Georges Gallet, 'Une Médaille de René, comte de Challant et seigneur souverain de Valangin in Suisse,' *Revue suisse de numismatique* 13 (1905): 113-22.

in response to their rudeness.[175] By this time, René was striking medals with his image and the inscription 'Rene . Co . A . Challan . Z . Valengin . Supr . D.' (René, Count of Challant and sovereign Lord of Valangin).[176] He had obviously given up no ground in his claims to sovereign status, a position facilitated by his transregional network of powerful supporters.

Matile's view that René had committed a 'felony' by refusing to swear homage to the Count of Neuchâtel simply accepts the Longueville claim at face value.[177] The sources indicate that the situation was more ambiguous, from the oath that René tried to swear to Jeanne (subject to certain concessions), to the one that he swore to her son, to the host of border conflicts and jurisdictional claims and counterclaims, to the procurations given to and rescinded from Collier, to the sale of sovereignty by a cash-strapped Jeanne that perhaps wasn't a sale after all. These kinds of disputes and the murkiness that surrounded them were typical of early modern political culture, and less clear-cut than the patriotic Neuchâtelois historians of the nineteenth century made them out to be. Thomas Maissen has described the difficulties in pinning down the pre-Bodinian meaning of the word 'sovereign', noting that, only in around 1600, did it lose its specific, concrete meanings (supreme appellate jurisdiction, especially) and become an abstraction, 'designating the general and universal competence of a sovereign in the modern sense'. In the Swiss area, Germanophone cantons 'learned such terms through their contacts with their Francophone neighbors'. In 1560, in Berne, there was reference to the *hochen oberkeyt* of an authority in the *pays de Vaud*, with the explanation that, in the local language, 'that was called sovereignty

---

175 AHR, FC 263, mz. 1, Granyer to René, Chambéry 20-V-?.
176 Frutaz, 'Notes,' 268-69; Gallet.
177 Matile, 244, cited in Vialardi di Sandigliano, 27.

['*souveränite in des orths sprach genant*']. Only in the seventeenth century did the Swiss Germans begin to use the term to mean something more rigid and vast than merely appellate jurisdiction.[178]

Thus, the operative concepts, the facts of the case, and the interpretation of those facts were all far from clear from the late 1530s onward. What does seem likely is that the territorial chessboard in the swath of Europe that had formerly been part of the Burgundian kingdom, from Flanders all the way down to the Mediterranean coast, was rapidly changing. The future of the Sabaudian lands was not clear: René had seen the French, Bernese, Fribourgeois, and Valaisans seize Sabaudian lands; witnessed the city of Geneva declare its independence; was aware of the treaty of Lorraine, which characterized that duchy as *liber & non incorpora(bi)lis* in 1542;[179] and then watched the French take over the *Trois-Évêchés* of Metz, Toul, and Verdun a decade later. Further Swiss incursions into the Franche-Comté or elsewhere were feared by Charles V and his allies. In such an unstable territorial context, it was to be expected for a transregional noble like René to take what he could and consolidate his gains before someone else did the same to him, especially given the ongoing fiscal and jurisdictional disputes that hounded Valangin. Even if he had to back down at some point, he would have bargaining power. Had there been a strong ruler of Neuchâtel who was physically present, rather than an older woman who resided at the French court, followed by a series of young absentee princes, René might have hesitated to press his claims. As it was, he seems to have reasoned that a powerful potential foe would take advantage of the situation were he not to act himself. 'Machiavellian' calculation was obviously neither limited to Italian urban elites, nor confined to lands south of the Alps.

Bibliography

Sophie Astier, 'Une défense de François Ier face à Charles Quint en 1542: Une pièce retrouvée de Guillaume de Quelques,' *BHR* 74, 2 (2012): 257-82

Maurice Barbier, 'Les rapports du pouvoir spirituel et du pouvoir temporel chez Vitoria,' *BHR* 66, 2 (2004): 297-310

Lionel Bartolini, 'Liberté de conscience dans le vocabulaire français: une genèse romande (1530-1560),' in *La Suisse occidentale et l'Empire*, ed. Jean-Daniel Morerod, Denis Tappy, Clémence Thévenaz Modestin, and Françoise Vannotti (Lausanne: Société d'histoire de la Suisse romande, 2004)

---

178 Maissen, 31, where he cites Quaritsch.
179 See https://fr.wikipedia.org/wiki/Traité_de_Nuremberg, 12 November 2019.

Edwin Bezzina, 'Caught between King, Religion, and Social Ambition: Marc-Antoine Marreau de Boisguérin and His Family (ca. 1560-1680),' *SCJ* 39, 2 (2008): 331-56

Arnold Biel, *Die Beziehungen zwischen Savoyen und der Eidgenossenschaft zur Zeit Emanuel Philiberts (1559-1580)* (Basel: Helbing & Lichtenhahn, 1967)

James Blakeley, '"Did the Pastor Buy You a Drink?" Religious Choice, Clerical Persuasion, and Confessional Elections in the Village of Goumoëns,' *SCJ* 44, 2 (2013): 345-66

Federico Chabod, 'Usi e abusi nell'amministrazione dello Stato di Milano' (1958), in *Carlo V e il suo impero* (Turin: Einaudi, 1985)

M.F.I. Dunod de Charnage, *Mémoire pour servir a l'histoire du comté de Bourgogne* (Besançon: Jean-Baptiste Charmet, 1740)

Antoine-Théodore du Prat, *Généalogie historique, anecdotique et critique de la maison Du Prat* (Versailles: Dagneau, 1857)

Fabrice Flückiger, 'Le choix de religion. Le rôle de l'autorité politique dans les disputes religieuses des années 1520,' *Revue suisse d'histoire* 60, 3 (2010): 277-301

Giovanni Fornaseri, *Le lettere di Renato di Challant, governatore della Valle d'Aosta a Carlo II ed a Emanuele Filiberto* (Turin: Deputazione subalpina di storia patria, 1957)

Marsha and Linda Frey, 'Fatal Diplomacy, 1541,' *History Today* 40, 8 (1990): 10-15

François-Gabriel Frutaz, 'Notes sur René de Challant et sur le passage de Calvin dans la Vallée d'Aoste,' *Musée neuchâtelois* 41 (1904): 242-67

Georges Gallet, 'Une Médaille de René, comte de Challant et seigneur souverain de Valangin in Suisse,' *Revue Suisse de numismatique* 13 (1905): 113-22

Charles Gilliard, *La conquête du Pays de Vaud per les Bernois* (Lausanne: Editions La Concorde, 1935)

Christine Isom-Verhaaren, '"Barbarossa and His Army Who Came to Succor All of Us": Ottoman and French Views of Their Joint Campaign of 1543-1544,' *FHS* 30, 3 (2007): 395-425

Benjamin Kaplan, 'Fictions of Privacy: House Chapels and the Spatial Accommodation of Religious Dissent in Early Modern Europe,' *AHR* 107, 4 (2002): 1031-64

Pierre Lambert de la Croix, *Mémoires de Pierre Lambert*, in *Monumenta Historiae Patriae edita iussu Regis Caroli Alberti Scriptorum*, vol. 1 (Turin: Regio Tipographeo, 1840)

Thomas Maissen, 'Qui ou quoi sinon l'Empire? Sources de légitimité en Suisse occidentale aux temps modernes,' in *La Suisse occidentale et l'Empire*, ed. Jean-Daniel Morerod, Denis Tappy, Clémence Thévenaz Modestin, and Françoise Vannotti (Lausanne: Société d'histoire de la Suisse romande, 2004), pp. 17-36

François Joseph Ferdinand Marchal, *Histoire politique du règne de l'Empereur Charles-Quint* (Brussels: H. Tarlier, 1856)

Charles Marchand, *Charles Ier de Cossé, comte de Brissac et maréchal de France 1507-1563* (Paris: Champion, 1889)

Georges-Auguste Matile, *Histoire de la seigneurie de Valangin jusqu'à sa réunion à la directe en 1592* (Neuchâtel, James Attinger, 1852)

Cédric Michon, 'Les richesses de la faveur à la Renaissance: Jean de Lorraine (1498-1550) et François Ier,' *RHMC* 50, 3 (2003): 34-61

W. Gregory Monahan, 'Between Two Thieves: The Protestant Nobility and the War of the Camisards,' *FHS* 30, 4 (2007): 537-558

E. William Monter, *A Bewitched Duchy: Lorraine and its Dukes, 1477-1736* (Geneva: Droz, 2007)

Richard Ninness, 'Protestants as Agents of the Counter-Reformation in the Prince-Bishopric of Bamberg,' *SCJ* 40, 3 (2009): 699-720

Dominique Quadroni, 'Jean Jacques de Bonstetten,' *DHS* (2004)

Helmut Quaritsch, *Souveränität. Entstehung und Entwicklung des Begriffs in Frankreich und Deutschland vom 13. Jh. Bis 1806* (Berlin: Duncker & Humblot, 1986)

Guillaume Ribier, *Lettres et memoires d'estat, des roys, princes, ambassadeurs, et autres ministres, sous les regnes de François premier, Henry II & François II* (Paris: Chez François Clouzier et La Vefve Aubovyn, 1666)

Brian Sandberg, *Warrior Pursuits: Noble Culture and Civil Conflict in Early Modern France* (Baltimore: The Johns Hopkins University Press, 2010)

Rémy Scheurer, 'L'évolution politique de la Réforme à 1707,' *Histoire du Pays de Neuchâtel*, vol. 2, pt. 2 (Hauterive, Switzerland: Editions Gilles Attinger, 1991)

Alexander Schmidt, 'Irenic Patriotism in Sixteenth- and Seventeenth-Century German Political Discourse,' *HJ* 53, 2 (2010): 243-69

Arturo Segre, 'Documenti di storia sabauda dal 1510 al 1536,' *MSI* 39 (1903): 3-296

Armando Tallone, 'Ivrea e il Piemonte al tempo della prima dominazione francese (1536-1559),' in *Studi eporediesi* (Pinerolo: Tipografia Chiantore-Mascarelli, 1900): 67-200

Luigi Vaccarone, 'Emanuele Filiberto principe di Piemonte alla corte cesarea di Carlo V imperatore (1545-1551),' *MSI*, 3rd ser., 5 (1900): 277-318

Tomaso Vialardi di Sandigliano, 'Un intruso tra i testamenti di Renato di Challant: Giuseppe Tornielli di Briona, novarese,' *Studi piemontesi* 41, 1 (2012): 23-40

Jeffrey Watt, 'The Reception of the Reformation in Valangin, Switzerland, 1547-1588,' *SCJ* 20, 1 (1989): 89-104

https://fr.wikipedia.org/wiki/Nicolas_de_Gilley, 12 November 2019

https://fr.wikipedia.org/wiki/Traité_de_Nuremberg, 12 November 2019

Eike Wolgast, 'Religionsfrieden als politisches Problem der frühen Neuzeit,' *Historische Zeitschrift* 282, issue JG (2006): 59-96

Cornel Zwierlein, 'Deutsche und Italienische Staatsbeschreibungskunst. Die Einkünfte aller Reichsstände, ca. 1547/48 nach einer unbekannten Quelle,' *ZHF* 39, 4 (2012): 593-660

4. René and Duke Emanuel Filibert

Abstract

In 1553, Duke Emanuel Filibert succeeded his father and named René de Challant lieutenant general of his lands. Weeks later, René was captured by the French when they attacked Vercelli, and he spent the next two years trying to arrange for his release. In October 1555, he returned to Issogne and immediately took up diplomatic activity in the service of Emanuel Filibert and the Valle d'Aosta. He arranged for the marriage of his daughter Isabelle to the nephew of the Cardinal-Prince-Bishop of Trent and lost his second wife in 1558. In 1559, he oversaw the return of the western Sabaudian lands to their natural ruler. He married twice more prior to his death in 1565. Historians' accounts of René's life are surveyed.

Key words: Emanuel Filibert, Vercelli, ransom, Madruzzo, Masino.

René and Emanuel Filibert

When Charles III died on 17 August 1553, René suddenly found himself the *de facto* head of Sabaudian government in the lands remaining under ducal control. For a few months, his constant movement across Europe came to a halt; from Vercelli, René 'took up this office with great zeal'.[1] That this transregional lord with sovereign claims of his own was willing to expend significant political capital in the service of a severely weakened northwestern Italian dynasty seems surprising. Episodes like this one raise questions about how loyalty, honor, self-interest, family identity, and passion intersected to inform this Renaissance noble's actions and caution us against simple assumptions.

As Charles' body was lying in state, René sent to Emanuel Filibert to warn him about corruption in the Sabaudian government. The death of Charles III, they reported, had set off a raid on the ducal treasury by unscrupulous

---

1 Segre, 'Il richiamo,' 197.

Vester, M., *Transregional Lordship and the Italian Renaissance: René de Challant, 1504-1565*. Amsterdam: Amsterdam University Press, 2020.
DOI 10.5117/9789463726726_CH04

officials. René seized whatever he could find in Vercelli 'in the hands of the officials repsponsible for these items, especially the rings'. There was no money for the deceased Duke's funeral. By handling this issue forcefully, Emanuel Filibert would show how committed he was to justice and the protection 'of your poor subjects', who would then be more likely to denounce corruption in the future.[2] René pushed for a purge of the ducal bureaucracy, but this did not occur immediately. Emanuel Filibert had been traveling and did not want to act precipitously.[3] He sent his first Chamberlain (Louis de Châtillon, Lord of Châtelard) to Vercelli,[4] while René kept Emanuel Filibert informed about events in Piedmont.[5] René struggled to retain control of the flow of information between Vercelli and Flanders, having learned that personal requests were being sent to the new Duke without the full council's knowledge. René urged him not to respond until more information was available.[6]

Three weeks later, René again alleged financial corruption among leading officials. Several recent letters had been penned by secretaries who were compromised; this one was carried by René's cousin, the Baron of Fénis. The only persons able to explain the treasury situation would be 'those who controlled it during the time of my said lord your father'. These people should thus be apprehended until an investigation was completed, but René did not wish to seize anyone himself without the Duke's express command:

> And it is very difficult for me to dissimulate in order not to expose the matter, and to deal with them carefully so that no on escapes, not only

---

2   At the end of their letter, René and St. Miguel identified the persons who were to be seized: 'Broissy, Valpergue, le cappitaine Dupuis et son frere, les deux Carrà, Locarno et Veillet' (Fornaseri, 113-15, René and Sebastiano St. Miguel [Spanish military commander in Vercelli; see Segre, 'Il richiamo,' 199] to EF, Vercelli 17-VIII-53). Note that René and St. Miguel were both outsiders with respect to the ducal council in Vercelli.

3   Ibid., 125-31, René to EF, Vercelli 19-X-53.

4   Segre, 'Il richiamo,' 197.

5   On 18 August, René appointed Carlo Malopera to receive loyalty oaths to the new duke from Cuneo and elsewhere (AST1, PD 185, f. 261, patents dated 18-VIII-53) and recommended his secretary Richard for a position in the *Chambre des comptes* (Fornaseri, 115-16, René to EF, Vercelli 19-VIII-53).

6   Ibid., 116-17, René to EF, Vercelli 22-VIII-53. He assured the Duke that no effort was being spared for 'the preservation of your authority and increase of your reputation', adding that the 'honors and ceremonies' of the deceased Duke's funeral were under preparation. He also asked Emanuel Filibert to discuss reinforcements for the castle of Nice with the Emperor (ibid., 117-19, René to EF, Vercelli 23-VIII-53). Noting that several Vercellesi had underwritten a 3,600-*écu* loan made by the Adda family (Lombard bankers) to Charles III, whose default had driven the Adda to collect from these underwriters, René sought the new Duke's intervention (ibid., 119-20, René to EF, Vercelli 31-VIII-53).

the key figures, whose responsibility it is to give a good accounting for everything, but also the servants who know whither the birds flew off, and helped cover their tracks.[7]

Rumors circulated about both the fraudulent administration of the treasury and the 'sudden death of the Duke'. René recommended appointing a special commissioner for this and other missing elements of the ducal patrimony (including 'the great unicorn horn') over which Louis de Gallier de Bressieu had had authority. René suspected that officials stole dynastic jewelry and then manipulated the inventory to cover for themselves. Chancery officials refused to submit the ducal seals, and, after René sealed the ducal archives ('the titles of the chamber of accounts'), the cameral officials likewise complained that 'it was their responsibility to seal the others, and that their offices were perpetual and irrevocable'. It seemed that almost every group of ducal officials was upset with René, who declared to the Duke that he focused only on his duty 'for the good and safety of your affairs' and the 'preservation of your *estat* with respect to past and future'.[8]

René painted a picture of the political environment among the Duke's impoverished subjects. 'The few lands that remain yours over here', would be 'abandoned and uninhabited' under continued fiscal pressure. This situation 'touches you,' wrote René, exhorting the Duke to consider his 'quality' compared to inferior Italian princes, and urging him to require Imperial officials to 'order and command others' to provide resources. Discretion in making official appointments (not naming new officials without René's input) would enhance the prestige of René's office, 'which would redound to your own honor, glory and authority'. René tied the Duke's authority to his own, positing a link between the ruler's honor and that of his leading nobles. René mentioned in passing that he had not been paid in three years, despite increased expenses in the Duke's service.[9]

---

7   Ibid., 120-24, René to EF, Vercelli 8-IX-53 (subsequent citations in this and the following paragraph from the same source).
8   Ibid. René's accusations, especially about financial malfeasance, cause one to wonder whether, as René was investigating these potential crimes, Sabaudian officials took advantage of the French capture of Vercelli (in November 1553) to claim that the property in question had been stolen by the French — or whether these officials even facilitated the French attack as revenge against René.
9   Ibid. In an undated, coded letter from sometime in September, René zeroed in on Bressieu, a former *gentilhomme de chambre* of Charles III who held the postmortem inventory of the dynastic jewels, as the source of the corruption (ibid.) On Bressieu see Uginet, 'Louis de Châtillon.'

Châtelard rode into Vercelli on 26 September 1553[10] with confirmation of René's position as lieutenant general and an order for the arrest of Bressieu and others. The towns of Vercelli, Biella, and Santhià all demanded fiscal exemptions; René reasoned that those who had enjoyed exemptions in the past (Vercelli) should now be required to pay taxes, while the others should now be exempted. Retaining the subjects' goodwill was fundamental. He applauded the Duke for his nominees to the 'private council', further recommending the Bishops of Aosta (Pietro Gazino) and Asti (Gaspare Capris), 'persons of state [*personnaiges d'estat*] who give wise and prudent advice in important matters'.[11] Declaring that honor 'drives me more than anything else' and citing the ducal patents which specified that 'I should hold this place, as if you were here in your own person', he wondered why the Duke had made appointments without consulting him. He hoped that Emanuel Filibert would trust him to 'apply such authority as demanded by the *estat* to which you appointed me'. He also wanted to know what others were writing about him, should it be necessary 'for the good of your affairs over here, because I have had no communication in any way about this'.[12] René de Challant's stature by October 1553 was that of an experienced, powerful, but slightly paranoid transregional aristocrat who was obsessed with what common people, city dwellers, officials, other nobles, and his Prince thought of him. His patronage power extended well beyond the Valle d'Aosta (where he was still the central political figure) and his fiefs abroad; from Vercelli, he dispensed favors to persons of influence from throughout the Sabaudian states and elsewhere.[13]

Bressieu and his wife, the treasurer Nicolas de Beaumont-Carrà, Carrà's brother Jean (a cameral official), Aubert Veillet, and others had been apprehended and were being questioned.[14] The trial began, in René's presence, on 13 November. About a month and a half later, an inventory of the documents (lists of jewelry and other precious items) that Bressieu had submitted to cameral officials was drawn up. These lists of jewels in Bressieu's possession

10   Segre, 'Il richiamo,' 197.
11   Fornaseri, 125-31, René to EF, Vercelli 19-X-53.
12   Ibid.
13   Valdostano communities looked to René for approval of their actions and various actors solicited him for passports or protection against Ferrante Gonzaga's fiscal demands; see AHR, FC 264, mz. 1, Vulliet to René, St. Pierre 28-X-?; ibid., Vulliet to Grandis, Aosta 19-XI-?; and Fornaseri, 131-32, René to EF, Vercelli 20-X-53.
14   Ibid., 132-33, René to EF, Vercelli 29-X-53. Veillet, formerly a ducal secretary, had accused René of criminal acts in Chambéry in 1531.

had been produced between Christmas 1539 and June 1553, in Genoa, Vercelli, and Nice, and were signed by the treasurers Carrà and Locarno. Another inventory of documents was put together a year later, indicating that that lower-level officials such as Claude Jacquier ('*argentier*'), and Jean Fillion ('*tapissier*') had had access to these items. In October 1555, Bressieu was exonerated of wrongdoing.[15]

Vercelli capture and efforts to get released

Four days into Bressieu's trial, during the night of 17-18 November, the French commander Brissac launched a surprise attack on Vercelli, capturing the citadel but failing to retain control of the city. Among those taken prisoner was René, who probably still owed money on his first ransom. A dozen soldiers from the garrison of Verrua (near the Po, on the edge of the Monferrato hills, about 35 kilometers southeast of Vercelli) began the assault, entering the city in disguise. Then the French floated down the Po from other places and marched overland to Vercelli under cover of darkness. They mounted the walls with ladders and, after some skirmishing, forced Colonel Giovanni Battista Dell'Isola back to the citadel with some of his soldiers. After Brissac himself arrived, they attempted a cannonade on the citadel, but their artillery failed. They did, however, take the life of Châtelard, the Duke's chamberlain. René was 'captured weapons in hand', according to some accounts, and 'surprised in bed' in others.[16]

Once the French broke into the city, Giovanni Francesco Costa d'Arignano went to René's lodgings to seek instructions, and, at that moment, about 100 enemy soldiers passed in front of the door, headed toward the main square.[17] Forthwith, several troops returned with the French Governor of Verrua, who was leading the attack. They threatened to break down the door, calling for the Count of Challant to exit 'as a gentleman'. René saw that resistance was futile and 'was forced to negotiate and open the door'.

---

15 AHR, FC 45, no. 5, 1554-1555 criminal case against Louis Gallier de Bressieu; ibid., FC 312, no. 5, judgment dated 24-X-55; ibid., FC 247, no. 21.
16 Marchand, 233-37; De Antonio, 176; Segre, 'Il richiamo,' 199. Arturo Segre, in 'L'opera politico-militare,' 11, assumed that the French success was due to 'un tradimento' (he also cited a report from the English envoy to Venice on this issue) and noted that the castle's governor, Tommaso Valperga di Masino, did not attempt 'alcuna difesa'. See also Frutaz, 'Notes,' 251.
17 AST1, LP, C.104, Arignano to EF, Ivrea 24-XI-53 (source for all of the citations in this paragraph)

He went out 'with many honorable words', was promised that 'together with the women and gentlemen and his household he would be kept safe and respected', and was given a guard of 30 men and a captain. Initially captured with him were Mencia, their daughters, and other ducal officials, including Carrà, Locarno, and Arignano. René would be taken to prison in Turin, but the others were set free a few days later, including Arignano, following a forceful intervention by Mencia on his behalf.[18]

The Governor of the citadel, Tommaso di Valperga, surrendered to the French when he saw that his cause was lost, and 'immediately the jewels and all the precious objects of the Duke of Savoy were stolen'. When someone urged Brissac to take the Holy Shroud, he declined, reportedly declaring that '"during my thirty years making war, I have never touched holy things, and I will neither start today"'. Imperial infantry from Asti was reportedly arriving, so Brissac and his forces withdrew from the city. His secretary later described the 'precious stones and other rings' that were taken, 'not counting the unicorn horn, which I carried away on my back'. Estimates of the ducal treasury's total losses in Vercelli ranged from 40,000 to 80,000 *écus*. Dell'Isola lamented these losses, including the death of Châtelard, but praised God for preserving Vercelli and 'His Holy Shroud, which is greater than any item of the treasury'. René was consigned to the castle of Valentino, on the outskirts of Turin, and denounced his imprisonment as a violation of the neutrality agreement, since he was a native of the Valle d'Aosta and a *bourgeois* of the Swiss cantons. The French confiscated 40 horses, clothing, gold chains, silverware, and other valuables from René. The French, aware of the extent of René's trans-European lands and authority, expected the principal return from their venture to be his ransom, projected at 'not less than 100,000 *écus*' (an overestimation, as we will see).[19]

The Vercelli disaster fueled discontent with the Imperial commander in Italy, Ferrante Gonzaga. Emanuel Filibert immediately dispatched the highly trusted Andrea Provana di Leynì to reassure his subjects and reestablish order over his affairs, appointing Masino to substitute René as lieutenant general.[20] René's capture destabilized the security of the valley as well, highlighting Mencia's crucial political role. Some ducal advisers worried that French ransom leverage over René would result in

---

18 Ibid.
19 For the citations, see Marchand, 233-37; see also the accounts in De Antonio, Segre ('Il richiamo' and 'L'opera politico-militare,'); and Frutaz, 'Notes.' For Dell'Isola's comment, see AST1, LP, I.8, Dell'Isola to EF, Vercelli 27-XI-53 [there are two letters from this date].
20 Chief among Gonzaga's critics were Antoine Perrenot and Emanuel Filibert (Segre, 'Il richiamo,' 200).

him convincing the Valdostani to accept Henry II as their Prince.[21] The council in Vercelli asked Mencia to accept a ducal garrison in the castle of Verrès, to facilitate René's rejection of French stratagems.[22] Mencia firmly resisted this innovation.[23] Adding to Sabaudian anxiety was the fact that Jean Carrà (brother of the treasurer imprisoned in Nice) had been captured and might be flipped. Carrà was a kinsman of Bressieu and of De Laudes, the Castellan of the key fortress of Bard. Taken together, one observer called 'the things of state [...] doubtful'.[24] The Bailiff of Aosta, Antoine de Leschaulx, convened the *Commis* and initiated efforts to have René released.[25] René's imprisonment had raised the political stakes. His release 'would be very helpful, in many ways, and especially for the Valle d'Aosta', wrote Dell'Isola. But Mencia's anger escalated as the suspicions surrounding her husband grew. The valley itself was politically divided, 'and some people say that the count of Challant had betrayed Vercelli, and willingly allowed himself to be captured. Others want to make him their duke. Others talk about becoming a canton with the Valaisans and the Swiss'.[26] Leynì's arrival in early January eased tensions; he met personally with Mencia in Issogne. From Turin, word arrived that the French did not consider themselves bound by the neutrality agreement or by René's status as a Swiss *bourgeois*.[27] René tried to escape, and, at one point, orchestrated a plot involving the wife of one of the prison guards. She was captured and executed along with her husband.[28] René pressed his immunity claims before the *Parlements* of Turin and Grenoble, and to the King himself, arguing that he had been in Vercelli not as a soldier, but as 'an officer of justice'. The French pointed to his capture with weapons in hand under the Spanish and Sabaudian banners.[29]

21   Segre, 'L'opera politico-militare,' 12-13, 31; see also Marchand, 248-49.
22   AST1, LP, I.8, Dell'Isola to EF, Vercelli 27-XI-53.
23   Ibid., Vercelli 3-XII-53; Segre, 'Il richiamo,' 201, 201 n.2. See also AST1, LP, I.8, Dell'Isola to EF, Vercelli 27-XI-53; ibid., Vercelli 3-XII-53.
24   Ibid., Vercelli 27-XI-53.
25   The Valdostani argued to the French that the neutrality required René to be set free; in the interim, they needed 'ung chiefz audit pays pour ladministracion gouvernement et protection' of the valley (ibid., L.17, Leschaulx to EF, Aosta 25-XI-53).
26   Ibid., I.8, Dell'Isola to EF, Vercelli 26-XII-53.
27   Ibid., Vercelli 14-I-54. Leynì brought the Duke a letter from Philiberte and Isabelle expressing the 'malheur que nous est advenu de la prinse le monsieur le Maréschal nostre père' (letter cited by Segre, 'Il richiamo,' 201, 201 n.3).
28   Frutaz, 'Notes,' 251.
29   Marchand, 251; Frutaz, 'Notes,' 252; 'Histoire généalogique'; AHR, FC 260, Dell'Isola to Mencia, Vercelli 24-II-54.

Family members and supporters were recruited to assist René,[30] the impact of René's capture on his patrimony was assessed,[31] and, at the Imperial court, Emanuel Filibert pushed for a prisoner exchange – even as Charles V was distancing himself, physically and psychologically, from affairs of state.[32] The prisoner swap initiative stalled as summer 1554 approached, but, in August, ransom negotiations established a *taille* of 26,000 *écus*.[33] Mencia's efforts to have the Bernese intervene with the King of France for sums owed to René did not succeed, and she prevented her Valdostano subjects from contributing to a subsidy voted by the valley estates, since they were already burdened by the payment of René's ransom.[34] As the year ended with René in prison, Emanuel Filibert's irritation with the Emperor and his advisers – concerning not only René, but also the governorship of Milan and military authority over nothern Italy, where the Duke had hoped to succeed Ferrante Gonzaga – increased. The Duke of Alva replaced Gonzaga in spring 1555, prompting Emanuel Filibert to send out feelers to the French via the Bishop of Aosta and René,[35] perhaps unblocking René's ransom discussions (see Chapter 7). Seeing an opening, based in part on his lands and connections across Europe, René empowered Mencia to alienate fiefs to raise funds, and mortgaged Valangin to the Bernese.[36] His release in late September or early October 1555 was based on a promise to pay most of the ransom in the future, or to negotiate another arrangement.

The twilight of a career

By 9 October 1555, René was freed and back in the Valle d'Aosta.[37] Without delay, he took steps to consolidate and expand his transregional authority, leaving for Flanders armed with a memoir to guide his discussions with

---

30 In April 1554, Mencia and her daughters borrowed 9,970 *écus* from various Bernese (SKB, *Schadlosbrief* dated 11-IV-54; debt confirmed by René on 18-III-56; see also Frutaz, 'Notes,' 252-53). Claude de Challant reported that a Diesbach from Berne was going to France to press René's case (AHR, FC 260, Claude de Challant to Mencia, Romont 29-IV-54).
31 Ibid., Alessandro Olgiato to Mencia, Vercelli 7-V-54.
32 Ibid., Hugues Richard de Montpon to Mencia, Brussels 21-V-54; see also AHR, FC 26, no. 31, EF to Mencia, Brussels 21-V-54.
33 AST1, LP, V.7, Masino to EF, Vercelli 13-VIII-54; ibid., C.25, Carrà to EF, Vercelli 27-VIII-54.
34 Ibid., I.8, Dell'Isola to EF, Vercelli 27-IX-54.
35 Merlin, 'Il Piemonte,' 281.
36 AEN, AS-K16, 14, copy of procuration for Jehan Robin and Blaise Junod, Vercelli 25-VI-55; for mortgage of Valangin, see Frutaz, 'Notes,' 253.
37 AHR, FC 260, Gio Giacomo Curbis to René (in Issogne), Vercelli 9-X-55.

Emanuel Filibert. First, he sought assistance in paying the ransom, or a reciprocal ransom-forgiveness plan with a current or former French prisoner. Second, he proposed himself as the new Imperial commander 'both in Milan and in the Franche-Comté'. Third, he asked permission from the Duke for his daughters to inherit from him, resolving 'to make use of fear in order to succeed' if necessary. Finally, he requested increased authority and salary, and a new title for himself as ducal lieutenant general.[38] After riding through French-controlled lands in Metz in February,[39] he entered Brussels and soon realized that his bid for an Imperial military command was unrealistic. Regarding the ransom, he learned that François de Coligny d'Andelot, a possible prisoner-swap candidate, had been or would soon be released. The Duke continued to rely on René for Swiss diplomacy, dispatching him to Berne in March to preserve the Swiss status quo regarding the Valle d'Aosta and to assure them of Emanuel Filibert's affection and 'neighborliness'.[40] By June, René was back in Brussels, reporting on his mission and elaborating on property-related and religious issues to be resolved with subjects in Vaud who wished to reconcile with the Duke.[41] From Brussels, René sent his own envoys to France to renew the Valdostano neutrality and to seek personal and commercial permits to travel through French territory.[42] He worked with the Imperial ambassador to France, Simon Renard, to prepare his own visit to the French court, but this was abandoned when Henry II decided to launch a new invasion of Italy in November 1556 – 'the fire has been lit', wrote Renard.[43]

In early 1557, René left Brussels for several months of traveling between the valley, Vercelli, Milan, and the Swiss cantons, where he negotiated for the Duke with Berne, Fribourg, and Valais.[44] The crushing Imperial victory

38 AEN, AS-K16, 16, undated advice paper [c. 1555-1556] for René at court (this memoir seems to be missing at least one page).
39 Ibid., AS-F16, 24, Vieilleville to René, Metz 19-II-56.
40 René told the Bernese that the duchy of Aosta wished to remain under 'la protection et subgection de leur prince naturel' and to 'maintenir et garder leurs libertez et franchises' (ibid., AS-K16, 10, copy of proposal made by René to lords of Berne, dated III-56).
41 Ibid., AS-H16, 23, Jean Réal 'general de la moneta [of Aosta]' to René, Aosta 25-VI-56.
42 He wrote letters for the Cardinal of Guise, the Constable, and mademoiselles Broissure and La Chambre (ibid., AS-I16, 25, undated copy of draft instructions for René's envoy ['baron des Guerres' – *Gruyère?*]).
43 Ibid., AS-G16, 8, Simon Renard to René, Ponssy [?] 16-XI-56.
44 René's credentials from the Duke described him as his cousin, counselor, Chamberlain, Lieutenant General, Marshal of Savoie, and Knight of the Annonciade and empowered him to collect loyalty oaths from all ducal subjects (AHR, FC 26, nos. 33-34, including patents dated 5-IX-57).

at St. Quentin, near Amiens (10 August), suddenly increased the likelihood of a Sabaudian restoration. René's daughter Isabelle married Giovanni Federico Madruzzo in Milan in November – René probably attended as he raced across northern Italy, strengthening Valdostano and Sabaudian defenses.[45] In late November, he left Vercelli, crossed the Simplon pass, and was greeted in Valangin by Arignano, Stefano Dell'Isola (nephew of the deceased Giovanni Battista), and several 'personal friends' as he prepared for talks with Berne and Fribourg.[46] Discussions with the Swiss took on a different valence as the international environment shifted, and René took advantage of his own position to make other claims.[47] He asked the Duke for more money for military expenses, renewed his request that Emanuel Filibert not issue privileges or exemptions without consulting him, and condemned Masino, who had substituted René as lieutenant general during his captivity and now refused to relinquish command, undermining 'my honor and reputation'. René forcefully demanded that the Duke put Masino in his place, threatening to withdraw from the Duke's service otherwise.[48] Emanuel Filibert, who might have developed suspicions about René's intentions as a result of his imprisonment,[49] waited before responding. René spent Christmas at Valangin, keeping abreast of affairs in Piedmont and the valley through his secretaries.[50] Some money finally arrived for Bard and Montjovet (Valdostano forts, whose garrisons had been threatening to abandon their posts), but René prohibited his own subjects in the valley from paying subsidies voted by the estates, since they were already funding the common defense through their payments to him. René also provided

---

45   Bassan Rua, Captain of Montjovet, called René 'nostro grande capitano' and 'bon protetorre apresso Soa Altessa', whose help was their last resort (AEN, AS-H16, 28, Bassan Rua to René, Montjovet 18-XI-57).
46   Fornaseri, 136-38, René to EF, Valangin 25-XI-57.
47   For René's proposal to fix a day with the Bernese to discuss the occupied lands, see Biel, 9.
48   René wrote that, if the Duke did not reinstall him as lieutenant general, he would assume that 'je soye noté a quelque meffaict'. He urged Emanuel Filibert to address matters quickly, 'que j'aye occasion de perseverer a l'affection et bonne voulenté que j'ay tousjours heu, car aultrement je seroye constrainct habandonner le tout et me retirer a la conduyte de petitz afferez, attendu qu'il me semble je ne demande que chose par trop raisonnable'. René reiterated this strong language in his own hand at the end of the letter, stressing that 'ma reputacyon et honeur [...] sont fort ynteressez' in the matter (Fornaseri, 136-38, René to EF, Valangin 25-XI-57).
49   Segre, 'L'opera politico-militare,' 73.
50   Ducrest was to have traveled to Sion to attend to a dispute with another of René's servants, but the weather prevented him from crossing the mountains, so he rescheduled the meeting (AEN, AS-F16, 14, Ducrest to René, Aosta 4-XII-57). Ducrest also reported on a dispute involving the Fribourgeois, who owed money to the hospice of St. Bernard of Montjoux (ibid.; also ibid., AS-H16, 8, Ducrest to René, Aosta 4-XII-57).

direction about disposing of the papers of Giovanni Battista Dell'Isola, who had been deeply involved in Swiss diplomacy.[51] René continued his work on that front in early 1558, negotiating for Bernese and Fribourgeois withdrawal from Sabaudian lands, and traveling to Uri to enlist the support of the Catholic 'forest' cantons.[52]

By mid 1558, when René was back in Vercelli, the military crisis in northern Italy had dissipated. The French had withdrawn and redeployed most of their army along the Flanders border. Their victory at Calais (January 1558) had brought both sides to peace negotiations. In Piedmont, though, René continued his bitter struggle with Masino over the lieutenant generalship. The Duke, mindful of René's authority, did not want to alienate him,[53] and so, in June, he informed Masino that René would resume his office,[54] sending the treasurer Carrà copious instructions for resolving the dispute. René would serve in Piedmont for a few weeks and then depart for Flanders to attend him there, and Masino would take over in René's absence; thus, 'each one would have his turn'.[55] In early September, as René and Mencia were traveling between Piedmont and Lombardy, the Countess fell suddenly ill and died near Novara.[56] René's grief was compounded by Masino's continued refusal to step down. René's sojourns in Lombardy were presumably planned to avoid being in a territory whose command he claimed but was not effectively exercising. He criticized the Duke for failing to stop what seemed an inevitable open conflict between the two grandees.[57] He called Emanuel Filibert's compromise 'more of an offense against my honor than a remedy', one that would damage his reputation. Masino even threatened to take up arms if René challenged his authority. René urged the Duke to send clear written

51 Dell'Isola's papers remained in Aosta after he died, before his nephew Stefano could claim them. The *Commis* decided to 'revoir et separer par liasses' these letters, 'mesmement celles qui font mention de deniers & cas d'estat'. Eventually, they decided to seek ducal instructions before leaving them to Stefano: 'Voyant qu'eles font mention des affaires d'estat & deniers venuz en ce pays na semblé ausd' s'rs commis ny a moy les espedier sans l'espres commandement de Son Alteze ou de vous.' They placed the papers 'dans les arches du pays [...] pour s'en servir toutes & quelquesfoys qu'il sera de bessoing' (ibid., AS-G16, 24 and 24a, Leschaux to René, Aosta 14-XII-57).
52 AST1, LP, C.104, Arignano to EF, Vercelli 24 I 58; Biel, 12.
53 Segre, 'L'opera politico-militare,' 73.
54 This would be done without prejudice to Masino's honor, since René had held the office until he was imprisoned and deserved to be restored to it (Fornaseri, 142 n. 2).
55 AST1, PD 223, ff. 168-73, instructions dated 17-VII-58.
56 Fornaseri, 139-40, René to EF, Novara [not 'Monace'] 8-IX-58.
57 René explained that he was not writing by his own hand since he feared that the Duke had been unable to read his letters (surely a cheeky criticism!). He acknowledged receipt of the Duke's most recent message but found it 'si ambigue et doubteuse' that Masino could effectively ignore it, 'et qu'ainsi en pourrons venir a grande diferrance' (Fornaseri, 142-44, René to EF, Pavia 26-XI-58).

instructions 'to prevent greater disorders amongst your minister and servants, because I am not someone who will put up with attacks on my honor and reputation'.[58] Emanuel Filibert promptly dispatched Andrea Provana di Leynì to Piedmont to inform Masino of his decision.[59] Leynì perhaps explained to both parties that the imminent peace treaty would result in a reorganization of commands anyway. In December, René informed Masino from Pavia that he would not return to Vercelli until sometime after Christmas.[60]

As his conflict with Masino escalated, valley leaders asked René to help renew their neutrality with the French. René viewed this as unnecessary given the peace negotiations and advocated waiting for the diplomatic outcome so as not to appear 'so fearful [...] without positioning ourselves as subjects who are going to request a truce in France as if we were terror-ridden and pusillanimous'.[61] The *Commis* sent envoys to France anyway, who argued that Brissac, by taking René prisoner, had violated the neutrality by excluding from it René and 'any other of his house and subjects'. The Valdostano envoys thus sought a royal injunction reversing Brissac's action.[62]

On 2-3 April 1559, the peace treaty was signed at Cateau-Cambrésis. It arranged for the double marriage of Emanuel Filibert to Marguerite of France (Henry II's sister), and Philip II to Elisabeth de Valois (Henry II's daughter). René reportedly witnessed the signing of the marriage contract and was present in Paris for the tragic death of the French King, who was mortally wounded in a tournament during the wedding celebrations.[63] His death at a critical moment created an environment of political uncertainty leading to decades of unrest and religious war in France. In this painful atmosphere, Sabaudian and French officials began implementing the peace agreement.[64] René resumed his position as *maréchal* de Savoie and received command of Chambéry and the other transalpine Sabaudian lands. On 8 July, Emanuel Filibert issued patents granting René extraordinary authority in his newly recovered states. Since the Duke could not take possession of his lands personally, he appointed 'our very dear, well-loved and faithful cousin the Count of Challant, Marshal of Savoie, knight of our order, and lieutenant

---

58 Ibid.
59 'Quella cessione di governo poi nella realtà non s'effettuò', according to Segre, 'perchè il Challant ebbe in quei giorni altri incarichi, per cui il Masino continuò a dirigere lo Stato' ('L'opera politico-militare,' 73).
60 René to Masino, Pavia 22-XII-58, cited in Claretta, *La successione*, 406-7.
61 AHR, FCC, mz. 6, P31, 868, René to Bailiff and *Commis*, Pavia 11-XI-58.
62 Ibid., P30, N855, *Commis* to Vallesa and Mistral, 29-III-59.
63 Frutaz, 'Notes,' 245.
64 Vester, 'The Piedmontese Restitution.'

general' to do so, 'which task belongs to him due to his *estat* of Marshal'. René was empowered to take possession of the 'country and duchy of Savoie, and our other lands and lordships on this side of the mountains', including 'the papers, documents, and other things to be restored to him' by French officials. He would also receive the homage and loyalty oaths due from the Duke's vassals, towns, and communities to 'their natural Prince'.[65]

On 3 August, René arrived in Chambéry and, a day later, formally requested from Guillaume Desportes, President of the *Parlement* of Chambéry, 'the restitution of the states', according to the royal agreement as his commission. On 7 August, possession was transferred

> in the great room of the castle of Chambéry, where President Desportes sat on the right, on a seat of purple velours, and the said Marshal sat on the left, where he received the keys of the city by the hands of the lord of Monterminod, first *syndic*, who gave them instantly to the Marshal, who then took the place of said president, who then retired.[66]

Later that day, the cameral officials Carrà and Michaud received 'all of the titles and papers from the chamber [of accounts]',[67] and, in the following days, René 'took actual possession of the places, [and] declared on 12 August that the Senate of Savoie was a sovereign court replacing the former resident council of Chambéry'. He reestablished Carrà and Michaud as the 'body of the chamber [...] to receive the titles and papers, and recover direction of the patrimony, and their prerogatives on this side of the mountains', and they began their work immediately. On 16 August, 'the lord master Carrà went to the *Saincte Chapelle* of the castle, to open the tomb of Philiberte of Savoie, Duchess of Nemours, inside of which had been hidden many important papers; as also had been done in the sacristy, and these were reinserted by inventory in the archives'.[68] In early October, as Emanuel Filibert drew near to his lands, Challant and other officials left Chambéry to meet him. After a couple of weeks in Bresse, the Duke floated down the Rhône on his way to Nice, where he would remain until his return to Piedmont about a year later.[69] René's reintegration into his office of Marshal of Savoie both concluded his struggle

---

65 Patents of EF dated Paris 8-VII-59, in Capré, 80-83.
66 Capré, 79.
67 Ibid.
68 Ibid., 83-84.
69 In Piedmont, Masino had been given 'la même authorité qu'avoit eu le Comte de Chalant' in the transalpine lands for the taking of possession. The Duke arrived in Lyon on 5 October 1559 and, from there, traveled to Bresse, before continuing to Nice (ibid., 84-85).

with Masino over the lieutenant generalship of Piedmont and positioned him in greater proximity to his fiefs in Virieu, Valangin, and Beaufremont (though marginally farther from the Valle d'Aosta). It also created an autonomous space for him with respect to the Sabaudian court, whose 1560 arrival limited Masino's authority as lieutenant general in the cisalpine lands.

Family matters and René's last years

The Sabaudian restoration offered René an opportunity to take stock of the state of his family's affairs. His eldest child was probably his illegitimate son François, for whom René had obtained clerical appointments in the Valle d'Aosta, since his illegitimacy prevented him from inheriting. One story suggests that René intended to have François legitimized and named Count of Challant, but that Mencia foiled the plan, and her husband acquiesced out of respect for his wife.[70] René's first testament was drawn up in September 1523,[71] followed by a second one in February 1546.[72] In the second document, René declared that, were he to have legitimate male heirs, the first would be Count of Challant and inherit his lands in the valley, while the second would be Count of Arberg and inherit Valangin and Beaufremont. If he had no legitimate male heirs, Philiberte and Isabelle, respectively, would inherit these titles and lands – at least, this was his plan.[73] His anxiety is apparent in lines written to Charles III just after Isabelle's birth:

> I was drunk with joy like you [the Duchess had recently given birth to a daughter, Catherine], because I had a daughter, though you had reason to be happier than I, because it pleased God to have given you males first, which is a great consolation to you and all your subjects and servants, but from here on I will no longer be drunk, so that, with God's help, the males will follow the females.[74]

By the time that Philiberte was in her early 20s, René was sounding out various marriage opportunities at the French court.[75] In early 1553, talks

---

70 'Histoire généalogique,' 54r.-v.
71 AST1, PD 188, f. 182, testament dated 15-IX-23.
72 AHR, FC 14, no. 11, testament dated 12-II-46.
73 Matile, 292-93; note that Matile incorrectly identifies the 1546 testament as René's first will.
74 Fornaseri, 34-35, René to Ch III, Chambéry 14-I-30.
75 Ibid., René to EF, Vercelli 26-II-51. One proposal was between Philiberte and Odet de Bretagne; simultaneously, another potential suitor worth 25,000 *livres* arranged to marry another woman to

were opened with Gian Giacomo Trivulzio, son of the Marquis of Vigevano, and René kept Charles III informed about the discussions.[76] The first set of proposals gave Philiberte a dowry of 30,000 *scudi*, titles to 'all his states' (René retaining usufruct), and set aside a dowry of 24,000 *scudi* for Isabelle. The firstborn male child was to bear 'the arms and name of Challant, and if he were to die with no sons and only daughters, the first-born would succeed and carry the arms of Challant and Trivulzio conjoined'. The contract was finalized in late May,[77] but Trivulzio's desire for the Emperor's approval delayed matters, and the match eventually fell through for reasons that are unclear.[78] So, in the mid 1550s, both daughters remained on the marriage market, with sizeable dowries. Someone urged René to accept a proposal from a suitor who was so 'honest and attractive' that 'if your daughter were already pregnant by him, by means that I could easily describe, you would not try to stop it'.[79] Was René perhaps uncertain about the intimate behavior of his eldest daughter? At around this time, the secretary Gautier wrote Mencia, a bit worriedly, about his desire for 'a marriage in your house, and I do not see anything that could stand in the way unless Mademoiselle does not wish to be married. But she should say so right away because she is already seen as a beauty'.[80]

In 1556, René's daughters were 28 and 26 years old. That August, Emanuel Filibert sweetened the pot for potential suitors by permitting René to pass all of his feudal power and authority to his children, whether male or female.[81]

---

whom he had long been attracted. Odet had more property 'mais l'on faict aussy bien difference des personnaiges, quoy que l'aultre soit ung beau & jeune seigneur' (AHR, FC 263, mz. 1, ? to René [?], s.d. [*c*. 1551-1553]).

76 Gian Giacomo's grandfather Giovanni Niccolo was the first Marquis of Vigevano; his father Gianfrancesco had married a Trivulzio cousin who brought the county of Maleo to the family and bequeathed it to Gian Giacomo. René notified the Duke, so he could 'me guyder sellon votre bon plaisir et comandement' (Fornaseri, 111-12, René to EF, Vercelli 23-IV-53).

77 The contract was drawn up in the presence of Gaspare Capris, Bishop of Asti. Gian Giacomo was willing to accept a dowry of 23,000 *scudi* worth of property from the Monferrato, with 6000 paid in cash and 1000 in jewels when the contract was signed. Charles III required that Gian Giacomo pledge 10,000 écus or the equivalent as dowry security, 'a la coustume de ce lieu' (AST1, PD 223, f. 4-30, marriage papers, including final version of contract [f. 4], Trivulzio to Ch III, Maleo 23-V-53 [f. 5], February 1553 proposals [f. 23], the Duke of Savoy's response [f. 28], and other notes [ff. 6, 8, 11, 30]).

78 Fornaseri, 112-13, René to EF, Vercelli 30-VI-53. Trivulzio married Antonia d'Avalos d'Aquino d'Aragona, daughter of the Marquis Del Vasto, but died in 1557.

79 AHR, FC 263, mz. 1, ? to René de Challant, s.d.

80 Ibid., FC 264, mz. 1, Gautier to Mencia, Vercelli 26-IX-?.

81 BCT, ms. 2154, f. 174, copy of act dated Brussels 14-VIII-56; see also AST1, PD 223 rosso, f. 119, act dated Brussels 14-VIII-56.

Fig. 4: Countess Mencia, Philiberte, and Isabelle, detail from altarpiece dated 1547-1548, by an artist close to Jakob Seisenegger. Source: Archivi dell'Assessorato Turismo, Sport, Commercio, Agricoltura e Beni culturali della Regione autonoma Valle d'Aosta – fondo Catalogo beni culturali. Photograph by Cesare Diego; used with permission of the Regione Autonoma Valle d'Aosta.

One scholar has suggested that the Cardinal Prince-Bishop of Trento, Cristoforo Madruzzo, who had lent money to René that was secured on his fiefs, saw a Challant match for his nephew Giovanni Federico as an opportunity to seize control of 'a feudal complex that, even if heavily indebted and difficult to manage politically due to its complex, tangled jurisdictional relations [...]

represented a strong international consolidation of the family's power'.[82] The view that the Madruzzo were the ones pushing the Challant match[83] seems corroborated by the correspondence of Madruzzo's agents in Brussels.[84] Still, the arrangement would enhance the prestige of both families.[85]

René gave mixed signals and was considered an unreliable interlocutor, according to Madruzzo's informants. There seemed to be suspicions that Philiberte did not want to get married, in which case Isabelle was considered as a substitute, but René wished to consult with Emanuel Filibert.[86] Despite the continued pessimism of the Cardinal's agent,[87] discussions advanced and a wedding date was set. Days prior to the scheduled wedding, though, the fears of many materialized as Philiberte absconded with a servant, eventually ending up in Venice. According to an account written 80 years later by a family historiographer, Philiberte had traveled to Milan from Aosta, where 'she could not resist giving herself as prey to a servant from Lorraine named Lespal with whom, in Issogne, while her father had been away, she had passed her time without anyone noticing'. Pregnant with Lespal's child, Philiberte made her way to Milan, stole the jewels of her mother and sister (worth 3000 *scudi*) and fled to Ferrara and then to Venice.[88] This left

---

82 Vialardi di Sandigliano, 24.
83 'Histoire généalogique,' 51v.
84 BCT, ms. 600, ff. 5, 112, 123, Pagnano to Madruzzo, Brussels 26-II-57.
85 When Charles V died in 1558, Francesco Robertello da Udine celebrated the Emperor's elevation of various Italian families to high honors, including the Doria, the D'Avalos, the Medici, the Colonna, the Farnese, the Sforza, and the Madruzzo (Spagnoletti, 28).
86 Pagnano reported in late February that he 'fece l'ufficio con *Mons'r de Scialand* [italicized words in code, decoded at end of document]'. René 'mi parlo asaj volendosi pur' far' credere grandiss'a volunta. Ma la fine fu che quando *lui sara in Italia intendera de la figliuola l'animo suo*, et al'hora fara quello che Idio lo inspirara'. Pagnano also reported that Emanuel Filibert had asked another of Madruzzo's agents 'se egli voleva che li facesse opera *perche quello che non si puo con la prima sia con la seconda*', apparently anticipating that Isabelle might be willing to substitute her sister. The other agent would keep Madruzzo informed following discussions between René and the Duke, 'benche no' mi pare potersene fidare' (BCT, ms. 600, ff. 5, 112, 123, Pagnano to Madruzzo, Brussels 26-II-57).
87 Following more talks a couple of weeks later, Pagnano called René 'homo che no' sta molto in proposito', again warning that 'no' me ne fido ponto' (ibid., f. 7, Pagnano to Madruzzo, Brussels 13-III-57).
88 'Histoire généalogique,' 52r; see also Weber, 165. The 'Histoire généalogique' was written by Vigilio Vescovi, a servant of the Prince-Bishop Carlo Emanuele di Madruzzo, in 1638. An Italian translation was published as Vescovi, 'Historia della casa di Challant et di Madruzzo.' Recently, Vialardi di Sandigliano (24-25) has cited an unidentified document at the Neuchâtel state archives to identify Philiberte's partner as '"[Michel] Honoré Collot originaire de Toul [Lorraine], soy disant de l'Espal"'. Admitting that 'storia e leggende s'intersecano', the author suggests that the two were married in Ferrara and that Collot had died by the end of 1558. Other

the Count and Countess of Challant deeply embarrassed, 'dealing with a Cardinal, a Governor and many Knights, who were immediately aware of the situation, the whole city remaining stupefied'.[89] René's hesitations during negotiations and the recurring questions about Philiberte's desire to marry raise the possibility that her pregnancy was not a surprise to her family. At any rate, René disinherited Philiberte in May, making Isabelle the universal heir, and pivoted to a match between Isabelle and Giovanni Federico.[90] It was agreed between the parties that, if possible, the rearranged wedding should be held in the presence of the Emperor, but, if not, it should be held quickly and simply in Vercelli. René also promised to assist Giovanni Federico's father, Niccolò, in finding a suitable position of command in Lombardy or Germany.[91] The wedding seems to have finally taken place in November 1557.[92]

With one daughter married, and the urgency of his governing responsibilities attenuated following the restoration, René thought again about producing a male heir. He took as his third spouse Marie de La Palud (daughter

documents suggest that there had been a marriage, but that the husband did not die until the early 1560s; see AST1, RLC, mz. 9, EF to Bobba [?], Nice 2-III-60; ibid., mz. 11, f 157r-v, EF to René, Chieri 19-XI-64.

89 'Histoire généalogique,' 52v.

90 Frutaz, 'Notes,' 253. Vialardi di Sandigliano argues (25) that, following Philiberte's disappearance, the Cardinal was the one who proposed the match with Isabelle and convinced René to disinherit his elder daughter, which René did in a new will written at the end of May; see also Frutaz, 'Notes,' 253. The will is in AHR, FC 14, no. 14, document dated 31-V-57; the Challant testaments have been edited by Orphée Zanolli and published as *Les testaments des seigneurs de Challant*. According to Segre, Emanuel Filibert wrote to his ambassador in Venice (Claudio Malopera) on 9 July, instructing him not to interact with Philiberte or her partner, but to ask the Venetians to arrest her and deliver her to her father. On 17 July, the Senate denied this request, an infraction of 'la libertà del Dominio', which permits people to come and go as they wish (Segre, 'Emanuele Filiberto,' 91, 91-92 n. 4).

91 BCT, ms. 2154, ff 102-4 (undated document).

92 There is some confusion about this; one source (http://genealogy.euweb.cz/italy/madruzzo.html, 23 May 2019) cites 21 November as the date of the marriage, and another indicates that the wedding took place in Milan in the presence of Giovanni Federico's father, Niccolò, and his brother Ludovico (the future Cardinal-Prince-Bishop), without specifying the date (Weber, 165). A letter from Giovanni Federico to the Duke dated 30 December 1557 supports a late November date; he refers to 'il nuovo legame del matrimonio ch'io ho contratto con la figliola di Mons. de Chiallant' (Giovanni Federico to EF, Pavia 30-XII-57, cited in Bianco di San Secondo, 106-7 – the original is in AST1, LP). Antoine Perrenot de Granvelle corresponded with Cristoforo Madruzzo in August (the letter carrier was René's secretary Ducrest) and warmly recommended René to Madruzzo, suggesting that the latter two were in proximity, presumably working on marriage arrangements (BCT, ms. 2900, f. 568, Antoine Perrenot to Cristoforo, Ralenfrainer [?] 4-VIII-57). Claudio Malopera wrote to the Duke from Venice in October and indicated that the marriage had not yet taken place (Malopera to EF, Venice 16-X-57, cited in Segre, 'Emanuele Filiberto,' 91 n. 1).

of Jean de La Palud, Count of Varax, and Claude de Rye) in May 1561.[93] The coresidence of René's daughters (Philiberte returned to the valley in 1559) and a stepmother of about their age in the valley might have generated conflicts of authority and precedence. René's third marriage took place during the same month when Emanuel Filibert visited the valley and stayed at Châtillon, apparently in René's absence.[94] From late 1559 until his death in 1565, René spent most of his time in Chambéry, Virieu, and other transalpine lands, making it easier for him to attend to his official business in the Duke's service, while also giving him relatively simple access to Valangin and enabling him to avoid his eldest daughter, Masino, and perhaps the Duke himself.[95] René assigned the title 'lieutenant general in the Valle d'Aosta for the very illustrious, high and powerful lord the Count of Challant' jointly to Isabelle and Giovanni Federico.[96]

Following the restoration, René reestablished contact with his eldest daughter, though apparently without a spirit of forgiveness. In October 1559, three of his officers met Philiberte in Vercelli and accompanied her back to the valley.[97] Over the next several years, René and Emanuel Filibert had a series of exchanges about her, the Duke urging René to reconcile and offer forgiveness. She eventually married a member of the lesser nobility from Novara named Giuseppe Tornielli, thanks to the Duke's support. The prospect of René's inheritance being divided between the two daughters and not transferred intact into the hands of the Challant-Madruzzo was likely preferable to Emanuel Filibert and may help explain his attitude.

In fall 1560, the Duke of Savoy left Nice and crossed the Maritime Alps in order to begin taking possession of his cisalpine lands. One source has both René and Giovanni Federico accompanying him at least in the initial

93 Marie was born in the early or mid 1530s, it appears. Jean de la Palud, Count of Varax, died in 1544, leaving Marie as his eldest daughter and heiress (Guichenon, *Histoire de Bresse*, pt. 3, 302). Various accounts suggest that Marie's sister Françoise was kidnapped by Jean-Amédée de Beaufort de Rolle in the 1540s and married to him, while others indicate that Marie herself was the one kidnapped; see Hisely, 397-98; De Charrière, 'La baronnie,' 86-87 and notes; Mugnier, 200; and *Dictionnaire historique & biographique de la Suisse*, 2: 26-27. An inventory from the subseries 7E of the departmental archives of the Doubs indicates that her mother Claude de Rye refused to give permission for Marie's marriage to Fernand de Lannoy in 1559, and that her 1606 testament expressed her wish to be buried in the church of Villersexel where her two daughters (Marie and Françoise) reposed; see Dornier, item 7E4002.
94 AEN, AS-I16, 13, accounts of Domenico Lescha, Castellan of Châtillon, for 1560.
95 In July 1560, René attended to the needs of the Reformed community at La Chaux de Fonds; see Frutaz, 'Notes,' 255.
96 Ibid., AS-I16, 13, accounts of Domenico Lescha, Castellan of Châtillon, for 1560.
97 They arrived in Châtillon on 23 October; days later, Philiberte left for Aymavilles (ibid., AS-K16, 11, 11a, 11b, expenses of the Castellan of Châtillon, October 1559).

stages.[98] In December 1561, the Venetian envoy Boldù reported that René, 'Grand Marshal of Savoie and regular Lieutenant General of the Dukes of Savoy [...] has now retired from affairs in order to rest, being fairly old'.[99] He carried on with his duties, inspecting the fortress at Montmélian in March 1562.[100] Three months later, the Duke asked him to ensure defenses in Savoie during the outbreak of the first religious war in France and the transit of Bernese troops across Sabaudian lands.[101] In January 1563, René was on diplomatic mission in Berne,[102] and, two months later, he was confronted with another tragedy – Marie de La Palud's death during childbirth.[103] René wasted no time taking a fourth wife, signing a contract with Péronne de La Chambre in June 1563 and residing with her at Virieu. Alas, within a year, Péronne also died. René's inheritance would have to pass through one or both of his daughters. When René met Emanuel Filibert and King Charles IX of France at Lyon and Crémieu in July 1564, René surely sought a reconfirmation from the Duke regarding the permission granted eight years earlier for his daughters to inherit his lands.[104]

The Count remained in Bugey and Bresse for the rest of his days, it appears, continuing his involvement in Swiss diplomacy. Soon after the death of Péronne, and just prior to the arrival of the French King in Lyon, a minor crisis erupted among the Sabaudian nobility, prompted by a Piedmontese noble named Annibale di Cocconato. In late April or early May, Cocconato was the victim (or believed that he was the victim) of some kind of attack on his honor, apparently by a Savoyard noble, and published a manifesto in response.[105] The Savoyard nobility seems to have taken offense at the manifesto and assembled together in protest. René managed to mediate between the Savoyards, whose assembly without permission threatened

---

98 Bianco di San Secondo, 107-8.
99 Boldù, 439.
100 Fornaseri, 146-47, René to EF, Montmélian 16-III-62.
101 AST1, RLC, mz. 10, EF to Challant, Fossano 28-VI-62. Perhaps as payment for this mission, 2,850 *lire* were transferred to René by the Duke's treasurer-general, 'a conto de soi crediti' (ASTR, art. 86, paragrafo 3, 1562, account of Treasurer-General Negron di Negro).
102 The Count's assignment was to try to detach the republic from its alliance with Geneva, in preparation for a conference to be held later that spring between Sabaudian and Swiss envoys regarding the restoration of the Sabaudian lands; see Cramer, 1: 101-2; Biel, 26.
103 Vescovi, 90-91.
104 AHR, FC 260, Giovanni Federico to Isabelle, Lyon 10-VII-64.
105 The manifesto, dated Turin 9-V-64, is preserved at the Biblioteca civica of Casale Monferrato. Another text published in Turin by Martino Cravotto in 1565 is entitled 'Manifesto del s. conte Annibale Coconato nella querella d'honore che vertisse tra lui et il s. Francesco di Manthone detto Roccaforte' (the university library of Pavia holds a copy).

ducal authority, and Emanuel Filibert, who expressed satisfaction with the Count's handling of the situation.[106]

Emanuele Filiberto and Giovanni Federico were on good terms, and the Duke began to employ him in important matters immediately following the restoration. This gave René another influential lobbyist at the ducal court, but it also gave the Duke leverage with respect to René. In September 1563, the Duke wrote to René on behalf of 'the Count of Avi your son-in-law', recommending 'the matter for which he is being sent to you'.[107] René continued to be politically active into 1565, especially in Swiss affairs.[108] In June 1565, he forwarded a report from the ducal ambassadors to the Swiss cantons to Emanuel Filibert.[109] He asked one of the diplomats (Louis Oddinet de Montfort, who was carrying the report) to request from the Duke letters of support 'touching my affairs in France'.[110] Until his last days, René pursued the aggrandizement of himself and the transregional reach of his house.

On 7 July 1565, René's secretary Gautier sent urgent news to Isabelle and Giovanni Federico from Chambéry about 'the sudden and ominous illness of my lord the Marshal'. Two days earlier, doctors had urgently been summoned from Chambéry to Virieu, but 'under the pretense that it was for an official', in order to conceal René's condition. Gautier urged Isabelle and her husband, 'with required dexterity, to put your affairs in order and attend to all necessities, and do not fail to send messengers here day and night to find out his state of health, which we pray God will be good'.[111] René breathed his last at Ambronay on 11 July 1565. Within two weeks, Isabelle

106 The Duke explained to René that he permitted Cocconato to publish the manifesto not to 'fere mettre en soupson, aulcuns nobles d'une ou d'aultre province, moins laisser esmouvoir aulcune partialité entre eulx', but simply to permit Cocconato to defend himself, nothing that 'messeigneurs noz predecesseurs [...] en heussent usé de mesme en semblable occasion' (AST1, RLC, mz. 11, f 124 r-v, EF to René, s.l. 9-VI-64). Cocconato was clearly a difficult character: in 1574, he, along with Boniface de La Môle, would be decapitated by Catherine de Medici for conspiring against the French crown.
107 Giovanni Federico had asked the Duke to support his request, as a sign of respect for his father in law. The Duke praised 'les bons deportement de luy & de la contesse sa femme votre fille', noting that 'leur bien & honneur c'est le votre propre' (AST1, RLC, mz. 11, f 24r-v, EF to René, Turin 26-IX-63).
108 His secretary Gautier collected information gathered 'par l'ung de mes gens, revenant maintent de Souisse' (Fornaseri, 148, René to EF, Virieu 16-I-65).
109 The other envoy was probably Giovanni Federico; both had helped negotiate the treaty of Lausanne, by which Berne agreed to relinquish the Sabaudian lands south of Lake Geneva that they had occupied in 1536.
110 Fornaseri, 148-49, René to EF, Ambronay 4-VI-65.
111 AHR, FC 131, Gautier to Giovanni Federico and Isabelle, Chambéry 7-VII-65.

summoned notaries and made out a procuration for Giovanni Federico so that he could, in her name, 'have celebrated an honorable funeral and the ecclesiastical obsequies required by the sorrowful trespass of said deceased lord'. The document referred to Isabelle as Countess of Challant and 'daughter and universal heiress appointed' by her father. It explained that she could not 'transport herself across the mountains to perform her duty as daughter and heiress' due to 'her pregnancy and imminent labor'. Her husband, 'Count of Challant and Avi', would also have power to settle accounts, recover property, receive credits and pay debts, gather documentation belonging to René, and appoint substitutes to carry out these tasks.[112] At this point, grief quickly gave way to political calculation, as the new Count and Countess of Challant scrambled to secure René's heritage for themselves.

Little is known about René's funeral and burial. One account indicates that a funerary monument to René was erected in the church of Notre Dame of Bourg-en-Bresse, and that, some years after his death, Emanuel Filibert visited the church. Seeing the monument, the Duke 'with his own dagger scratched out the the words "*hault et puissant*" and affirmed that only he held such rank in his domains'.[113] If René's body were laid to rest in Bresse, though, his heart seems to have remained in the Valle d'Aosta. A 1578 inventory of the property of the sacristy of the cathedral chapter of Aosta indicates, among many other items, 'a small wooden box where the heart of the magnificent Lord *monsieur* René de Challant is contained in a small box of lead'.[114] The physical division of René's body in death, in lands that he commanded on either side of the Alps, is a powerful reminder of his political position on the edge of the Italian Renaissance. The safekeeping of his heart in the sacristy of the Aosta cathedral also highlights his ambiguous status as the Duke of Savoy's greatest vassal and potential competitor who claimed sovereign rights of his own.

Historiographic perspectives of René's life

René de Challant has been mentioned by many writers, beginning in his own lifetime. While he was still in his mid thirties, Pierre Lambert de La

---

112 Ibid., FC 40, no. 17, procuration by Isabelle for Giovanni Federico dated 26-VII-65.
113 De Antonio, 235-36.
114 Archivio del Capitolo della Cattedrale di Aosta, Boîte 17a, cart. 1, doc. 20, 'Inventaire des biens, livres et parements de la sacristie' (2 June 1578), 8r. Many thanks to Roberto Bertolin for this reference. On the practice of extracting the heart and other organs and burying them separately from the body, see Giesey, 19-24. This practice was widespread among late medieval kings.

Croix referred to him in his memoirs,[115] and, in around 1560, the author of an advice paper given to Emanuel Filibert stressed René's influence in the Sabaudian lands.[116] About a year later, the Venetian ambassador to the court of Savoy, Andrea Boldù, acknowledged René's wealth and influence, but noted that he was 'fairly old' and had retired from an active political life.[117] As we have seen, René's eventful life also attracted attention from writers appealing to public audiences, such as Bandello. Among his *Novelle* was the story 'The Countess of Challant Has the Count of Masino Killed and Her Own Head Cut Off' (1554). For Bandello, René's first marriage was a tragedy about spouses from different stations, a wife with '"unbridled desires"', and a husband who coolly seized her inheritance after she died.[118] François de Belleforest's French version of the story (1566) faults René for having granted too much freedom to his wife and having been unable to control her. When Bianca Maria understood that '"with her Count it was impossible to have her garden watered by another gardener than he who was the true possessor who had usufruct"', she fled. Despite his partial responsibility, Belleforest presented René as 'good, wise, virtuous, and of noble family', and as one who loved his wife 'honestly and ingenuously'. This French version of the story spread throughout Europe and was published in England by William Painter in his *Palace of Pleasure* (1567).[119] Even before he had died, René was a kind of celebrity who elicited a range of contradictory responses, having been portrayed as skillful, incompetent, faithful, disloyal, trusting, crafty, virtuous, ambitious, and naïve. While Lambert had alluded to some of René's specific activities, other writers described his great influence in a geopolitically important region or focused on the Bianca Maria tragedy.

There were two early seventeenth-century accounts of some of René's activities. François Boyvin du Villars, a younger contemporary of René who had been Brissac's secretary during the 1550s, left a set of memoirs in 1610. By that time, after a long period as French ambassador in Turin, he was serving Henry IV as Bailiff of Gex, and seems to have shared his master's commitment to a Franco-Sabaudian anti-Habsburg alliance. Boyvin depicted René as a politically astute, dedicated servant of the French King in all

115 *Mémoires de Pierre Lambert*, 502-3, 513-17.
116 Probably Cassiano dal Pozzo; see his biography by Stumpo and the discussion of this memoir in Barberis, *Le armi del Principe*. For the text of the memoir, see 'Memoriale del Presidente Niccolò Balbo,' in Ricotti, 1: 334 and following; esp. 329-33.
117 Boldù, 439; see also 414, 430-34. Boldù mistakenly referred to René as the count of 'Colegno', but the context makes it clear that he was describing René.
118 Pavesio, 36-37; also 29, 31.
119 Ibid., 36-39.

ways that did not compromise his primary fidelity to the Duke of Savoy. His discussion of René focuses on his capture at Vercelli and subsequent imprisonment and ransom negotiations.[120] The Trentino writer Vigilio Vescovi (1610-1679), secretary of Charles Emanuel Madruzzo, Prince-Bishop of Trent and Count of Challant, translated into Italian and updated a fifteenth-century family history by Pierre du Bois, entitling his new work the *Historia della Casa di Challant e di Madruzzo* (1638-1639).[121] Vescovi offered the most comprehensive account to date of René's life, describing René as 'known throughout Italy as a most noble and rich lord'.[122] Absent from his story is René's involvement in Swiss diplomacy, a description of how he managed his various fiefs, or any details about his role in Valdostano politics. More than earlier writers, though, Vescovi attempted to explore René's personality and inward dilemmas. After his first wife had 'cuckolded the good Count without him knowing or realizing it', the Count, then in Paris, 'moved by a noble shame, pretended to be ill so as not to appear in public', until he learned of her death.[123] He returned to the valley 'without wanting to hear the *Gaspardona* mentioned'.[124] René grew in fortitude from this experience, so that, in 1536, he 'did not lose spirit' but remained faithful to Charles III.[125] Likewise, when Philiberte absconded in 1557, René was able to 'sustain and digest the sorrow and affront' but failing to be reconciled with her after she returned to the valley, 'caring no more for his wealth or titles, as if out of his mind, he retired to Ambronay [...] wishing to pass the rest of his life far from home, brooding'.[126] Vescovi portrayed René as a melancholic *par excellence*, a man who 'had no light-heartedness or happiness in his life, despite holding the highest honors, being very wealthy, well-esteemed, and considered as a prince by everyone, including foreigners'. René was more of a 'man of state and government' than a soldier, 'prudent, and of few words'.[127]

Over the centuries, there have been various assessments of René's political, diplomatic, and military abilities. Pierre Lambert de La Croix described the Duke's displeasure with René's performance at the Payerne negotiations,

---

120   Boyvin, 526-27, 632, 658, 662, 684-88, 725.
121   For the purposes of this historiographic discussion, I refer to the Italian version of Vescovi published in the *Archivum Augustanum* rather than the French-language manuscript version in AST1.
122   Vescovi, 91-92.
123   Ibid., 83-84.
124   Ibid., 84-85.
125   Ibid., 85-86.
126   Ibid., 90-91, 93.
127   Ibid., 94.

which had led the Swiss to expect the *pays de Vaud* as security for their agreement, an interpretation of René's Swiss diplomacy that became standard.[128] Lambert was more charitable about René's role in subsequent Sabaudian diplomacy, especially during the talks at Nice involving the Pope, the King of France, and the Emperor, where Lambert gave René a leading role in easing tensions between the Nice castle garrison and Imperial authorities.[129] Boyvin offered a detailed account of a peace proposal concocted by René in discussions with the French secretary Plancy. René hoped that the plan would result in his release, but Boyvin represents it as an astutely crafted potential solution to the conflict in Europe.[130]

The nineteenth-century historian Ercole Ricotti relied on Lambert and Boyvin for René's diplomatic service,[131] mentioning his work in defense of the valley after 1536 and a few other actions serving the dynasty, dismissing his post-1559 activities as those of a weakened man.[132] The diplomatic historian Domenico Carutti, following Lambert, faulted René for the Payerne talks.[133] The Valdostano historian, priest, and patriot François-Gabriel Frutaz (1859-1922) saw René was 'a very capable negotiator' who was placed in an impossible position with respect to the Swiss prior to 1536.[134] In 1928, Carlo De Antonio added a new archival dimension to the story of René's diplomacy based on the correspondence of Giovanni Battista Dell'Isola during the mid 1550s. If Dell'Isola was an 'obstinate alarmist' and 'suspicious of everyone about everything', René's very powerful position in the valley perhaps explained the paranoia.[135] For De Antonio, family tragedies and prison experiences undoubtedly made René feel 'abandoned by everyone, so he created around himself an atmosphere of diffidence', which left him unmistakably embittered.[136] Giovanni Fornaseri was the first to read René's

---

128 *Mémoires de Pierre Lambert*, 502-3.
129 Ibid., 513-17.
130 Boyvin, 526-27, 632, 658, 662, 684-88, 725. René, a 'seigneur de marque' (658), criticized earlier peace proposals that had failed to take into account 'les consequences de l'estat, à la prosperité duquel les plus petites choses servoieint plus que les grandes' (ibid.) The Count supported a marriage between Emanuel Filibert and Marguerite, and the Duke's neutrality between France and the Habsburgs would be guaranteed 'à cause du mariage et de la proximité de ses estats, de tous costés environnés des fleurs de lis' (ibid.) due to the common knowledge that 'la maison de Savoye a tousjours prosperé tandis qu'elle s'est bien entretenue avec la France' (687).
131 Ricotti, 1: 200-1, 203.
132 Ibid., 265; ibid. 2: 286, 41, 99-100, 106, 107, 129.
133 Carutti, 275, 323.
134 Frutaz, 'Notes,' 245-46.
135 De Antonio, 175-76, 177-78.
136 Ibid., 237.

correspondence in Turin, and finally upended Lambert's interpretation, concluding that René had been shrewd and effective as a negotiator with the Swiss.[137] He placed René's career within its historical context, pushing back against historians who assigned him personal responsibility for events like the loss of Geneva and the Bernese invasion of Vaud. These events were driven by much more complex circumstances (such as economic and commercial ties that bound Geneva to the Swiss) that 'cannot be controlled by one man', he argued. At any rate, René had to operate within the constraints of religious policies established by the Duke.[138] Most recently, François-Charles Uginet highlighted the importance of personal relationships in René's career as a leader. He viewed the Count's appointment as Marshal of Savoy in 1528 as an attempt by Charles III to gratify Francis I, partly, at least. Uginet argued that René's Swiss diplomacy was strengthened by his lordship of Valangin, his knowledge of German, and his kinship tie to the Governor of Vaud (Aymon de Genève-Lullin). René never gave up his commitment to an eventual 'Sabaudian revenge against Geneva', and Uginet stressed his proximity to Charles III (crediting him with suggesting that the Duke send his son to the Imperial court) and his long relationship with Emanuel Filibert.[139]

Over the centuries, many historians also remarked on René's attitudes toward the House of Savoy, and toward his own Challant dynasty. Samuel Guichenon, seventeenth-century historiographer of the Savoy family, observed that, as Marshal of Savoy, René wielded 'a strong absolute power over military men', leading Emanuel Filibert to abolish the office after René's death.[140] Guichenon had little else to say about René's life, a discussion of which might have undermined his representation of the ruling dynasty's power. Two centuries later, Giovanni Battista Adriani stressed René's political influence among 'the few Piedmontese nobles who remained faithful to the long-suffering house of Savoy'.[141] His contemporary Gaudenzio Claretta drew attention both to Challant power and to the

---

137 Fornaseri represented the 1564 treaty of Lausanne (by which the Bernese restored Chablais, Gex, and Ternier but kept Vaud) as a replay of the 1529 decision of Payerne, which he called 'il [...] trionfo più bello' of René. In Fornaseri's view, René understood better than most the importance of instrumentalizing the religious differences between the Bernese and the Fribourgeois (xxvi-xxvii, xxviii-xxix). Arnold Biel briefly mentioned a few of René's diplomatic efforts between 1557 and 1563; see Biel, 9, 12, 18 n. 65, 26.
138 Fornaseri, xxviii-xxx, xxxiv-xxxv.
139 Uginet, 'René de Challant.'
140 Guichenon, *Histoire genealogique*, 115-16.
141 'Sanctacrucii Cardinalis Prosperi,' 686.

family's devotion to the House of Savoy. He concluded that the Duke of Savoy carefully avoided alienating René, who was 'fearsome, because he was Valdostano' and married to a formidable, politically connected second wife.[142] For Arturo Segre, the 'feudal ties' that linked the valley to René and thereby to the House of Savoy were crucial.[143] Fornaseri situated the Challant family in a European context, citing the observation that it was '"not only the most noble Valdostano house, but one of the most illustrious of Europe"'.[144]

Fornaseri's focus on historical context was also emphasized, in a different way, by Luigi Bruzzo, who seems to have been an independently wealthy, amateur historian who also wrote poetry, drama, and religious texts, and was probably a monarchist. His 1959 study of the ancestors and descendants of René and Mencia places the Count in a historical period of 'corruption' that he compared to his own postwar times. During René's life,

> all moral principles were collapsing: the Church under the assault of the Reform, the knightly spirit due to the disappearance of traditional values. [...] All this helps us to understand René de Challant, whose world was quite dissimilar from that of his heroic, knightly ancestors and more like that of today.[145]

René's political psychology differed from his ancestors' in that his goal was not to be a faithful vassal so much as to imitate kings who sought to increase their dominions at any cost: 'In all things, including the matter of his wife, René acted as a king.'[146] Bruzzo underscored René's strong religious sentiment, his devotion to the church and to the Sabaudian dynasty, and the strong reciprocal attachment linking him to the Valle d'Aosta and its inhabitants. He viewed René as a ruler of multiple, spatially discontinuous lands, showing how events in one of his lands informed his actions in another. For example, he argued that the rapid advance of the Reform in Valangin had led him to ensure that the Valdostano estates took preventative action against any religious change there. His prestige, his influence over the *Commis*, and his leadership 'rendered the duchy practically independent

---

142 Claretta, *Notizie storiche*, 17-18, 18-19, 20, 22, 197-98, 407 n. 1.
143 Segre, 'L'opera politico-militare,' 9, 11-12, 24-25. René was 'faithful', though 'perhaps without great abilities' and, toward the end of his life, 'so malcontent' that he abandoned his government, 'withdrawing to his own lands'.
144 Fornaseri, ix, citing the Abbé Henry.
145 Bruzzo, 28.
146 Ibid., 31.

and autonomous'. For Bruzzo, René both supported the House of Savoy and tirelessly advanced his own family's interests.[147]

Bruzzo probably came closer than any other historian to appreciating how René's collection of lordships, scattered from northwestern Italy to Lorraine, established him as a transregional noble operating within a European, not just Sabaudian, political context. His reflections on the moral environment of the times are idiosyncratic. But his understanding of Renaissance nobles as actors who saw themselves not in relation to an inevitably dominant state apparatus but as heads of families eager to defend ruling claims of their own, helpfully avoids anachronism. The following four chapters will explore the transregional dimension of René's activities as a Renaissance noble in Italy and beyond. Specifically, they examine the spatially distinct ways in which René's kin relations, political networks, financial activities, and practices of lordship were configured.

Bibliography

Walter Barberis, *Le armi del Principe: La tradizione militare sabauda* (Turin: Einaudi, 1988)

Ernesto Bianco di San Secondo, 'Giovanni Federico Madruzzo ambasciatore di Emanuele Filiberto,' *Studi trentini di scienze storiche* 28, 2 (1928): 103-32

Arnold Biel, *Die Beziehungen zwischen Savoyen und der Eidgenossenschaft zur Zeit Emanuel Philiberts (1559-1580)* (Basel: Helbing & Lichtenhahn, 1967)

Andrea Boldù, 'Relazione della Corte di Savoia' (12 December 1561), in *Relazioni degli ambasciatori veneti al Senato*, ser. 2, vol. 1, ed. Eugenio Albèri (Firenze: Tipografia all'insegna di Glio, 1839), pp. 401-70

François Boyvin du Villars, *Mémoires*, in *Choix de chroniques et mémoires sur l'histoire de France*, ed. J.A.C. Buchon (Paris: Librairie Charles Delagrave, 1884)

Luigi Bruzzo, *Ascendenti e discendenti di Renato di Challant e di sua moglie Mencia di Portogallo* (Genoa: Giorgio di Stefano Editore, 1974 [1959])

François Capré, *Traité historique de la Chambre des comptes de Savoye* (Lyon: Chez Guillaume Barbier, 1652)

Domenico Carutti, *Storia della diplomazia della corte di Savoia*, vol. 1 (Torino: Fratelli Bocca, 1875)

Gaudenzio Claretta, *Notizie storiche intorno alla vita ed ai tempi di Beatrice di Portogallo duchessa di Savoia* (Turin: Tipografia Eredi Botta, 1863)

---

147 Ibid., 32-36.

Id., *La successione di Emanuele Filiberto al trono sabaudo e la prima ristorazione della casa di Savoia* (Torino: Eredi Botta, 1884)

Lucien Cramer, *La seigneurie de Genève et la maison de Savoie, de 1559 à 1603*, 3 vols. (Geneva: A Kündig, 1912-1950)

Carlo De Antonio, 'La Valle d'Aosta ed Emanuele Filiberto,' in *Lo stato sabaudo al tempo di Emanuele Filiberto*, ed. Carlo Patrucco, vol. 1 (Turin: Miglietta, 1928), pp. 153-237

M.L. de Charrière, 'La baronnie de Rolle et Mont-le-Vieux. Étude féodale,' *Mémoires et documents publiés par la Société d'histoire de la Suisse romande* 34 (1879): 33-122

Dictionnaire historique & biographique de la Suisse, ed. Victor Attinger, vol. 2, 'Baroffio-Équey' (Neuchâtel: Administration du Dictionnaire historique et biographique de la Suisse, 1924)

A. Dornier, *7E Titres de Familles. Repertoire Sommaire [7E3667-7E4062]* (Besançon, 1931)

Giovanni Fornaseri, *Le lettere di Renato di Challant, governatore della Valle d'Aosta a Carlo II ed a Emanuele Filiberto* (Turin: Deputazione subalpina di storia patria, 1957)

François-Gabriel Frutaz, 'Notes sur René de Challant et sur le passage de Calvin dans la Vallée d'Aoste,' *Musée neuchâtelois* 41 (1904): 242-67

http://genealogy.euweb.cz/italy/madruzzo.html, 12 November 2019

Ralph Giesey, *The Royal Funeral Ceremony in Renaissance France* (Geneva: Droz, 1960)

Samuel Guichenon, *Histoire de Bresse et de Bugey* (Lyon: Iean Antoine Huguetan and Marc Ant. Ravaud, 1650)

Id., *Histoire genealogique de la royale maison de Savoye* (Lyon: Chez Guillaume Barbier, 1660)

J.J. Hisely, *Histoire du comté de Gruyère*, vol. 2 (Lausanne: Georges Bridel, 1857)

Pierre Lambert de la Croix, *Mémoires de Pierre Lambert*, in *Monumenta Historiae Patriae edita iussu Regis Caroli Alberti Scriptorum*, vol. 1 (Turin: Regio Tipographeo, 1840)

Charles Marchand, *Charles Ier de Cossé, comte de Brissac et maréchal de France 1507-1563* (Paris: Champion, 1889)

Georges-Auguste Matile, *Histoire de la seigneurie de Valangin jusqu'à sa réunion à la directe en 1592* (Neuchâtel, James Attinger, 1852)

'Memoriale del Presidente Niccolò Balbo al Duca Emanuele Filiberto,' in Ricotti, *Storia della monarchia piemontese*, pp. 291-340

Pierpaolo Merlin, 'Il Piemonte nel sistema imperiale di Carlo V,' in *Sardegna, Spagna e Stati italiani nell'età di Carlo V*, ed. Bruno Anatra and Francesco Manconi (Rome: Carocci, 2001), pp. 265-88

François Mugnier, *La vie et les poésies de Jean de Boyssonné* (Paris: Champion, 1897)

Monica Pavesio, 'La "vie désordonnée" di Bianca Maria di Challant: dalla IV novella di Bandello *all'histoire tragique* di Belleforest,' in *I novellieri italiani e la loro presenza nella cultura europea: Rizomi e palinsesti rinascimentali*, ed. Guillermo Carrascón and Chiara Simbolotti (Turin: Accademia University Press, 2015), pp. 28-39

Ercole Ricotti, *Storia della monarchia piemontese*, vol. 1 (Firenze: G. Barbèra, 1861)

Arturo Segre, 'Emanuele Filiberto e la Repubblica di Venezia,' *Miscellanea di storia veneta*, ser. 2, vol. 7 (1901): 65-513

Id., 'L'opera politico-militare di Andrea Provana di Leynì nello Stato sabaudo dal 1553 al 1539,' *Atti della Reale Accademia dei Lincei*, 5th ser., *Classe di scienze morali, storiche e filologiche* 6 (1898): 5-123

Id., 'Il richiamo di D. Ferrante Gonzaga dal governo di Milano e sue conseguenze (1553-1555),' *Memorie della Reale Accademia delle Scienza di Torino*, 2nd ser., 54 (1904): 185-260

'Sanctacrucii Cardinalis Prosperi de vita atque rebus gestis ab anno MDXIV ad MDLXVII,' ed. with notes by G.B. Adriani, *MSI* 5 (1868): 477-992

Angelantonio Spagnoletti, *Le dinastie italiane nella prima età moderna* (Bologna: Il Mulino, 2003)

Enrico Stumpo, 'Cassiano dal Pozzo,' *DBI* 32 (1986)

Les testaments des seigneurs de Challant, ed. Orphée Zanolli, 2 vols., *Bibiothèque de l'Archivum augustanum* 3 (1974) and 9 (1979)

François-Charles Uginet, 'Louis de Châtillon,' *DBI* 24 (1980)

Id., 'René de Challant,' *DBI* 24 (1980)

Tomaso Vialardi di Sandigliano, 'Un intruso tra i testamenti di Renato di Challant: Giuseppe Tornielli di Briona, novarese,' *Studi piemontesi* 41, 1 (2012): 23-40

Vigilio Vescovi, 'Historia della casa di Challant e di Madruzzo,' ed. Lin Colliard, *Archivum Augustanum* 2 (1969): 1-118

Matthew Vester, 'The Piedmontese Restitution: Franco-Savoyard Diplomacy in 1562,' M.A. thesis, University of Virginia (1992)

Simone Weber, 'Emanuele Filiberto di Savoia e il cardinale Cristoforo Madruzzo,' *Studi trentini di scienze storiche* 28, 2 (1928): 133-72

5. Kinship and noble life

Abstract

The formal and informal political authority of René de Challant was rooted in his kin relations. He inherited titles, lands, and relationships through the ancestors of both of his parents, and through affinal kin. The territorial dimension of the connections spread from northern Italy to the transalpine Sabaudian lands, and from Iberia to the Swiss lands and the Franche-Comté. René's family interacted socially with other nobles in the Valle d'Aosta and elsewhere, consolidating their shared position as members of the elite but also engaging in sharp legal conflicts when their landed or jurisdictional interests collided.

Key words: kinship, marriage, noble sociability, law

The idea that family members were political assets for early modern nobility is taken for granted by historians. Noble diplomats, for example, depended heavily on the assistance of kin. Noble diplomatic networks were 'family firms', whose existence 'demands a more broadly-conceived notion of "the political" – one marked more by the informal social politics of families, factions, and negotiation'.[1] Cardinal Jean de Lorraine (1498-1550) was one such noble who was more than just a diplomat; he was the brother of Duke Antoine de Lorraine and Duke Claude de Guise and played a key role in holding together the fragile mosaic of jurisdictions ruled by the different branches of his family. A favorite of Francis I, he participated in Franco-Imperial conferences in Roussillon and Nice in 1538 and exemplifies the idea of the noble 'family firm'.[2] René was also part of such a family grouping that offered support in a variety of ways.

However, within noble families, there was a constant tension between individual desires and interests and the structural pressure to defend the

---

1 Williams, 48, 362-63.
2 Michon, 36.

Vester, M., *Transregional Lordship and the Italian Renaissance: René de Challant, 1504-1565.*
Amsterdam: Amsterdam University Press, 2020.
DOI 10.5117/9789463726726_CH05

well-being of the family as a whole. This operated both in terms of individual members and with respect to various branches of a kin group.³ Relations between collateral lines were like relations between brothers – these inevitably involved mutual service and solidarity, but also conflict. This was true both for noble families and for ruling dynasties: 'A dynasty was in effect a lineage, and not immune from either demographic constraints or kinship relations.'⁴ The decision by Jean-François de Mahuet to resign his high office and subordinate his 'individual desire' to his 'familial duty' was described by his historian as an example of the 'dark side of a dynastic culture'.⁵ Setting aside the question of whether contemporaries would have viewed such action as 'dark' or 'heroic', the practice of collective decision-making by family councils in early modern Europe indicates a shared understanding of the importance of the interests of the lineage. William of Orange justified his marriage to the Lutheran Anne of Saxony by noting that it conformed to '"the advice and counsel of my family"'.⁶ While few have studied relations between non-coresident members of kin groups among commoners (due to the overwhelming nature of the sources),⁷ it has been shown that some lineages might actually privilege cadet branches in the event of a problem of some sort with the elder branch.⁸ The idea of sacrificing individual interests for the sake of the whole was a powerful force in early modern noble families, even if there were family members who resisted it for the sake of other passions.

René's own marital and family relationships were most explicitly represented by Bandello and his literary successors, while Vescovi also described the personal impact of Bianca Maria's unfaithfulness and Philiberte's disrespectful behavior on the Count of Challant. Adriani's assessment was that Bianca Maria had been 'of low blood and modest lineage', and that the couple had married secretly, without obtaining proper guidance. Bianca Maria's 'unbridled and dishonest desires', and the excessive liberties granted to her by René, only made matters worse.⁹ Claretta's assessment of Mencia was that she was 'a headstrong woman with a powerful following'.¹⁰

3   Members of the Balbi family lived and worked in Genoa, Milan, Madrid, Antwerp, Alicante, Sicily, Venice, and elsewhere while preserving 'i loro riferimenti unitari' (Grendi, xiii [for quotation], xxi-xxii).
4   Nassiet, *Parenté, noblesse et États dynastiques*, 233 (for quotation), 73.
5   Lipp, 'Power and Politics,' 49-50.
6   Geevers, 'Family Matters,' 475.
7   Levi.
8   Nassiet, 'Parenté et pouvoir local.'
9   'Sanctacrucii Cardinalis Prosperi,' 674-78.
10 Claretta, *La successione*, 197-98, 407 n. 1.

Luigi Vaccarone's (1849-1902) discussion of René's life focused more on his family interests than on his service to the House of Savoy. Regarding Bianca Maria, he noted that her will of December 1525 showed that she had already broken from her husband by this date, since he was not mentioned, and she expressed a wish to be buried alongside her first husband.[11] This was irrelevant in the sense that René seized her inheritance anyway. Vaccarone also portrayed René as a subverter of Valdostano customs, claiming that Mencia had persuaded him to contravene Challant policy and local practice by obtaining permission for his daughters to inherit. René was thus accused of 'bad faith' and a desire to 'supplant the male cousins', despite his own Aymavilles branch having risen to power through agnatic inheritance. Vaccarone argued that René cherry-picked from among his family papers, 'not mentioning anything that could favor the agnates', in order to make his case to Emanuel Filibert (who had reasons of his own to gratify René).[12] Taken together, these pieces depict a noble who ruthlessly pursued his interests, either by working with custom or circumventing it.

Frutaz picked up on Vaccarone's critique, acknowledging that, while René had defended the valley effectively during the turbulent sixteenth century, he had disregarded the Challant 'family pact' regarding his daughters' inheritance, 'leading to interminable lawsuits, and the ruin of this illustrious family'. But Frutaz also recognized René's bind, given his reliance on financial help from the Madruzzo (who wanted to marry into the Challant inheritance) to pay his second ransom.[13] Bruzzo echoed Adriani's perspective about the absence of strong male guidance leading to René's first marriage, pointing that Bianca Maria was fourteen years older than the eighteen-year-old René when they married. This, combined with René's absences due to his widespread family and his official duties, led to tragedy – a situation to which René responded as a 'modern practical man', who simply kept working and then asserted his right to the Gaspardone inheritance with stoic deliberation. 'Count René did not cry over the woman who threw his name into the mud: he remained impassive. Of course he suffered as any other man would, but he never showed it.'[14] He was more attentive to the prestige of his second wife's lineage, which added royal blood to his own line, and could tie him to all of the ruling houses in Europe, including the House of Savoy.

11   Vaccarone, 'Bianca Maria di Challant,' 90-91.
12   Vaccarone, 'Le questioni di successione,' 31-32.
13   Frutaz, 'Notes,' 252-53.
14   Bruzzo, 29, 30.

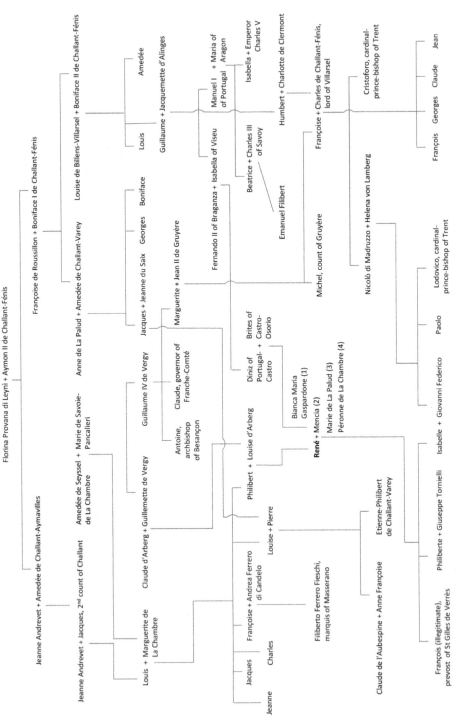

Table 1: A simplified genealogy of the Challant. Table by author.

This chapter builds upon scholarly work on noble kinship in general and René's kin relations in particular by situating kinship, noble sociability, and household management in a transregional perspective. It considers René's family in the context of interactions with other noble families, in the Valle d'Aosta and beyond. René's considerable authority in different parts of Europe did not guarantee, however, that relations with kin and other nobles remained friendly; in closing, the chapter looks at the ways in which René used the legal system to address conflict.

Kin relations

Over the course of the centuries, the Challant family had divided into several branches: the viscounts of Aosta and the lords of Cly, of Ussel, of Fénis, of Varey, of Châtillon, of Verrès and Graines, and of Aymavilles. In 1424, the head of the main line, François de Challant-Verrès, was made 'count of Challant' by the Duke of Savoy, but his death without male heirs in 1442 caused a succession dispute, which, as we have seen, was ultimately won by Jacques de Challant-Aymavilles. The Challant-Aymavilles thus became the most powerful branch of the family, even though Jacques' cousin Boniface II de Challant-Fénis was technically senior to him (the founder of the Aymavilles line was a younger brother of Boniface II's father). Jacques' son, Louis, married Marguerite de La Chambre, daughter of Aymon, in 1477. She brought a dowry of 12,000 florins.[15] Louis was a key figure in Sabaudian politics, serving as Governor of Nice during the 1480s. After he died in early 1489, his second cousin Georges de Challant-Varey, an apostolic protonotary, became the tutor for his sons. Louis's children included Philibert (René's father), Jacques (Lord of Aymavilles, Verrès, Ussel, and St. Marcel), Charles (apostolic protonotary and prior of St. Gilles[16] and St. Ours), Françoise (married to Andrea Ferrero di Candelo in 1500), Louise (married to Pierre de Challant-Varey in 1506), and Jeanne (religious at the monastery of Saint Catherine of Aosta).[17] Almost immediately, conflicts arose between Georges, the tutor, and Louis's widow, Marguerite. These seem to have been over Marguerite's claim that Louis had bequeathed Aymavilles to her.[18] In 1494,

---

15 AHR, FC 5, no. 23, 1477 marriage contract.
16 On Charles, see C. Passerin d'Entrèves.
17 For the marriage of Louise and Pierre de Challant-Varey, see AHR, FC 6, no. 5.
18 Ibid., FC 35, no. 5, ducal letter dated 4-X-1489; this letter identifies Pierre de Leschiel as the procurator of Georges de Challant.

a ducal letter declared the majority of Marguerite's second son, Jacques, Lord of Aymavilles.[19] Then, in 1508, mother and son reached an agreement over Aymavilles.[20]

Philibert de Challant, son of Marguerite and Louis, married Louise d'Arberg, daughter of Claude, and of Guillemette de Vergy, in 1502. Louise was the universal heir of her parents and brought a dowry of 15,000 florins.[21] At the time of his marriage, Philibert and his brothers were already involved in litigation with Antoine de Gingins, Lord of Divonne, over their claims to the dowry of Bonne de Gingins, widow of François de Challant.[22] Gingins seems to have contacted Marguerite to ask if she would like to join his suit against her children, and also urged her to assert her jurisdiction over the matter. An agreement between Gingins and Jacques was reached in March 1503.[23]

Meanwhile, over the course of the fifteenth century, the Challant-Fénis had acquired multiple fiefs in the *pays de Vaud* and adjacent to the counties of Romont and Gruyère. Humbert de Challant-Fénis (1460-1515) had three sons. The eldest, Gaspard, inherited Fénis; the second, Georges, became a cleric; and the third, Charles (1513-1556), married Françoise de Gruyère and inherited all his father's lands after Gaspard died in 1534. These lands included Fénis, St. Marcel, Montbreton (in Dauphiné), and a number of fiefs north of Lake Geneva, including Villarsel.[24] In accordance with a family tradition of egalitarian partibility,[25] Charles passed on these fiefs to his four sons François, Georges, Claude, and Jean.[26] However, the invasion of the *pays de Vaud* and nearby areas by the Bernese and Fribourgeois in the 1530s placed their authority in these lands at risk, increasing the incentive for the brothers to stake their claim to the lands and titles in the valley that, according to them, had been usurped by the junior Aymavilles branch in the fifteenth century.

19 Ibid., FC 28, no. 13, ducal decree of 11-IX-1494.
20 Ibid., FC 31, no. 6, transaction dated 29-VIII-08.
21 Ibid., FC 6, nos. 1-3.
22 Ibid., FC 3, no. 3, 1499-1500 litigation; see ibid., FC 5, no. 7 for the Gingins-Challant marriage contract dated 30-IV-1441. The François who married Bonne was not the first Count of Challant but seems to have been a generation or so later, perhaps a descendant of Yblet de Challant (1330-1409) by Yblet's son Pierre.
23 Ibid., FC 263, mz. 1, Anthoine de Gingins (Lord of Divonne and President of the Council of Savoie, c. 1515) to Madame de Challant, Turin 10-VI-?; ibid., FC 6, no. 4, March 1503 agreement.
24 Villarsel, le Châtelard (above Montreux), Attalens, Billens, Châtel-St-Denis, Torny-le-Grand, and Villargiroud.
25 Barbero points out that the Challant-Fénis did not begin to practice primogeniture until the seventeenth century; see 'Principe e nobiltà,' 210.
26 De Tillier, *Historique*, 289; ibid., *Nobiliaire*, 102-38.

René relied on his extended kin for support, especially early in his career. In 1517, he named his uncle Charles de Challant the 'lieutenant, governor, and administrator of his property in the Valle d'Aosta'.[27] As noted above, Charles was Philibert's brother, an apostolic protonotary, and prevost of St. Gilles from 1484 until *c.* 1520. Charles had himself been a protegé of his father's second cousin Georges, who had helped him acquire several ecclesiastical positions in the valley and elsewhere, including the priory of St. André de Bellentre in Tarentaise.[28]

The Challant-Varey branched off from the Fénis line in the early fifteenth century. As we have seen, Pierre de Challant-Varey married René's aunt Louise in 1506. In 1528, he made a donation of all his property and rights to René, reserving for himself the amount of 1,200 *scudi*.[29] Seven years later, René gave permission to Pierre to mortgage his property in order to borrow 1000 *francs* necessary for the dowry that his daughter Anne Françoise (René's cousin) brought to her marriage with the French secretary of state, Claude de L'Aubespine.[30] This marriage took place on 9 February 1536 (in the midst of the Franco-Swiss invasions). Years later, in 1561, Anne Françoise's brother Etienne-Philibert donated to René all the property on which the mortgage for his sister's dowry had been taken out.[31]

René also maintained cooperative relations with members of the Challant-Fénis line. One member of this line, a lord of Châtillon, wrote to René in the early sixteenth century about intervening on his behalf with respect to Duke Charles III.[32] Charles de Challant, mentioned above, frequently interacted with René, especially on Swiss matters. He helped René borrow money from various parties, including the King of France,[33] and acted as a financial broker and factor of sorts, transferring cash from one place to another for him.[34] In an undated letter from Varey, he wrote to René that, while God 'has sent me a ton of problems', at least they had made him 'wise enough to desire to serve my lords and relatives when they wish to make use of me'.[35] The mutually supportive relationship between Charles and René culminated

27   AHR, FC 194, no. 11, letter dated 8-VIII-17.
28   Ibid., FC 263, mz. 1, Georges de Challant to his nephew Charles, Issogne 7-I-? [early 1500s?].
29   Ibid., FC 22, no. 14, donation dated 14-III-28.
30   Ibid., FC 6, no. 9, letter dated 4-X-35; see also ibid., FC 225, no. 1.
31   Ibid., FC 103, no. 17, donation dated 21-VIII-61.
32   Ibid., FC 263, mz. 1, Châtillon to René, Nice 7-XII-?.
33   Ibid., Villarsel to René, Romont 27-VI-?.
34   AEN, AS-F16, 27, Villarsel to René, Romont 8-X-?.
35   Villarsel then related his troubles interacting with his Challant-Varey cousins and uncle; see ibid., AS-H16, 10, Charles de Challant to René, Varey 19-XI-? and Guichenon, *Histoire de Bresse*, pt. 3, 72-78.

on Christmas Eve in 1555 when the two made an agreement – Charles in his name and that of his four sons, and René in the name of his eldest daughter Philiberte – by which Charles ceded to René all of his rights of property and succession in the county of Challant and its dependencies, as well as Aymavilles, St. Marcel, Ussel, and other lands. Charles also ratified René's testament, which named Philiberte as his universal heir. For his part, René ceded to Charles his rights over Fénis and Monbreton (near Vienne) and agreed to pay Charles 20,000 *écus*.[36] It does not seem that this payment was ever effected, judging by the inheritance dispute between René's daughters and Charles' sons in the later sixteenth century.

René's relations with his paternal grandmother's family, the La Chambres, were sometimes contentious due to competing claims on his grandmother's inheritance. In 1534, he empowered Bellegarde to negotiate on his behalf with one of his La Chambre relatives (probably one of his grandmother's nephews, either Jean, Count of La Chambre, or Charles de La Chambre-Sermoyé). René made it clear that, in the property dispute at issue, he would defend his rights.[37] But René had a good working relationship with Marguerite herself. In one of his earliest letters, the eighteen-year-old René asked his grandmother to send him 'my big rope chain to do me honor at the baptism of the beautiful son that it pleased God to send us'. This was a reference not to his own son (he had only married Bianca Maria three months earlier), but to Adriano Giovanni Amedeo, the first son of Duchess Beatrice, who was born on 19 November 1522 but died two months later. It was important to René to wear this necklace at the baptism (held in Ivrea on 14 December), 'because there will be many embassies from various places and a large company of other great lords'. René also issued a receipt to Marguerite for the 'large gold chain [...] that she is keeping for us'. He also promised to send her news about a matter that he had discussed with the Duke upon her request.[38]

Interactions with René's maternal grandmother, Guillemette de Vergy, and her family seemed warmer. Guillemette named René her universal heir in her 1522 testament.[39] She effectively gave René control over her inheritance in exchange for his promise to see to her upkeep. In 1537, René noted in a letter to Bellegarde that 'Madame', which seems to have been a

---

36   AHR, FC 35, no. 10, agreement dated 24-XII-55; see also ibid., FC 31, no. 8.
37   AEN, AS-C4.2, d, René to Bellegarde, Beaufremont 15-V-34.
38   AHR, FC 260, no. 5, René to Marguerite de La Chambre, Ivrea 6-XI-22 ('jeudy appres toussaintz') and receipt dated the same day; for the baptism, see Brero, 7-8. René and Bernardino I di Savoia-Racconigi (head of a cadet branch of the dynasty) held the baby's gold-embroidered blanket at the baptism; both Bianca Maria and Mencia marched in the procession (ibid., 203, 215).
39   AHR, FC 14, no. 8, testament dated 24-V-22.

reference to his grandmother, had been asking him for money 'with her usual lamentations' – a critique that was softened by his instructions to provide her with anything that she might need.[40] He kept his grandmother updated about his activities, such as when he visited the Imperial court in 1540, and passed along the greetings of other nobles, like the Count of Gruyère.[41] Sometimes, Guillemette felt isolated, though, such as when she wrote to Prangins about her dispute with the Lord of Vaumarcus (Prangins's wife was Isabelle de Vaumarcus). 'I feel quite melancholic and unhappy at this hour', she wrote, 'because of the bad luck that has struck me suddenly, as you know'. She thus sought the help of her 'good kin and good friends'.[42] René's second cousin François de Vergy, Count of Champlitte (Guillemette's grandnephew) contacted him one May from Metz, when René was at Valangin, expressing regret about his inability to visit.[43] Another cousin Rose de Vergy wrote similarly that, if she had known that René 'was passing through this area, together with Madame my cousin [...] I would have gone to seek you along the way'.[44] Elene or Eqeme de Vergy announced to René the death of her husband in 1556, consoling herself that the deceased had had 'an end that was as beautiful as possible'.[45] Another acquaintance who lived in the vicinity of Beaufremont was Odette Lhuillier, a noblewoman whose first husband had been Louis de Stainville, Seneschal of Barrois. Odette sent René news of the marriage between her daughter Louise and Jean VII, Count of Salm, and promised to do her best to obtain for René the hunting dogs about which he had inquired.[46]

Relations with wives and children

When spouses married down, there was a risk that hypogamy would become '*mésalliance*', that is, that the social distance between the partners

---

40 AEN, AS-H16, 12, René to Bellegarde, Issogne 18-X-37.
41 Ibid., AS-G16, 23, René to Guillemette, Valenciennes 24-I-40.
42 Ibid., AS R5.10, vvv, Guillemette to Prangins, Valangin 24-VI-?.
43 AHR, FC 264, mz. 1, Francoys de Vergy to René, Metz 19-V-?. Another cousin, François's aunt Pauline de Vergy, wrote to René in 1541 about the Archbishop of Besançon (Antoine, Pauline's brother) and the visit to him by her husband (Michel de Viry) (ibid., FC 260, no. 11, Pauline de Vergy to René 'mon cousin,' Valangin 21-VIII-41). For Michel de Viry, Baron de Coppet, see De Charrière, 'La baronnie,' 78-79.
44 AEN, AS-G16, 27, Rose de Vergy to René, Champlitte 1-VII-?.
45 Ibid., AS-I16, 7, Elene/Eqeme de Vergy to René, Gye [?] 17-VI-56.
46 Ibid., AS-F16, 4, Oudete de Luliere to René, Stainville 7-III-?. On the Stainville family in the seventeenth century, see Spangler, 141.

would be unacceptably great. Sometimes daughters married down in order to maintain a balance between entering dowries (that of his wife) and exiting dowries (those of his daughters); hypogamy could be useful for the father since it permitted him to acquire clients from her affinal kin. When the model shifted toward homogamy in seventeenth-century France (as defending one's bloodline became more important), the balance was maintained by sending some daughters to convents.[47] But the possibility of varied social status within the couple raises questions about the emotional relationship between husband and wife, a theme that scholars have begun to investigate. Marriage has long been recognized as a social space in which power relations were negotiated interpersonally, socially, and symbolically,[48] but it was also a moment when a new set of shared interests was created.[49]

René's first wife, Bianca Maria, thanks to the enormous wealth inherited from her father, had a remarkable propensity to find herself in complicated situations. Her first husband, Ermes Visconti, was the second-born son of Battista Visconti di Somma. He had been intended for a clerical career but abandoned this path 'at an uncertain date, due to an extremely lucrative *mésalliance* with a stratospheric dowry of 25,000 *scudi* and a beautiful and lively young woman, daughter of a Monferrato financier'.[50] The death of Ermes in 1519 opened the door for the Gonzaga family to strengthen its ties to the Monferrato through a Gaspardone marriage.[51] In early 1522, Bianca Maria wrote to the Duke of Mantua, Federico II, about 'the negotiations initiated with the illustrious lord Sigismondo [Gonzaga di Vescovato] your cousin', thanking him for considering her.[52] She signed a subsequent letter, about ten days later, as 'Bianca Maria Gonzaga Vesconta', again expressing her happiness 'for having sought me out as kin through the contract with

47 Nassiet, *Parenté, noblesse et États dynastiques*, 142, 144-47, 148, 173.
48 Wunder.
49 Demade. See Broomhall and Van Gent for an appeal for study of how families' emotional lives and interests were intertwined. Erica Bastress-Dukehart has shown how both emotional and legal concerns drove inheritance strategy (Bastress-Dukehart). For intimate correspondence and the complexity of marriage bonds, see James, 338, 341-42.
50 Arcangeli.
51 The Paleologue rulers of Monferrato were tied to the House of Gonzaga when Marquis Guglielmo IX of Monferrato married his daughter Maria to Federico II Gonzaga in 1517. After Guglielmo died the next year, his widow Anne d'Alençon ruled as regent in the name of her young son Bonifacio. An alliance with the influential Gaspardone family would have improved the Gonzaga position in the Monferrato.
52 ASMn, Archivio Gonzaga, b. 746, cart. 15, Bianca Maria to Federico II Gonzaga, Casale 25-I-22.

the illustrious lord Sigismondo'.[53] It appears that Bianca Maria had gotten ahead of herself, however, as her remarriage had become a political issue reflecting the competition between the houses of Savoy and Gonzaga for influence over the Monferrato. Perhaps the regent Anne d'Alençon preferred René, the Sabaudian candidate, or perhaps Sigismondo himself backed out. In any event, what seems to have been Bianca Maria's first choice did not materialize.[54]

The marriage contract with René was signed on 4 August 1522. It stipulated a dowry of 25,000 ducats, which was secured on property in Frassineto, Guardapasso, San Salvatore, and Occimiano for 9000 ducats; on St. Maurizio for 2000; on Verolengo for 3000; and in Casale for 10,000.[55] On the same day, Bianca Maria signed an instrument naming René as her procurator; in it, she was identified as the daughter of Jacobi Gaspardone 'citizen of Casale and counselor and treasurer-general of the marquisate'.[56] Following the marriage, Bianca Maria brought from Casale to Ivrea (where she apparently resided, at least temporarily) an amount of jewelry, clothing, and household items whose inventory was eight pages long. These included emeralds, pearls, gold rings, rubies, diamonds, sapphires, *jacynto*, gold bracelets and necklaces (some with 'circles for holding perfume'), gold hems, 'a gold crown with a gold apple at the end for hoding perfume', 'a gold image of the Annunciation' to wear on a hat, 21 pairs of gold *pontali*, a black crown, a white alabaster crown, and eighteen small gold *paternostri*. There were also silver serving bowls, cups, salt holders, knives, and spoons; gold coins, and 73 gold clothing fasteners. She had a number of dresses (crimson satin with 85 *gropoi d'oro*, black satin with fourteen pairs of gold *pontali*, white with gold thread, purple velours with wolf's fur, a white wool dress with gold thread, a damask robe with gold thread, a crimson velours robe, a crimson satin robe, a black satin dress '*a la Portughesa*', a gray velours dress, and a black damask dress with gold thread) and petticoats of white and green damask, along with overcoats and capes of white and black damask, and a coat of white fabric with a crimson velours hood. The inventory also listed linens, towels, napkins, tablecloths, bedsheets, bedcovers, various pieces of fabric, 'an *officio* of the Madonna covered with crimson satin with shapes and buttons of gold-plated silver',

---

53 Ibid., Casale 2-II-22.
54 Rosselli.
55 AST1, PD 188, f. 242, 246, marriage contract of Bianca Maria, dated 4-VIII-22. See also ibid., f. 243, for a different dowry structure.
56 Ibid., ff. 254-56, instrument of Bianca Maria naming René as her procurator, dated 4-VIII-22. A month earlier, Bianca Maria had given her Calamandrana property to the convent and friars of Santa Croce of Casale (AHR, FC 17, no. 18, donation dated 9-VII-22).

twelve beds and a mattress, tin plates, six candleholders, leather chairs, wooden stools, washbasins, bedcushions, bed warmers, and bedpans.[57]

In April 1523, Bianca Maria named as her procurators (with René's consent) Eusèbe Gamache (Castellan of St. Marcel) and Raphael de Dugnano of Milan.[58] About three weeks after her husband was captured at Pavia (24 February 1525), Bianca Maria's procurator farmed all of her property in Nizza Monferrato and Calamandrana to Laurent and Antoine de Bogiis for 90 *scudi*, perhaps as part of René's ransom payment.[59] The subsequent efforts made by René's agents, such as Giovanni Battista Royer (Roero?) to manage Bianca Maria's inheritance created friction with members of her family. Royer wrote from Ternavasso to 'the magnificent sister-in-law and sister Madonna Margarita Gaspardona'[60] in Casale, about efforts by these family members to seize control of this property.[61] On another occasion, Margarita invited Royer and his wife, Elena, to come visit her, but they were unable to do so without 'a great burden and shame', since Elena 'as a sister-in-law and niece is in mourning with her kin'. But, if Margarita could come keep Elena company, it would be a 'great pleasure and honor'.[62]

René's attitudes toward his wife and relatives were, to some extent, reflected in the first will that he left as a nineteen-year-old, prepared as he was about to leave Issogne to go to war with Francis I against the Duke of Milan. He left to his grandmother Marguerite her dowry, his property in Ussel and St. Marcel, the 'tower and farm of San Stefano' in Pinerolo, all his property in the diocese of Aosta, and the usufruct of the castles of Châtillon and Issogne, together with their revenues. To Guillemette, he left the usufruct of Valangin and Beaufremont. To Bianca Maria, he left 1,300 *écus*, her own dowry, clothes, jewels, and moveable property, and the lifetime usufruct of all of his jewelry, clothes, silverware, and moveable property. He also gave her six each of a variety of silver table items. Gaspard de Challant-Fénis and his brother Charles, Lord of Villarsel, received a cash payment (amount unclear), while his aunt Françoise de Challant (wife of Andrea Ferrero, Lord of Masserano and mother of Filiberto Ferrero Fieschi, Marquis of Masserano) received 1000 *écus*. All of his other property would go to his son born of Bianca Maria, and, if there were no male heirs, his

---

57 AST1, PD 188, ff. 238-39, 249-50, 'La descriptione e inventario [...],' dated Ivrea 29-XII-22.
58 Ibid., f. 243, document dated 28?-IV-23.
59 AHR, FC 110, no. 12, farm contract dated 20-III-25.
60 Margherita degli Inviziati, Bianca Maria's mother?
61 AHR, FC 264, mz. 1, Jo. Baptista Royer [Roero?] to 'la mag'ca cugnata et sorella Madona Margarita Gaspardona, in Casale,' Ternavasso 2-VII-?.
62 Ibid., same to same, Asti 2-II-?.

universal heir would be Jean de Challant-Varey, 'his first cousin by blood'. If he had daughters, each would receive 10,000 *scudi* for dowries.[63]

René's second marriage was contracted on 7 January 1528 in the presence of the Duke's brother, Philippe de Savoie-Nemours, 'in the private room of the Infanta Beatrice of Portugal'.[64] This union with Mencia was greatly desired by Duchess Beatrice, who had married Charles III in 1521. Mencia's grandmother Isabella of Viseu was the sister of King Manuel I, father of the Duchess of Savoy, making them first cousins once removed. René's marriage to Mencia was accompanied by a variety of gifts and privileges offered by the Duke and Duchess of Savoy.[65] Surviving correspondence does not shed much light on the nature of the emotional relationship between René and Mencia. They wrote each other occasionally, giving news about their health and about other family members. René expressed confidence, upon hearing that Mencia was improving from a recent illness, that 'with God's and the doctors' help you will soon be back on your feet, as well as ever, if spring comes soon and you take care of yourself'. A stoic demeanor on the part of René was also expressed when he reacted to the news that a certain 'Annibal' (perhaps René's uncle, illegitimate son of Louis de Challant), had been captured by corsairs, by observing laconically that 'one must praise God in everything, and that his health and honor are preserved' and hoping that Annibal's uncle the Cardinal would be able to ransom him. In response to Mencia's wish to go away (from the valley, where she was?), René insisted that the danger would soon pass and that 'the truce will soon be general and widespread', without many more comforting words of reassurance.[66]

René's eldest child seems to have been his illegitimate son, François. Several scholars have indicated the ways in which illegitimate children could play important political roles in noble families.[67] Bastards were liminal members of families but potentially important assets.[68] François received a dispensation in December 1536 from the Bishop of Aosta enabling him to receive his 'first tonsure'.[69] Fifteen years later, the Bishop of Ivrea granted François entry to the 'order of acolytes'.[70] After becoming prevost of St. Gilles in 1544, François acquired authority over a vast array of property and rights in

63 AST1, PD 188, ff. 274-81, René's will, dated 10-IX-23.
64 AHR, FC 6, no. 7, contract dated 7-I-28.
65 AST1, PD 203, ff. 8, 15, 17, 33v, 7/8-I-28 acts in favor of Mencia.
66 AHR, FC 263, mz. 1, René to Mencia, s.l., s.d.
67 See Oresko; Coolidge, '"A Vile and Abject Woman",' 197, 201.
68 Byars; Van Steensel, 'Kinship, Property, and Identity,' 255; Bestor, 554-55, 559, 580.
69 AHR, FC 65, no. 9, dispensation dated 23-XII-36.
70 Ibid., FC 65, no. 15, permission dated 21-V-51.

the valley, including in the castellany of Cly.⁷¹ There are a handful of mentions of François in conjunction with René's fief of Virieu (see below), but few other references to him remain. An outstanding question concerning François is why René does not seem to have attempted to have him legitimated and made his legal heir. One story has it that Mencia convinced François that his father wanted him to take holy orders before returning from one of his trips to Flanders, and that the youth was thus ordained before the father had the opportunity to try to have him legitimated.⁷² Other possibilities, however, are that René judged François incapable of being an effective family leader, or that the Count wanted his son to construct his own ecclesiastical power base in order to complement the family's temporal authority.

The marriage negotiations for René's daughters and the circumstances of their marriages have been outlined above. In concluding this discussion of René's kin relations, it is helpful to place René's inheritance challenges in a broader historiographic context. Scholars have recognized that inheritance regimes and marriage practices varied across Europe and even within particular regions.⁷³ This variety was due in part to the contradictory goals faced by noble families: they wanted to provide for all of their children, but they also wanted to see their family name continue. Alongside the structural tensions in family interests was another dialectic between customary norms and lived practice. A family's decisions in the areas of inheritance or marriage alliance depended on their economic and demographic situations, or on moments in individual life cycles. Jérôme-Luther Viret has concluded that norms and practices largely coincided in these matters, rejecting the argument of Bernard Derouet that different juridical systems nonetheless resulted in similar forms of property transmission.⁷⁴ For Viret, customs grew out of 'the daily social practice of country people'. He goes so far as to refer to these customs as the '"natural law" of peasants, opposed to positive law'.⁷⁵ In some parts of France, one could act contrary to custom

71   Ibid., FC 116, no. 14, acts of possession-taking of two meadows dated 25-V-59; P.-E. Duc, 188-89. In 1564, François urged his father to act on his behalf on a privilege related to St. Gilles, before it elapsed (AHR, FC 260, François to René, 17-VII-64).
72   Vescovi, 93-94. Vescovi also identifies a second bastard son named Claude (ibid.)
73   Van Steensel, 'Nobility Identity and Culture;' Delille, 'Représentation,' 147. Delille raises the interesting question of what European society would look like if one followed only feminine lines of descent, stressing that official representations of families often differed from actual alliance patterns (147) and masked the continual redefinition of kinship networks (157).
74   Élie Haddad, 'Faire du mariage,' 74; see also Van Steensel, 'Kinship, Property, and Identity,' 247-48.
75   Cited in Haddad, 'Faire du mariage,' 75. Haddad and others think that customary statutes came from towns, not the countryside.

in marriage contracts, giving families 'a real latitude in organizing the devolution of a part of their patrimony'. Parisian customs also gave families significant flexibility in inheritance questions, though certain social norms still provided boundaries.[76]

Such exceptions might have been occasioned by fathers' wishes that their daughters inherit their lands and titles, as was the case with René. There were various grounds on which an argument for female inheritance could be based, even if it contravened local customs. One operative legal principle was that of 'equity', which suggested that a higher principle of justice might require the law to be adjusted in a given case. This was frequently invoked in supplications to princes.[77] Princes sometimes granted exemptions for customary inheritance law to help nobles keep their estates together and enable all their children to live nobly.[78] The Renaissance dukes of Milan claimed a 'plenitude of power' enabling them 'to override any particular law when the need arose'.[79] During the Renaissance, the Visconti, Trivulzio, and Borromeo families practiced partible inheritance, but, in the absence of male heirs, the female daughters of the last legitimate male heir could inherit. In exceptional cases, women were even designated as heirs.[80] Elsewhere in Italy (Naples, for example), Lombard and Frankish customs of dowries substituting for inheritance portions could complicate efforts to pass fiefs on to women.[81] But, to return to the general problem of the degree to which customs or norms determined inheritance practices, these exceptions point toward the conclusion that contingencies (mainly political context and immediate family needs), rather than structures, governed behavior in most cases.[82]

Nobles and domestic life

René's family papers also offer various insights into interactions among nobles in the Valle d'Aosta and his own domestic life. The Challant were

76 Ibid., 79 (for quotation), 78, 88.
77 J. Shaw, 55-56.
78 Van Steensel, 'Kinship, Property, and Identity.'
79 Black, 1.
80 Arcangeli notes that the rulers of Milan favored partibility, since it prevented the emergence of strong noble rival dynasties but that 'una società politica fatta di agnazioni scarsamente dinastizzate poneva troppe richieste alle limitate possibilità del patronage principesco'.
81 J. Shaw, 14, 17.
82 Gérard Delille insists that general rules for kinship remained; see 'La France profonde,' 912-13. Sandro Guzzi-Heeb views alliance patterns non-structurally, in terms of social and political networks; see Guzzi-Heeb.

at the center of a news network by which the valley nobility learned from and informed each other. In an undated letter, one Challant official passed along to Mencia the regards of Gabriel de La Tour, and those of 'madame the wife of the Bailiff Lostan', who had just given birth to a baby boy. He also gave news of Jean François Vaudan and his wife Nycoline, who was pregnant. Unable to obtain a certain 'work' from Mademoiselle de La Croix, he enlisted the assistance of Castellamonte.[83] In June 1539, the Bailiff of Aosta, Roz Favre (father-in-law of Vaudan), wrote to René that his daughter Nycoline 'had a beautiful baby boy on Saturday the last of May' and that mother and baby were doing well.[84] Guichard passed along word to René that, while waiting in Milan, he had sent the secretary Cavet away and was lodging with Geronimo Cattaneo in the room of the treasurer Carrà, who had gone to Nice.[85] The Lord of Chevron kept René abreast of his sister's marriage plans,[86] and René Lostan reported to Mencia about a group of 'Burgundian nobles' who passed through the valley.[87] Examples of this kind of information-sharing could be multiplied. Correspondents obviously considered it important to share information about family developments and social contacts between members of the nobility.

Nobles and elites frequently cooperated with each other, lending each other money, hunting together, having meals together, and even sharing each other's servants. In 1540, Louis de Vallesa asked René's permission to use Fagnano as his representative in Mantua, where Fagnano was going soon, to see the Gonzaga duke. Vallesa took the opportunity to update René on his affairs in the Monferrato and the Valle d'Aosta.[88] During the same years, the Lord of Chevron suggested that his brother's teacher might be a good tutor for Challant's illegitimate son, François.[89] On the other hand, as one might expect, conflicts divided the nobility in every possible direction. In 1540, Louis de Vallesa urged Challant's secretary Grandis to avoid contact with the nephew of Bellegarde (René's Governor of Valangin), Nicolas (who was then at court), in order to avoid a repeat of the outburst between them that had recently occurred in Aosta.[90] The Castellan of Bard reported some kind

83 AHR, FC 263, mz. 1, a Challant official [at Casale?] to Mencia [?], s.l., s.d., [c. 1540].
84 AEN, AS-H16, 20, Roz Favre to René, Aosta ?-VI-39; De Tillier, *Nobiliaire*, 256-60.
85 AHR, FC 264, mz. 1, Gichar [?] to René, Milan 20-XII-42 [?].
86 Ibid., FC 263, mz. 1, Chevron to René, Gye, 3-IX-?.
87 Ibid., FC 264, mz. 1, Lostan to Mencia [?], Aosta 2-X-?.
88 Ibid., FC 260, Louis de Vallesa to Grandis, Ivrea 1-IV-40.
89 Ibid., FC 263, mz. 1, Chevron to René, Gye, 3-IX-?.
90 Ibid., FC 260, Louis de Vallesa to Grandis, Ivrea 1-IV-40.

of dispute between the noble Philibert Mistralis and Jehan de Rua; there had been reports that a compromise had been reached between them, but Mistralis was appealing the case to the Duke.[91]

Undoubtedly, many of these disputes had to do with money. Nobles in and around the Valle d'Aosta frequently lent each other money, or owed money to each other for various reasons. Sometimes money was owed for fiscal purposes, like the sixteen-florin debt that Lady Margherita Montalto owed to René for her part of a subsidy.[92] Sometimes, nobles like René owed money to their officers, such as the 45 *écus* that René owed to Guillaume Vulpin of Villara in 1551 for almost three years' worth of unpaid service. By October 1551, René had paid Vulpin back all but seven *écus*.[93]

Among this group of nobles, credits and debts were often tied to clothing purchases. René's grandmother Marguerite apparently borrowed eight *écus* from Sebastiano Ferrero, Bishop of Ivrea, for silk that the Bishop delivered to Marguerite's sons.[94] Eusèbe Gamache entered ten florins, six *gros* into his accounts for the purchase of five and a half *rups* of black satin in 1524.[95] When Granyer asked to borrow money from Ludovico Davalle in Casale, he also asked for 'a high Spanish collar'.[96] René sent Jeronimo Fagnano to find black velvet for him in Milan in 1537 and thence to Cuneo or Nice to try to borrow money.[97] In July 1540, Mencia promised to repay her secretary Aynard Sappin, who delivered 195 *aulnes* of fabric from Autun (Burgundy) to her. The material cost ten *sols* per *aulne*. She also agreed to pay her servant Collini four *écus* for having transported it from Autun to Beaufremont, and to settle the combined account of 105 *livres* 10 *sols* by Epiphany 1541.[98] An undated letter to a Countess of Challant identified a variety of expensive clothing items in her chests, including Flemish cloth with gold and silver

---

91   Ibid., FC 263, mz. 1, Castellan of Bard to René, 5-X-?. For a conflict between the Baron of Vallesa and his son-in-law, Alardet, see ibid., FV 295, mz. 1, Baron de Vallaise to 'Monsieur mon cousin Mons'r de la Bone [?] Mons'r Leonard cez la tent [?]' [back of letter reads 'la l're de Mons' de la Court mandee par mons'r le baron'] Aosta 3-IX-?.

92   Ibid., FC 263, mz. 1, Gamache to René, Ivrea 8-IV-?.

93   AEN, AS-I16, 8, notes signed by René dated 25-VII-51 and 12-X-51.

94   AHR, FC 263, mz. 1, La Chambre to his sister [Marguerite de La Chambre, grandmother of René, wife of Louis de Challant], Chamox 22-IV-?.

95   Ibid., FC 172, no. 11, 1526 accounts of Eusèbe Gamache.

96   Ibid., FC 263, mz. 1, Granyer to Ludovico Davalle (in Casale), Aymavilles 25-X-?.

97   Ibid., FC 260, no. 7, Jeronimo Fagnano to René, Vercelli, Feast of the Ascension [V-19?] 1537.

98   AEN, AS-H16, 30, receipt issued by Mencia to Aynard Sappin, a secretary, Beaufremont 12-VII-40.

thread, scarlet silk velvet, etc.[99] In the early 1540s, a servant named Guichard was sent to Milan to look for

> four arms of velours [...] and six of taffeta, two of the finest *estamet* that could be had, and a velours hat, two pairs of velours shoes, and your sword well sharpened and your belt which is already quite dirty, which is why I thought that I should send you another one of simple velours.[100]

From Casale in 1542, Fagnano promised René that he would bring Mencia's 'slippers' with him when he came to see them.[101] In 1554, when Mencia was in the midst of efforts to raise money to pay for René's ransom, Alessandro Olgiato wrote to her from Vercelli to discuss fabric and a vase that he had purchased for her and Philiberte.[102] After he was released from captivity, René received news from the secretary, Perret, about some fabric in which he was interested, which cost six florins per *aulne*.[103]

The costly clothing worn by the Challant, their servants, and other nobles in the valley obviously distinguished them from members of other social groups and from each other. Nobles and elites interacted in a variety of social settings in which one's clothes could set one apart. One year at Carnival, a lord named Panthaleon (Vaudan?) and his wife held a 'great banquet', attended by Monsieur d'Avise, Monsieur Anthoine (Vallesa?), Lady Marguerite (Vallesa's wife?), and Monsieur Francoys (René's son?). After dinner, 'they all retired together in a room where they had a long discussion'.[104] In November 1541, René sent Castellamonte to the Sabaudian court to discuss some business on his behalf with the Duke. Castellamonte was also to invite the Prince of Piedmont to come and 'visit this district, and to have some recreation by watching the horses run across the mountains, where you can really wear yourself out before catching them'.[105] Writing from across the Alps one summer, René lamented the heat and his sunburn, and expressed his wish to return to the valley 'where the women are'. He

---

99 AHR, FC 263, mz. 1, ? to [Countess of Challant?], s.d.
100 Guichard's language suggests that some of these items had previously been pawned; he noted that, while in Milan, he also asked the armorer to 'accoustrer votre harnois' (ibid., FC 264, mz. 1, Gichar [?] to René, Milan 20-XII-42 [?]).
101 Ibid., FC 263, mz. 1, Hieronimo da Fagnano to René, Casale 21-X-42 [?].
102 Ibid., FC 260, Alessandro Olgiato to Mencia, Vercelli 30-V-54.
103 AEN, AS-H16, 19, Perret to René, Antwerp 21-VI-56. For more on René's moveable property, see Frutaz, 'L'inventaire.'
104 AHR, FC 263, mz. 1, Gamache to René, Bard 7-II-?.
105 Fonaseri, 100-1, René to EF, Issogne 16-XI-41.

also instructed his 'head waiter' to pay three *écus* for 'the portrait that he made' and to give it to Mencia.[106] Gambling was another important social activity for René and other valley nobles. René played while serving the Duke in Vercelli and in other places,[107] and, on one occasion, his officer Granyer asked a contact in Casale to have his 'dagger' sent back to him, lamenting the fact that he had lost eighteen *écus* while gambling with the treasurer Fontavel and the *escuyer* Bellegarde.[108] After the Sabaudian restoration, a household account identified nobles and elites who had passed through, dined, or stayed at Issogne in 1561. These included the Colonel Lostan, Friar Bonaventure, a fiscal official named Lucas, Pierre Foldon, the Castellan Chandiou, Mathieu Lostan, 'Monsieur Roncax', the Prevost of St. Gilles and a monk from Verrès, the Lord and Lady of La Tour, and Bartod L'Aliod.[109] In May 1561, the Duke of Savoy himself visited the valley and stayed at Châtillon; Isabelle seems to have been pregnant, indisposed, and unable to host the ducal suite at Issogne. If Philiberte were at Châtillon at the time and played hostess to Emanuel Filibert in her sister's stead, this might help explain his subsequent positive disposition toward her.[110]

Along with banquets, gambling, and visits, hunting was a social activity through which valley nobles expressed their status. In 1539, René boasted to Charles III that 'I am a good hunter, especially of deer'. 'And to remove any doubt', he wrote, 'I put together a barrel of boar's meat, knowing that you like it'.[111] Hunting also meant maintaining stables of horses, kennels of hounds, and birds of prey. Castellamonte took René's dog Constantin and two other small dogs that the Castellan of Verrès had given him to his residence of Castellamonte in 1539. His nephew, 'who is the best in the country at breeding dogs', was raising a hunting dog there and planned to breed puppies for René. His nephew was also feeding a *levrier* and a *levrière*, who were born of the *levrière* who was still at Verrès, and they were 'very beautiful but look more like mastiffs than greyhounds'.[112] A few years later, Chevron updated René on his hunting dogs and about the horse of Grandis, which they planned to send from Gruyère.[113] A positive report was received

---

106 AEN, AS-I16, 3, René to Tolleni (procurator-general in Savoie), Conflans 1-VIII-?.
107 AHR, FC 65, no. 13, 1549-1552 register listing René's gambling profits.
108 Ibid., FC 263, mz. 1, Granyer to Ludovico Davalle (in Casale), Aymavilles 25-X-?.
109 AEN, AS-I16, 14, account from Issogne, by nephew of the person responsible (Generiis, who was at Aymaville?), 11-XI-61.
110 Ibid., 13, accounts of Lescha for Châtillon for 1560.
111 Fornaseri, 98-99, René to Ch III, Virieu 9-IX-39.
112 AEN, AS-K16, 20, Castellamonte to René, 8-V-39.
113 AHR, FC 263, mz. 1, Chevron to René, Gye [Savoie] 3-IX-?.

by René in January 1548 from one of his officials in Valangin about his herd of horses there.[114] A few years earlier, Le Bretton had sent a falcon or a hawk from Valangin across the Alps to René. Unfortunately, as René subsequently wrote to Bellegarde, the bird 'was beautiful but died on the way, on this side of the mountains'.[115]

The western Alps, including the Valle d'Aosta, was a dangerous region during most of René's adult life, and not just for birds. Even aristocrats and their officers took their lives into their own hands when they traveled between the valley, Monferrato, Piedmont, and Lombardy during the Franco-Habsburg wars. One of René's officials wrote to Mencia in around 1540 about leaving Casale to go to Fontaneto to try to obtain cash from Filippo Maria Visconti. He was between Romagnano and Gattinara when he met 'an innkeeper from Busto Arsizio' who made him turn around 'because of bandits who were a mile away from there'. These exiles comprised a group of about 50 horses and soldiers. The innkeeper had been captured by them, but, since he had given supper to one of them one night and lent a *teston* to them, they let him go. The innkeeper also reported having seen fifteen dead people 'in the woods and so many weapons that they would not fit in a room' and had also seen them kill 'two merchants'. At that point, the officer turned around, thanking 'God and Our Lady' and went back to 'Gayanin' and then Masserano. The Lord of Candia (Candelo?) did not want him to leave 'because of the bandits around there'.[116]

As dangerous as traveling through war zones could be, the greatest threat to health and safety experienced by René and other sixteenth-century people was illness. René fell gravely ill at numerous points in his life. In 1530, he reassured the Duke of Savoy that he was feeling better after 'my illness, so that I now take air regularly and the doctor ordered me to change it'. He planned to leave Virieu the next day to go 'to the mountains, to see how I feel'. While there, 'I will have my people hunt, because I still feel too weak to do so myself, and whatever we take (or that which we took before I fell ill) we will keep for when you come, or will send it to wherever you would like'.[117] The only recourse that nobles like René had was to seek care from doctors with good reputations. In 1540, someone in René's household was ill and the attending physician, who was from Moncalieri, needed a

---

114   AEN, AS-K16, 19, Valangin officer to René, s.d. [I-48?].
115   Ibid., AS-H16, 17, 17a, René to Bellegarde, Ivrea 26-IX-45. For more on hunting with birds, see Kettering, *Power and Reputation*, 28-30.
116   AHR, FC 263, mz. 1, a Challant official [at Casale?] to Mencia [?], s.l., s.d., [c. 1540].
117   Fornaseri, 74-75, René to Ch III, Virieu 11-VIII-30.

remedy that was not available in the valley. However, neither the doctor nor Castellamonte was willing to cross the mountains to bring back the medicine.[118] The secretary Pierre Ducrest wrote to Lescha, 'my good and honest brother', in September 1560, shortly before he died. He thought that his fever was gone, but his illness had returned. 'I will no longer keep this diet and abstinence that has been imposed on me', he wrote, 'but will take the air bit by bit and when I am a bit better will go seek the best of my health by visiting my lady', the countess of Challant. He and his wife commended themselves to 'our mistresses [Philiberte and Isabelle] and the entire company' and to Lescha and his wife.[119]

Somewhat surprising is how infrequently the Challant records refer to religious devotion. In his will of 1523, René stated his desire to be buried in the Franciscan convent of Aosta and set aside 300 *écus* to pay for his transport there, were he to die 'on this side of the mountains'. If, however, he were to die 'across the mountains', he wanted to be buried in the collegial church of Valangin. He also left money for funeral masses, for the convent of St. Gilles in Verrès, for the dowries of poor girls, and for the hospitals of Aosta, Châtillon, Verrès, and Bard.[120] In 1540, an officer reported to Mencia that the Mass that she had arranged was being said every day 'here at Notre Dame [of Aosta, the cathedral]', and that the priest at Aymavilles was doing the same. Clerics in both places were also praying for Mencia 'and for my lord and my mistresses'.[121] Following Mencia's death in September 1558, René lamented that, in her, the Duke of Savoy had lost 'a very humble and obedient servant, who desired nothing more in this world than to see you in your states. She prayed for this restoration and had others pray continuously to our Lord by devout people who were totally dedicated to spiritual things'.[122] Aside from other occasional references to people praying for each other, the faith of René and those around him was not a frequent topic of conversation in written records. It is also possible that these were matters about which people spoke in person, or that were important but taken for granted, and thus not openly discussed. It is also possible that René and his circle (possibly excepting Mencia) were just not very spiritually minded.[123]

One way to try to construct an intellectual history of René de Challant would be through an examination of his library. The inventory performed at

118 AHR, FC 263, mz. 1, a Challant official [at Casale?] to Mencia [?], s.l., s.d., [c. 1540].
119 AEN, AS-K16, 9, Ducrest to Lescha 'mon bon et honneste frere,' Aosta ?-IX-60.
120 AST1, PD 188, f 274-81, René's will, dated 10-IX-23.
121 AHR, FC 263, mz. 1, a Challant official [at Casale?] to Mencia [?], s.l., s.d., [c. 1540].
122 Fornaseri, 139-40, René to EF, Novara 8-IX-58.
123 For lists of religious objects at Issogne, see Frutaz, 'L'inventaire,' 219-20, 243-47.

Issogne following his death in 1565 indicates that he had around 90 books, including 24 in French, 24 in Spanish, and the remainder in other languages. These included Bartolus and a variety of law books, *Lancelot of the Lake*, Petrarch's *Sonnets* (presumably, in French), Petrarch's *Triumphs*, Cicero's rhetoric, Quintilian's *Institutes*, Cicero's letters, a book on architecture, a book of French royal statutes, a Latin vocabulary, *Amadis de Gaule* and *Galeanus de Grecia* (both in Spanish), and Livy.[124] Of course, it is difficult to know which of these works were acquired by René, which by his wife and daughters, and which were inherited – not to mention whether they were read or used. Judging by his surviving correspondence, it appears that René's identity expressed itself more through governance and martial activities than through reflection, perhaps partly due to an unconscious appropriation of contemporary ideas about masculinity.

In recent years, just as scholars of early modern dynasticism have pointed to the important role of women in noble families, other historians have also benefited from insights in gender studies in order to show how practices of masculinity contributed to the formation of a noble identity. In their work on early modern Spanish nobles, Elizabeth Lehfeldt and Grace Coolidge have examined models of masculinity for different social groups and over a long chronological period. Such models could be contradictory, though: military valor, moderation, and sexual restraint were important for nobles,[125] but, among the high nobility, both men and women could have sexual affairs without a loss of social status (though this was riskier for women than for men).[126] Mistresses, writes Coolidge, 'occupied a flexible moral space in the Spanish patriarchy' and could use status, child-bearing ability, and the legal system to maneuver for themselves and affect their lovers' families.[127] Other scholars have linked different periods in the life cycle to masculinity. Acting boyishly could connote femininity for nobles, as could being raised exclusively by women, as opposed to a more balanced boyhood that involved 'competition with other young males in the venues of drinking, violence, and sexual exploits'.[128] Male honor was often tied to one's parental authority

---

124 Ibid., 234. See Colliard; also see Zanotto for printing practices in the valley as a whole. Giulio Romero Passerin d'Entrèves and Paulette Taieb are currently engaged in a larger project, *Bibliothèques Nobiliaires Valdôtaines* (https://www.taieb.net/bnv/page11.html, 12 November 2019), a digital mapping effort to identify and locate the dispersion of books and archives belonging to the early modern Valdostano nobility.
125 Lehfeldt.
126 Coolidge, '"A Vile and Abject Woman".'
127 Ibid., 196; also id., 'Contested Masculinity.'
128 Koabel, 599.

and ability to manage dependents, although Sandra Cavallo has shown that expectations in these respects could differ across Europe.[129]

But the proper management of one's estates and family was generally accepted as a key element of noble masculinity.[130] Perhaps more than any other practice, hunting on one's estates exemplified nobility for a male lord[131] – as we have seen, it was of great importance to René de Challant. Sharon Kettering's discussion of the importance of hunting with birds in the relationship between the Duke of Luynes and Louis XIII offers a more nuanced view of hunting and masculinity. Luynes served as the King's falconer, and, for Kettering, this tells us something about the Duke's character. 'A falconer had to be patient, good-tempered, shrewd, and inventive with keen eyesight, sharp hearing, a strong voice, and a habit of sleeping lightly in order to hear his birds at night if they became agitated. [...] Patience and intelligence, [...] [and] reliability and gentleness' were also necessary. Noting a difference between these traits and the warrior-like character stressed in other works on nobility, Kettering wondered if the falconer's temperament was viewed as 'unmanly and weak'.[132] It seems more likely that noble masculinity was more complicated than many accounts would have it, and that perception of it changed over time, varied from place to place, and was not even necessarily uniform at a given time and place.[133]

Something about which René and his aristocratic contemporaries did feel strongly was honor. This concern took a variety of forms. René made sure, following the birth of his second daughter, Isabelle, in 1530, that the Duchess of Savoy, Beatrice, would be willing to serve as her godmother, since this redounded not only to the honor of his daughter, but to his own.[134] Later that same year, while serving as Marshal of Savoy in Chambéry, he was happy to extend a warm reception to the 'Count Hermont and the English ambassadors'. This honor was compounded by the Duke's invitation to 'show them the Holy Shroud', located in the Sainte-Chapelle of the castle (two years later, a fire in the chapel would damage the Shroud).[135] René, like any noble, was very sensitive to slights to his honor. In the early 1540s, his officer Guichard was trying to obtain money from a Milanese senator and judicial official named Giovanni

129 Dialeti; see also Cavallo.
130 Coolidge, 'Contested Masculinity,' 68.
131 Della Misericordia, 'Gusti cavallereschi,' 808-11; Monter, 59-60.
132 Kettering, *Power and Reputation*, 20-30.
133 See Wintroub, 405-6.
134 Fornaseri, 31-33, René to Ch III, Chambéry 13-I-30.
135 Ibid., 45-46, René to Ch III, Chambéry 9-IV-30.

Battista Speciano, who held various posts in the financial administration of the duchy of Milan. Guichard was certain that Speciano 'would try to take advantage of you in your affairs', an assessment based on 'an understanding that his were only words and mockeries and that you are not a person who is moved by such things'. Guichard knew that Speciano misjudged René: 'They think that they can treat you like a Piedmontese or Savoyard and [...] they are very mistaken. Because they have a German in front of them who will not put up with such treatment.'[136] This is an interesting example of how René's Germanic heritage, through his mother, Louise d'Arberg, could serve as a point of honor in his eyes and that of his servants. René's dispute with Masino over the lieutenant generalship, described elsewhere, was an obvious instance of the imperative not to be dishonored. He expressed his displeasure to the Duke in September 1558 about this issue, complaining that Emanuel Filibert had not replied 'to what I had already written to him concerning my honor and his service'.[137] René deferred to no one, not even the Duke, when it came to safeguarding his honor, prestige, and status.

For a Renaissance noble, defending one's reputation also meant demonstrating to the world that one effectively maintained order in one's own household. We have seen that entertaining and banqueting were important moments of social interaction for valley nobles – and indeed for local notables in all of René's lands.[138] Behind such events was a logistical organization that had to be effectively managed by René, his wife and daughters, and their servants. This was true, above all, for the provisioning of the Count's table. Not long after René moved to Chambéry, in June 1530, he was told that a local named Hubodi had wine that belonged to the Duke of Savoy, from a vineyard belonging to *'madame la grant maistresse'* (Madeleine de Savoie?). René arranged for the wine to be brought to the cellar of the chateau.[139] His officials corresponded with each other about obtaining food and other household items, and René sometimes gave explicit instructions about where to obtain game or other meat, 'such as venison and other kinds', for his table.[140] It was important to be aware of how seasonal weather

---

136 AHR, FC 264, mz. 1, Gichar [?] to René, Milan 20-XII-42?.
137 Fornaseri, 139-40, René to EF, Novara 8-IX-58.
138 For the variety of people passed through Valangin in 1536-1537 and what they ate, see AHR, FC 172, no. 16, account of Antoine Mothery.
139 Fornaseri 67-69, René to Ch III, Chambéry 17-VI-30.
140 AEN, AS-G16, 13, René to Loranze, Ducrest, and the Castellan of Aymaville, Vercelli 11-IV-58; see also AHR, FC 263, mz. 1, Loys de Castellamont to an unnamed castellan, Morgex 2-XI-?; ibid., René to the Castellan of Challant, Issogne 6-IV-?.

conditions affected provisions, such as when Lostan wrote to Mencia about how expensive butter was due to a drought.[141]

Household accounts from 1559 through 1561 give a more specific sense of the nature and cost of food provisioning. In October and November 1559, an official named Turrillia spent 132 florins for Philiberte's table and a few other expenses, presumably at Châtillon. The money was spent on beef, bread, candles, *'ung sallignyon'*, butter, lard, spices, *'manthon'*, sugar, fish, eggs, paper, salt, partridge, oil, oranges, tripe, *'ung pigne'*, and scissors.[142] Turrillia also paid for the transport of wine from 'Pallex' (Palazzo Canavase, which is where Lescha was from – though he was also described as a citizen of Ivrea) to the secretary Ducrest. To 'master Humbert, cook' at Issogne for Christmas 1559, he delivered salt, pears, apples, cabbage, *'sallignions'*, sugar, and other things.[143] Another list of provisions for Issogne for late 1559 and early 1560 accounted for an expenditure of 90 florins for food (including eight *émines* and six *quartanees* of onions, a large amount of lard and nut and olive oil, and also oats and hay for horses). The account, which was signed by Isabelle, also indicated income of 131 florins received from the *lods* of Issogne, and an additional expenditure of 562 florins for eighteen *muys* and five *sestiers* of wine, at a rate of 30 florins per *muys*.[144] That fall, Ducrest gave Lescha more explicit instructions about wine provisioning.[145] In January 1564, Paolo Madruzzo informed René that 'in Montjovet there is someone who has twenty-five *mogia* of wine to sell, and if Your Illustrious Lordship would like me to make arrangements I will', at a lower price than the other fifteen *mogia* that Paolo had already purchased.[146]

The provisioner Loys Bonini submitted another account for expenditures at Issogne from April 1561. Bonini was identified as 'provisioner of the castle of Issogne' and supplied veal, chicken, spices (pepper, cloves, ginger, cinnamon, saffron, *noys muscatte*), lard, beef, *chevrot*, butter, capons, eggs, tripe, fish, white bread, and rye bread for Isabelle's table. Jean de Vaudagne helped provide many of these items. Isabelle signed the account for 224 florins that

---

141 Ibid., FC 264, mz. 1, Lostan to Mencia [?], Aosta 2-X-?.
142 AEN, AS-K16, 23, Turrillia expense account for voyage with 'Mlle de Challand,' X/XI-59.
143 Ibid., 12, Turrillia expense account, VIII- through XII-59.
144 Ibid., AS-I16, 4, food provisions for Issogne, late 1559-early 1560. Another account for Issogne, submitted by its Castellan Antoine de Generys, listed sums spent on a variety of items by command of Isabelle, La Fontaine, and Ducrest, amounting to 163 florins; see ibid., 5, account of Generys, 1560.
145 Ducrest ordered preparations for muscat wine, for the 'vins de Pallas et Pivron', and for wine from Donnas (ibid., AS-K16, 9, Ducrest to Lescha 'mon bon et honneste frere,' Aosta ?-IX-60).
146 AHR, FC 131, Paolo Madruzzo [?] to René [at Virieu], St. Marcel 25-I-64.

Fig. 5: The courtyard of the castle of Issogne. Photograph by Attilio Locati; used with permission.

fall when it was reviewed.[147] For the first week of May 1561, Isabelle spent 137 florins on food, and another 315 florins for the following two weeks. Large amounts of bread were purchased from four different women ('Loyse *bolongiere*', 'la Beatrix', 'la Doye', and 'Marie de Marc'); on 16 May, 25 florins were spent on bread. This was also the month when Emanuel Filibert came through the valley and stayed at Châtillon, which undoubtedly explains the enormous expenditures.[148] Accounts for Issogne for that November and December list similar kinds of expenses for food and for having bread made, including special items for Christmas, such as snails, partridge, oranges, a sheep, a deer, a barrel of mustard, fruit, cheese, 'a half *quarteron* of Ypocras [*spiced wine*]', candles, sausages, tripes, spices from Ivrea, two cabbages, a hare, and a pound of rice.[149] In November, while Isabelle 'was in Ivrea with His Highness [the Duke], the Castellan of Issogne still purchased 20 florins' worth of bread and two *sestiers* of wheat.[150]

These and other accounts also refer to other kinds of labor that underpinned the smooth running of René's and his daughters' households. In 1535, the Count had left a 'household ordinance' that he wished to be implemented

---

147   AEN, AS-K16, 5, account of Loys Bonini for expenses at Issogne, IV-61.
148   Ibid., 6, account of expenses at Issogne when EF visited, V-61.
149   Ibid., AS-I16, 4, account from Issogne, by nephew of Generiis, 11-XI-61.
150   Ibid., 15, receipt for Castellan of Issogne, 19-XI-61.

at Beaufremont, listing key officers for the barony and outlining their duties. There was to be a captain whose job was to receive various dues and revenues owed to 'the said house, and everything in the way that a master of the household and receiver should do'. He was to have two servants and a chamberlain working under him. One servant would collect fees and oversee *corvée* labor, and the other would serve the said 'master of the household and captain'. The captain would have two horses, one of which would be designated for work on the estate. He would be required to travel 'for the affairs of the said house' and would submit expense accounts. The captain would carry out only those repairs to the estate that were necessary and would contract out the work for cash payments by days of labor or by job 'as will be most profitable for the said house'. The roof of the house and the fishpond were to be prioritized, and any necessary work would be put out for bids. Firewood for the house would be provided for him, though he was not permitted to sell any without René's permission. He could use René's wood to make any necessary repairs. For his upkeep, he would be paid 50 *francs* per year and would receive a specified amount of provisions annually.[151] The captain was also to oversee the *corvées* of the subjects in the vineyard and had to feed them during their days of work. He was to take wheat from the granary 'to bake the bread to distribute' to the *corvée* laborers and to transport manure from around the house to the vineyard when necessary. The servant who kept accounts would be paid 25 *francs* per year and was subject to the orders of the captain. Twelve *bichets'* of wheat were to be set aside annually to bake bread 'for the poor'. A 'gatekeeper' under the captain's command would receive a wage of fifteen *francs* and a *vigneron* would be paid eighteen *francs*. The captain would also be responsible for taking care of the Count's dogs.[152] This is the most explicit statement of the sort of work that René expected from his castellans and household officials; scattered evidence provides other details of his servants' activities.[153]

There are few indications of the personal nature of René's interactions with his servants. When the son of 'Jehan the muleteer' died, he expressed his sadness to Bellegarde, adding that 'it's something that we all have to go through'.[154] Others did not always have a positive opinion of René's servants;

---

151 Details in ibid., AS-S26, 48, orders for Beaufremont from 1535.
152 Ibid.
153 AHR, FC 263, mz. 1, a Challant official [at Casale?] to Mencia [?], s.l., s.d., [c. 1540]; AEN, AS-K16, 12, Turrillia expense account, VIII- through XII-59; ibid., AS-I16, 5, account of Generys, 1560; ibid., 4, account from Issogne by Generiis's nephew, 11-XI-61; AHR, Fonds Roncas, categoria 16B, no. 9, account dated 1559-1564.
154 AEN, AS-G16, 12, René to Bellegarde, Issogne 12-X-?.

the Bishop of Aosta, Pietro Gazino, called René's man Boullet a 'man without reason' and asked the Count no longer to use him to send messages.[155] A certain Pierre was close enough to Mencia to be entrusted with the delivery of a book and the exchange of a key.[156] One of René's officers at Valangin (perhaps Trolliet?) was devastated to learn from one of René's letters 'that you say that I make fun of you, and similar things' when this officer didn't go to Beaufremont 'as you had ordered me to at Virieu'. The officer had had every intention of doing so, and asked René to believe that he would have carried out his instructions had it been at all possible, begging René to excuse him.[157]

Finally, it is important to note how many expenditures and how much effort was linked to the mobility of René's household. In 1540, an officer asked Mencia to have a servant named Petit Jehan ready the 'tapestry and also the furnishings for the camp beds, the altar cloth, mule blankets, and silverware together with the two *plasantins* and other things listed in the memoir that I am sending you'.[158] René related to Emanuel Filibert in 1553 how he and 'my whole household' had moved to be with Charles III in Vercelli, 'to carry out my service to him'.[159] Expenses for hay, food, and lodging made such travel a burden on René's budget.[160] In 1560, the Castellan of Issogne paid fourteen florins to Ducrest 'for my lord's mules, but to Maurix and to Jehan de Reymond and Jory, in the amount of twelve *faix* of hay' at a rate of fourteen *gros* per *faix*. He also paid eighteen florins for six *sestiers* of oats 'purchased in Champdepraz [...] and delivered to the grooms of the Count of Avi [Giovanni Federico] in Aosta'.[161]

Such traveling could be exhausting, and certainly weakened those who were already in a fragile state of health. René learned this through bitter experience. In September 1558, together with Mencia 'and the entire company', he decided to 'have a visit' near Novara 'and engaged in some *recreation*'. Mencia then wished to greet the Duke of Sessa in Milan, and, as they returned, 'she was suddenly taken by a persistent high fever'. The Count brought her to Novara as quickly as he could, despite the danger of her illness and that posed by the French, who were in the area. Notwithstanding everything done 'by means of many good doctors, whom I summoned from

---

155 AHR, FC 260, Gazino to René, Aosta 17-IV-37.
156 Ibid., FC 264, mz. 1, Pierre [?] to Countess of Challant, Châtillon 12-XII-?.
157 AEN, AS-K16, 19, Valangin officer to René, s.d. [I-48?].
158 AHR, FC 263, mz. 1, a Challant official [at Casale?] to Mencia [?], s.l., s.d., [c. 1540].
159 Fornaseri, 111-12, René to EF, Vercelli 23-IV-53.
160 AEN, AS-I16, 13, accounts of Lescha for Châtillon, 1560.
161 Ibid., 5, account of Generys, 1560.

everywhere', she did not recover, expiring on 3 September 1558, after having received the Sacrament. 'I do not wish to describe to Your Highness the sorrow that I experienced, since nothing is greater than the separation of two people who have live so long together in such friendship', he wrote to Emanuel Filibert.[162]

Legal issues

The kinds of family relationships, noble sociability, and household management described in the preceding sections were mediated by noble property and made possible by the possession of land, houses, and other goods in multiple regions. Such property was routinely the subject of legal action between René and others, whether kin or not. Martha Howell has recently reminded us of the various, and often regionally specific, ways in which European legal traditions dealt with property. Roman law distinguished between immoveable and moveable goods (defining the former as land), a distinction that northern customary law treated in terms of property that produced income versus things that were produced by property. Immoveable property, which produced income, 'was not subject to individual ownership [...] because its productive life far exceeded that of any individual. It was thus intended to serve generations, not individuals'. This was patrimony, not property, and this explains why nobles like René de Challant went to such lengths to protect related claims through legal means. They were fighting not for individual property, but for dynastic patrimony. Some buildings could fit into either the immoveable or moveable category, as could things like jewelry and even *rentes constituées*, since they could be passed on to heirs.[163]

These issues have been among those examined within a recent outburst of scholarship on the uses of the law in early modern France. Jeremy Hayhoe has argued that, in eighteenth-century Burgundy, there was far more contact between ordinary people and the court system than there is today. People then stood before judges multiple times a year and were involved in about four suits per decade. Much of this litigation took place in seigniorial courts, which he describes as effective institutions of local justice.[164] Rafe Blaufarb has discussed the litigation between early modern Provençal communities and their lords, pointing out that conflict was not just violent, but also legal.

---

162 Fornaseri, 139-40, René to EF, Novara 8-IX-58.
163 Howell, 540-41, 556.
164 Hayhoe, ix.

A case study of one community's struggle with its lord during the seventeenth and eighteenth centuries leads him to characterize such litigation as 'a forum for negotiation and dialogue'.[165] Michael Breen has described recourse to the legal system as a form of social collaboration, noting that civil litigation was far more common than criminal litigation during the early modern period, despite the tendency of historians to focus on the latter.[166] Caroline Castiglione is among those who has carefully studied the ways in which Italian lords used the courts to advance their claims.[167] This body of work shows that the nobility of René's time were not only warriors who tried to settle disputes violently, but that they and their subjects employed a variety of means, including legal ones, to defend their patrimonial claims.

When Emanuel Filibert became Duke of Savoy, René sent him a long letter that included his views on the Sabaudian judicial system.[168] He observed that

> in earlier times there had been a resident council, in addition to the councils of Turin and Chambéry, before which, once a case had been settled by a definitive sentence, the losing party would claim a legitimate reason to appeal, and would do so to the resident council, which was the court of final appeal.

But this procedure had not been observed for several years, due to the wars and to the fact that 'most of the judges retired to their houses'. In René's view, this context explained the introduction of a custom in what became the Senate of Piedmont that had given it a negative reputation. Now, when a decision was rendered, if the losing side wanted to appeal, it appealed to the same Senate but without the Senators who had presented the case. This meant that the same judges were called upon to hear the case a second time, 'which has been the source of much injustice', since the judges simply reiterated their earlier judgments, 'to the great prejudice of those appealing'.[169]

This problem led to 'infinite quarrels' for Charles III, who hit upon a solution just prior to his death. He decided to appoint appellate judges and

---

165 Blaufarb, 526.
166 Breen.
167 Castiglione.
168 Fornaseri, 125-31, René to EF, Vercelli 19-X-53. For a focused study of the Piedmontese Senate, see Merlin, 'Giustizia.' For the criminal justice system in Savoie, see Laly. Françoise Briegel and Sylvain Milbach have also coordinated two important volumes on Sabaudian justice: *Le Sénat de Savoie* and *Les Sénats des États de Savoie*.
169 Fornaseri, 125-31, René to EF, Vercelli 19-X-53.

had sent word about this to Emanuel Filibert before his passing. The order had been introduced 'in public council' and approved; all that was left was to 'complete the number of the senators and the said appellate judges'. Most observers thought that more magistrates still needed to be named.[170] Now, however, some ducal officials wanted to reserve all such cases for the Senate, arguing that it was too great an expense to pay extra appellate judges. For René, the extra cost to the pocketbook would be easier to bear than the cost to the soul, and he was convinced that 'the country' would be willing to bear this expense if 'the result were that justice was administered'. He urged the new Duke to move ahead with the reform proposed by Charles III, whose 'conscience was heavy, having been unable to attend to this in time'. He had informed several 'good, wise, and well-informed men who are not moved by passion or any interest in the Senate or appellate courts' about this proposal. They approved, 'desiring only that justice be done, and that our reputation in neighboring states improve from what it has been'.[171]

René was concerned about judicial reform not only out of a principled commitment to a system of justice that seemed fair to him, or because (more cynically) he was interested in the patronage power that went along with nominating new magistrates who were sympathetic to his interests. Rather, he, like every great aristocrat of his time, was constantly involved in multiple legal disputes for which he sought efficient resolution. When he was in his early 20s, following the death of his first wife, he, his former Gaspardone in-laws, and others began wrangling over Bianca Maria's Monferrato inheritance. These disputes, heard before the Bishop of Casale and the Senate of Monferrato, included a variety of elements. In an undated letter that appears to be from early 1527, the Castellan of Bard wrote to a certain Raphaello, 'like a brother to me', about René's litigation with Francesco Visconti (a relative of Bianca Maria's first husband) over the inheritance of the deceased.[172] In 1527, members of the Gaspardone family claimed that they should inherit from Bianca Maria 'as closer agnates' of her father, Giacomo, pointing to a supposed agreement between them and René dated 3 June 1527.[173] The dispute was settled in a way that was favorable to René, and subsequent suits were brought against René by individuals who claimed

170 Ibid.
171 Ibid.
172 AHR, FC 263, mz. 1, Castellan of Bard to Mess'r Raphaello, 'mio como uno fratello,' Aymaville, 22-III-?.
173 This case was filed in the episcopal court and was mediated by Benvenuto, Count of San Giorgio, and by Don Pietro di Saluzzo, apostolic protonotary; ibid., FC 45, no. 2, 1527-1528 litigation; ibid., FC 79, no. 3, 1527-1528 litigation.

to have inherited credits on the Gaspardone estate, or by René against those who owed payments for property that he had acquired.[174] In early 1540, Grat Rolin, one of René's officers, was criticized by Louis de Vallesa for having 'left all of his cases before the council while he went to Casale' apparently to attend to René's interests there.[175] Later that year, the Senate of Monferrato ordered the community of San Salvatore, part of the inheritance, to cease its requests that René make payments of certain 'victuals and wine' to the marquisate's fisc, and that they pay the amounts themselves.[176] The Gaspardoni appear to have appealed the case to the Senate of Monferrato, where litigation was initiated in 1541.[177] René successfully protected his claims; during the war years he and his kin mortgaged the Monferrato property to meet various financial obligations.[178]

Of course, René and his family were involved in a host of other inheritance disputes, in places farther afield than the Monferrato. An exhaustive account of such litigation will not be made here, but a few examples give a sense of the range of the Challant interests. Prior to his death, Philibert (René's father) had fought over the inheritance of his 'uncle', Georges de Challant, who had been the prior of St. Ours and also a canon of the cathedrals of Lyon and Aosta.[179] René also had claims on the castle of Miolans (Savoie), inherited from his grandmother, Marguerite de La Chambre – Luigi di Castellamonte was working on this litigation for René along with Jacques Cachot and Niccolò Balbo.[180] Some of René's claims involved him in litigation in Swiss jurisdictions, in the *pays de Vaud*, for example, and against the Abbot of St. Maurice in Chablais (Jean Miles).[181] Conflicts involving Valangin led René to arrange meetings with legal experts in Besançon and to instruct his servant Bellegarde to bring money for the 'other jurists who will consult with him'.[182]

---

174 Ibid., no. 2, register of litigation of René before the Senate of Casale against the Gaspardoni and others who claimed to be creditors of René, 1513-1550; ibid., FC 103, no. 16, acts before the Senate of Monferrato (1518-1541) between René as heir of Bianca Maria and Venetiano Cavallo, who owed an annual payment for a garden located 'nelle fini di S. Salvadore'.
175 Ibid., FC 260, Louis de Vallesa to Grandis, Ivrea 1-IV-40.
176 AST1, Protocolli Monferrato 34, 41r, order dated ?-IX-40.
177 AHR, FC 79, no. 6, litigation dated 1541-1542. René's legal advsers included the famous jurists Andrea Alciato, Giovanni Francesco Porporato, and Niccolò Balbo (ibid., FC 263, mz. 1, Hieronimo da Fagnano to René, Casale 21-X-42?). See Abbondanza; Alliaudi; Busino.
178 This process itself engendered more litigation, however; see AHR, FC 263, mz. 1, a Challant official [at Casale?] to Mencia [?], s.l., s.d., [c. 1540].
179 Ibid., 'Challant' to the Countess of Challant, Issogne 28-I-?.
180 Ibid., Bernard Boulet? to René?, Turin 9-X-?.
181 AEN, AS-I16, 12, Bernese approval of procurators for Guillemette and René, 12-VIII-37; AHR, FC 222, no. 24, 7-II-58 ligitation against the Abbot of St. Maurice. On Miles, see Roduit.
182 AEN, AS-C4.2, b, René to Bellegarde, Besançon 5-IV-34 [?].

Soon after the Sabaudian restoration, René began to press his claims to inherit Varey, in Bugey, against the pretensions of his cousin Etienne-Philibert de Challant-Varey. In February 1561, he requested the Duke's support for his position and, later that year, submitted documentation to the Senate of Savoie that resulted in a ducal order for the arrest and transfer of Etienne-Philibert to the prisons of Chambéry.[183] Within a year, a merchant named Baptiste Navarrin, who had guaranteed loans taken out by Etienne-Philibert, had sued René. Presumably, when René acquired the fief, he also acquired the debts that had been secured on it. Emanuel Filibert worked with the Senate to ensure that René did not suffer any damages as a result.[184] In a letter from around 1563, another of René's officers pointed out that the recent death of the Countess (Marie de La Palud died in late March 1563) would affect a case between René and the Countess of Varax, and, some months later, the Duke of Savoy sent a letter to the Senate of Savoie instructing them to bring a quick and just conclusion to this dispute.[185] René was, unsurprisingly, also involved in other property disputes that were not strictly related to inheritance.[186]

René also found himself the target of criminal proceedings. For example, in June 1531, a ducal secretary named Aubert Veillet accused him of having engaged in an 'violent invasion' of a house belonging to him and then expelling his servants and workers from it, 'knowing that I was the true possessor'.[187] In late 1530 or early 1531, Velliet had became involved in a conflict with two other persons, Claude Collier and Bonne Pigniere, before an unidentified tribunal. Pigniere's identity is unknown, but Collier was a protegé and later agent of René.[188] René had supported Collier and Pigniere, in whose property he seems to have had some interest, but they lost their case. Nonetheless, René continued to maintain that Collier and Pigniere were the rightful owners.[189] He petitioned the Duke about this, requesting his property

---

183 AHR, FC 247, no. 23, request dated 25-II-61; ibid., FC 224, nos. 6-7, documentation from 1561-1562.
184 ADS, B 1789, EF to Senate, Rivoli 14-II-62; ibid., EF to Senate, Rivoli 13-III-62.
185 AHR, FC 263, mz. 1, Charlene? to Gilles de Brion, Chambéry, 17-VI-?; ADS, B 1789, EF to Senate, Nice 20-I-64.
186 AHR, FC 45, no. 1, 1520-1521 litigation; ibid., FC 263, mz. 1, Bernard Boulet? to René, Aosta, 18-VI-?.
187 AEN, AS-K6, 28, ducal response to petition dated 26-VI-31; Fornaseri, 59, René to Ch III, Aymavilles 26-V-30.
188 In 1525, Collier had been accused of poisoning someone, but René protected him; see AEN, AS-C1.8 for 1525 register; also see Matile, 249-50 and Fornaseri, 14, René to Ch III, Chambéry ?-XI-29. By the 1530s, Collier was working for René in Valangin and was named Prevost of the collegial church there.
189 AEN, AS-K16, 26, register of Veillet litigation dated 30-VI-31.

not be prejudiced, and the Duke responded favorably on 26 June 1531.[190] According to Veillet, four days later, René's servants 'violently invaded and entered into my house and property and expelled my servants and workers from it for a time'. Veillet's servants were only able to reenter the house later through the intervention of the ducal council. In late July, the council gathered testimony from René, having been summoned by ducal letters two weeks after arriving in Chambéry. He defended his right 'peacefully to hold that which belongs to him' and asked the Duke to pronounce him 'the true lord with direct dominion, proprietor and legitimate possessor of the property'. René agreed to have his case heard by the Duke but not by the Council President,[191] urging Charles III not to make him 'retreat from my rights in any way', so 'that my honor and reputation not be sullied'.[192] This episode was not immediately resolved; in 1534, René instructed his officers to expedite a conclusion of the litigation.[193] At first blush, it is surprising that Veillet chose to initiate a dispute with such a powerful figure. However, it is also true that Veillet was a ducal secretary who likely had his own network of supporters in Chambéry. Perhaps he thought that the great number of pressing affairs in which René was involved in various places would distract him from this specific matter. If so, he miscalculated: as his letter to the Duke shows, for René, the property conflict unavoidably invoked his honor and reputation. The dispute itself and the procedures by which it would be resolved took on existential dimensions, making it impossible for René to back down. Nor did he forgive the offense caused by Veillet: in 1553, when Emanuel Filibert appointed him lieutenant general, Veillet was among those whom René accused of corruption and had detained.

This was not the only case of litigation between René and other officials. In 1537, he complained to the Bishop of Aosta, Pietro Gazino, about a certain 'citation' issued in his regard, and was assured by the Bishop that the matter would be resolved.[194] In 1542, René was involved in a suit in Chambéry against Marc Antoine, and, in a *transsumpt* [?] affair' in Grenoble, involving *parlementaires* from Chambéry.[195] In the 1550s, René litigated with the Castellan of his fief of St. Marcel (in the valley) over the accounts of his

---

190   Ibid., 28, ducal response to René petition dated 26-VI-31.
191   Ibid., 26, register of Veillet litigation dated 30-VI-31.
192   Fornaseri, 57-59, René to Ch III, s.d. [1530?].
193   AEN, AS-C4.2, d, René to Bellegarde, Beaufremont 15-V-34.
194   AHR, FC 260, Gazino to René, Aosta 17-IV-37.
195   Ibid., FC 263, mz. 1, Granyer to René, Conflans 14-I-42.

revenues.[196] René also found himself involved in disputes with his own agents. The Bernard Boulet who had served as his procurator in the Veillet case eventually filed suit against René in the episcopal court of Sion (and seems to have been countersued in the diocese of Aosta), claiming that René was demanding certain documents of him that René in fact had in his own possession.[197]

René de Challant depended on his family and his circle of noble friends, in Italy and across the Alps, for support. However, in addition to offering assistance and encouragement, these relationships could also create conflicts. René did not to hesitate to turn to the law for the resolution of such conflicts, even viewing 'legal jurisdiction' as a mechanism for defending his honor. The next chapter will examine in more detail how René's networks of support operated, pointing out how the spatial distribution of these networks enhanced his standing as a transregional lord.

Bibliography

Roberto Abbondanza, 'Andrea Alciato,' *DBI* 2 (1960)

Camillo Alliaudi, *Notizie biografiche su Gian Francesco Porporato* (Pinerolo: Giuseppe Chiantore, 1866)

Letizia Arcangeli, 'Ragioni di stato e ragioni di famiglia: strategie successorie dell'aristocrazia milanese tra Quattro e Cinquecento (Visconti, Trivulzio, Borromeo),' *Mélanges de l'École française de Rome – Italie et Méditerranée modernes et contemporaines* 124, 2 (2012), https://journals.openedition.org/mefrim/775, 12 November 2019

Alessandro Barbero, 'Principe e nobiltà' in id., *Valle d'Aosta medievale* (Naples: Liguori, 2000), pp. 179-209

Jane Black, *Absolutism in Renaissance Milan: Plenitude of Power under the Visconti and the Sforza 1329-1535* (Oxford: Oxford University Press, 2009)

Erica Bastress-Dukehart, 'Sibling Conflict within Early Modern German Noble Families,' *JFH* 33, 1 (2008): 61-80

---

196 AHR, FC 46, nos. 3-4, ligitation of I/II-60. René had named Carlo di Loranzè di San Martino Castellan of St. Marcel, and, when Loranzè refused to render accounts of the fief's revenues, René sued him. René brought the case before the Bailiff of Aosta, Antoine de Leschaux, arguing that Loranzè still owed him 1,200 florins for the farm of St. Marcel. Claude Excofferi acted as René's procurator. The case was eventually appealed to one of the Senates.

197 AEN, AS-H16, 20, Roz Favre to René, Aosta ?-VI-39.

Jane Fair Bestor, 'Bastardy and Legitimacy in the Formation of a Regional State in Italy: The Estense Succession,' *Comparative Studies in Society and History* 38, 3 (1996): 549-85

Rafe Blaufarb, 'Conflict and Compromise: *Communauté* and *Seigneurie* in Early Modern Provence,' *JMH* 82, 3 (2010): 519-45

Michael Breen, 'Law, Society and the State in Early Modern France,' *JMH* 83, 2 (2011): 346-86

Thalia Brero, *Les baptêmes princiers. Le cérémonial dans les cours de Savoie et Bourgogne (XV-XVIe s.)* (Lausanne: Université de Lausanne, 2005)

Susan Broomhall and Jacqueline van Gent, 'Corresponding Affections: Emotional Exchange Among Siblings in the Nassau Family,' *JFH* 34, 2 (2009): 143-65

Luigi Bruzzo, *Ascendenti e discendenti di Renato di Challant e di sua moglie Mencia di Portogallo* (Genoa: Giorgio di Stefano Editore, 1974 [1959])

Giovanni Busino, 'Niccolò Balbo, *DBI* 5 (1963)

Jana Byars, 'From Illegitimate Son to Legal Citizen: Noble Bastards in Early Modern Venice,' *SCJ* 42, 3 (2011): 643-63

Caroline Castiglione, *Patrons and Adversaries: Nobles and Villagers in Italian Politics, 1640-1760* (Oxford: Oxford University Press, 2005)

Sandra Cavallo, *Artisans of the Body in Early Modern Italy: Identities, Families and Masculinities* (Manchester: Manchester University Press, 2007)

M.L. de Charrière, 'La baronnie de Rolle et Mont-le-Vieux. Étude féodale,' *Mémoires et documents publiés par la Société d'histoire de la Suisse romande* 34 (1879): 33-122

Gaudenzio Claretta, *La successione di Emanuele Filiberto al trono sabaudo e la prima ristorazione della casa di Savoia* (Torino: Eredi Botta, 1884)

Lin Colliard, 'La bibliothèque du château d'Issogne d'après l'inventaire de 1565,' *Bulletin de l'Académie Saint-Anselme* 37 (1960): 61-68

Grace Coolidge, 'Contested Masculinity: Noblemen and their Mistresses in Early Modern Spain,' in *Contested Spaces of Nobility in Early Modern Europe*, ed. Matthew Romaniello and Charles Lipp (Farnham, UK: Ashgate, 2011), pp. 61-84

Id., '"A Vile and Abject Woman": Noble Mistresses, Legal Power, and the Family in Early Modern Spain,' *JFH* 32, 3 (2007): 195-214

Gérard Delille, '*La France profonde*: Relations de parenté et alliances matrimoniales (XVIe-XVIIIe siècle),' *AHSS* 70, 4 (2015): 881-930

Id., 'Représentation, généralisation, comparaison: Sur le système de parenté européen,' *AHSS* 62, 1 (2007): 137-57

Massimo della Misericordia, 'Gusti cavallereschi, stili residenziali e temi figurativi. Aspetti della cultura aristocratica nella Lombardia alpina alla fine del medioevo,' *Quaderni storici* 51, 3 (2016): 794-96

Julien Demade, 'Parenté, noblesse et échec de la genèse de l'état: le cas allemand,' *AHSS* 61, 3 (2006): 609-31

Androniki Dialeti, 'Defending Women, Negotiating Masculinity in Early Modern Italy,' *HJ* 54, 1 (2011): 1-23

Jean-Baptiste de Tillier, *Historique de la Vallée d'Aoste* (Aosta: ITLA, 1994 [1742])

Id., *Nobiliaire du duché d'Aoste*, ed. André Zanotto (Aoste: Editions de la Tourneuve, 1970 [1733 ms])

Pierre-Etienne Duc, *La prévôté et la paroisse de St-Gilles Abbé à Verrès diocèse d'Aoste* (Ivrea: Imprimerie du séminaire, 1873)

Giovanni Fornaseri, *Le lettere di Renato di Challant, governatore della Valle d'Aosta a Carlo II ed a Emanuele Filiberto* (Turin: Deputazione subalpina di storia patria, 1957)

François-Gabriel Frutaz, 'L'inventaire du château d'Issogne en 1565,' ed. Joseph-César Perrin, *Bulletin de l'Académie Saint-Anselme* 40 (1963): 199-248

Id., 'Notes sur René de Challant et sur le passage de Calvin dans la Vallée d'Aoste,' *Musée neuchâtelois* 41 (1904): 242-67

Liesbeth Geevers, 'Family Matters: William of Orange and the Habsburgs after the Abdication of Charles V (1555–67),' *RQ* 63, 2 (2010): 459-90

Edoardo Grendi, *I Balbi: Una famiglia genovese fra Spagna e Impero* (Turin: Einaudi, 1997)

Samuel Guichenon, *Histoire de Bresse et de Bugey* (Lyon: Iean Antoine Huguetan and Marc Ant. Ravaud, 1650)

Sandro Guzzi-Heeb, 'Kinship Transition and Political Polarization: The Spread of Radicalism in the Swiss Alps,' *JIH* 47, 1 (2016): 27-51

Élie Haddad, 'Faire du mariage un acte favorable. L'utilisation des coutumes dans la noblesse française d'Ancien Régime,' *RHMC*, 58, 2 (2011): 72-95

Jeremy Hayhoe, *Enlightened Feudalism: Seigneurial Justice and Village Society in Eighteenth-century Northern Burgundy* (Rochester, 2008)

Martha Howell, 'Movable/Immovable. What's In a Name?' in *Money, Markets and Trade in Late Medieval Europe*, ed. Lawrin Armstrong, Ivana Elbl, and Martin Elbl (Leiden: Brill, 2007), pp. 538-71

Carolyn James, 'Marriage by Correspondence: Politics and Domesticity in the Letters of Isabella d'Este and Francesco Gonzaga, 1490–1519,' *RQ* 65, 2 (2012): 321-52

Sharon Kettering, *Power and Reputation at the Court of Louis XIII: The Career of Charles d'Albert, duc de Luynes (1578-1621)* (Manchester: Manchester University Press, 2014)

Greg Koabel, 'Youth, Manhood, Political Authority, and the Impeachment of the Duke of Buckingham,' *HJ* 57, 3 (2014): 595-615

Hervé Laly, *Crime et justice en Savoie (1559-1750). L'élaboration du pacte social* (Rennes: Presses Universitaires de Rennes, 2012)

Elizabeth Lehfeldt, 'Ideal Men: Masculinity and Decline in Seventeenth-Century Spain,' *RQ* 61, 2 (2008): 463-94

Giovanni Levi, 'Family and Kin in Italy: A Few Thoughts,' *JFH* 15 (1990): 57-67

Charles Lipp, 'Power and Politics in Early Modern Lorraine: Jean-François de Mahuet and the *Grand Prévôté* de Saint-Dié,' *FHS* 26, 1 (2003)

Pier Paolo Merlin, 'Giustizia, amministrazione e politica nel Piemonte di Emanuele Filiberto. La riorganizzazione del Senato di Torino,' *BSBS* 80 (1982): 35-94

Cédric Michon, 'Les richesses de la faveur à la Renaissance: Jean de Lorraine (1498-1550) et François Ier,' *RHMC* 50, 3 (2003): 34-61

E. William Monter, *A Bewitched Duchy: Lorraine and its Dukes, 1477-1736* (Geneva: Droz, 2007)

Michel Nassiet, *Parenté, noblesse et États dynastiques, XVe-XVIe siècles* (Paris: Éditions de l'EHESS, 2000)

Id., 'Parenté et pouvoir local en Méditerranée occidentale,' *AHSS* 61, 3 (2006): 633-45 (review of Delille, *Le maire et le prieur*, 2003)

Robert Oresko, 'Bastards as Clients: The House of Savoy and Iis Illegitimate Children,' in *Patronages et clientélismes 1550-1750 (France, Angleterre, Espagne, Italie)*, ed. Roger Mettam and Charles Giry-Deloison (Lille: Publications de l'Institut de recherches historiques du Septentrion, 1995), pp. 39-68

Charles Passerin d'Entrèves, 'La Collégiale de St-Gilles de Verrès,' *Bulletin de l'Académie Saint-Anselme* 29 (1951): 91-101

Giulio Romero Passerin d'Entrèves and Paulette Taieb, *Bibliothèques Nobiliaires Valdôtaines* (https://www.taieb.net/bnv/page11.html, 12 November 2019)

Olivier Roduit, 'Entre Bernois réformés et Valaisans catholiques: L'Abbaye de Saint-Maurice de 1520 à 1572,' pt. 3, 'L'abbatiat de Jean Miles, 1550-1572,' *Annales valaisannes*, n.s. 64 (1989): 99-145

Donatella Rosselli, 'Bianca Maria Gaspardone, contessa di Challant,' *DBI* 52 (1999)

'Sanctacrucii Cardinalis Prosperi de vita atque rebus gestis ab anno MDXIV ad MDLXVII,' ed. with notes by G.B. Adriani, *MSI* 5 (1868): 477-992

Le Sénat de Savoie: archives, historiographies, perspectives. XVIe-XIXe siècles, ed. Françoise Briegel and Sylvain Milbach (Chambéry: Université de Savoie, 2013)

Les Sénats des États de Savoie. Circulations des pratiques judiciaires, des magistrats, des normes (XVIe-XIXe siècles), ed. Françoise Briegel and Sylvain Milbach (Rome: Carocci, 2016)

Christine Shaw, *Barons and Castellans: The Military Nobility of Renaissance Italy* (Leiden: Brill 2015)

James Shaw, 'Writing to the Prince: Supplications, Equity and Absolutism in Sixteenth-Century Tuscany,' *PP* 215, 1 (2012): 51-83

Jonathan Spangler, 'Points of Transferral: Mademoiselle de Guise's Will and the Transferability of Dynastic Identity,' in *Dynastic Identity in Early Modern Europe*, ed. Liesbeth Geevers and Mirella Marini (Farnham, UK: Ashgate, 2015), pp. 131-51

Luigi Vaccarone, 'Bianca Maria di Challant e il suo corredo,' in id., *Scritti sui Challant*, pp. 79-102

Id., 'Le questioni di successione ai feudi,' in id., *Scritti sui Challant*, pp. 31-78

Id., *Scritti sui Challant* (1893), ed. and reprinted by Lin Colliard and Andrea Zanotto (Aosta: ITLA, 1967)

Arie van Steensel, 'Kinship, Property, and Identity: Noble Family Strategies in Late-Medieval Zeeland,' *JFH* 37, 3 (2012): 247-69

Id., 'Noble Identity and Culture: Recent Historiography on the Nobility in the Medieval Low Countries III,' *History Compass* 12, 3 (2014): 287-99

Vigilio Vescovi, 'Historia della casa di Challant e di Madruzzo,' ed. Lin Colliard, *Archivum Augustanum* 2 (1969): 1-118

Megan Williams, 'Dangerous Diplomacy and Dependable Kin: Transformations in Central European Statecraft, 1526-1540,' PhD dissertation, Columbia University (2009)

Michael Wintroub, 'Words, Deeds, and a Womanly King,' *FHS* 28, 3 (2005): 387-413

Heide Wunder, 'Matrimonio e formazione del patrimonio nella prima età moderna. Un contributo sulla relazione tra la storia di genere e la storia economica,' *Studi storici* 50, 3 (2009): 747-78

André Zanotto, 'Aperçu sur le début de l'art typographique en Vallée d'Aoste,' *Bulletin de l'Académie Saint-Anselme* 37 (1960): 113-20

6. The Challant political networks

Abstract

The political networks of René de Challant were spatially diffused across what had been called the Lotharingian 'Middle Kingdom', reaching from northwestern Italy across the Alps into Savoie and the Swiss cantons, and, from there, northward to Lorraine and Flanders. René interacted with other leaders across this area as both a patron and a client and was assisted in his network by officers who sometimes served him for decades. To these, were added networks of ecclesiastical influence and circles of influence manipulated by his second wife, Mencia. These political relationships were maintained through complex strategies of information exchange and distribution and were simultaneously threatened and reinforced by René's interactions with Sabaudian, French, and Imperial officers.

Key words: political network, women as patrons, information, officials

Since René's lifetime, Valdostano and Piedmontese historians have remarked on his tremendous political influence in the Valle d'Aosta and beyond. In around 1560, an anonymous memorialist stressed the geostrategic importance of the Valle d'Aosta and René's great wealth and authority there. But he also questioned René's fidelity to the dynasty (based on his subjects' refusal to pay wartime subsidies being raised by the valley for the Duke) and pointed to the dangers of a powerful foreign family – the Madruzzo – inheriting René's position through the inheritance of his daughter Isabelle. This would enable the Prince-Bishop of Trento to 'build a good project in said valley, where he could reach an agreement as a confederate with the Swiss at little cost, since he is of the German nation'.[1] Foreign diplomats likewise remarked on René's power within the Sabaudian lands, albeit on the wane by the early 1560s.[2]

---

1 'Memoriale del Presidente Niccolò Balbo,' 334; see also 329-33.
2 Boldù, 439; see also 414, 430-34. The relations of Boldù's compatriots Sigismondo Cavalli in 1564 and Giovanni Correr in 1566 did not mention René (see Cavalli; Correr).

Vester, M., *Transregional Lordship and the Italian Renaissance: René de Challant, 1504-1565*. Amsterdam: Amsterdam University Press, 2020.
DOI 10.5117/9789463726726_CH06

This appreciation of René's influence within the valley and beyond was highlighted by Jean-Baptiste de Tillier, an eighteenth-century Valdostano historian, secretary of the valley estates, and fierce defender of the valley's autonomy. Although René played a surprisingly modest role in De Tillier's *Historique de la Vallée d'Aoste* (1742), the author did stress the number of important secular and ecclesiastical offices held by the Challant in the valley, their numerous fiefs and castles, and the fact that they had always held 'a very high rank and the first place in the whole jurisdiction of this duchy'.[3] He discussed René's role in the *Conseil des Commis*, his family relationships (leaving out the scandalous details), and the offices that he held for the Duke of Savoy.[4] De Tillier also highlighted René's skill in interacting with Rome, in terms of obtaining patronage rights over the prevosture of St. Gilles and various parishes. This happened 'during a time when the heresies of Luther and Calvin were spreading in the neighborhood of this duchy' – De Tillier seems to think that René knew how to leverage the religious crisis to his own ends.[5]

Frutaz, another Valdostano historian writing about 150 years later, created a nuanced image of René as a local hero, the 'most noteworthy character of the Sabaudian states during the turbulent period from 1530 to 1565', and simultaneously devoted to the Catholic cause, the 'interests of his country', and the House of Savoy.[6] Gaudenzio Claretta underlined the massive influence of the Challant in the Valle d'Aosta and their landed holdings elsewhere, which enabled them to 'aspire to the sovereignty of their native valley'.[7] Likewise, Domenico Carutti described René as the 'patron' of the Valle d'Aosta.[8] Segre agreed with other historians that, after 1555, 'Challant was so powerful in the Valle d'Aosta that it was in the duke's interest to keep him happy' in the context of the competition with Masino over the lieutenant generalship.[9] Carlo De Antonio described the variety of offices and functions held by René in the valley, which was characterized, citing a medieval chronicle, as a place '"that is neither in Gaul, nor in Italy, but between the borders of Burgundy and Lombardy"'.[10] He portrayed René as a 'quasi-sovereign' who 'concentrated all powers in himself', creating some

3   De Tillier, *Historique*, 111-12.
4   Ibid., 308, 491-92.
5   Ibid., 184.
6   Frutaz, 'Notes,' 243.
7   Claretta, *La successione*, 15-16 n. 1.
8   Carutti, 1: 275, 323.
9   Segre, 'L'opera politico-militare,' 73.
10 De Antonio, 209.

anxiety for Emanuel Filibert.[11] De Antonio catalogued the range of historians' assessments of René, positive and negative, noting appreciation for René's disinterested service and constant devotion to the House of Savoy despite that fact that he 'could have easily made himself lord' of the Valle d'Aosta.[12]

More recent scholarship has examined how early modern nobles were able to establish and spread their political influence. There is a sizeable scholarly literature on patronage, clientage, affinities, and various forms of networking among early modern elites, and historians have disagreed over what language should be used to analyze various kinds of relationships.[13] Janie Cole's remark that 'the difference between friendship and clientelism, or kinship and patronage ties, was often blurred'[14] seems sensible, given (a) the variety of contexts in which these relationships existed, and (b) the fact that early modern correspondents themselves used language inconsistently. Many elites served multiple patrons, albeit in less mobile environments than that studied by Cole. Still, there are relatively few 'high-quality case studies describing the precise nature of noble affinities' during the late Renaissance.[15] Brian Sandberg briefly describes the networks of warrior nobles, who 'needed to be able to count on the quick responses of their clienteles, since the civil warfare in [early seventeenth-century France] was characterized by sharp religious divisions and localized confrontations'. Violence thus shaped the way in which such nobles understood friendship and clientage – a setting far removed from literary circles in Baroque Rome. Sandberg distinguishes between 'prestige clientage', military clientage, administrative clientage, urban clientage, and seigneurial clientage.[16] Some relationships, like that between Jean de Lorraine and Francis I, were difficult to categorize. The King trusted the Cardinal, because they kept each other company while hunting, playing tennis, feasting, and debauching women. Although Jean did not have the means to create numerous clients, he had agents and was able to use networks that were weaker than factions but could still be influential.[17] Perhaps part of his appeal to the King was through the equestrian expertise developed by his Guise brother and nephews. Marjorie Meiss-Even stresses how frequently horse-raising and -trading is discussed in the Guise correspondence, a topic about which not much is

11   Ibid., 175-76, 177-78, 235-36.
12   Ibid., 236-37.
13   For a brief discussion of these debates, see Vester, *Renaissance Dynasticism*, 188-90.
14   J. Cole, 738, 784.
15   Milstein, 21-22.
16   Sandberg, 80.
17   Michon, 38.

known. Horses used by the French high nobility usually came from other lands, such as Lorraine, Germany, and the Netherlands, creating important brokerage possibilities for the Guise.[18]

The case of René de Challant invites us to expand our understanding of early modern political networks through the example of a transregional and spatially diverse set of relationships. The scope of René's influence is made clear through consideration of the geographic breadth of his networks. He had so many clients and supporters within the Valle d'Aosta, rooted in his fiefs, feudal officers, and official positions there, that he could have perhaps seized control of the duchy of Aosta for himself. Moreover, he wielded tremendous influence in the other places where he had lands and authority (the transalpine Sabaudian lands, Piedmont and the Monferrato, the Swiss area, and Beaufremont and Lorraine). His political authority thus roughly followed his landed position, though not perfectly. René employed a core of close officials through whom individuals and families within his lands (and beyond them) were bound to him in varying degrees of allegiance. What follows is a partial listing of some of René's friends, clients, and contacts in different parts of Europe, as revealed through surviving correspondence and other papers. It is not meant to be complete, but rather to offer a sense of the geographic reach of René's network.

René's network

The regional scope of René's ties

René's following was most dense within the valley itself. This Valdostano network could be documented in other ways, through identifying the envoys sent to the valley estates by the communities subject to René, making a comprehensive list of all of his correspondents from the valley, or identifying all of his subjects as listed in the *reconnaissances* from his fiefs. This chapter will offer a few examples to illustrate his following in the valley.

In 1531, the Veillet litigation in Chambéry identified Jean Bartholomé Riquering (Ricarand) as one of his procurators.[19] Many members of the Ricarand family, which appears to have originated in Settimo Vittone (just outside of the valley on the road to Ivrea), served as local and Valdostano officials over the course of the sixteenth century.[20] Jean Ricarand was Castellan

---

18   Meiss-Even.
19   AEN, AS-K16, 26, register of Veillet litigation, statement by Riquarand on f. 80r.-v.
20   AHR, FC 263, mz. 1, Gamache to René, Bard 9-IV-?.

of Montjovet in the 1540s and 1550s and was the first husband of Peronnette Mistralis, a noble lady from St. Vincent (within the castellany). After Jean's death, Peronnette remarried and had another daughter named Marie, whose first husband was Pierre Ricarand, son of Bernardin, from Settimo Vittone.[21] Marie's second husband, Vincent Regis, was one of the most powerful officials in the valley at the time of René's death: he was secretary of the valley estates, and later treasurer of the valley. When Marie made out her will in 1588, she did it in the house of 'noble François Ricarand notary' in Montjovet.[22] In the 1560s, this François Ricarand was a procurator for various individuals in cases heard before the tribunal of Montjovet.[23] In 1579, another Ricarand (Bernard) held local office in Montjovet. His precise relationship to Francesco, Pierre, and the other Ricarands is unknown.[24] Various members of the Ricarand family continued to play key roles in valley politics in the second half of the sixteenth century.[25] They enjoyed considerable political success over the course of the sixteenth century, and it seems likely that the protection initially extended by René de Challant had a good deal to do with this. After having moved from Settimo to Montjovet/St. Vincent, the Ricarand established multigenerational alliances with local elite families and continued to serve not only the dukes of Savoy, but also the House of Challant from their strategic position at Montjovet, a fortified defile in the central valley.

René's network in the valley also included individuals such as Roz Favre, Castellan of Quart, and René's lieutenant general in the valley.[26] In June 1539,

21 AHR, FC 253, mz. 1, no. 15, 'Espletti dalla visita fatta et infor'ni tolte [...] in San Vincenzo,' 3r.-4r.; APSV, cart. 10, 1565 register 'Processo della comunita et huomini di Mongioetto,' copy of Ch III to Jean de Richerand, Nice 24-XI-?; ANA, CT 340, 1st numbering, 1587-1588 acts, ff. 90r.-91r., act dated 26-VI-88; ibid., CT 131, 2nd numbering, ff. 173r.-175r., act dated 11-II-65.
22 Ibid., CT 136, 8th numbering, ff. 66v.-69r., act dated 7-VII-88.
23 Ibid., CT 758, acts before Michiel Andrion, Castellan of Montjovet dated 3-III-64; AHR, FC 253, mz. 1, no. 15, 'Espletti dalla visita,' 3r.-4r.
24 APSV, cart. 22, 1579 litigation, act dated 24-X-79.
25 Ibid., cart. 4, 'Processo della communità et huomini di San Vincentio contra il Sr Procurator Patrimoniale [1565-1566],' procuration dated 16-X-65.; ibid., cart. 10, Giovanni Giacomo Ricarando to Francesco Mistralis, Turin 19-X-66; ASTR, art. 86, paragrafo 3, Tesoreria Generale di Piemonte, 1576b account of Giovanni Fauzone and Ludovico Bruno 'tesoreri generali di SA di qua da monti' for the last six months of 1576; ANA, CT 133, act dated 13-II-79; AST1, Archives Passerin d'Entrèves, cart. 66 (Famille Mistralis), 1024, 19-VI-92 transaction between Panthaleon Mistralis and Jean Boniface d'Avise; AHR, FC 295, mz. 1, Ricarand to the baron of Valesa, Ivrea 22-IV-98; ibid., FC 262, mz. 1, Ricarand to Emanuel René, Bard 25-VI-97; ibid., same to same, Donnas 21-V-97; De Tillier, *Nobiliaire*, 300-1, 459-69.
26 De Tillier also identified Favre as the husband of Claudine, a natural daughter of René; see *Nobiliaire*, 256-60. It seems more likely that Claudine was René's half-sister, given the dates at issue here.

Favre wrote to René about a vacancy in a particular office in the valley, expressing his wish that René 'could have an acceptable servant in this office once its current occupant is gone'. He also promised to send Castellamonte to inform René if that person, the father of 'maistre François', were to die. 'I know that my son-in-law would much prefer to be appointed by other means', he wrote.[27] The 'son-in-law' was Jean François Vaudan, husband of Favre's daughter Nicoline.[28] The office that was about to fall vacant was that of vice-bailiff, and indeed, on 12 July 1539, René (himself 'grand bailiff of Aosta') constituted Vaudan as Vice-Bailiff. Vaudan swore his oath of office between the hands of Roz Favre, his father-in-law, 'as lieutenant general' of René.[29] Vaudan was also appointed vice-castellan of Châtelargent.[30] Through Favre, René's influence permeated the highest levels of political authority in the valley and, through his children and affines, reached to other members of the valley nobility as well.

For example, in the early 1540s, René consolidated ties with the Vulliet de St. Pierre family. The St. Pierre (together with the Challant, Vallesa/Vallaise, Nus, Sariod d'Introd, and Sariod de la Tour) belonged to the Valdstano peerage – they enjoyed the judicial privilege of being judged only by the sovereign and by other peers.[31] Jean Vulliet, a leading Sabaudian magistrate for Charles III, moved to the valley and married Guilliermine, daughter and heiress of Jacques de St. Pierre, the last member of that family. The day after his father-in-law died in 1529, Jean was granted investiture for the fief of St. Pierre; already in 1516, the Duke had granted to Jean and his male heirs the status of noble peers in the valley. He became a member of the *Conseil des Commis* in 1541 and served on various diplomatic missions.[32] Influence between René and people like Vulliet worked in two directions. In an undated request that seems to date from 1540, René asked the Duke for an assignation as compensation for underwriting a loan for him, an action that he took 'having been persuaded by Monsieur de Musinens, master of the horse, and Monsieur the master Vulliet, Lord of St. Pierre, master of the household and first secretary of Your Excellency'.[33] A couple of years later, René intervened on Vulliet's behalf with the wife of the Governor of Neuchâtel, who had underwritten a loan for Vulliet but then wanted to back

---

27 AEN, AS-H16, 20, Roz Favre to René, Aosta ?-VI-39.
28 Ibid., AS-G16, 22, Vaudan to René, Aosta 17-V-39; De Tillier, *Nobiliaire*, 256-60.
29 *Recueil*, 45.
30 De Tillier, *Nobiliaire*, 256-60.
31 Roddi, 58.
32 De Tillier, *Nobiliaire*, 653-67.
33 AHR, FC 25, no. 15, request by René to Ch III, s.d.

out. Over the course of several months, René and his officers energetically interceded for Vulliet, promising that, if Madame de Prangins would grant a delay for Vulliet's repayment, he would personally guarantee it.[34] By operationalizing René's relationship with Prangins and his wife, Vulliet demonstrated his own importance to René as a key client in the valley, and perhaps also at the Sabaudian court. René's willingness to use his political capital on Vulliet's behalf was a way of demonstrating his influence to other political actors in the valley and elsewhere, and also obviously a means by which he could guarantee the allegiance of a new member of the *Commis* and a leader of the Valdostano nobility.

René's network in the valley also included members of his own family. His cousin Charles de Challant-Fénis, Lord of Villarsel, sometimes operated as a go-between for René and Emanuel Filibert. In August 1552, Charles brought him a letter from Charles III, instructing him to 'stay in this country, to put affairs in order', a command which prevented René from otherwise going to 'do reverence' to the Prince. Charles pledged to bring Emanuel Filibert news from the valley on his return trip.[35] Michel de Villette, Baron of Chevron (whose grandmother was Marguerite de Challant, daughter of Amédée de Challant-Varey), was a leading noble from Savoie who served René in a variety of ways, especially diplomatically. He sent news to René one December that the Countess and '[the Count's] entire suite' were at Issogne and doing well, and that 'we are nearing our goal'.[36] Since the letter is undated, it is difficult to know what the 'goal' was, but Chevron's use of the first person plural is an indication of how he and many nobles and clients in the valley identified René's interests and concerns with their own. He also served as a link between René and the Savoyard nobility, discussing with him, for example, the 'kennel boy' of Monsieur de Menthon.[37]

Outside of the valley, the ducal court was the most important site for René's political network. As a trusted counselor for Dukes Charles III and Emanuel Filibert, René was present at court when circumstances permitted. The fact that Duchess Beatrice was a kinswoman of Mencia and had facilitated the Count's second marriage set the tone for their relationship as well. He sometimes corresponded directly with the Duchess, exchanging

---

34 AEN, AS-R5.10, vv, René to Mme de Prangins 'ma grosse mere,' Aosta 25-II-42; ibid., d, René to Prangins, Aosta 25-II-42; ibid., eee, Bellegarde to Prangins, Valangin 5-III-42; ibid., u, René to Prangins, Valangin 9-IV-43.
35 Fornaseri, 110-11, René to EF, Aosta 13-VIII-52.
36 AEN, AS-G16, 26, Chevron to René, Paris 4-XII-?.
37 AHR, FC 263, mz. 1, Chevron to René, Gye 3-IX-?.

letters in late 1530 about his negotiations with the Swiss.[38] René's epistolary interactions with the Dukes of Savoy were routine, given the offices that he held. One exchange sheds light on his relationship with Charles III. In 1549, René sent the Lord of Laudes and other envoys to court in response to a ducal request to send his 'master of the house Martine' to him. René understood that the Duke wished to make use of Martine, who was, by all accounts, an effective officer – this underscores the close relationship between the Count and Charles III, and René's ability to employ members of his network to generate political capital for himself at court.[39]

René's connections at court included former or current officers or clients of his who acquired positions within ducal institutions, as secretaries or magistrates. In late 1529, when René had just started his appointment as Marshal of Savoie in Chambéry, a ducal secretary named Baptendier passed away. René subsequently urged the Duke to replace him with one of his own secretaries (not named in the correspondence), and, just over a month later, Charles III granted this request.[40] Ducal servants who subsequently found themselves involved in valley politics might also be pulled into René's network. Giovanni Battista Dell'Isola was sent to the valley by the Duke to oversee strategic matters, while René was in prison. Although René thus spent little time with Giovanni Battista, he did get to know Dell'Isola's nephew, Franco. In 1557, the Bailiff of Aosta sent Franco 'the moveable property left by the deceased lord Colonel Dell'Isola his uncle', including some but not all of his correspondence with the Duke, part of which remained in the valley and was accessible to René and his associates.[41] On another occasion, not long after Mencia's death, René had returned to Novara from 'a devotional site, where I went, not far from here' and found a letter from the ducal secretary Hugues de Richard de Montpon, a former secretary of René who was then serving as a Sabaudian envoy to Rome.[42] Montpon wrote of the imminent death of Pierre-Hercule Vulliet de St. Pierre, an official in the *Chambre des comptes*, and implicitly invited René to nominate him (Montpon) as Vulliet's replacement. René took up Montpon's cause

---

38 Fornaseri 84-85, René to Beatrice, Aymavilles 11-XII-30; ibid., 85, same to same, Aymavilles 23-XII-30.
39 Ibid., 105-6, René to Ch III, Beaufremont 19-VI-49.
40 Ibid., 13, René to Ch III, Chambéry 13-XI-29; see also ibid., 25, same to same, Chambéry 20-XII-29; ibid., 26-28, same to same, Chambéry 27-XII-29.
41 AEN, AS-G16, 24 and 24a, Leschaux to René, Aosta 14-XII-57.
42 Fornaseri, 140-41, René to EF, Novara 18-IX-58; Abbé Coutin, 'Comment les Prêtres de la Mission établirent le Grand Séminaire d'Annecy en la rue du Bœuf, vers 1650,' *Mémoires et documents publiés par l'Académie Salésienne* 47 (1929), xi-xii.

wholeheartedly.[43] Pierre-Hercule Vulliet de St. Pierre was the second son of Jean, mentioned above.[44] He had been named a counselor in the *Chambre* by Emanuel Filibert in July 1555, along with Albert Veillet, Jean Carrà, and Hugues Michaud. In 1560, Carrà and Michaud were still in their positions, and, not only had Montpon been added to their number (in late 1559), so had Pierre Gautier d'Hostel, another former secretary of René.[45] Shortly after his lobbying of the Duke for a position for Montpon, René did the same for 'my lord the attorney Curbis', who desired to fill the vacancy of 'my lord the collateral Borre, of your council in Vercelli', who had also recently died.[46] Finding 'someone more capable or efficient in said office' than Curbis was impossible, according to the Count. He stressed Curbis's long and faithful service to both Emanuel Filibert and his father. Once more, René placed his chips on the table on behalf of his protégé, noting that

> Your Highness has not yet placed anyone in office over here, but for love of me I beg you to do so now, so that the said Curbis, whose hope has been placed first in Your Highness and then in me, and those who know that I am working on his behalf will know that I have some credit with Your Highness.

He announced that he was also seeking the support of Claude-Louis Alardet, Abbot of Filly, and of Pierre Maillard du Bouchet (one of Emanuel Filibert's closest advisers in Brussels) for the appointment of Curbis. René even urged the Duke to appoint Curbis 'before there is any competition', since the Duke's service would surely suffer if someone else were appointed.[47]

René also sought, usually successfully, the support of the Duke of Savoy and other rulers for his various affairs. Shortly before René's death, Emanuel Filibert wrote to the King and Queen of France, noting that the Count held many credits with respect to the French Crown and requesting that they be honored.[48] Emanuel Filibert also asked the Swiss ambassadors to the King to

---

43 Montpon had long served both Emanuel Filibert and René as a secretary and intermediary, dating back to the 1540s (Fornaseri, 104-5, René to EF, Beaufremont 17-VII-48). For René's support of him see also ibid., 140-41, same to same, Novara 18-IX-58; ibid., 141, same to same, Novara 3-X-58). Interestingly, René's archrival Masino also urged the Duke to appoint Montpon to this vacancy; see AST1, LP, V.7, Masino to EF, Vercelli 29-IX-58.
44 De Tillier, *Nobiliaire*, 653-57.
45 Capré, 284-85.
46 Fornaseri, 144-45, René to EF, Milan 7-XII-58 (same source for following citations).
47 Ibid.
48 AST1, RLC 11, f. 250r.-v., EF to King and Queen of France, Turin s.d. (draft).

present his letter to the French court. Since 'the Count of Challant my cousin' had told him about the money owed to him by the King, he requested that they instruct 'your delegates for other matters to His Majesty to mention this as well'. Both the Duke and the Count would be 'greatly obliged' if they agreed to perform this service.[49] Finally, the Duke also instructed his envoy to the Swiss to explain René's request and present the letters to them on this topic when they gathered at the upcoming Diet in Baden.[50]

René was able to press Emanuel Filibert hard on the issue of recommending clients to vacant bureaucratic positions, thereby obtaining a public display of the Duke's goodwill toward him. This probably represented the apogee of René's influence – it seems clear that the Duke of Savoy preferred to grant the Count's wishes rather than provoke a potentially damaging rupture. Nowhere is Emanuel Filibert's admission and reinforcement of Rene's power clearer than in the authority granted to him during the restitution of the Sabaudian lands in 1559. When Emanuel Filibert appointed René to take possession of his transalpine domains on his behalf in 1559, he gave the Count

> full power, authority, and special and general commission to order, establish, constitute, and deputize all officers and ministers of lower, ordinary, middle, and sovereign justice; to make and create commissioners and inspectors of our domain and feudal declarations, notaries, sergeants, and all other officers, of every place and office, in such a number and with such power and wages that he will reasonably determine to be of service to us and benefit to our said subjects.

What is more, René was granted the authority 'to order and dispose of our patrimony and revenue, both ordinary and extraorindary, as necessary'. He could also 'appoint, confer, and dispose of all benefices that might have gone vacant during our absence', except for bishoprics and abbeys, which the Duke reserved for himself. Further, he was permitted to 'sub-delegate and appoint one or more persons as subsitutes where needed in these matters, with such power, or a portion thereof, as required'.[51] This was a remarkable degree of authority, and René used it to consolidate his already strong networks of support in the transalpine lands.[52]

---

49 Ibid., f. 250v., EF to ambassadors of the Leagues, Turin s.d.
50 Ibid., ff. 251r.-252r., EF to Gauvain de Beaufort, Turin 27-VI-65 (draft).
51 Patents of EF dated Paris 8-VII-59, in Capré, 80-83.
52 See AHR, FC 290, no. 47, for an order dated Chambéry 12-VIII-62 to all ducal officers and subjects to assist Captain Beaufort.

Since his initial appointment as Marshal of Savoie, and thanks to his paternal grandmother's family, René had been building a political network in the transalpine lands, where he also held a number of fiefs. He cultivated and maintained that support in part by serving as a broker between transalpine subjects and the Duke of Savoy. In June 1530, he interceded on behalf of Antoinette de Pontbriand, wife of Marin de Montchenu, French ambassador to the Swiss, with respect to a Savoyard noble who was their creditor.[53] In the same letter, he observed that a notary who had been a subject of his kinsman Pierre de Challant-Varey had died, and asked the Duke to give the notary's papers to Varey. René thereby both did his cousin/uncle a favor and helped himself, since, a little over a year earlier, Varey had donated his lands to René, effective upon his death.[54] René was on good terms with the Chambérien Pierre Lambert de La Croix, President of the *Chambre des comptes* in the 1530s and 1540s. As early as 1525, during René's first imprisonment, his servant Jehan Jacques was sent to Cuneo to meet with Lambert.[55] Their correspondence shared confidential information about court politics – so secret, in fact, that they sometimes indicated to each other that they would only discuss key matters in person. Once, Lambert had important news that he wanted to give to René but was prevented from sharing it due to a sharp attack of gout that made it impossible for him to travel.[56] René also acted as a protector for Lambert's daughter, who seems to have been a member of Mencia's suite.[57] The noble family of Charles de La Forest, another of René's allies, had long resided near Chambéry and remained dedicated to the House of Savoy during the occupation. Charles wrote to René in the 1550s about trying, unsuccessfully, to send a messenger to Emanuel Filibert due to the unsafe 'passages'.[58]

René's influence also extended into Piedmont, the Monferrato, and nearby areas of northwestern Italy. The Castellamonte were one of the most powerful families of the Canavese, the district just southeast of the Valle d'Aosta, on the road toward Turin. Luigi di Castellamonte was among René's most faithful servants, from the 1520s until the 1540s, serving him on many diplomatic and financial missions.[59] Twelve or fifteen miles from Castellamonte is the community of Azeglio, one of whose lords, Manfredo,

---

53 Fornaseri, 60, René to Ch III, Chambéry 1-VI-30.
54 Ibid.; also AHR, FC 22, no. 14, donation dated 14-III-28.
55 Ibid., FC 172, no. 11, accounts of Eusèbe Gamache (1526).
56 Ibid., FC 264, mz. 1, Lambert? to René, Nice 10-II-? [c. 1536-1537].
57 AEN, AS-K16, 20, Castellamonte to René, Issogne 8-V-39; De Tillier, *Nobiliaire*, 306-11.
58 AHR, FC 263, mz. 1, La Forest to René, Chambéry? 2-VI-?.
59 Ibid., FC 40, no. 15, procuration for Luigi di Castellamonte dated 8-VIII-26.

was also a client of René and an intermediary with princes elsewhere in Italy. He seems to have accompanied René on the Pavia campaign and subsequent imprisonment and remained at the French court as René's procurator after René returned to the valley in fall 1526. The two men corresponded about political and social matters, especially about animals and hunting.[60] Another contact, Luca Cambiano, was sent by René to Casale Monferrato to look at the horses of the Archbishop of Sanseverino, which he was selling for 200-300 *écus* each.[61] René also corresponded directly with Federico II Gonzaga, sending him 'some *malinois* [Belgian shepherds] and arquebuses' in 1531.[62] A certain Claude Jacquier was René's factor in Milan,[63] and Filiberto Ferrero Fieschi, Lord of Masserano, sought news from the Count of Challant, his 'cousin,' about the arrival of the Duke of Savoy, 'our Prince', and about visiting and drinking wine together.[64] By the late 1550s, one of René's key Piedmontese allies was Carlo Malopera, cousin of the brothers Claudio, Sabaudian envoy to Venice and then to Rome, and Giorgio, who farmed the Duke's salt monopoly for several years. Carlo referred to himself as a faithful servant of René and reciprocated political favors with him.[65]

Due to his position in Valangin and his extended family's other holdings in the *pays de Vaud*, René also had an extensive network of support in the Swiss area. This enabled him to represent the interests of the Valle d'Aosta there, such as when he offered to assist Mathieu Lostan, Bailiff of the valley, when a Valdostano envoy was sent to Fribourg in early 1539. A herald from the Swiss city had passed through Aosta on his way to see the ducal official Carlo di Mombello, Count of Frossasco. This envoy had told Lostan

> that there was a very learned astrologer and a master builder, and having spent time with both of them, he told me that the *docteur astrologue* was more reliable but that he didn't dare to put his *science* into practice without the permission of the lords of Fribourg.

60 Fornaseri, 67-68, René to Ch III, Chambéry 17-VI-30; AHR, FC 263, mz. 1, Momfrey d'Azeglio to René, Azeglio, 3-VI-?). Azeglio discussed with René how he could 'metera su una bellissima falconaria [...] una falconaria da principe' (AEN, AS-F16, 19, Manfredo d'Azeglio to René, Azeglio 14-II-39).
61 AHR, FC 263, mz. 1, Luis [Luc?] Cambiani [Cambrain?] to René, Casale 25-II-?.
62 ASMn, Archivio Gonzaga, b. 747, cart. 15, René to Federico II Gonzaga, Casale 16-IV-31.
63 AHR, FC 263, mz. 1, Claude Jacquier [?] to René, Milan 24-IX-?.
64 Ibid., FC 264, mz. 1, Masserano to René, Masserano 15-XI-?; the county of Masserano was erected into a marquisate by Pope Paul III in 1547.
65 AEN, AS-F16, 13, Carlo Malopera to René, Milan 12-XI-57. Malopera helped René try to secure the governorship of Pavia for Nicolò Madruzzo, while René helped secure Malopera's appointment as *podestà* of Milan; see Ghinzoni, 357.

So, Lostan asked René to intervene with the Fribourgeois authorities on his behalf, in order to obtain the assistance of this *astrologue*. He also took the opportunity to thank René for his concern about 'the loss suffered by my wife and me'.[66] René's assistance was also requested, via Bellegarde, from a certain Jaques Golye (?), who had had his property confiscated by the Genevans. Authorities in Berne had subsequently been badly informed about his case, so he came to René for help.[67] Among René's papers at Valangin was a list (dated 1543) of property that had formerly been held by Aymé du Rosey in the mandament of Monthey, on the left bank of the Rhône above the lake of Geneva. The property listed included a house, stable, meadows, tithes, fields, rents, and *censes*. It is not clear whether René was perhaps helping Rosey in some dispute related to this property, or if he had acquired it and was hoping to use it as leverage in his dispute with the Longueville over Valangin, which was in arbitration in Berne in the spring of 1543.[68] René's friends and clients in the Swiss lands (including Aymon de Genève-Lullin; Urbain Quisard, Lord of Crans; members of the Erlach family, and others) advanced his interests there in various ways.[69]

One of René's key contacts in the Swiss area was Michel, Count of Gruyère, a second cousin whose mother was Marguerite de Vergy, niece of Guillemette de Vergy (René's grandmother). Michel's father, Jean II, Count of Gruyère, died in 1539, and Michel spent his youth at the court of King Francis I and was a supporter of the Duke of Savoy. He engaged in military and diplomatic service both to the French and to Charles V – this is perhaps what eventually brought on a series of financial difficulties for him. Still, in 1548, the Swiss recognized him as an ally.[70] Gruyère was an influential figure in Swiss politics in the 1540s and a close associate of René's cousin Villarsel. In November 1540, Gruyère served as a kind of postal intermediary for René, whose letters for Villarsel were passed along by servants of Gruyère. On this occasion, Gruyère also took it upon himself to defuse some sort of minor conflict involving Villarsel and the Countess of Challant. He also noted that the ten *écus* that René had sent had not been received.[71] Although well-connected, Gruyère

---

66 Ibid., AS-G16, 29, Lostan to René, Aosta 11-II-39.
67 Ibid., 6, René to Bellegarde, Virieu 23-IX-39.
68 Ibid., 11, property list of Aymé de Rosey, taken by René to Berne, 18-III-43?.
69 AHR, FC 264, mz. 1, Lullin to René, 'Damsprug' [Innsbruck?] 25-III-46?; AEN, AS-K16, 19, Valangin officer to René, s.d. [I-48?]; ibid., AS-F16, 16, Martine to René, Valangin ?-V-49; ibid., AS-H16, 1, B. Erlach to René, Beaufremont 16-XII-56). On the lord of Crans, see Tappy.
70 Birchler.
71 Villarsel had apparently given the impression of having slighted Mencia over the use of a certain horse; see AEN, AS-F16, 12, Gruyère to René, Echallens [?] 10-XI-40). A letter discussing

was also a demanding character. In late September 1549, he asked René to 'lend me Martine your master of the household' for a few months (this was three months after the Duke of Savoy had made the same request) for business of his in France.[72] A month later, he wrote René again, criticizing him (half-jokingly, it seems) for having 'been so stingy not to send me a piece of paper with news from you – but I do not wish in response to display my prodigality toward you by so freely describing my happenings, perils, and fortunes on so much paper'. He then thanked René for having lent him Martine, 'and for not being upset with me for having sent him back to you before the time that you had assigned'. He added that since he was 'was short of personnel', he would be grateful if Martine could continue to serve him for another few months. But then, he immediately complained that, after Martine had returned from France, he had gone to Valangin 'for your affairs, for a sum of money that had to be delivered by All Saints' Day' that was owed to 'the treasurer Steiger', even though he was still supposed to be serving Gruyère. He thus asked René to order Martine not to attend to René's business during this period.[73] Not long after this, Gruyère's financial troubles (which were perhaps related to a deficit in interpersonal skills) caught up to him; in 1554, Fribourg seized his fief of Corbières, which he had mortgaged to them. When he was unable to pay his other debts to Fribourg and Berne, he fled to Burgundy and the Swiss seized and divided his other lands.[74]

René also benefited from the networks of members of his network. Bellegarde, for example, was well-connected in the Swiss lands. Jehan Maville wrote to him apologetically in September 1541 about some troubles that he was having in sending letters from Soleure to Paris, but stressed that 'I did my loyal best, as one who greatly desires to serve my lord the Marshal' and urging Bellegarde to inform him 'how I could serve my lord and you'.[75]

René's relationship to the French Crown dates back to his participation at Pavia on behalf of Francis I and his subsequent imprisonment. He maintained his ties in France thereafter, and continued to collect a pension from the King. He wrote to Charles III in early 1530 about a contact at the royal court who had informed him about an upcoming journey by Francis I to Dijon and then Lyon, where he was to arrive in a couple of weeks.[76] His envoys to the

Gruyère's wish to purchase the horse might shed light on this episode (ibid., AS-I16, 27, Gruyère to Villarsel, 31-X-?).
72 Ibid., AS-F16, 20, Gruyère to René, Berne 28-IX-49.
73 Ibid., AS-H16, 21, Gruyère to René, La Bastie 29-X-49.
74 Birchler.
75 AHR, FC 260, no. 11, Jehan Maville? to Bellegarde, Neuchâtel 13-IX-41.
76 Fornaseri, 35-37, René to Ch III, Chambéry 26-I-30.

French court not only gave him news, they also transmitted communications from René to the King, the Constable, and the Chancellor, and helped him obtain letters of support from figures like the Duke of Guise.[77] An officer in Valangin urged René to write to the Duke and Duchess of Guise (probably in the course of the conflict with Neuchâtel over Valangin) to ask for support in René's 'matter, since they have authority in it'.[78] René's correspondents in France included 'the Countess of Valence', which seems to have been Louise de Clermont-Tallard, Countess of Tonnere, Lady of Crussol from 1556, and lady-in-waiting of Catherine de' Medicis. René asked her to assist him with respect to those 'who keep my money without reason', offering, in return, to 'do something even better to please you on another occasion when the opportunity arises'.[79] Another French contact was François, Cardinal of Tournon, a leading French prelate and statesman who agreed to send someone to René to discuss his concerns (probably his claim for back pensions owed to him).[80]

Over time, René sent a variety of individuals to the French court to solicit his affairs. His officer Granyer was received by Francis I himself, who promised him (via the Constable and the Duke of Aumale) that he would help compensate him 'for my expenses [*interestz*]' during his embassy.[81] Another of René's envoys to France was François de Riddes. In Paris, he set out to purchase clothing for René's family members (such as *chaussons* 'for the little ladies', his daughters). He also reported on the King's movements and coordinated letter exchanges between people passing through.[82] Another time while in Paris, De Riddes was in communication with the Constable, the Chancellor, and the Cardinal of Tournon about certain unnamed affairs of René's. De Riddes assured the Constable (Anne de Montmorency) that René was 'a good man, and that if the King had reason to suspect otherwise, he would justify the Count with respect to any doubters if need be'. Then the Constable told him: "'Wait my friend, don't go away until I have spoken to the King tomorrow morning and raised this matter with him, and I am very happy to do it because I am the Count's good friend.'" The royal council then reached some resolution, and De Riddes sent René a coded version of it.[83]

---

77 AHR, FC 263, mz. 1, Aymard to René, Paris 5-VII-? [1530s?].
78 AEN, AS-K16, 19, Valangin officer to René, s.d. [I-48?].
79 AHR, FC 74, no. 43, René to 'la comtesse de Valence,' Beaufremont 16-IV-?.
80 Ibid., FC 264, mz. 1, Tournon to René, Lyon 21-X-?.
81 AEN, AS-H16, 4, Granyer to René, Paris 26-VI-?.
82 AHR, FC 264, mz. 1, François de Riddes to Grandis, Paris 19-VI-?.
83 Ibid., François de Riddes to René, Chambéry 4-VIII-?. De Riddes also took care of textile purchasers and other matters for René; see ibid., François de Riddes to 'Sire Pierre Bauge marchant de draps de soyes a Lyon,' Romilly-s-Seine 22-IV-?.

The Baron of Chevron also served René in France, including after René's capture at Vercelli. Chevron exploited contacts at court with the royal secretary Claude de L'Aubespine (husband of René's first cousin), with Honorat II de Savoie, Count of Villars, and with Anne de Montmorency (Villars's brother-in-law). In the early 1550s, he found the Constable leaving the King's *lougis* and tried to speak to him but was unable to do so effectively due to 'the mass of people who are always there'.[84] After *souppé*, however, the Constable sent for him and gave him an audience in his room; he spoke very honestly about René's affairs, both those involving Brissac, who had already departed for Piedmont, and the others 'being managed by the lord Constable'. The Constable exhibited a good disposition toward René, but expected an appropriate dispatch (that is, an appropriate payment?). Chevron also recommended René's affairs to the Cardinals of Lorraine and Guise and to Nemours. Granyer was also in Paris at the time, but Chevron had been unable to speak to him. Chevron transmitted letters from René to the Imperial ambassador to the French court, Simon Renard (ambassador there from 1549-1553). The Constable had asked for news of Monsieur de Martigues, who apparently had been captured by the Imperials, but Chevron had none. The Constable expressed his hope that he would be released 'with an honest ransom'. Chevron planned to attend on the King in Paris and then travel to Blois 'by post to see *messieurs* his children', where he would stay 'in your usual lodgings'.[85] These examples show that René had very well-placed contacts at the French court, and could exercise considerable influence there, at least with respect to his own interests.

René's network also extended across what might be called the 'Middle Kingdom' – the borderland territories between the Valois and Habsburg dominions that stretched from the western Alps up through the Franche-Comté, the Rhineland, Alsace, Lorraine, and the Low Countries. Tom Scott has argued that, during the late fifteenth century, political culture along the Upper Rhine was marked by Burgundian expansionism and by conflict between southwest German princes (or feudal nobles) and the 'republican Swiss'. For Scott, though, there was a 'cultural integrity' in this area that might also have been matched by a 'regional economic identity'.[86] The barony of Beaufremont was situated in the heart of the old Middle Kingdom, and provided a base from which René reached out to other lords and rulers

---

84   AEN, AS-H16, 25, Chevron to René, St. Germain en Laye, 14-XI-53? (following citations from the same source).
85   Ibid.
86   T. Scott, 8-9.

in the area. In 1530, he recommended to the Duke of Savoy his cousins, the lords of St. Pol (perhaps a reference to François II de Bourbon and his kin), who were going to see the Duke, calling them 'your very humble servants who are inclined, as is their duty, to serve you'.[87] Pierre de la Baume, Bishop of Geneva (1522), Cardinal (1539), and Archbishop of Besançon (1541) was one of René's correspondents. After his expulsion from Geneva, Pierre took up residence at Arbois, in the Franche-Comté, whence he wrote with news from Spain and the Empire and sent René barrels of the local red wine.[88] Claude de Ray was from a leading Franc-Comtois family and his uncle had been a member of the Savoyard order of the Annonciade.[89] He wrote to René about the death of Pierre de La Baume in 1544. 'I know that you will not be bothered by the advancement of my house', he wrote, pointing out that the Cardinal's death was 'a disaster for his kin and friends, which include me'. Since this left many benefices vacant, he asked René to say a good word to the Duke of Savoy on behalf of his brother, 'who is studying in Bologna, and both of us will obliged to serve you as humble relatives and friends'.[90]

As we have seen, René also counted on various members of the House of Lorraine for support and assistance. Martine sometimes served as his interlocutor with the Duke of Guise, working to arrange meetings between René and the Guise at Joinville, for example.[91] René traveled to Lorraine in 1545 in order to meet the Duke of Guise, with whom he thought that 'my entire affair can be resolved'.[92] He sent dispatches from Beaufremont to Emanuel Filibert at the Imperial court via nobles in the service of the Count of Vaudémont and with other local merchants from Lorraine and Strasbourg.[93] An unknown correspondent pledged service to René in 1556, writing from Nancy, seat of the Lorraine court, and alerting him to letters sent via the Baron of Agneres and a valet of the Duchess of Lorraine.[94]

In Flanders, René's circle of allies included the financier Gaspard Schetz (see Chapter 7), and the noble Nicolas de Croÿ, who congratulated René when he was released from prison in 1555 and planned to come to Brussels

---

87 Fornaseri, 69, René to Ch III, Chambéry 23-VI-30.
88 AEN, AS-I16, 9, La Baume to René, Arbois 20-III-?; AHR, FC 263, mz. 1, La Baume to René, Arbois 13-XI-? [after 1539].
89 Guillaume, 79-80.
90 AEN, AS-H16, 3, Claude de Ray to René, Ray 19-VI-?.
91 Ibid., AS-I16, 6, ? to Martine, Moûtiers 10-IV-?.
92 Ibid., AS-H16, 17, 17a, René to Bellegarde, Ivrea 26-IX-45.
93 Fornaseri, 104-5, René to EF, Beaufremont 17-VII-48.
94 AEN, AS-I16, 22, ? to René, Nancy 13-III-56.

(whither René was traveling) to offer his service.[95] Also crucial were his ties to the Perrenot family. Thomas Perrenot (brother of Antoine, Bishop of Arras and future Cardinal of Granvelle) thanked him in 1556 for having sent his officer La Fontaine to visit his wife and him when his son was born, and pledged his service to René just as his father (Nicolas Perrenot de Granvelle) had done.[96] Although there are few surviving indications of René's network in Iberia (thanks largely to Mencia's family), we know that René went there twice: following his capture at Pavia, and then again in 1538 in the context of Habsburg-Valois negotiations. His servant Jeronimo Fagnano wrote to René from Toledo in November 1538 to give him an update on happenings at the Spanish court.[97] Another unknown correspondent produced a memoir in 1564 concerning René's affairs at the court of Spain.[98]

René's ecclesiastical network

René's networks of supporters, patrons, kin, and correspondents thus extended from the areas where his own lands were located to regions across Europe. These far-flung ties of reciprocity crisscrossed boundaries and offered access to resources and decision-makers in ways that gave him considerable leverage in his interactions with other political actors. The broad territorial scope of these connections was replicated in the array of ecclesiastical privileges and Church-related contacts that he enjoyed. Most of this ecclesiastical influence was regional, to be sure, and focused on the Valle d'Aosta and the Sabaudian lands. In 1533, Pope Clement VII gave René patronage rights over the Augustinian convent of St. Gilles at Verrès, enabling him to name the provost of the house, which held benefices and rights all over the valley.[99] In 1539, the provost whom René had appointed in 1535, Augustin Ferraris, wrote to him soon after his return from a mission that had taken him longer than he expected. He presented his excuses to René and promised to 'live as a good religious and upright man, applying myself to every virtue'.[100] In 1544, Ferraris stepped down so that René could appoint his illegitimate son François as provost.[101] At the other end of the valley, on the Grand-St-Bernard pass leading into the Valais (also referred to

95 Ibid., AS-G16, 5, Nicolas de Croye [?] to René, Brussels 24-XI-55.
96 Ibid., AS-I16, 18, Thomas Perrenot to René, Cantecroix [?] 8-VII-56.
97 Ibid., AS-F16, 17, Fagnano to René, Toledo 26-XI-38.
98 AHR, FC 290, no. 53, memoir dated 24-VII-64.
99 Ibid., FC 116, no. 13, execution (I-35) of 14-II-33 bull of Clement VII.
100 AEN, AS-F16, 7, 'mag'r de Verres' to René, 19-VI-39.
101 P.-E. Duc, 188-89.

as 'Montjoux'), was another Augustinian house. Provosts there were also in communication with René; either Philibert de La Forest (Provost, 1524-1552) or his cousin Benoît de La Forest (who succeeded Philibert until 1563) wrote to the Count from near Rome one summer to request an 'address in Berne'.[102]

The map of ecclesiastical jurisdictions in and around the valley did not respect secular political boundaries. The abbey of St. Maurice d'Agaune in the Valais had a variety of rights over parishes in the valley. For example, the Lords of Challant declared *reconnaissances* for property held from the church of St. Maurice, and, in 1552, the Abbot of St. Maurice granted René the investiture of the castle and jurisdiction of St. Martin de Graines.[103] Prior to 1536, the Duke of Savoy, with René's assistance, made ecclesiastical appointments involving men and institutions in various of his lands, thereby creating ties of dependence. René asked him on behalf of a local lord to grant a vacant canon's post in the Sainte-Chapelle to a son of the 'Banner Lord of Romont' and to assign 'a bastard from Valangin' to another canonry at Aiguebelle.[104] René stayed in close touch with the Bishop of Lausanne through correspondence carried by trusted servants such as Castellamonte, and he was also involved in other kinds of ecclesiastical disputes in the *pays de Vaud*.[105]

René's ecclesiastical ties extended farther abroad. His servant Jeronimo Fagnano was in contact with Benedetta Spinola Carretto about an unidentified 'deal concerning the things of My Lord of Challant', which Carretto had discussed with a high cleric (possibly Cardinal Agostino Spinola, from Savona), reaching the conclusion that the matter should wait.[106] At around the same time, the cleric Gaspare Capris, future Bishop of Asti and one of René's protégés, sent news about happenings at the Sabaudian court (the Duke was said to be on his way to Savona), and in Rome (whence the Bishop of Ivrea, Filiberto Ferrero, future Cardinal, had just left to take up his position as papal nuncio in France).[107] A few years later, Gamache enlisted the support of Ferrero's uncle, Bonifacio Ferrero (also a cardinal) in Rome, to

---

102 AHR, FC 264, mz. 1, Prevost of Montjoux to René, Bibiana 30-VIII-?.
103 Ibid., FC 211, I, no. 4, investiture dated 27-I-52; ibid., FC 141, no. 1, *reconnaissances* from various years.
104 Fornaseri, 31-33, René to Ch III, Chambéry 13-I-30.
105 AHR, FC 263, mz. 1, Castellamonte to René (in Aosta), Turin 23-II-?. For René's mediation of a conflict between clergy from Romont and the archdeacon of the collegial church there (Jean de Marnix, secretary of a former Duchess of Savoy, Margaret of Austria), see Fornaseri, 56, René to Ch III, Romont 7-V-30. On Jean de Marnix and Margaret of Austria, see Eichberger, 50-52; Cauchies, 368-69, 374; Bruchet, 43-50.
106 AHR, FC 260, Benedetta Spinola Caretto to Fagnano, Savona 18-IV-37.
107 Ibid., FC 263, mz. 1, Gaspar Capris? to René, Vercelli 18-V-37?.

raise money for a particular project. Gamache also sent René updates about the Bishop of Aosta, who suggested that the Count not solicit 'the matter of St. Gilles' (the appointment of François as provost?) yet, since the Cardinal was old and might have other intentions.[108] Jean de Frainel, Abbot of the Augustinian monastery of Chaumousey (in the Vosges, about 50 kilometers from Beaufremont), thanked René in 1556 for his letter and his assistance, and sent his nephew to see Mencia to thank her personally.[109]

René's key subordinates

As one reads the papers produced by René over the course of his 45-year career, one encounters a small group of officers who served faithfully for long periods in various regions: Castellamonte, Bellegarde, Granyer, Martine, Gautier, Chevron, Ducrest, De Riddes, Grandis, and some others, such as the castellans Gamache and Grat Rolin. It is difficult to find biographical information on these individuals. Some of them perhaps inherited family service to the Challant. In 1478, René's grandfather Louis named Fernando della Porta di Castellamonte as one of his procurators, though this might simply have been a resident of Castellamonte rather than a family member.[110] 'Granyer' was likely the same person as or a relative of Bernardin de Granier, an official in the Genevois, *maître d'hôtel* of Jacques de Savoie-Nemours and father of Claude de Granier, Bishop of Geneva (1579-1602), who was, in turn, uncle of St. François de Sales. He traveled to the Low Countries on behalf of René in the 1550s, writing about his arrival in Zeeland and his efforts to get from there to Antwerp prior to René's arrival.[111] He also served as an envoy to Paris, exchanging letters with secretaries such as Aynard Sappin, who 'spent a lot of money in order not to lose his office' – a sacrifice that René's interests might lead him to recognize. If René were to treat him well, Granyer suggested, 'he wants to support your rights and always remain your humble servant'.[112]

In his first will of 1523, René made a number of bequests to his officers and servants: 100 *écus* to Luigi di Castellamonte, 100 to his *maître d'hôtel* Francoys Feste, 200 to Michel Vercellon (Castellan of Challant), 100 to Gamache, 50 to Grat Rolin (Castellan of Aymaville), 50 to Guillaume Tollein

---

108 AEN, AS-G16, 28, Gamache to René, Aosta 3-VII-43?.
109 Ibid., 2, the Abbot of Chaumousey 'Franelz' [Jean de Frainel] to René, 'de votre maison de Chaumosey' 1-VII-56.
110 AHR, FC 73, no. 27, procuration dated 29-X-1478.
111 Ibid., FC 263, mz. 1, Granyer to René, Bruges 18-V-?.
112 AEN, AS-H16, 4, Granyer to René, Paris 26-VI-?.

(Castellan of Châtillon), etc. He also left money in smaller amounts to other servants, including 'Guyot Jacques the groom, Jacques the muleteer', the ordinary servants of Bianca Maria, and the servants of his grandmother Marguerite.[113] We occasionally glimpse the relationships between these officers, and with their Lord. François de Riddes wrote to René's secretary Grandis from Paris during the 1530s, expressing surprise that their Lord 'is unhappy with me' and asking Grandis to intervene on his behalf. He pointed to the limited resources at his disposal and a recent illness that prevented him from completing his mission, asking Grandis to 'speak for me' and to be 'my advocate', just as he would do for Grandis in a similar situation. He also recommended himself to 'all my companions and to the young ladies of the house' and asked Grandis to tell his mother Claudine 'that she not make anything of my not writing her, since I am so upset not to have been able to complete the deal for my said lord'.[114] By early August, he was back in Chambéry, whence he described to René the 'stomach illness and fever' that he had endured in Paris.[115] A March 1541 letter offers another example of René's officers supporting each other. Jeronimo Fagnano informed Roz Favre and Grat Rolin about the death of Grandis, advising them 'of all the arrangements for the obsequies or funeral, and [...] burial of poor deceased Grandis'. He also promised to have this carried out by Friar Felice and 'at least a dozen other priests [...] according to your will, to satisfy the honor and benefit of his soul'.[116]

Officers like Gautier were constantly confronted with the challenge of coordinating information transfers between different people who were often in motion between Italy and transalpine Europe. In late May 1543, Gautier wrote to René (then traveling between Berne and Aosta) that he was going to send a dispatch to René in Valangin (where the Count had been at the beginning of the month). But, when Gautier had recently been in Chambéry, he learned from Madame de La Croix that René was on his way to Aosta. So, Gautier was sending his letter there. He had already sent another packet via one of Mencia's servants, who had been in Chambéry. That dispatch included news about business with a merchant named Pierre Saugey and a report of the response of the President of the Chambéry *parlement* to a communication from René.[117]

---

113   AST1, PD 188, f. 271, bequests made by René in his 1523 will.
114   AHR, FC 264, mz. 1, François de Riddes to Grandis, Paris 19-VI-?; ibid., FC 263, mz. 1, Aymard to René de Challant, Paris 5-VII-?.
115   AHR, FC 264, mz. 1, François de Riddes to René, Chambéry 4-VIII-?.
116   Ibid., FC 260, no. 11, Jeronimo Fagnano to Roz Favre and Grat Rolin, Vercelli 5-III-41.
117   AEN, AS-H16, 24, Gautier to René, Virieu 23-V-43.

Officials engaged in a wide variety of work for the Count. The 'Doctor' Jacques Cachiot (whether he was a physician or a lawyer was unclear) was involved in a range of activities. In Casale Monferrato, he worked with Grat Rolin and others on René's property interests. One of these officers reported that a certain Rafaello da Lugnano was willing to purchase some documents that were in René's possession. The officers also tried to meet in Milan with the 'master foundryman [...] to learn about the metal [related to weapons production?]' but this artisan was out of town.[118] Rolin, Cachiot, and the Bishop of Aosta kept abreast of financial disputes; in one involving a feudal official in Aymavilles, heard before the Duke's 'resident council', they were able to minimize René's exposure.[119] In May 1530, Cachiot was also a go-between for René, then in Romont, and the Duke of Savoy.[120]

Some of René's officers and servants appear only fleetingly in the records: Nicolas d'Avise was René's *maître d'hôtel* in 1563 but seems to have acquired that position only toward the end of René's life.[121] Servants of René's relatives, such as the 'Chamberlain' of Guillemette de Vergy, Henrys Damours, also served René. Damours helped the Count locate muleteers in Lorraine; while some servants were quite mobile, others were bound to one or another of René's transregional holdings.[122]

Mencia's network

Sharon Kettering recently observed that early modern nobles placed clients in princely households to try to win influence and information but remarked that historians had not examined the practice closely.[123] Kettering was especially interested in ladies of the court, but subsequent work indicated that there was still no extensive study of noble female households, for which it was difficult even to identify members. This has been the case despite scholarly interest in the social and political

---

118 AHR, FC 263, mz. 1, ? to René?, s.l., s.d.
119 Another case involving a certain Francoys Savyoz had been set aside until the Bishop would be able to attend to it; ibid., FC 264, mz. 1, Grat Rolin? to René, Aosta 26-XII-?.
120 Fornaseri, 55, René to Ch III, Romont 7-V-30 [2 letters].
121 *Recueil*, 193-94, entry dated 9-III-63. A certain 'Belmond' submitted an account of travel expenses incurred in René's service in 1560-1561, but does not appear in earlier sources; see AHR, FC 70, no. 6, account of Belmond (1560-1561).
122 Ibid., FC 263, mz. 1, Henrys Damours 'chambrier de madame de Valengin' to René, Bar 12-II-?.
123 Kettering, 'Strategies of Power.'

roles of early modern women, and in the transnational nature of female courtly service.[124] Indeed, within the past fifteen years or so, noble and princely consorts, and the political activity of noblewomen in general, have begun to receive sustained scholarly attention. Judith Aikin has studied Aemilia Juliana of Schwarzburg-Rudolstadt, highlighting not only her production of heirs, but also her networking through correpondence, offering of political advice, and oversight of the household.[125] The political roles of the female members of the Medici dynasty, as consorts, regents, communicators, and patrons have recently been the subject of scholarly study.[126] Grendi's work on the Balbi focused on the role of family's women, which extended beyond juridical limits as both widows and daughters lent money or exerted financial influence by renouncing their dowries.[127] Some attention has been given to the influence of widows on a family's destiny, including by directing the confessional orientation of sons and daughters.[128] As a widow, Louise de Savoie exerted considerable authority in France, ruling as regent for her son in 1515 and 1525 without encountering any objections.[129] Widows might hold or govern lands in their own right, and even wives could act as guardians for their children or govern lands for absent husbands or sons (though they do not seem to have been members of feudal consortia). Some widows 'became formidable matriarchs'.[130]

While the surviving source material does not permit an exhaustive and comparative study of Mencia of Portugal-Braganza, there are enough records to indicate that her own political network was a crucial element of the Challant family's European position. René's consort for 30 years, Mencia exercised a great deal of authority, both thanks to her own political relationships, and by serving as René's proxy during periods when he was abroad or in prison (1553-1555). Mencia's circle of correspondents included other powerful princesses, like Antoinette de Bourbon, who, sometime prior to 1550, thanked Mencia for 'the powder' and the medical recipe that Mencia had sent her prior to her coming to see Antoinette in person, in Lorraine.[131] She received a letter from a Portuguese princess in the 1550s,

---

124 Akkerman and Houben, 5, 9, 23.
125 Aikin.
126 Brown; see also Ferrari.
127 Grendi, xviii.
128 Nassiet, *Parenté, noblesse et États dynastiques*, 192.
129 De Waele, 211; on this topic, see also Taylor, 561-62.
130 C. Shaw, 17.
131 AHR, FC 263, mz. 1, Antoinette de Bourbon to Mencia, Joinville 18-IV-?.

expressing a desire for René's release and offering other news.[132] Philibert de Marcilly, Lord of Cypierre, was captured by the Imperial army and imprisoned in Milan, which was probably whence he wrote to Mencia as 'your very humble servant', expressing his hope for release.[133] Jean, Count of Salm, thanked her from Brussels for the messages that she had sent him via François-Prosper de Genève-Lullin and Pierre Maillard du Bouchet, two of Emanuel Filibert's most trusted servants.[134] Bouchet corresponded with Mencia fairly frequently. In 1551, he thanked her for commending him to René and sent her news from Milan about the capture of François de Coligny d'Andelot and Cypierre by the Imperials. He had seen Cypierre himself and reported that one of the two French lords 'said to hell with the deal and the dealers', apparently indicating an unwillingness to negotiate for their release.[135] On another occasion, he promised to try to send her a 'fairly powerful' gray horse that Monsieur de La Chaulx had given to him. Giovanni Francesco Costa d'Arignano and Antoine de Cusinens confirmed that it would not be a problem for him to send it to her in Beaufremont.[136] Bouchet also wrote to Mencia from Flanders in October 1554 to encourage her about efforts to have her husband released.[137] René's secretary Gautier reported to Mencia from Vercelli about his efforts to find her citrus fruit and about her husband's whereabouts.[138]

Other influential members of the Savoyard and Vaudois nobility, such as Cusinens and François de Riddes, also exchanged letters with Mencia. The former purchased clothing for her in Brussels,[139] and the latter corresponded with her about Spanish ladies in her suite, about creditors, about marriage rumors (such as the Marquis of Saluzzo, Gian Gabriele [?] marrying the sister of King Francis I's mistress, Anne de Pisseleu, Duchess of Étampes), and about his cooperation with the Duke of Guise to advance the affairs of René.[140] Other contacts sent her information about military developments (including the army's finances); conversations with key leaders such as

132 Ibid., Dona Francesca [Teresa?] to Mencia, Rivore? 14-XI-? [c. 1555] (the author was perhaps Mencia's niece, daughter of her brother Fernando-Ruiz, or perhaps Fernando-Ruiz's wife; see http://genealogy.euweb.cz/capet/capet61.html, 12 November 2019).
133 AHR, FC 264, mz. 1, Sipierre 'v're bien ungble serviteur' to Mencia, s.l., s.d.
134 Ibid., FC 260, Jean, Count of Salm to Mencia, Brussels 20-IX-55.
135 Ibid., FC 263, mz. 1, Bouchet to Mencia, s.d. [internal evidence suggests 1551].
136 Ibid., Bouchet to Mencia, s.d.
137 Ibid., Bouchet to Mencia, 'Du camp de l'empereur a Meyni' [Meyri?] 12-X-54 [year by internal evidence].
138 Ibid., FC 264, mz. 1, Gautier to Mencia, Vercelli 26-IX-?.
139 Ibid., FC 263, mz. 1, Cusinens to Mencia [two letters, one dated Brussels 24-IX-?].
140 Ibid., FC 264, mz. 1, François de Riddes to Mencia, Romilly-s-Seine, 21-IV-?.

Ferrante Gonzaga, Imperial commander in Italy; and reports on influential individuals who were ill or close to death.[141]

At various times throughout her married life, Mencia exercised authority over the Challant fiefs and among political actors in the valley and beyond. This role seems to have begun for her by the mid 1540s; there are few indications of her political activity from the time of her marriage through the 1530s. An unknown correspondent wrote to 'Madame' in an undated letter about the arrival of the ducal secretary Montpon, informing her that he had communicated with the Duke and promised to carry out his charge faithfully. This correspondent also appealed to his service to the convent of St. Bernard as evidence that he would be a worthy servant of hers.[142]

In 1545, René expressed his frustration to Bellegarde that he had not been better informed about the fiscal and financial situation of Valangin. He was angry that the instructions on these matters recently issued by Mencia had been disregarded.[143] Having obviously learned his lesson, in October 1547, Blaise Junod wrote the Countess a long account about the state of affairs in Valangin, updating her on revenues and construction projects there and blaming the receiver Trolliet for things that had gone wrong.[144] At this point, Junod worried that, if René decided to 'rent out the seigniory to avoid the expense', their cash flow would dry up. The receivers, including himself, would then have to lend money to René to enable him to cover building expenses. He thus sought Mencia's advice about how to proceed. He also reported that Martine had passed through Valangin, given him a message from her, and upbraided him for having tried to collect too much 'with great disturbance of the poor people'. Trolliet had replied that, regardless of how much he collected, he would follow René's instructions never to take anything out of the *seigneurie*. Junod did not know if Trolliet would really stay 'in his district [Thonon, apparently]' until Lent, or whether he would return with Bellegarde. Understandably, Junod asked Mencia not to discuss the contents of this letter with Trolliet.[145] This correpondence demonstrates how deeply involved Mencia was with the administration of the Challant fiefs and with the political relationships among members of their clientele. She seems to have been particularly attached to Junod. A few years later, Mencia sent Claude Amyod to see Junod about fifteen *écus*

---

141 Ibid., Marcot? to Mencia, Lavaie? 22-VIII?-? [mid 1550s?].
142 ? to Mencia [?], s.l., s.d. [before 1553?].
143 AEN, AS-G16, 14, René to Bellegarde, Issogne 14-XII-45.
144 Ibid., AS-H16, 26, Blaise Junod to Mencia, Valangin 17-X-47.
145 Ibid.

that he was to collect for her. In response, Junod apologized for the fact that what he had been able to gather was insufficient but explained that the 'good people' could give no more, and that he had even included five *écus* of his own money. He had already sent her another 25 *écus*, which she should have received, and planned to collect 40 more, hoping to have most of them 'by the next fairs'.[146]

After René was captured at Vercelli in November 1553, Mencia was more actively involved in politics. This is most apparent in records of the *Conseil des Commis* and other authorities in the Valle d'Aosta, although it is also true that Sabaudian and Imperial authorities sent Giovanni Battista Dell'Isola to attend to strategic matters in the valley soon after the Count's capture.[147] In February 1554, Dell'Isola sent Mencia news of military developments in Piedmont and elsewhere, and also asked her to have Ducrest send a receipt to the Spanish treasurer Fornaro for the 1000 *scudi* that Ducrest had received from Dell'Isola in Milan. It was important that Mencia have Ducrest send the receipt 'so the Imperial chamber will enter it into the said treasurer's accounts'.[148] Montpon reported to Mencia from the Imperial court a few months later with details about prisoner-exchange efforts and a message of gratitude from Emanuel Filibert about her help to collect a subsidy from subjects in the valley.[149]

Giovanni Francesco Costa d'Arignano explained to the Countess the Duke's reaction to the collection of the subsidy 'in that area'.[150] He had read Mencia's recent letter about the subsidy out loud to the Duke 'to disabuse him of any evil impression that he might have imagined'. Most likely, this was related to an initial effort by Mencia to shield her own Challant subjects from having to contribute, given their already considerable efforts to provide for René's expenses. However, after Arignano explained the situation to the Duke 'he trusted and believed what I reported' and 'took everything very well'. The Duke also told Arignano that he had always respected both Mencia 'like a blood relative of his [through his mother Beatrice]' and René, 'whom he holds as one of the great and principal lords of his *estat*'. Emanuel Filibert stressed his confidence in René, 'having placed everything in his hands, including the administration of his lands, vassals, and the authority of

---

146 Ibid., AS-F16, 23, Blaise Junod to Mencia, Valangin 16-III-51.
147 See AHR, FCC, and AST1, LP, correspondence of various individuals (especially Dell'Isola in I.8).
148 AHR, FC 260, Dell'Isola to Mencia, Vercelli 24-II-54.
149 Ibid., Montpon to Mencia, Brussels 21-V-54.
150 Ibid., FC 263, mz. 1, Arignano to Mencia, Brussels 20-V-54 (following citations from same source).

lieutenant over all of them'. However, the Duke was somewhat preoccupied by 'the contrariness and irresolution of your subjects regarding the said subsidy, given that it is for the common good and conservation of the *pays* and for profit and advantage'. Emanuel Filibert would have preferred 'that you had required them to agree right away without permitting them to raise any objections that might incite others'.[151] Mencia found herself in the middle of a sharp political dispute between her Challant subjects, her husband, valley authorities, and the Duke of Savoy. For the time being, though, her immediate focus was on the valley's safety and her husband's release from prison.

In early 1555, Mencia expressed impatience with Dell'Isola for taking so long to attend to the defenses at the castle of Bard. The valley was in the midst of trying to renew its neutrality agreement with the French, and the President of the Chambéry *Parlement*, who was overseeing this task, was creating obstacles. Mencia saw the military situation as urgent, and implored Dell'Isola to come soon so as not to 'lose the whole country'.[152] Meanwhile, she continued to oversee her husband's fiefs and financial affairs. In June 1555, she issued a procuration for Blaise Junod and Jehan Robin to alienate 'the seigniory of Bourjod in the *pays de Vaud* and bailiwick of Yverdon', in order to provide for sums owed by the Count of Gruyère to René. Mencia began the procuration with the words: 'We, by the charge and administration that we hold in the regime and government of the property of the lord my husband, according to his rights and claims in this respect, well informed and advised and by our free and good will.' She clearly saw herself as a lieutenant for René, endowed with the full authority that such an office entailed, not only in the Valle d'Aosta but in multiple regions.[153]

In a letter sent (probably from Valangin) soon after his release from prison, René showed that he had come to appreciate his wife's abilities and desired to continue to rely on her help. He asked Mencia to 'order as well as you can all of the necessary matters and arrange everything so that we can put together as much money as we can over there'. He directed her to command the secretary Ducrest as she saw fit: 'I appointed him master of the household and chief accountant and hope that he does the job to my satisfaction and yours.' He intended for all their officers to be at her service, with no exceptions, 'neither my daughters nor any others'. He informed her that he was going to have more blank letters with her signature on them

151 Ibid., FC 263, mz. 1, Arignano to Mencia, Brussels 20-V-54.
152 Ibid., FC 260, copy of Mencia to Dell'Isola, Issogne 22-II-55.
153 AEN, AS-K16, 14, procuration by Mencia for Robin and Junod, Vercelli 25-VI-55.

made so that he could send them to 'my ladies of Lorraine and Escott', and to others who would otherwise find it strange that she had not written to them. Only two of these blanks remained, one of which he sent to the King of England (Philip). He was waiting to receive from her 'the legal documents of [Pierre?] Hoteman' and expressed his satisfaction that the Portuguese came, along with his hope that 'this journey will be very profitable for us'. While he was away, she was to order their houses and their fiefs' revenues, and to be attentive to the fact that the prices of their agrarian products might drop due to the truces currently holding (because of lower demand than would have been the case with armies campaigning, presumably). He also sent her 'the titles' that he had brought with him after having had them examined by La Fontaine, who was optimistic about them. Along with those, he also shipped her a clock and some cheese from Gruyère, promising to send more news 'via Besançon or Milan'.[154]

In March 1556, René conceded to Mencia the ability to 'dispose of her dowry property' by an act notarized in the presence of Pierre Maillard du Bouchet and two other witnesses. This act gave her complete authority over 'all of her dotal property and rights, and others belonging to her, both moveable and immoveable of whatever kind' with power to assign them 'to whomever she wishes as it pleases her'.[155] A year later, René granted her the faculty of appointing a commissioner for the renewal of the feudal *reconnaissances* of Aymavilles.[156] In December 1557, she issued a receipt to the Castellan of Graines, Gamache, for 25 *écus*, which he had given her from the fief's revenues.[157] Mencia's involvement in the political affairs of the family enabled her to mobilize her own networks – in Italy, Portugal, and Spain – and it continued after René's liberation from captivity, right up until the end of her life.

Letters and information

René's communications with Mencia and with his officers required the efficient production, transmission, and storage of information. These are problems that have begun to receive scholarly attention within early modern

---

154   AHR, FC 263, mz. 1, René to Mencia [?], s.l. [Valangin?], s.d. Perhaps the Lady of Escott/Estott was Adrienne d'Estouteville, sister-in-law of Antoinette de Bourbon.
155   Ibid., FC 290, no. 38, act dated St. Rémy 6-III-56.
156   Ibid., FC 180, no. 20, act dated 12-X-57.
157   AEN, AS-K16, 21, receipt from Mencia to Gamache, Vercelli 19-XII-57.

studies, though not necessarily from the perspective of spatially dispersed lordship. Some work has focused on the history of archival practices and the ways in which feudal lords organized their own familial and administrative records.[158] Lords were aware of the importance of archival documentation for the establishment of rights claims or social status that could be passed on to subsequent generations. In the early modern Netherlands, 'a culture of record-keeping' served as an 'anchor of identity' for the nobility.[159] By the late seventeenth century, archives had become associated with the verification of a document's authenticity. Expert knowledge was developed by those working with the records possessed and jealously guarded by sovereigns or lords.[160] Markus Friedrich examines seigneurial administration during the eighteenth century, including the creation and management of archives. He highlights the role of the *'feudistes'*, who had expertise in reading old handwriting, especially in Latin, and who worked for lords across France as legal and informational consultants. Friedrich shows how knowledge about record repositories within local districts, about 'which notaries had worked where and for how long and who owned the old registers now' and about 'what had happened to a family's papers once a family died out or moved' effectively dispersed seigneurial power within a community.[161] The necessity of such geographically specific knowledge for officials serving local lords raises the related question of how families with multiple, geographically dispersed fiefs, like the Challant, managed their documentation, especially in earlier centuries prior to the emergence of the *feudistes* as archival experts.

Information was not only stored away in the archives of the politically powerful; it was also circulated. Scholars have recently argued that the English, beginning in the late sixteenth century, were increasingly well-informed about politics.[162] Other historians have studied letter-writing and postal services during the sixteenth century. For Jay Caplan, writing, sending, and receiving letters through the mediation of postal structures created 'epistolary spaces' that brought distant places closer and blurred the boundaries between public and private.[163] Fritz Glauser has examined

158 Walsham.
159 Buylaert and Haemers, 133.
160 Head.
161 Friedrich, 67.
162 Lloyd Bowen claims that the Welsh, who circulated information in their mother tongue, were part of this process, and had the advantage of being 'bilingual brokers who could readily access and circulate information' (Bowen, 127). Likewise, Paul Slack viewed seventeenth-century England as a laboratory for the use of information, including quantitative kinds; see also Slack; Zwierlein.
163 Caplan, 7, 173-75.

such postal structures more specifically, in the sixteenth-century Swiss confederation. This Swiss structure developed out of an earlier system in which lords, cities, religious orders, banks, and other entities had their own messenger services. Commercial, financial, political, and religious interests drove the development of a unified system. Glauser discusses specific postal routes and identifies postal agents in the Swiss area during the 1500s.[164] At that time, letters took five or six days to go from Brussels or Malines to Innsbruck during the summer (a day longer in winter) and two or three days to Paris. The Malines-Innsbruck postal route was set up in the 1490s, and, at about that time, there was also a regular service between the Bishop of Geneva and the Duke of Savoy.[165]

Throughout his lifetime, but especially during the tumultuous years of the 1530s and 1550s, René struggled to send and receive timely and accurate information from his own officials and from the Duke and Imperial authorities. He wrote to Charles III in May 1535 that 'according to the news arriving here, we should warn you not to be surprised if we send you changing opinions, since as things change, we have to respond and order them differently, acting as diligently as possible in everything as the case requires'. The urgency of having reliable information quickly was tied to the problem of where to assign scarce resources. On this specific occasion, René sent the letter with an envoy named Baptiste, and asked that the Duke send him right back, along with 500 to 700 *écus*, 'and more if possible, to try to organize your affairs [...] for the military campaign and other things' and other things. Two responses to the problems of coordinating information and reacting to rapidly changing situations were blank letters and credential letters – crucial forms of sixteenth-century political technology. Blank letters were official missives signed by the ruler with portions left blank so that agents could fill in key bits of information according to circumstances that had changed or had been unanticipated. Credentials empowered an envoy to make agreements with the full faith of the principal, again permitting him to adjust to a changed environment. In the letter discussed here, René and others were about to embark on a mission to visit towns in the Monferrato, to advance the Duke's interests there, and asked both for letters 'that trustworthily identify us' as the Duke's ambassadors, and for 'blank letters, so that we can insert above what is required, to address to the towns were we go, which will be necessary for us to assure them that everything is according to your will'. In closing, René noted that the Duke was 'at Chivasso in the middle of the

164 Glauser.
165 Ibid., 7, 12; Caplan, 30.

Monferrato' and proposed that, since 'seeing you will encourage everyone', they would travel there to visit him. Spending time with the ruler, physically in the same place, was important for a host of reasons, not least because it provided the opportunity to exchange information directly, without time delays, and to communicate about what circumstances demanded while minimizing ambiguities or misreadings.[166]

As he was on the move from one region to another, René constantly sent and received information about Sabaudian and European events. Key topics included the health and well-being of important individuals,[167] and diplomatic and military developments.[168] Much of the news about international events came from the Imperial court. In March 1546, René was updated on the Emperor's negotiations with France, on Charles V's relations with his brother and the other German princes, and on recent fighting with the Turks near Buda.[169] A couple of months later, Stroppiana sent the Duke a long report from court, which ended up in René's hands. This text included a reflection on Frederick II, the Elector Palatine, who, malcontent with Charles V due the latter's refusal to support his claims to the Danish throne, had openly declared himself Lutheran. Stroppiana's sense was that the Count had been leaning that way 'since the first time we were in Speyer, when he was already listening to the Lutherans' and that 'beneath this dissimulation he heard many secrets which will perhaps be revealed'. The report indicated that Claude-Louis Alardet was to address the Imperial Diet, perhaps to request support, and that Emanuel Filibert had had a 'beautiful and honorable meeting' with Cristoforo Madruzzo, Prince-Bishop of Trento. Military preparations in northwestern Italy were also outlined.[170]

Closely tied to military news was financial news of various sorts. In May 1546, word arrived of peace talks between France and England

---

166 Fornaseri, 92-93, René to Ch III, Mont Cenis 6-V-35.
167 In 1539, De Riddes reported from the French court on the impending death of the Duke's ambassador, so De Riddes 'persuada a l'ung des principaulx de ses gens de retyrer secretement tous ces papiers et scriptures concernantz voz afferez' (Ibid., 98-99, René to Ch III, Virieu 9-IX-39). For other health news, see AHR, FC 264, mz. 1, Lambert to René, Nice 10-XII-?; ibid., Lullin to René, Nice 23-VII-38?; ibid., Lullin to René, 'Damsprug' [Innsbruck?] 25-III-46?; Fornaseri, 107-8, René to EF, Vercelli 26-II-51.
168 AEN, AS-F16, 3, Lambert to René, Nice 25-XI-38; ibid, AS-R5.10, ccc, note s.l., s.d., but the next document in the bundle, dated 13-VIII-42, refers to it; Fornaseri, 98-99, René to Ch III, Virieu 9-IX-39; AHR, FC 263, mz. 1, Castellan of Bard to René [?], 11-II-?.
169 Ibid., FC 264, mz. 1, Lullin to René, 'Damsprug' [Innsbruck?] 25-III-46?.
170 AEN, AS-I16, 29, copy of Stroppiana to Ch III, Regensburg 24-V-46; ibid., 30, Lullin to Ch III, Regensburg 24-V-46.

– including a French offer of 1.8 million ducats to the English for the recovery of Boulogne.[171] An undated letter, perhaps from 1552, reported that the Fuggers were trying to raise 600,000 *scudi* for Charles V, but that no money could be had from Flanders, since the roads were all blocked by the Emperor's enemies.[172] Sometimes René's financial interests suffered due to communications problems. One of Bellegarde's agents informed him in 1541 that he had sent letters to Soleure 'to send by the post to the *Sieur* Pattoulles, a banker in Paris', but the letters were returned to him because 'the King prohibited anyone from sending letters through his *postes* that were for their own affairs'. From now on, 'ordinarily, every packet dispatched must be addressed not to the overseer of the post riders, but to the King'.[173]

Other topics of correspondence related to who was going where and when,[174] and to the happenings at various princely courts.[175] Occasionally, letters sent to the Duke of Savoy ended up in René's hands, either because the Duke read them and forwarded them, or because René or one of his agents was supposed to relay them to the Duke, but the communications broke down and they remained in René's possession. For example, in May 1546, two letters addressed to Charles III by Stroppiana and Lullin, from the Imperial court at Regensburg, were received in Valangin and remained there.[176] Had the Duke already read them? Or were they supposed to have been passed along to Vercelli or Nice, and were somehow neglected?

The issue of making sure that letters reached their desination, and could later be accessed when necessary, was related to the broader problem of information storage and access. In 1529, René reported to Charles III that he needed certain documents, could not find them in the *Chambre des comptes*, and thought that Lullin might have them. They were related to the

---

171 Ibid., 29, copy of Stroppiana to Ch III, Regensburg 24-V-46.
172 AHR, FC 263, mz. 1, ? to 'Mons de Rie,' s.d. [1552?].
173 Ibid., FC 260, no. 11, Jehan Maville [?] to Bellegarde, Neuchâtel 13-IX-41.
174 Fornaseri, 100, René to Ch III, Virieu 16-X-39; AHR, FC 263, mz. 1, Hieronimo da Fagnano to René, Casale 21-X-42 [?]; ibid., Granyer to René, Conflans 14-I-42; ibid., ? to 'Mons de Rie,' s.d. [1552?]; AEN, AS-I16, 29, copy of Stroppiana to Ch III, Regensburg 24-V-46.
175 Granyer informed René when Jacques de Savoie-Nemours made his first entry into Annecy, 'laquelle sera belle car ilz font grandes preparatives' (AHR, FC 263, mz. 1, Granyer to René, Conflans 14-I-42). For other courtly news, see ibid., FC 260, Granyer to René, Châtillon [Dombes] 25-VIII-42; AEN, AS-I16, 30, Lullin to Ch III, Regensburg 24-V-46. Gichar compared reactions to the failed 1541 expedition of Charles V to Algiers to what had been done in Lyon after the French loss and the King's capture at Pavia in 1525. On that occasion, the French had demonstrated 'asseurance et fermete de vouloir et propoz aux adversitez. [...] Qui donne congnoissance de la diversité des complexions et mode de vivre' (ibid., FC 264, mz. 1, Gichar? to René, Milan 20-XII-42?).
176 AEN, AS-I16, 29, copy of Stroppiana to Ch III, Regensburg 24-V-46; ibid., 30, Lullin to Ch III, Regensburg 24-V-46.

THE CHALLANT POLITICAL NETWORKS   211

interest of the Lord of Monaco in purchasing 'one of your places near Nice'.[177] On another occasion, Pierre Bachet, a ducal official in Bresse, notified René that the Duke had given him an inventory containing various titles. He would give it to René if the Duke gave him permission.[178] A key challenge was the transfer of crucial documentation, whether fiscal, jurisdictional, or otherwise, from one of René's fiefs to another. The Count did not have a central archive, and so his papers moved in unexpected directions depending on immediate needs, making it difficult to keep track of them. One summer, Grat Rolin and René coordinated the shipment of inventories of documents from Verrès and Aosta that related to Virieu, Coligny, and other places in the transalpine lands (many of which concerned the La Chambre inheritance) over the mountains. Rolin oversaw the packing of 'the chests and all the baggage' to send to Virieu. He made arrangements with a muleteer from Morgex to transport everything to the 'Three Kings' in Montmélian for a fee of 16½ florins. From there, 'big Jacques' would deliver everything to Virieu. He went through Boulet's *coffre* and packed everything that he could find concerning 'the rights of Virieu, Coligny, and the marsh of Chavelley (Chavoley), and the rights against *monseigneur* de La Chambre through his marriage with deceased Madame'. He placed these documents in a burlap sack in the middle of the mattress roll to protect them from the rain and to keep them secret, reminding René to have the unpackers retrieve them carefully. These papers were organized 'bundle by bundle' as indicated in the copy of the inventory that Rolin had already sent.[179] At another time, an author had to correct a false account of what had happened to an envoy named Perruchon who was carrying important information. A 'miscreant' had spread the word that Perruchon had been robbed and injured after leaving on his trip, but this was not at all true, and he had arrived safely at Beaufremont.[180]

Relations with officials

While much of René's time and energy was spent attending to his fiefs and to his family's interests, his princely service was dedicated, for the most

---

177 Fornaseri, 9-11, René to Ch III, Chambéry 9-XI-29.
178 AHR, FC 263, mz. 1, Pierre Bachet to René, Bourg 11-I-?.
179 AEN, AS-H16, 15, Grat Rolin to René, Aosta ?-VII-?; ibid., AS-G16, 3, Rolin to René, Aosta 21-VI-?.
180 AHR, FC 264, mz. 1, ? to René, Bard 6-IV-?.

part, to the House of Savoy. Historians have had relatively little to say about relations between René and state authorities, however. Patriotism inspired much Sabaudian historical writing in the years during and immediately following the Risorgimento. Ercole Ricotti, whose monumental multivolume *Storia della monarchia piemontese* was published in the same year as the foundation of the kingdom of Italy under Sabaudian rule (1861), celebrated Piedmontese leadership in general and Emanuel Filibert, who 're-established the state and Italianized it', in particular. For Ricotti, this Duke 'changed the government from a feudal to an absolutist one', and figures like René, who seemed to be a throwback to the old feudal order that was being superseded, were ignored.[181] Claretta acknowledges René as someone who took his work as a ducal officer seriously, while being frustrated by 'the laziness of the persons with whom he had to interact' in the ducal administration. He applied himself as an 'impartial minister zealous for the good of all social classes', despite having to confront corruption and episodes of stubbornness in dealings with personalities like Masino.[182] One has the impression that Claretta was describing, through René, the kind of functionary that he wished to see serving the new Italian state.[183] Another Risorgimento-era historian, Domenico Carutti, hailed René for having 'preserved [the Valle d'Aosta] under the dominion of Charles III, and transferred it intact, without foreign occupation, to Emanuel Filibert'.[184] A two-volume biography of Emanuel Filibert on the the 400th anniversary of his birth (1928, year six of the fascist era) had little to say about René; the authors were concerned with celebrating the dynasty and its state-building efforts, not in drawing attention to a figure who complicated those themes in many ways.[185]

As a great aristocrat with pretensions to sovereignty and ties to courts across Europe, René found it frustrating and demeaning to be constrained by ducal or Imperial officials for procedural or institutional reasons. Resource allocations, often for military purposes, were often approved by the Duke or the Emperor, only for access to the money to be blocked by bureaucratic procedures. In the 1530s, the power to release payment of René's pensions or other sums owed by the Duke to René was held by the President of the *Chambre des comptes*, Pierre Lambert de la Croix.[186] In 1539, Roz Favre

---

181 Ricotti, 1: 7, 41.
182 Claretta, *La successione*, 17-18, 18-19, 20, 22.
183 Ibid., 135-36.
184 Carutti, 275, 323.
185 Segre, *Emanuele Filiberto*; Egidi, *Emanuele Filiberto*.
186 AEN, AS-F16, 3, Lambert to René, Nice 25-XI-38; AHR, FC 263, mz. 1, Gamache to René, Bard 6-IX-?.

informed René that he had sent 'to Nice to have your payments for Quart and Cly redone'. Quart and Cly were ducal castellanies in the valley; it appears that René was expecting payments assigned to their revenues. Favre both sent envoys for this purpose and 'I also wrote to the president Lambert asking him on your behalf' to approve disbursal of the money.[187] These delays could be costly, especially when geographic distance already presented challenges during critical moments.

A report that Castellamonte sent to René in May 1539 gives a detailed sense of how cameral officials influenced ducal business and controlled the flow of resources in ways that could frustrate great lords. As soon as Castellamonte arrived in Nice, he spoke with Lambert and showed him the instructions given to him by René. The President said that he strongly disapproved of René's idea of requesting that the King of France grant Montréal and Matafelon (two fiefs in Valromey, currently occupied by the French) to him. Lambert declared that the Duke 'would absolutely never concede this, which could ruin all his other affairs'.[188] Hearing this, Castellamonte adjusted his approach and obtained Lambert's approval for 200 *écus* to be delivered to René by Monsieur de La Croix, 'assigned to the gabelle', but Lambert would not approve the 100 *écus* 'on the castellany of Cly'. Castellamonte countered that René's pension as marshal was 600 *écus*, half of which were assigned to Cly (in the Valle d'Aosta) and half to Valromey (near Bugey, also occupied by the French), but that, during the war, René had not received the 300 from Valromey. This surprised Lambert, who said that the Castellan of Valromey had told him that he had paid René at least part of this sum, but finally agreed to make out the assignation for Cly 'according to custom'. Castellamonte forwarded this to the Castellan Roz Favre (in Aosta), and then set about trying to find the treasurer Locarno to have letters issued. When Castellamonte arrived in Vercelli from Nice, Locarno had already left Vercelli for Ivrea to see the Duke. Castellamonte hoped that, even though the assignations lacked Locarno's countersignature, the castellans would agree to pay the sums indicated once they saw that the Duke himself had signed them. Finally, Castellamonte spoke to Lambert about the case of Jean Guillet, whose appeal for repayment of sums owed to him by the Duke was supported by René. Lambert suggested that René not request anything on behalf of Guillet and proposed writing another letter promising payment in three months. Castellamonte thought that

---

187 AEN, AS-H-16, 20, Roz Favre to René, Aosta ?-VI-39.
188 Ibid., AS-K16, 20, Castellamonte to René, Issogne 8-V-39 [dated by internal evidence] (following citations from same source).

this would be useless and argued that Guillet was 'a good man and *home de prince*'. Lambert refused to admit as much and again urged René not to do him any favors.[189] Examples like this are abundant.[190]

Having to depend on legal or financial officials not only made it difficult to access resources, it also created situations in which procedural requirements threatened aristocratic honor, disrupted social hierarchies, or compromised jurisdictional claims. When the Castellan of Montjovet detained one of René's subjects, René responded right away. He instructed Roz Favre to write the Castellan of Verrès about it, as had René, urging the latter also to write to Montjovet, as did René, 'in favor of our subject, the prisoner'. He did not appear to criticize the Castellan's actions, noting that 'the denunciation gives him jurisdiction'.[191] But his actions suggest that he was troubled by the fact that a lesser ducal official was detaining one of his subjects. Another case shows how problematic it was for princes to permit other princes to effect judicial inquiries over their subjects. René wrote to Charles III from Casale in 1533 about a group of soldiers from the Monferrato who had allegedly attempted to launch an attack on Mondovì. They were being detained in Casale, where the Duke of Savoy sent a commissioner to interrogate them, but the men 'would not testify without permission from the Marquis [of Monferrato]'. René asked the Marquis to order the men to give depositions, 'and have my attorney communicate them to his secret counselors'. The Marquis agreed to this mechanism, but then 'had his counselors hinder the examination of the witnesses'. However, 'the deposition was copied by my attorney secretly in my house'.[192] One of René's secretaries, Delompnes, compared René's mode of acting to that of princes who did not think that procedural niceties should stand in the way of them executing their will. He wrote to a Savoyard noble that René 'acts naturally as a grandee behaving according to his will [*pro ratione voluntas*]'.[193]

René's interactions with officials were often mediated by court politics. Not enough is known about Charles III's court to be able to assess the structure of factionalism there,[194] but the 1539 letter from Castellamonte

---

189 Ibid., AS-K16, 20, Castellamonte to René, Issogne 8-V-39 [dated by internal evidence].
190 AHR, FC 263, mz. 1, Granyer to René, Chastellard 19-V-?; ibid., FC 264, mz. 1, Gichar [?] to René, Milan 20-XII-42?; ibid., FC 263, mz. 1 ? to René [?], s.l., s.d. [1554?].
191 Ibid., René [?] to Castellan of Verrès, Aosta 5-IX-?.
192 Fornaseri, 86, René to Ch III, Casale 15-IV-33?.
193 AHR, FC 263, mz. 1, Delompnes to La Tornette, Virieu 20-II-?.
194 According to Lino Marini, the basic factional division in the sixteenth-century Sabaudian lands was between Savoyards and Piedmontese; see L. Marini; see also Barbero, 'Savoiardi e Piemontesi.'

cited above indicates some of the divisions. The Prince (Emanuel Filibert) was affectionate toward René, wrote Castellamonte, and others at court (the protonotary Provana, Monsieur le Grand, Bressieu, and Lambert) all sent their good wishes. 'Le Galier', however, did not. Castellamonte urged René to serve the Duke and '*tout son estat*' by coming to the Valle d'Aosta, so that he would be able to meet the Duke, who planned to be in Vercelli or Ivrea in May. In that case, Lambert would also go meet with René in Aosta. Being in direct contact with the Duke and his key officials was crucial. René could go to the valley 'with a small following', and, if he did, 'things would be ordered for your favor and profit', especially given René's preeminent position there. Otherwise, Castellamonte was concerned that René would be outmaneuvered by a certain person who pretended to be René's friend and wrote him letters but was not to be trusted. If René were to wait to be summoned by the Duke, 'you will be there on judgment day, given that the man who governs [the court] fears nothing else in this world'. Castellamonte had 'seen and heard about things that I will tell you in person'. René had seen before how this person operates. 'He has never had good words for you except to deceive you, and I promise you that every day he schemes at his master's expense.' The person in question had his own councillors with him, including a 'Mudry', his own chief official, and other followers who met with him for an hour each day.[195]

Within the valley, where René's influence was unmatched, his relations with officials seemed smooth. His interactions with the *Commis*, the Bishop, and others were characterized, for the most part, by deference toward him.[196] In 1552, he named Pierre Ducrest, his secretary, as his procurator to work with the *Commis* on the neutrality agreement, an arrangement that proceeded without a hitch.[197] Although there were some conflicts between René and the *Commis* over the participation of René's subjects in certain *tailles* voted by the valley estates, their financial relationship was less contentious than René's dealings with the *Chambre des comptes*.[198] There was at least one example of a complaint by officials in Chambéry over René's administrative abilities when he was serving as *maréchal de Savoie* there in the late 1520s. Some of the council members had apparently solicited from the Duke a

---

195 AEN, AS-K16, 20, Castellamonte to René, Issogne 8-V-39. The person in question might have been Louis de Châtillon; see Uginet, 'Louis de Châtillon.'
196 The political landscape of the sixteenth-century Valle d'Aosta will be examined in detail in a separate work.
197 AHR, FC 194, no. 15, letter dated 12-I-52.
198 For cooperation between René and the valley estates, see AEN, AS-I16, 20, receipt dated 22-III-59.

letter that instructed them to render justice more quickly. René defensively assured the Duke that, while he had been in Chambéry, the council had acted expeditiously. He also asked the Duke to identify the complainants, so that he could address their cases at once (or maybe so that he could teach them a lesson about going behind his back).[199] René had cooperative relations with other officials, who even served as brokers for him sometimes, such as the secretary Regard – an intermediary between René's agent the Baron of Chevron and the President of the Senate of Savoie.[200]

René's interactions with administrative and judicial officials, like his political networks, extended from Monferrato and Piedmont into the Valle d'Aosta, Savoie, Valangin and the Swiss lands, Lorraine, and elsewhere. These relationships both offered benefits and posed challenges that were both logistical and symbolic. The next chapter will show how the transregional and spatial dimensions of René's lordship created opportunities for him as a financial broker.

Bibliography

Judith Aikin, *A Ruler's Consort in Early Modern Germany: Aemilia Juliana of Schwarzburg-Rudolstadt* (Farnham, UK: Ashgate, 2014)

Nadine Akkerman and Birgit Houben, 'Introduction,' in *The Politics of Female Households: Ladies-in-Waiting Across Early Modern Europe*, ed. Nadine Akkerman and Birgit Houben (Leiden: Brill, 2014), pp. 1-27

Alessandro Barbero, 'Savoiardi e Piemontesi nel ducato sabaudo all'inizio del Cinquecento: un problema storiografico risolto?' *BSBS* 87 (1989): 591-637

Ursula Birchler, 'Michel de Gruyère,' in *DHS* (2006)

Andrea Boldù, 'Relazione della Corte di Savoia' (12 December 1561), in *Relazioni degli ambasciatori veneti al Senato*, ser. 2, vol. 1, ed. Eugenio Albèri (Firenze: Tipografia all'insegna di Glio, 1839), pp. 401-70

Lloyd Bowen, 'Information, Language and Political Culture in Early Modern Wales,' *Past and Present* 228, 1(2015): 125-58

Judith Brown, 'Introduction,' in *Medici Women: The Making of a Dynasty in Grand Ducal Tuscany*, ed. Giovanna Benadusi and Judith Brown (Toronto: Centre for Reformation and Renaissance Studies, 2015), pp. 17-57

Max Bruchet, *Marguerite d'Autriche. Duchesse de Savoie* (Lille: L. Danel, 1927)

---

199 Fornaseri, 18-21, René to Ch III, Chambéry 4-XII-29.
200 AHR, FC 263, mz. 1, Chevron to René, Chambéry 28-X-?.

Federik Buylaert and Jelle Haemers, 'Record-Keeping and Status Performance in the Early Modern Low Countries,' *PP* 230, supplement 11 (2016): 131-50

Jay Caplan, *Postal Culture in Europe, 1500-1800* (Oxford: Voltaire Foundation, 2016)

François Capré, *Traité historique de la Chambre des comptes de Savoye* (Lyon: Chez Guillaume Barbier, 1652)

Domenico Carutti, *Storia della diplomazia della corte di Savoia*, vol. 1 (Torino: Fratelli Bocca, 1875)

Jean-Marie Cauchies, 'Marguerite d'Autriche, gouvernante et diplomate,' in *L'itinérance des seigneurs (XIVe-XVIe siècles)*, ed. Agostino Paravicini Bagliani, Eva Pibiri, and Denis Reynard, *Cahiers lausannois d'histoire médiévale* 34 (Lausanne: Université de Lausanne, 2003), pp. 353-76

Sigismondo Cavalli, 'Relazione della Corte di Savoja' (1564), in *Relazioni degli ambasciatori veneti al Senato*, ser. 2, vol. 2, ed. Eugenio Albèri (Firenze: Tipografia e calcografia all'insegna di Clio, 1841), pp. 27-56

Gaudenzio Claretta, *La successione di Emanuele Filiberto al trono sabaudo e la prima ristorazione della casa di Savoia* (Torino: Eredi Botta, 1884)

Janie Cole, 'Cultural Clientelism and Brokerage Networks in Early Modern Florence and Rome: New Correspondence between the Barberini and Michelangelo Buonarroti the Younger,' *RQ* 60, 3 (2007): 729-88

Giovanni Correr, 'Relazione della Corte di Savoja' (1566), in *Relazioni degli ambasciatori veneti al Senato*, ser. 2, vol. 5, ed. Eugenio Albèri (Firenze: Società Editrice Fiorentina, 1858), pp. 1-46

Abbé Coutin, 'Comment les Prêtres de la Mission établirent le Grand Séminaire d'Annecy en la rue du Bœuf, vers 1650,' *Mémoires et documents publiés par l'Académie Salésienne* 47 (1929): xi-xii

Carlo De Antonio, 'La Valle d'Aosta ed Emanuele Filiberto,' in *Lo stato sabaudo al tempo di Emanuele Filiberto*, ed. Carlo Patrucco, vol. 1 (Turin: Miglietta, 1928), pp. 153-237

Jean-Baptiste De Tillier, *Historique de la Vallée d'Aoste* (Aosta: ITLA, 1994 [1742])

Id., *Nobiliaire du duché d'Aoste*, ed. André Zanotto (Aoste: Editions de la Tourneuve, 1970 [1733 ms])

Michel De Waele, 'La fin des guerres de Religion et l'exclusion des femmes de la vie politique française,' *FHS* 29, 2 (2006): 199-230

Pierre-Etienne Duc, *La prévôté et la paroisse de St-Gilles Abbé à Verrès diocèse d'Aoste* (Ivrea: Imprimerie du séminaire, 1873)

Pietro Egidi, *Emanuele Filiberto*, vol. 2 (1559-1580) (Turin: Paravia, 1928)

Dagmar Eichberger, 'Margaret of Austria,' in *Women of Distinction: Margaret of York – Margaret of Austria*, ed. Dagmar Eichberger (Davidsfonds-Leuven: Brepols, 2005), pp. 48-55

Catherine Ferrari, 'Kinship and the Marginalized Consort: Giovanna d'Austria at the Medici Court,' *Early Modern Women* 11, 1 (2016): 45-68

Giovanni Fornaseri, *Le lettere di Renato di Challant, governatore della Valle d'Aosta a Carlo II ed a Emanuele Filiberto* (Turin: Deputazione subalpina di storia patria, 1957)

Markus Friedrich, 'The Rise of Archival Consciousness in Provincial France: French Feudal Records and Eighteenth-Century Seigneurial Society,' *PP* 230, supplement 11 (2016): 49-70

François-Gabriel Frutaz, 'Notes sur René de Challant et sur le passage de Calvin dans la Vallée d'Aoste,' *Musée neuchâtelois* 41 (1904): 242-67

http://genealogy.euweb.cz/capet/capet61.html, 12 November 2019

Pietro Ghinzoni, 'Cronaca semestrale pervenuta dall'archivio di stato di Milano. I.º semestre, 1878,' *Archivio storico lombardo* 5 (1878): 352-60

Fritz Glauser, 'Kommunikation und Innovation im 16. Jahrhundert. Zu den Anfängen der Post in der Schweiz,' *Revue suisse d'histoire* 53, 1 (2003): 1-33

Edoardo Grendi, *I Balbi: Una famiglia genovese fra Spagna e Impero* (Turin: Einaudi, 1997)

Jean-Baptiste Guillaume, *Histoire généalogique des sires de Salins au comté de Bourgogne* (Besançon: Chez Jean-Antoine Vieille, 1757)

Randolph Head, 'Documents, Archives, and Proof around 1700,' *HJ* 56, 4 (2013): 879-907

Sharon Kettering, 'Strategies of Power: Favorites and Women Household Clients at Louis XIII's Court,' *FHS* 33, 2 (2010): 177-200

Lino Marini, *Savoiardi e piemontesi nello Stato sabaudo (1418-1601)* (Rome: Istituto storico italiano per l'età moderna e contemporanea, 1962)

Marjorie Meiss-Even, 'The Guise "Italianised"? The Role of Italian Merchants, Intermediaries and Experts in Ducal Consumption in the Sixteenth Century,' in *Aspiration, Representation and Memory: The Guise in Europe, 1506-1688*, ed. Jessica Munns, Penny Richards, and Jonathan Spangler (Farnham, UK: Ashgate, 2015), pp. 47-60

'Memoriale del Presidente Niccolò Balbo al Duca Emanuele Filiberto,' in Ricotti, *Storia della monarchia piemontese*

Cédric Michon, 'Les richesses de la faveur à la Renaissance: Jean de Lorraine (1498-1550) et François Ier,' *RHMC* 50, 3 (2003): 34-61

Joanna Milstein, *The Gondi: Family Strategy and Survival in Early Modern France* (Farnham, UK: Ashgate, 2014)

Michel Nassiet, *Parenté, noblesse et États dynastiques, XVe-XVIe siècles* (Paris: Éditions de l'EHESS, 2000)

Ercole Ricotti, *Storia della monarchia piemontese*, vol. 1 (Firenze: G. Barbèra, 1861)

Giuseppe Roddi, *Il 'Coutumier' Valdostano (1588)* (Quart: Musumeci, 1994)

Brian Sandberg, *Warrior Pursuits: Noble Culture and Civil Conflict in Early Modern France* (Baltimore: The Johns Hopkins University Press, 2010)

Tom Scott, *Regional Identity and Economic Change: The Upper Rhine, 1450-1600* (Oxford: Clarendon Press, 1997)

Arturo Segre, *Emanuele Filiberto*, vol. 1 (1559-1580) (Turin: Paravia, 1928)

Id., 'L'opera politico-militare di Andrea Provana di Leynì nello Stato sabaudo dal 1553 al 1539,' *Atti della Reale Accademia dei Lincei*, 5th ser., *Classe di scienze morali, storiche e filologiche* 6 (1898): 5-123

Christine Shaw, *Barons and Castellans: The Military Nobility of Renaissance Italy* (Leiden: Brill 2015)

Paul Slack, 'Government and Information in Seventeenth-Century England,' *PP* 184 (2004): 33-68

Denis Tappy, 'Pierre Quisard,' in *DHS* (2009)

Craig Taylor, 'The Salic Law, French Queenship, and the Defense of Women in the Late Middle Ages,' *FHS* 30, 4 (2006): 543-64

François-Charles Uginet, 'Louis de Châtillon,' *DBI* 24 (1980)

Matthew Vester, *Renaisance Dynasticism and Apanage Politics: Jacques de Savoie-Nemours 1531-1585* (Kirksville MO: Truman State University Press, 2012)

Alexandra Walsham, 'The Social History of the Archive: Record-Keeping in Early Modern Europe,' *PP* 230, supplement 11 (2016): 9-48

Cornel Zwierlein, 'Deutsche und Italienische Staatsbeschreibungskunst. Die Einkünfte aller Reichsstände, ca. 1547/48 nach einer unbekannten Quelle,' *ZHF* 39, 4 (2012): 593-660

7. Finance and brokerage

Abstract
René's influence was rooted in his role as a financial broker, which was based, in turn, on his role as a transregional lord. Borrowing money, whether for himself or for others, depended on the lands and rights that he could offer as collateral. The attractiveness of this collateral depended on whether potential lenders saw benefits in acquiring it. The spatial situation of René's lands (and their productivity) with respect to the location of various lenders was thus crucial, as were his personal relationships with various Swiss creditors. René instrumentalized his landed position and became a key financial broker for the House of Savoy and others. His two imprisonments seriously harmed his financial position, but he eventually recovered.

Key words: finance, loans, Swiss, ransom

Nobles and finance

Recent studies of the nobility have argued, based partly on assessments of their strong financial position, that this social group remained socially and politically influential during the early modern period. While it is true that there is a paucity of records that might offer a clear picture of nobles' financial status, documentation of noble borrowing, or sales of seigniories, 'does not necessarily mean that a noble lineage was on the verge of bankruptcy'. Noble revenue streams were often diverse (including non-landed investments and office-holding).[1] In late medieval Franconia, the financial strength of the nobles led princes to grant them governorships in exchange for loans. Holders of such *Pfandschaften* might even include princely debt as part of their daughters' dowries, thereby binding their heirs to the princely state over which they could continue to exert significant influence.[2] The

---

1   Buylaert, 'The Late Medieval "Crisis",' 1119, 1126-27.
2   Zmora, 623-25.

Vester, M., *Transregional Lordship and the Italian Renaissance: René de Challant, 1504-1565*. Amsterdam: Amsterdam University Press, 2020.
DOI 10.5117/9789463726726_CH07

active engagement of the early modern nobility in financial activities naturally extended into other dimensions of their lives. In France, nobles 'used complex investment and fiscal strategies to manage large monetary fortunes', navigating exchange rates, making investments, engaging in commerce, and borrowing from and lending to clients, other nobles, and the Crown.[3] Marriage strategy and kin relations included important financial components. Heads of families assumed debt in order to provide dowries for daughters, and they also 'depended on the financial support and decision making of their allies, and especially on the contributions of "houses" that had died out'.[4] Language relating to finance also colored relationships between nobles.[5]

The financial position of a noble family derived largely from its property, in ways that illustrate the connections between material possessions and noble identity. Customary law often viewed property that produced income as something 'not subject to individual ownership […] because its productive life far exceeded that of any individual. It was thus intended to serve generations, not individuals'.[6] Such property was really patrimony, not property, and included not only land, but also things like jewelry and even *rentes constituées* that could be passed on to heirs. The patrimony, although a source of financial strength, belonged to the family line and was not 'freely available to the market'.[7]

Rulers borrowed not only from the landed nobility, but also from merchant-bankers, some of whom had claims to nobility. Urban republics had an advantage over princes with respect to public finance in that it was easier for them to create excise taxes and tolls while avoiding the pitfalls of trying to collect direct taxes. Cities, whether in the Mediterranean zone or in transalpine regions, encountered fewer obstacles taxing their subjects than did monarchs.[8] Thus, during the late Middle Ages, southern German merchant bankers created the financial structures that permitted emperors and kings to carry out their spending plans.[9] These Germans, however,

3   Sandberg, 57-58.
4   Haddad, 'Kinship,' 589.
5   Claire Crowston argues that two dimensions of the word 'credit', one with an interpersonal connotation and the other privileging abstract status, overlapped during the early modern period (Crowston, 10-13).
6   Howell, 540-41.
7   Ibid., 558.
8   Kellenbenz, 335, 340-41. Kellenbenz generally classifies financiers as either 'German' or 'Italian', without regard for bankers functioning in between those realms.
9   Zwierlein argues that it was in the early 1500s that rulers began to prioritize knowledge of their own revenue streams and those of other states.

lost their dominant positions to Italian financiers by the mid-sixteenth century.[10] Southern Germans had been the largest creditors of the French, Spanish, and Portuguese monarchs who went bankrupt in 1557-1560; their loss of position in international credit markets also had a negative economic impact in southern Germany, but many of them invested in land and titles and began to serve at princely courts.[11] Among the Italian lenders who subsequently became involved in French and Spanish state finance were patrician families like the Gondi and the Balbi.[12] Edoardo Grendi's study of the latter found that scholars had exaggerated the influence of bankers on sovereigns, attributing to the banker 'the dominant role' and reducing 'the sovereign to a postulant'. Honor was a key element of the relationship between the ruler and a patrician banker, and was the ruler's to give, in terms of prestige and titles.[13] Grendi identified a triangular relationship in the 1590s between the Spanish Crown, Genoese lenders, and 'the creditors of the creditors', an important reminder that state finance was never simply a bilateral affair.[14]

Scholars have recently begun to examine the practical logistical details of war financing,[15] and William Caferro has described how mercenary captains and soldiers borrowed from bankers, from rural innkeepers, and from their employers.[16] There have been few detailed studies of how nobles helped to finance wars or how they served as financial brokers for princes, however.[17] Sabaudian state finance prior to 1559 has not been extensively studied.[18] Nothing has been written about René's role as a financial broker. Matile commented misleadingly that René was perpetually trying to raise revenues due to 'the feeble state of his finances', resulting from his extravagant military, diplomatic, and courtly expenditures.[19] Frutaz noted sensibly that René's financial problems stemmed from his first imprisonment after Pavia, but then criticized him, again on questionable grounds, for the size of his following and 'his feasting with a princely attendance'.[20]

10   Hildebrandt, 211-12.
11   Ibid., 213-14, 224.
12   For the Gondi, see Milstein.
13   Grendi, xv-xvi.
14   Ibid., 41.
15   Parrott.
16   Caferro, 'Warfare,' 181-83.
17   Erik Swart does not mention the nobility's role in war financing; see Swart.
18   But see Ostoni on the finances of Charles III and Gravela for public finance in fourteenth-century Turin.
19   Matile, 268.
20   Frutaz, 'Notes,' 251.

In fact, analysis of René's case not only shows how his lands and offices provided him revenues that gave him financial authority and solidifed his family's prestige, but also how he grew into a role as a financial broker for the Duke of Savoy and other princes. His borrowing, whether for himself or on behalf of others, brought him into close relationship with Imperial and Sabaudian financial officials, and with urban patricians and bankers in the Swiss cantons and elsewhere. The fact that his fiefs were spatially dispersed meant that he had access to credit markets in different parts of Europe where lenders were more likely to make loans secured by property that was proximate to them. This facilitated their gathering of information about such collateral and made loans based on it more attractive, since, if the borrower defaulted, repossession would be easy and would fit into the lender's own regional landholding position. One of the most important ways in which René embodied a bridge between the Renaissance in Italy and elsewhere in Europe was through his financial activity, which was based on his multiple, spatially dispersed lordship.

René as borrower and broker

The financial situation inherited by René

Like any great noble dynasty during the Renaissance, the Challant family met its urgent expenses, whether military, courtly, diplomatic, or otherwise political in nature, through borrowing. These loans were most often secured on the future revenues from their estates, on the estates themselves, or on future pensions or salaries. What resulted was an extremely complex web of financial relationships whose key factors included the political identity and interests of the lenders, the precise value and location of the lands on which loans were secured, the jurisdictional status of those lands, the position of the Challant in regional and European politics and the shifting strategic environment.

Borrowers and lenders also interacted within a historical context of past relationships between their families. In particular, the Challant had a long history of borrowing from the Swiss cantons, on the basis of their lands near the Swiss area and their income from the House of Savoy.[21] Lenders were willing to engage in credit relationships with the Challant partly because

---

21   For Louis de Challant's debts to the Fribourgeois and other Swiss, see AHR, FC 73, no. 24, document dated 25-I-1474. René's great-grandfather Jean d'Arberg borrowed from creditors in Basel and Berne; see AEN, AS-S26, 1 and annexes. On Jean d'Arberg, see Hausmann; on the general problem of inheriting debt, see Kuehn.

the family's ties to the House of Savoy guaranteed future income streams. For example, by the late 1490s, in addition to his own lands, Philibert also enjoyed the revenues of the Duke's castellany of Bard (and assigned these for his mother's upkeep).[22] Such income helped guarantee loans from the Swiss; in 1500, Claude d'Arberg, René's grandfather, repaid a sum to Guillaume Felga of Fribourg.[23] It is also crucial to note here that the landed position of the Challant in the Swiss area – specifcially, their seigniory of Valangin – gave them equity with which to secure loans from the Swiss, whose proximity made it easier for them to gauge the value of the Challant holdings and, if necessary, to occupy those lands in the event of a default.

René thus stepped into a family history of borrowing, especially from Swiss sources. Charles III assigned him an annual pension of 1200 florins in 1518 (an amount matching that received by his grandfather Louis), and, a few years later, René borrowed 1000 florins from the Bernese Hans von Erlach.[24] In 1523, René and his grandmother Guillemette made a financial arrangement to permit the young Count of Challant to embark on his political and military career. The 10,000 gold Rhenish florins that had comprised Guillemette's dowry and were assigned to Beaufremont and its dependencies would be made available to her through the usufruct of the residences and revenues of Valangin and Beaufremont for the rest of her life. It was also acknowledged that there were many loans that her husband, Claude d'Arberg, had taken out on Valangin (which was burdened by annual rent payments owed to lenders). Guillemette promised to 'stop [using resources] and leave' the seigniory of Valangin, renouncing her usufruct and rights there, while retaining her dowry on Beaufremont, which would pass completely to René after her death.[25] This arrangement made it easier for René to borrow more from the Swiss with Valangin as his security. In 1524, he borrowed 2000 *gulden* from Wendell Sonnenmeyer of Lucerne, a loan that would only be paid off in 1581.[26] At around the same time, shortly before he left for the Pavia campaign, he sought to establish a summary view of his financial situation.[27]

---

22   AHR, FC 209, no. 8, documents from 1497 and 1499; ibid., FC 24, no. 18, donation dated 23-XII-1497; for Louis's annual pension from the Duke, see AHR, FC 24, no. 13, document dated 6-IX-1483; for other revenue grants, see ibid., no. 14, documents from 1485, 1487, 1490, 1497; for the pension of Louis's widow, Marguerite, see ibid., no. 17, document dated 7-IX-1496.
23   AEN, AS-S26, 7, receipt dated 1500.
24   AHR, FC 194, no. 12, document dated 12-XII-18; AEN, AS-Z8, 11, document dated 1521.
25   AEN, AS-S26, 43, copy of a financial arrangement made between Guillemette and René, 1523.
26   Ibid., AS-Z8, 1, loan dated 1524. Sonnenmeyer was a wealthy cloth merchant; see 'Henrich Küssenberg's Chronik,' esp. 445, 448.
27   AHR, FC 263, mz. 1, Castellan of Bard to Raphaello, Aymavilles, 22-III-? [c. 1525].

1526-1536: Finances and Swiss negotiations

René's first imprisonment after the battle of Pavia and subsequent ransom demands created the first financial crisis for him to manage. Already in August 1526 he got to work, appointing Luigi di Castellamonte to collect pensions and other sums owed to him by the Duke of Savoy.[28] While his wife's execution in Milan was obviously deeply embarrassing for him in many respects, it also created an opportunity for him to access resources that could help him meet his financial obligations – even if Bianca Maria's Gaspardone relatives contested René's ability to dispose of her inheritance. About five months after her death, René complained to the Marquise of Monferrato, Anne d'Alençon, and to Charles III about 'the extortions carried out against me' in the Monferrato, where soldiers seem to have been trying to collect payments from the Gaspardone inheritance.[29] The substantial dowry brought by the marriage to Mencia in 1528 helped resolve some of these problems.

Several undated letters testify to the preoccupation with financial considerations amidst René's political, military, diplomatic, and administrative activities. In a typical letter, Eusèbe Gamache, one of René's castellans in the Valle d'Aosta, mentioned several different issues, indicating how many different tracks a lord like René had to follow at any given time. Gamache reported that he was gathering money for René, some of which was supposed to come from *Monsieur* Vallesa. Roz Favre claimed that he could not provide any more and suggested that some of what he had was being given to Vallesa for a diplomatic mission. Vallesa owed additional money, which he was trying to satisfy by selling his part of the jurisdiction and *censes* of Carema and Quincenay for 244 *écus*, with a right to repurchase within two years. Gamache was also trying to collect sums owed by a certain Poncet and opined that the sale of two mules that had been contemplated would not generate even ten *écus*. At the same time, René owed sums to various other people, including the Castellan of Bard, who would not be satisfied with the grant of the Bard toll as his reimbursement. The community of Bard owed 40 *écus*, and Gamache would try to hold the Castellan responsible for them. A certain Jaquete, who was in prison, owed 200 florins to René, who, in turn, owed 30 *écus* to the 'good fathers' in Casale. Gamache concluded his letter with a pledge to send 100 *écus* to René from Turin or Vercelli.[30]

---

28 AHR, FC 40, no. 15, procuration by René for Luigi di Castellamonte dated 8-VIII-26.
29 Fornaseri, 6-7, René to Ch III, 23-II-27?.
30 AHR, FC 263, mz. 1, Gamache to René, Ivrea 8-IV-?. For a similar example from one of René's agents in Vercelli and Milan, see ibid., Claude Jacquier [?] to René, Vercelli 30-III-?; ibid., same

René's financial brokerage on behalf of Charles III quickly became a key element of his early administrative and diplomatic career in Savoie and in the Swiss cantons. Here, it is important to note that about two-thirds of the Duke's annual revenues were already committed to payments to the widows of previous dukes (Blanche de Montferrat, Claudine de Brosse, and Marguerite d'Autriche) and to the Duke's brother for the apanage of the Genevois.[31] René, like all diplomatic envoys of the time, had to front his own expenses and later seek repayment from the Duke: in June 1529, he asked for money 'to support the expenses that I incur continuously away from my house'.[32] To cover his costs, he had had to pawn his 'tableware' in Lyon, and, once installed in the chateau of Chambéry, where Mencia was about to give birth, he wished to recuperate these household items 'to celebrate the birth honorably'. He thus asked the Duke for the 1000 *écus* necessary to redeem it – a sum that had been owed to René since Christmas 1528. He also asked for the other 1000 *écus* currently owed to him 'so that I will no longer have to pay such interest as I have in the past; I would prefer to use the money for your service than for interest payments'.[33] To obtain payment from the Duke, he tried to leverage Bianca Maria's inheritance in the Monferrato, cutting his losses in those lands where he was encountering resistance.[34]

In early 1530, as René continued to try to collect sums owed to him by Charles III, the Duke asked him to underwrite a new loan from Hans Settimalier/Sentimachre.[35] Five months later, René warned the Duke that, if he failed to pay his debts to the Fribourgeois, 'your ambassador and I will be forced to underwrite them ourselves, which will dishonor you'. If the Duke's agents failed to reach an arrangement with Settimalier by the next scheduled meeting, 'he is such a man as to detain our ambassadors until he is repaid', according to René. He also urged the Duke to have a ducal treasurer pay him the '*estat* with which it pleased you to endow me, so that I could repay my provisioners'.[36]

to same, Vercelli 2-IV-?.
31   Brero, 14-15.
32   Fornaseri, 7-8, René to Ch III, 10-VI-29?. Later that month, the Duke gave René permission to build an irrigation canal near Verolengo (AHR, FC 194, no. 13, document dated 25-VI-29).
33   Fornaseri, 9-11, René to Ch III, Chambéry 9-XI-29.
34   Ibid., 18-21, René to Ch III, Chambéry 4-XII-29.
35   Ibid., 33-34, René to Ch III, Chambéry 13-I-30. René apologized for not being able to assist the Duke owing both to political circumstances in Fribourg and to his own debts; see also AHR, FC 289, no. 24, declaration dated 5-IV-30.
36   René would have to find out if one of his own creditors would be willing to have his credit assigned to the revenues of Ternier. He also corrected the Duke, who underestimated the amount that he owed René (Fornaseri, 67-68, René to Ch III, Chambéry 17-VI-30).

Financial concerns were thus at the heart of René's negotiations with the Swiss on behalf of Charles III during the summer and fall of 1530. René frequently brokered loans by the Duke of Savoy from the Swiss, sometimes intervening personally in order to maintain goodwill between the parties. This meant that René's 'personal' financial status was inextricably linked to the Duke's financial diplomacy. By 1 July, money had arrived for René from the Duke. This was welcome 'with respect to the interest payments that I had to support in Lyon', which, over the two years that had passed since repayment had been due, had risen to 400 *écus*.[37] In early August, he wrote to Duchess Beatrice from Lyon about the same matter. A ducal treasurer had given 500 *écus* to a creditor in Lyon, but whether this was on René's or the Duke's behalf was unclear. The merchant, Pierre Saugey, also owed money to the Duchess, but René pledged to use some of his revenues from Crescentino (in Piedmont) to repay Beatrice for that. He asked the Duchess to restrain another treasurer (Carrà) who was pressuring Saugey for repayment. Saugey also reported that the merchant to whom Beatrice had pawned rings in Lyon was threatening to melt them down if he did not receive repayment by the end of August. René believed that losing the rings either this way or through their sale at auction would bring 'shame' upon the dynasty. He offered to make payments himself but had no cash and was struggling for his own part to put together 2000 *écus* to repurchase a piece of mortgaged land in the Monferrato (Guardapasso) before the contract expired in September.[38] By late August, the Duke resolved to mortgage one of his fiefs to René for 4000 *écus*, and so the latter began beating the bushes for investors. From Virieu, he wrote to Prangins, the Governor of Neuchâtel, asking him to underwrite a loan for three years and sent Castellamonte to draw up the paperwork. The next day, he traveled to Chambéry and called in a pledge of 1000 *écus* from Duchess Beatrice, reminding her that he was owed another 1500 by the end of September, in addition to the sums still owed from his marriage to Mencia.[39]

Despite his frustrations with the Duke and Duchess over their failure to keep up with his pensions and reimbursements, René retained good credit among Swiss lenders, on the basis of his lands in Valangin and elsewhere,

---

37   Ibid., 69-71, René to Ch III, Chambéry 1-VII-30.
38   Ibid., 73-75, René to Duchess of Savoy, Lyon 4-VIII-30 and René to Ch III, Virieu 11-VIII-30.
39   AEN, AS-R5.10, g, René to Prangins, Virieu 31-VIII-30?; Fornaseri, 75-76, René to Beatrice, Chambéry 1-IX-30. René continued to borrow for the Duchess of Savoy that fall; see ibid., 81-82, René to Beatrice, Chambéry 23-X-30; also see AEN, AS-R5.10, e, René to Prangins, 13-XI-30?.

and thanks to his political connections.[40] Often, René's financial brokerage was difficult to follow and involved complicated and simultaneous loan guarantees. For example, in June 1533, he provided a guarantee for his cousin Villarsel, who was, in turn, guaranteeing a loan of 2300 *écus* made by the Fribourg city council to René.[41] Later that year, Charles III appeared to have settled his debt to René, subsequently acquiring more cash from him through the sale of Coligny-le-Neuf. In November 1533, René wrote that the Duke's ambassadors had received 6000 *écus* from him, including 2000 from a canceled debt. He also asked the Duke to issue letters that would permit him to force the Count of Crescentino to pay what he owed to René, 'so that my right will be upheld'.[42] Bellegarde was quite involved in René's financial business,[43] and so were his agents in France, who continued to lobby on the Count's behalf for the collection of pensions and revenues from the French Crown.[44]

Finance during the war years to 1545

After the invasion of the Sabaudian lands in 1536, René continued to be deeply involved in financial brokerage, borrowing and lending for himself and for others, at perhaps an even greater level of intensity. He sent agents (in one case, Gaspare Capris, future Bishop of Asti) to try to collect money

---

40 Ibid., AS-Z8, 12, 2500-*écu* loan from Ludwig Rundig dated 1532; ibid., AS-S26, 11, payment to Geronime de Lucernolo of Soleure dated 2-III-32; AHR, FC 289, no. 30, receipt issued by René to Antoine Cauda (Castellan of Bard), 18-IX-32. René's creditor, Wendell Sonnenberg, reminded him that one of his guarantors had died and needed to be replaced (AEN, AS-G16, 19, Sonnenberg to René, Lucerne 25-XI-32 [see also AS-S26, 12 for copy of letter in German]). René borrowed 1200 *gulden* from Doctor Zwincker of Basel, and 1500 *écus* from Bartholomey Ammann (ibid., AS-Z8, 13 and 8, loans dated 1533).

41 AHR, FC 74, no. 3, loan guarantee by René dated 2-VI-33; for another example, see AEN, AS-F16, 11, Claude de Challant to Bellegarde, s.l., s.d.

42 Fornaseri, 90-91, René to Ch III, Valangin 30-XI-33.

43 In 1534, Bellegarde gathered revenues from René's feudal agents to pay *censes* so that 'il n'y aura point de fraiz ny ostages' (AEN, AS-C4.2, b, René to Bellegarde, Beaufremont 5-IV-34 [?]). The sixteenth-century Swiss took hostages (*Geiselschaft* in German) in order to guarantee repayment of debts. It was considered an honor to be chosen as a hostage. If the debtor failed to repay, the creditor could summon the hostage or their servant to appear at a given place and time, and to live there at the debtor's expense until the debt was repaid; see Dubler. René empowered Bellegarde to negotiate for him in other financial and legal matters (AEN, AS-C4.2, d, René to Bellegarde, Beaufremont 15-V-34).

44 Francis I assigned René revenues in Arnay-le-Duc, which René rented out (ibid., AS-I16, 21, farm agreement dated 7-V-35). René's royal pension amounted to 2500 *livres* in 1535 (AHR, FC 247, no. 16, royal payment order dated 19-VI-35).

owed to him in Piedmont,[45] while his creditors likewise hounded René to pay his own debts.[46] In October 1537, he sent 500 *écus* to Bellegarde for the payment of *censes* in the Swiss area (instructing him first to change these coins 'in the Franche-Comté where they are exchanged for *escus sol*'), and apologized for not being able to send more. He hoped to be able to supplement this sum in the future with revenues from Beaufremont, from the 'castle of Coligny', and from his own *cens* receipts.[47] For the next few years, he and his envoys worked in Italy, the Swiss lands, and even in Spain to collect sums owed to René, to borrow money, and to mortgage property.[48]

In early 1540, René was sent as Sabaudian envoy to the Emperor in Flanders, and was undoubtedly pleased to receive a payment order for 400 *écus* for his expenses,[49] although the IOU that he issued to Philibert de la Baume de Montfalconet in April, for 100 *écus*, suggests that it was not enough.[50] Things seemed to be looking up a few months later, when Charles V granted René an annual pension of 1000 *écus*,[51] and then Charles III confirmed one for 150 *écus*, assigned to the revenues of Santhià. This was to recompense René for his guarantee of a 6000-*écu* loan that the Swiss had made to the Duke, and for the fact that the Duke's gift of Coligny-le-Neuf only produced 150 *écus* for him (5 per cent interest on the 6000-*écu* loan that René had underwritten for Charles was costing René 300 *écus* per year).[52] But, despite this good news, that fall, René began to despair of ever collecting what he was owed from the French Crown.[53] He also sought

---

45   AHR, FC 263, mz. 1, Gaspar Capris [?] to René, Vercelli 18-V-? [*c*. 1537].
46   Ibid., Bernard Boulet? to René?, Turin 9-X-?.
47   AEN, AS-H16, 12, René to Bellegarde, Issogne 18-X-37.
48   Ibid., AS-F16, 17, Fagnano to René, Toledo 26-XI-38; ibid., AS-Z8, nos. 2, 4, 3, 9, loans from creditors in Aarau and Lucerne dated 1539; ibid., AS-K16, 20, Castellamonte to René, Issogne 8-V-39 (for sums borrowed in the Monferrato); ibid., AS-G16, 22, Jean-François Vaudan to René, Aosta 17-V-39; Matile, 270-71; SKB, Staatliche Sammlungen, Urkunden [C 1 a], Neuenburg Fach Neuenburg [1214-1995], letters dated 17-IV-39, 25-VII-39 (for loans from private individuals, and the almshouse of Berne, secured on Valangin and Beaufremont).
49   AST1, PD 174, f. 5v., payment order dated 12-II-40.
50   AHR, FC 289, no. 59, obligation by René to Philibert de la Baume de Montfalconet dated 14-IV-40. René's castellans Roz Favre and Gamache each sent a creditor named Marguerite de Fers to the other to try to collect (AHR, FC 262, mz. 1, Marguerite de Fers to René, Montalto 18-V-40).
51   AHR, FC 341, no. 1, patents dated 12-VII-40.
52   AHR, FC 25, no. 9, patents dated 14-VII-40; ibid., no. 15, undated request by René to Ch III.
53   Since his envoy at the French court was getting nowhere, he decided to ask the Bernese to intervene for him (AEN, AS-I16, 1, René to Guillemette, Beaufremont 8-X-40). A new potential lender, 'Mons de Setours,' had credit 'de deux costez' of the Alps (AHR, FC 264, mz. 1, De Riddes to René, Chambéry 10-X-?).

permission from the Duke to sell Coligny, along with the Santhià revenues (with a permanent right of repurchase reserved for the Duke and his heirs). René made this request 'to facilitate repayment of debts owed to the Swiss', thereby enjoying 'a much improved ability to serve Your Excellency'.[54] This was not mere rhetorical flourish, but a frank acknowledgment of the fact that René's ability to broker loans from the Swiss for the Duke depended on his own solvency. While René was away, one of his agents reported to Mencia about continued efforts to raise money in the Count's absence, including by mortgaging lands in the Monferrato in order to make payments to Swiss lenders.[55] When René returned, he empowered several of his officials to sell his farm of Guardapasso near Casale (purchased only about a decade earlier). He later asked for the help of the young Prince Emanuel Filibert to help him pay off the Swiss debts that he had contracted 'for [the Duke's] service, in order subsequently to be able to serve him and you'.[56]

In spring 1542, despite a promise to pay René 1000 *écus* for various credits,[57] the Duke of Savoy still owed him at least 2445 *écus* and issued a payment order for 122 *écus* to reduce that debt.[58] Later that year, René encountered problems with the revenues assigned to him at Santhià and complained to Charles III about the 'scant reputation shown to me in this Santhià matter'. These problems made him suspect 'that you have some sinister and evil opinion toward me, based on false reports'. If this were so, René asked the Duke to reveal what the accusations were, 'for I am a man of integrity and I will show you the evil of those who behave this way'. He implored the Duke to

> take pity and consider the great expenses and losses that I suffer due to these damnable rents and interest payments to the Swiss, most of which I have taken on by your command, in your service, and do me the favor of examining the accounts and satisfying me for that part of my credit that will cause the least prejudice to your affairs while helping me avoid the danger of losing my property.

René's tone softened by the end of the letter, and he asked for forgiveness 'If my passion forces me to write in this way'.[59]

---

54 AHR, FC 25, no. 15, undated request by René to Ch III.
55 Ibid., FC 263, mz. 1, unnamed Challant officer [at Casale?] to Mencia, *c.* 1540.
56 AHR, Fonds Roncas, categoria 16B, no. 7, sale of Guardapasso dated 16-I-41; Fornaseri 100-1, René to EF, Issogne 16-XI-41.
57 AHR, FC 264, mz. 1, Vulliet to René, Nice 12-II-? [1541-1542].
58 AST1, PD 211, f. 12, payment order dated 12-V-42.
59 Fornaseri, 101-2, René to Ch III, Aymavilles, 14-IX-42.

In an undated letter that may have been from late 1542, an unidentified writer initiated a discourse around the need to reestablish financial order in René's affairs – language that would continue in subsequent years. He urged René to limit his travel to princely courts over the next three years and to encourage his revenue collectors, who had lent their own money to René and even borrowed with interest on his behalf but were barely covering their costs from what they collected in grain. Just as René's ability to support the Duke financially depended on his own good credit, so did that of René's officers who underwrote his activity.[60] The pressures were mounting: René was trying to make payments on his loans from the 'gift granted me by my subjects [in Valangin, it seems]' in order not to have to borrow more money 'in *Allemagnie*' (the Swiss cantons) for this purpose.[61] Hieronimo da Fagnano, one of René's procurators for the Guardapasso (Monferrato) sale, needed René to repay him because his own creditors were demanding their money.[62]

Efforts to find cash while delaying payments continued in 1543. Pierre Saugey and his associates, who had lent money to the House of Savoy in the late 1520s, now owed René money, perhaps for failing to have provided proper accounts for purchases allegedly made for him. He seemed to have disappeared.[63] In August 1543, René's secretary Gautier was in Chambéry, where he discovered that Saugey had fled to Toulouse. He also began talks to restructure the Count's debt to a lender named Cornellio.[64] Gautier then found Saugey and brought him back to Virieu. Saugey claimed that there had been accounting errors concerning sums that he had spent on René's behalf, for such items as a diamond belt, a red hat, dogs, and loans repaid to various creditors of René. He denied that he had made unseemly profits at René's expense and claimed that, of the 3000 *écus* that he had provided for René, no more than 600 or 700 were for 'mechandise' (which was not even 'from my shop'), and everything else had been in cash.[65] During roughly the same period, René wrote from Vercelli to Bellegarde about the absence of financial help from ducal officials to help with the rent payments for the Swiss. Bellegarde was to ask the Bernese for a loan and, failing that, to 'sell

---

60   AEN, AS-K16, 19, Valangin officer to René, s.d. [I-48?].
61   Ibid., AS-G16, 12, René to Bellegarde, Issogne 12-X-?.
62   AHR, FC 263, mz. 1, Hieronimo da Fagnano to René, Casale 21-X-42 [?].
63   One correspondent noted that Saugey 'est a present vacabond' (AEN, AS-G16, 9, Mache/Malet to René, 8-V-? [1543?]). Another advised the Count to settle for 1500 *écus* to cover the entire debt (ibid., AS-H16, 24, Gautier to René, Virieu 23-V-43).
64   Ibid., AS-F16, 26, Gautier to René, Chambéry 4-VIII-43.
65   AHR, FC 264, mz. 1, Pierre Sougey to René, Virieu 29-VIII-43 [?].

new rents or mortgage the best and most attractive property if you can find a lender'. Finding money to pay the Swiss rents was of the highest importance. 'Look for individual lenders', suggested René, 'in Fribourg or wherever you can find people with 200 or 300 *écus* at some honest rate, and collect what is needed, or mortgage specific properties', such as tithes and other things. If Bellegarde would do this, and if he could also obtain Bernese support for obtaining the back pensions owed to him from the French court, then he was hopeful that 'I will have the means to repay everything wherever I have borrowed', and that, within three or four months, there would be 'a way [...] to settle and disengage'.[66]

That fall, René took the first steps to try to bring order to his finances. His officials Jacques Cachiot, Louis de Vallesa, and Grat Rolin drew up a memoir about disposing of his property in the Monferrato.[67] In late 1544, Charles III borrowed another 4000 *écus* from René and then assigned another 200 to him in annual payments (a rate of 5 per cent) on the revenues of Santhià.[68] Although he was subsequently able to make a payment of 75 *écus* to one of his Swiss creditors (one of the rent payments that were constant sources of concern),[69] he wrote in September of that year that, with respect to the *cens*, 'there was disorder'. René was unable to find money for himself, 'nor for others, not even at the rates that I pay in Flanders, for the money that I had to borrow to sustain my recent expenses', which debts were much larger than Bellegarde had indicated. René was in 'great straits' and unable to get anything from the Duke of Savoy. He thus resolved to 'order things over there' and raise the money, if necessary, by borrowing (although not 'in *Allemaigne*'). New debts were to be assigned to the revenue of Valangin rather than to the 'gift granted by my subjects', from which René had not yet received anything. He instructed Bellegarde to 'implement the organization decided for the Valangin revenues'.[70] At about this time, René fell victim to a 'pestilential quartan fever' that left him 'at death's door' and unable to 'cross the mountains'. Perhaps this experience fortified his resolution

66 René had sent Martine to Chambéry via the Valle d'Aosta, and thence to Valangin (AEN, AS-H16, 2, René to Bellegarde, Vercelli 14-VIII-43).
67 AHR, FC 290, no. 14, memoir dated 20-XI-43; items up for potential liquidation included certain documents in the Count's possession (ibid., FC 263, mz. 1, Louis de Vallesa [?] to [René?], s.d.). For the activities of these agents in the Monferrato, see also ibid., FC 264, mz. 1, Grat Rolin to René, Aosta 18-X-43 [?]; ibid., Grat Rolin [?] to René, Aosta 26-XII-?.
68 AHR, FC 247, no. 18, assignation dated 24-IX-44; ibid., FC 25, no. 15, copy of ducal edict mentioning 1544 assignation, dated Turin 12-III-67; AST1, PD 175, f. 115, order for annual pension of 200 *scudi* in deduction of ducal debt, dated 24-XII-44.
69 AEN, AS-S26, 13, receipt issued by Conrad Clauser of Lucerne to René, 1545.
70 Ibid., AS-H16, 17, 17a, René to Bellegarde, Ivrea 26-IX-45.

to recover his financial health in addition to his physical well-being. He ordered his Captain of Beaufremont to make a renewed attempt at the court of Lorraine to recover the pension of 1000 *francs* that René had formerly received from the Duke.[71] Charles III's decision in November to assign an extra pension of 50 *scudi* to Mencia, as interest on a 'dowry security' of 1000 *scudi*, seemed promising.[72]

From the 1545 'restructuring' to the second imprisonment

In a long letter to Bellegarde written from Issogne in December 1545, as he was slowly recovering from his illness, René laid out his intentions about an exhaustive restructuring of his financial affairs. He referred stoically to his medical travails, and then noted how his financial struggle stemmed from his borrowing on behalf of rulers. He resolved to disengage from such service, 'no longer trusting in said princes', for a time. His own landed income should suffice, meanwhile, to pay off his debts, as Bellegarde had often counseled. To 'order my *estat*', he issued instructions for those administering his fiefs. Martine would deliver these rules, which focused on keeping more clear accounts and on seeing that his and Mencia's orders were carried out. He ordered that 'in your governance of my said lordship you explain to me what you have done in order to ensure my profit and advantage without any loss', adding that he expected his officers to prove by their actions that he was right to trust them. He was particularly dismayed that Valangin had not produced similar revenues as other seigniories in the area, and that Bellegarde's failure to wait for the right moment to sell his grain had cost him so much that he had had to borrow money to make his mortgage payments. He insisted, however, that he continued to have confidence in Bellegarde, and 'that you have always been faithful in serving me, for my good and profit'. But he expected Bellegarde to find a way to reimburse Martine for the sums borrowed for the mortgage, so that Martine's own credit would not suffer. He concluded that 'my will is that he be repaid'.[73]

From this point on, René was determined that the recovery of his finances and health should progress in tandem. In 1546, he farmed out the revenues of Valangin to Jean Robin, Blaise Junod, and Jean Clerc dit Vulpe, for 2000

---

71 The Captain was to seek the assistance of the Count of Salm in this matter (AEN, AS-S26, 46, memoir to Captain of Beaufremont, Issogne 26-X-45).
72 AST1, PD 219, f. 42, pension grant dated 26-XI-45.
73 AEN, AS-G16, 14, René to Bellegarde, Issogne 14-XII-45.

écus per year, an arrangement that continued until René's death.[74] René made a bit of headway with the new French King, Henry II, who promised to assign to particular revenues the amount owed to him, which René placed at 4500 *écus*.[75] However, his contact in Berne, Hans Jakob von Watteville/Wattenwyl,[76] was of the opinion that it would have been better if the King had given him cash, noting that it 'it will not profit your affairs over here, which require cash'.[77]

In early 1548, Martine wrote several letters to René, then in Beaufremont, about finances. René had summoned him to Beaufremont, but Martine explained his inability to go and deflected claims that he and other Valangin officers (to whom Martine referred as hardworking) were ignoring his commands.[78] Martine was, in fact, in the midst of a frantic effort to renegotiate René's debts by meeting with creditors in Basel, Lucerne, and elsewhere in the Swiss lands, a project that would save the Count money but would require some short-term support from his Valdostano fiefs.[79] Martine thought it possible to pay off the debts on Valangin to his Swiss creditors within two years – a prospect that he called 'a beautiful and great breakthrough'. That year's harvest seemed abundant, and the revenue collectors were doing all that they could, 'but it is a big problem that the people are so short of money in this country'. This made it difficult to collect even a quarter of what was owed from 'those who have been freed from feudal obligations', and Martine suspected that this problem was compounded by local malcontents undermining René's interests.[80]

---

74 AHR, FC 56/B, no. 8, contract dated 30-X-46; see also Matile, 270-71.
75 AHR, FC 292, no. 35, undated request by René to King of France.
76 Jean Jacques de Watteville, Lord of Colombier, had been educated as a page at the court of Savoy, taken prisoner by the Imperials (along with René) while fighting for the French at Pavia in 1525, and served as Governor of Dijon. He was a member of the large and small councils of Berne from the 1520s and *avoyer* from 1533. Watteville married a Franche-Comtoise noblewoman and oversaw the cession of Gruyère to Berne and Fribourg in 1555; he died in 1560 (see Braun, 'Wattenwyl').
77 AEN, AS-F16, 15, Watteville to René, Berne 9-VIII-47.
78 Ibid., AS-K16, 19, Valangin officer to René, s.d. [I-48?].
79 Martine secured loans in Basel; settled with '*le changeur*'; bought time from Sonnenberg in Lucerne; tried (unsuccessfully) to identify new underwriters in Lucerne, Basel, Berne, or Soleure; secured a loan from the town counselors of Neuchâtel; and extended a loan from Watteville. These operations saved René 130 *écus* annually but required 1000 more *écus* from the valley and the balance from Valangin (ibid., AS-F16, 5, Martine [his handwriting] to René, ?-I-48).
80 Someone had reportedly told these subjects that they owed more than they really did, and that, if they failed to pay, 'ne seront point admis ny receuz au nombre des bourgeois'. This provoked a 'mutination entre vous subietz dressee par le meschant conseil de ne scay quelles gens' and created difficulties for the collectors (ibid.).

Martine was soon able to secure a loan from the Lucernois Sonnenberg, guaranteed by 'the Neuchâtel councilors', and to report that 872 *écus* had arrived from the Valle d'Aosta. In the interim between the time René ordered the transfer of funds, Martine had managed to make certain payments, but new obligations had arisen (including liquidating a loan for which Watteville had presented himself as hostage), and so the cash was applied to these ends. Watteville was Reformed and well-disposed toward René. He and Martine both were being pressured by other Reformed ministers concerning the situation of the preacher of La Chaux de Fonds, which added another dimension to these financial negotiations.[81] For the next year, Martine continued to work on straightening out René's finances, negotiating with the Swiss Hans Steiger, the banneret Wingarten, Lady Barbe Amman, Louis and Felix de Diesbach, and Sebastian Nägeli.[82]

From June 1550 through his capture in November 1553, René seems to have been mainly in Vercelli and in Piedmont, except for a trip to Brussels in June 1551 and time spent in the Valle d'Aosta in late spring and summer 1552. He does not seem to have experienced any financial crises during this period, and it even appears that he and Mencia became interested in trying to exploit the manganese mines at St. Marcel.[83] The only indication of a problem was a claim by the Imperial Captain Cesare Maggi that René owed him money. Maggi threatened that, if he were not repaid, 'I will no longer consider Your Lordship the friend that I have always held you to be, and will be forced to provide for myself and end our friendship, and the

---

81 Martine warned that, if they did not repay the loan for which Watteville had provided security by the end of April, 'vous perdes le credit d'ung de vous meillieurs amis [Colombier] et d'ailleurs moy que luy suis obligé pour ladite somme'. Other underwriters in Fribourg and Berne were also demanding repayment (ibid., AS-G16, 20, Martine to René [in Beaufremont], Valangin 19-II-48).

82 In May 1549, Martine held talks with 'Steigeher' (Hans Steiger) and with the banneret 'Vingart' (Steiger was a member of the large and small councils from 1538 and 1545, respectively, and, beginning in 1548, was 'trésorier du Pays romand'; see Hans Braun, 'Steiger'). Barbe Amman had offered to take over the security guarantee of the Diesbachs, who had apparently mortgaged their house to raise the money, and Steiger then purchased the house. No more arrangements could be made with those of the 'Ligues, sans ce que je me oblige par la dedans', before these debts were repaid. Here, we see Martine in the same situation that René had been in when he had brokered Swiss loans for Charles III (AEN, AS-F16, 16, Martine to René, Valangin ?-V-49). That fall Martine collected money from Valangin to repay Steiger (ibid., AS-H16, 21, Gruyère to René, La Bastie 29-X-49).

83 AHR, FC 166, no. 1, permission dated 14-XII-50 from René for Mencia to take manganese from the St. Marcel mines. In early 1551, the Count received a payment assigned to 'la recepte generalle de Lion' (ibid., FC 260, Jacques David to René [in Vercelli], Lyon 'en votre maison' 26-IV-51 [?]).

fault will be yours, not mine'.[84] It is difficult to know what to make of Maggi's pretensions, since René seems to have been fairly solvent during these years. This was due to his ability to use lands and revenues in one region to support financial activities in other ones, and to the proximity of his various fiefs to sources of credit.[85]

The financial implications of ransom

Early modern nobles who had the misfortune of being captured in combat were forced to finance extravagant ransom payments. The greater a prisoner's prestige, the higher the ransom demanded, such that ransom finance created an ironic inverse relationship between high status and future patrimonial solvency. Being captured did not, in itself, imply any dishonor for prisoners,[86] although it often resulted in uncertainty about who had the right to demand the ransom. After the battle of Pavia, Robert III de La Marck was ransomed for 2000 *écus*, while Anne de Montmorency's ransom was 10,000. In 1557, after St. Quentin, Jacques d'Albon de Saint-André's ransom was set at 60,000.[87] During the 1550s, Emanuel Filibert, Imperial commander in the Low Countries, turned the trade in prisoners and ransoms into 'a real war business. During the Picardy campaigns, he purchased prisoners from captors at low prices and then held them for juicy ransoms'.[88] In 1553, the French monarchy, working together with commanders in the field, tried to regulate the ransom problem, and the treaty of Vaucelles (1555) stipulated that a ransom would equal a year's worth of a prisoner's revenues, according

---

84   Ibid., FC 264, mz. 1, Cesare de Mayo to René, Volpiano 6-VII-51 [?]. Cesare Maio (or Maggi) da Napoli fought for Charles V in Piedmont in the early 1550s; see Teodori.
85   Indeed, he was called upon by his kinsmen Charles de Challant-Villarsel and Claude de Challant-Fénis (son of Charles' brother Gaspard?; see De Tillier, *Nobiliaire*, 102-38) to pledge security for them on loans that they had taken out from Swiss lenders (AHR, FC 74, no. 14, obligation by Villarsel to Conrad Clauser dated 7-III-52; ibid., FC 74, no. 15, guarantee by Challant-Fenis freeing René and Villarsel from obligation to pay loan security to Heinrich Bichereit of Lucerne dated 18-IV-52).
86   John Lynn notes, however, that surrendering during a battle was more acceptable for a combatant than doing so during a siege; see Lynn, 100-1.
87   Deruelle, 539. After Pavia, the Queen-Regent of France, Louise de Savoie, helped prisoners pay ransoms; see Contamine, 227.
88   Deruelle, 534-35. The author notes that, in 1553, 'après le siège de Thérouanne, il rachète, par exemple, Sébastien de Baugé à un capitaine pour 15,000 écus avant de le mettre à rançon pour 40,000 écus', citing a work by Ambroise Paré for this detail. Baugé is identified as Sébastien de Luxembourg, second son of François II de Luxembourg, Viscount of Martigues following the death of his elder brother.

to the prisoner's good-faith declaration.[89] Paul Vo-Ha, following Philippe Contamine, thus described the history of 'ransom economics' as 'the slow intervention of a regulating State, by the turn of the seventeenth century, in a hitherto ultra-liberal market'.[90] Noble captives were expected to submit to the ransom demands of their captors and, if they had given their pledge, were not to try to escape, subject to dishonor and ostracism.[91] Captors had to provide appropriate hospitality and might release a prisoner on the basis of his promise to pay the ransom. Sources detailing prisoners' living conditions are few, however.[92]

According to Matile, after René was taken prisoner at the battle of Pavia, he asked his subjects in Valangin to pay two florins per person in order to raise money for a ransom. Some of the subjects paid, but others did not, and, 20 years later, he was still trying to collect. These revenues helped him pay off the mortgage that he had taken out in 1533, on Beaufremont, from Pietro de Valle and Giovanni Donato for 2000 *scudi*, in order to provide the first ransom.[93] From the 1530s on, military commanders in Piedmont on both sides were concerned about the financial threat posed by heavy ransoms.[94]

Eleven months after René's capture at Vercelli, Pierre Maillard du Bouchet, one of Emanuel Filibert's closest advisers, assured Mencia that René was not forgotten and that he and others continued to work for the Count's release. Mencia's Iberian network had been activated.[95] Bouchet noted that Louis de Silly, Lord of La Roche Guyon (potential subject of a prisoner exchange), had been captured at the battle of Renty (August 1554) but had been given to

---

89   Vo-Ha, 210; Contamine, 229, 232.
90   Vo-Ha, 210. Contamine described this as part of 'un processus plus large de prise en charge par l'État de ses militaires dans tous les aspects de leur condition' ('Un contrôle étatique croissant,' 235).
91   Lynn, 101.
92   Deruelle, 534-37.
93   AHR, FC 65, no. 8, mortgage dated Vercelli 16-I-33; Matile, 262; De Antonio, 236.
94   In August 1553, the French commander Brissac and the Imperial general Ferrante Gonzaga reached an agreement to 'fixer d'avance le taux de ces rançons [for captured officers and nobles] d'un commun accord'. French officers had sometimes been fighting *incognito*, as common soldiers, in order to avoid having to pay burdensome ransoms in the event of their capture – a practice that the Italians, Spanish, and Germans disdained. As we shall see, the agreement was not very helpful for René; see Marchand, 180-82; and BNF, Mss. Fr. 20449, f. 229 for the agreement (cited by Marchand).
95   The Bishop of Salamanca (Mencia's brother, Pedro de Castro Lemos) had recently arrived in England to meet with King Philip, the Duke of Braganza had written to the Duke of Savoy about René, and Mencia's other brother (Fernando-Ruiz, Marquis of Sarria) and the Portuguese ambassador were on their way to see the Emperor.

Guillaume de Croÿ, Marquis of Renty, to trade for Renty's brother, Philippe III de Croÿ, Duke of Aarschot. But prisoners taken at Hesdin the year before might be included in another trade, and Challant 'will not be forgotten' in this case. Bouchet promised that they would obtain René's release one way or another, and 'his affairs will improve so much' that Mencia would have reason to be happy.[96] Mencia also asked Ferrante Gonzaga (Imperial Governor of Milan) to speak to Charles V about René's imprisonment and to stress René's role in 'the preservation of the Valle d'Aosta' and other places.[97] One candidate for a prisoner swap was François de Coligny, Lord of Andelot, who had been captured by Imperial forces in 1551.[98] Giovanni Francesco Costa d'Arignano spoke to Charles V on behalf of René in late November, and was told that the Emperor had placed the matter in the hands of his sister, Mary of Hungary, and of Antoine de Perrenot (the Bishop of Arras and future Cardinal of Granvelle).[99] In December 1554, as anxiety about the safety of the Valle d'Aosta heightened due to the French capture of Ivrea, Mencia turned her attention away from the prisoner-exchange strategy to the problem of raising ransom funds. Investors in Lyon did not want to lend money on property (like Beaufremont) that was so far away, so, in January, she sent agents to Paris to request payment of back pensions owed to René by the Count of Vaudémont (who would soon marry Jeanne de Savoie, sister of Jacques de Savoie-Nemours). She also sought out potential lenders in Lucerne.[100]

In Brussels, Arignano continued to work for a prisoner exchange, winning the support of Mary of Hungary and Ruy Gomez. He also explained to the Emperor the strategic vulnerability of the valley (and northern Italy) due to the recent loss of Ivrea, and urged 'an exchange for the Count of Challant, for the sake of the country's safety'.[101] Later that spring, Arignano acknowledged receipt of Mencia's reports about 'the rigorous treatment of the Marshal', promising that the Duke of Savoy had spoken to Charles V about this.[102] At about the same time, René wrote to the Duke, via the secretary Ducrest, from prison in Turin to express his happiness about Emanuel Filibert's arrival in

---

96 AHR, FC 263, mz. 1, Bouchet to Mencia, 'Du camp de l'empereur a Meyni' [Nomeny?] 12-X-54.
97 Ibid., Mencia [?] to Ferrante Gonzaga, s.l., s.d. [after 1553].
98 Ibid., ? to [Mencia?], s.l., s.d.
99 AST1, LP, C.104, Arignano to EF, Brussels 7-XI-54.
100 Marchand, 249; AHR, FC 263, mz. 1, Chevron to Mencia, Annecy 25-XII-54 [?]; ibid., FC 260, Chevron to Mencia, Annecy 30-I-55.
101 Charles V 'voleva far [the prisoner exchange] ma bisogniaria aspetar vera risposta da francesi' (AST1, LP, C.104, Arignano to EF, Brussels 6-I-55).
102 AHR, FC 263, mz. 1, Arignano to Mencia, Brussels 20-V-55 [?].

Vercelli (news of which had been given to him by Brissac). This gave him hope that he would soon leave 'this hateful place and long detention', and promised to come see the Duke as soon as he was free, to 'discuss my affairs with you in detail'.[103] The Duke's visit to his lands in 1555 was marked by frustration with Charles V's failure to end the war and restore his Sabaudian patrimony. Accounts based on the memoirs of Brissac's secretary suggest that the Bishop of Aosta, Pietro Gazino, had advised Emanuel Filibert to open a diplomatic gambit with the French that involved his marriage to Marguerite, the King's sister. René reportedly favored this move, which may have created pressure for the Emperor to change his policy in a way that afforded Emanuel Filibert more control over his own destiny.[104]

On 10 September 1555, René and Brissac signed a contract concerning René's ransom and liberation. René was required to pay a ransom of 24,313 *écus*, 5000 of which were paid right away, another 2000 via a promise from a certain 'Breton Gros', and possibly 2000 more if Henry II would approve the sale by René of 'village revenues in the Captainate of Santhià' to Jehan Maure (Giovanni Antonio Mauro), resident of Milan. For the balance of the sum, René pledged to mortgage to Brissac the barony of Beaufremont and any other property owned by René in Lorraine, the diocese of Toul, or the *ressort* of Paris, with the proviso that René could redeem this property if he were to pay the balance of the ransom by other means within one year of the day of his liberation. Should he fail to do this or to provide 'someone to take his place [as a hostage]', Brissac would acquire those properties as if they had been sold to him. Each side appointed two procurators to attend to any matters arising from the agreement, and, on 25 September, René was 'freed and delivered from prison'.[105] By 9 October, the Count was back at Issogne, and immediately began planning a trip to Brussels to meet with the Duke.[106]

---

103 Fornaseri, 134-35, René to EF, 'Chatyau de Thurin' 21-V-55.
104 Gazino reportedly met with the Governor of Ivrea, Montbasin, and discussed the Franco-Sabaudian diplomatic opening, to which Brissac was favorable (Marchand, 267-70, 268 n.1). According to Boyvin, René had, on several occasions, urged the Duke to reconcile with France (Boyvin, 683-84).
105 The accord was notarized by Jehan Baptiste Ghignonis, a citizen of Turin and secretary for a French court there. René's procurators were Jean Guillaume de Santhusen, his Captain of Beaufremont, and Bernard de La Fontaine (procuration notarized by Pierre Foldon of Aosta), and Brissac's were François de l'Aubespine (royal counselor, Lieutenant General of Berry for the King, and President of the Council of Justice of Metz) and Jacques du Val (*advocat du Roy* and *greffier* at Metz) (AHR, FC 56B, no. 12, notarial act dated 15-XI-55).
106 Ibid., FC 260, Gio Giacomo Curbis to René [in Issogne], Vercelli 9-X-55. The Bishop of Aosta wrote to the Duke on the next day that 'Mons di Chiallant e usito dalle mani di francesi con la

In late 1555, soon after René was released from prison, valley authorities began their efforts to renew their neutrality agreement with the French. They asked René to be involved, but the Count, understandably, replied that 'seeking the confirmation of this truce seems ill-advised, given its inefficacy for him while he was imprisoned or for his subjects'.[107] René was more preoccupied with the transfer of financial authority over Beaufremont to Brissac's procurators, which was taking place simultaneously.[108] A few days later, Giovanni Fabri – Emanuel Filibert's chief secretary and a native Valdostano – congratulated René on his release.[109]

Over the course of the next year, one of René's most pressing concerns was thus to raise the money required to pay the balance of his ransom to Brissac, in order not to lose Beaufremont, which had already been mortgaged to the Duke of Lorraine and then repurchased in 1540. Before René had been released from prison, Mencia and her daughters had borrowed 9970 *écus* from the Bernese, secured on Valangin, an arrangement confirmed by René in March 1556.[110] René also set about raising money on his other lands as well, mortgaging Ussel and St. Marcel to Paolo Madruzzo, illegitimate nephew of Cardinal Cristoforo Madruzzo, for 12,000 *scudi*. He used his palaces in Casale and Verolengo to secure 2000 *scudi* from Guglielmo Gonzaga, Duke of Mantua and Marquis of Monferrato, and sold his other houses in Casale, his farms in San Salvatore, and his jurisdictions of Settimo Vittone, Quincinetto, Carema, and Montalto.[111]

In early 1556, René traveled to Brussels, where his central concern in his discussions with the Duke was the ransom payment. Significantly, an element of the Treaty of Vaucelles, dated 19 December 1555 (six weeks prior to the treaty's official signing) had just made provisions for the ransoms to

---

tagli de 24,000 scudi e me dissi nel mi venir chio feci in qua che passata la festa de tutti santi si voleva incaminar da VA' (AST1, LV, Aosta, mz. 20, Gazino to EF, Milan 26-X-55).

107 The Bishop of Aosta asked Emanuel Filibert to instruct René in this regard, 'no' essendolj qua altro principe che VA' (ibid., Aosta 30-XI-55).

108 In mid November, procurators for René and Brissac traveled to Beaufremont, examined the places in question, and effected a transfer that resulted in the Captain's maintenance of possession of the barony, whose revenues would be gathered and submitted to René during the year in question, without Brissac's interference (AHR, FC 56B, no. 12, notarial act dated 15-XI-55).

109 AEN, AS-G16, 25, Fabri to René, Brussels 20-XI-55.

110 Matile wrote that it was Beaufremont that had been mortgaged to the Bernese in this respect, but this would not make sense given that René had also mortgaged Beaufremont to Brissac (Matile, 271-72). Vialardi di Sandigliano links the 9970-*scudi* loan to Valangin, which is surely correct (Vialardi di Sandigliano, 24).

111 Ibid.; also Frutaz, 'Notes,' 252; Bianco di San Secondo, 105; 'Histoire genealogique,' 51r.

be paid by prisoners of war held by each side.¹¹² René thus brought up 'the matter of the exchange' for Andelot (who was being held in the castle of Milan), an issue requiring Philip's involvement prior to his departure for England. The question was to determine the quality of the French prisoners then being held, whether they had been assigned ransoms, and if an exchange were possible that would amortize René's mortgage of Beaufremont. Since René had arranged for his release prior to this general agreement, he needed to ascertain that he would not have to pay more than the new treaty required. He also stressed that, while in prison, he had been forced to make payments to many guards (and not only his own servants) beyond their wages – something that the French prisoners had not had to do. Further, Andelot's good treatment at the castle of Milan was to be compared to the 'rudeness' with which René's French captors had handled him.¹¹³

René also continued to pursue ransom funding in other ways. First, prior to his release from prison, René had received Emanuel Filibert's approval to sell the revenues of the *capitanato* of Santhià, which had been granted to him by Charles V, to the Milanese Mauro.¹¹⁴ Second, in December 1555, a treasury official from Milan issued an attestation that René would receive payment for back pensions owed to him (1000 *scudi* per year beginning in 1538) amounting to 51,774 *lire*.¹¹⁵ Whether this payment was ever effected is not clear – perhaps it was and was also applied to the ransom. Third, René tried to squeeze more from his fiefs. In early 1556, he urged Bellegarde to collect everything due from that year's harvest at Valangin and from the past ones (under Trolliet's watch) when 'the harvests were so good that they have no excuse, nor should we heed those who refused to help me

---

112 Prisoners were to be 'mis à rançon, pour une fois paier, au seûr & prix du revenu d'une année de leurs biens, ensemble des gages, soldes, pensions, & traictemens annuels qu'ils ont de leurs Princes: & pardessus cela seront pesées & estimées raisonnablement les qualitez d'un chacun,' by deputies appointed by each side. The prisoners were to be notified of this agreement right away, and they were to declare on their honor 'combien ils ont de revenu par an, ensemble des traitemens, soldes & pensions, charges & qualitez qu'ils ont, & l'envoieront écrit & signé de leurs mains,' with a declaration of whether they accepted this agreement or not. Not included in this arrangement were the dukes of Bouillon, Montmorency, and Arscot, who were making their own arrangements. The prisoners were also to be responsible for any expenses incurred by them during their captivity (*Recueil des traitez de paix*, 507-8).
113 If a French prisoner who was a candidate for exchange had been assigned a ransom of 'leur revenu d'un an tant en biens comme de leur estatz', and the individual did not have the cash on hand, then they would need to work out an arrangement; René had already paid more than a year's revenue (AEN, AS-K16, 16, memoir s.d. for René at court).
114 AHR, FC 39/B, no. 10, approval dated 17-VII-55.
115 Ibid., FC 74, no. 18, attestation by Giovanni Battista Cotta dated 4-XII-55.

FINANCE AND BROKERAGE 243

escape from debt'.[116] Fourth, René approached the Count and Countess of Vaudémont for their help in securing unpaid pensions from the Duke of Lorraine, and offered to sell them part of Beaufremont.[117] Then, perhaps through the intercession of the Vaudémont, René's Captain in Beaufremont (Santhusen) began negotiations with other potential purchasers.[118] Fifth, René even explored involvement in the grain and spice trades as ways of raising money.[119] Sixth, he turned to his own subjects in the Valle d'Aosta, collecting a subsidy from them.[120] Finally, René tried to borrow from other nobles.[121]

By the fall of 1556, it appears that the Bishop of Arras (Granvelle) had agreed to relieve René of the balance of his debt to Brissac. Without specifying the amount of the sum, René asked Emanuel Filibert, now Governor-General

116   AEN, AS-G16, 1, René to Bellegarde, Brussels 4-II-56.
117   Santhusen visited the Count of Vaudémont on René's behalf and noted that the Duchess of Lorraine had also promised an annual pension of 1000 *francs*, but was now refusing to make back payments (ibid., AS-F16, 21, Santhusen to René, Beaufremont 6-VI-56). The Duke of Lorraine had asked René to settle for 800 *francs*, but René instead sought help from the Vaudémont, offering to sell them 'sa piece de Boffroymont', in recognition of 'la grande afection qu'il a a sette mayson de Loreigne' (ibid., AS-I16, 24, request by René to the Count and Countess of Vaudémont, s.d. [after 1555?]). Santhusen thought that the real obstacle to the pension payment was the Countess, Jeanne de Savoie, whose brother Jacques had claims on Neuchâtel (ibid., AS-G16, 7, Santhusen to René, Vézelise 12-VII-56). In September, Vaudémont finally announced that he was unable to make the payments requested (ibid., AS-F16, 30, Nicolas de Lorraine [?] to René, Nomeny 18-IX-56).
118   One of the counts Palatine of the Rhine put Santhusen's agent in touch with Colonel Reiffemberg, who was interested in lending money to René 'pour satisfaire a ranson'. A series of negotiations followed; see ibid., AS-S26, 41, De Bildsonge [?] to Santhusen, Rambervillez [?] 30-V-56; ibid., AS-F16, 21, Santhusen to René, Beaufremont 6-VI-56; ibid., AS-G16, 7, Santhusen to René, Vézelise 12-VII-56.
119   René sent an agent to request a passport permitting him to transport 6000-8000 sacks of grain along the Moselle, through the *Trois-Evêchés*, sale of which would support his ransom payment (ibid., AS-I16, 25, copy of draft instructions for René's envoy to French authorities to request passport, s.d.). Etienne Perret wrote from Antwerp about a plan involving the 'poix des espicez de Portugal', and another one involving the coommercialization of 'sucrez' (ibid., AS-H16, 19, Perret to René, Antwerp 21-VI-56). Later, Perret reported a discussion with Gaspard Schetz about a venture with Gilbert van Schoonbeke, 'comys des finances du Roy', to invest in a spice-distribution business (ibid., AS-G16, 18, Etienne Perret to René [in Brussels], Antwerp 11-VIII-56 [?]).
120   Ibid., AS-K16, 3, receipt issued by René to Ducrest, Novara [?] 23-IX-58.
121   He asked Ponthus de Lalaing, Lord of Bugnicourt and Marshal in the Imperial army, for 16,000 *écus* to be deducted from the ransom of the Constable Montmorency and secured by Gaspard Schetz (ibid., AS-F16, 8, copy of Bugnicourt to René, Villers 13-VIII-56). Emanuel Filibert also borrowed from Schetz (AST1, Minute Registri Lettere della Corte, mz. 9, f. 32, EF to CdC, Brussels 23-III-57). Perret also remained in the Low Countries working with different financial contacts on René's behalf (AEN, AS-H16, 6, Perret to René, Antwerp 14-VIII-56).

of the Netherlands, to find a revenue source with which to repay Granvelle for his help, 'so my debt can be settled, as it is toward Brissac, thanks to God and you, so my house is now *en liberté*'. In a postscript, René noted that both he and Emanuel Filibert were now obliged to Granvelle.[122] After having gone through the ordeal of prison and ransoms on two separate occasions, René was sought out by those who found themselves in similar predicaments.[123] Ultimately, his escape from his ransom burden was facilitated by numerous transregional lands and relationships situated along an axis running from Italy to Flanders.

Financial recovery

In early 1557, Philip II confirmed the annual pension of 1000 *scudi* that Charles V had assigned to René on the revenues of Vespolate (near Novara) and nearby places, and increased it by 200 *scudi*.[124] Although he continued to collect from his lands in the Valle d'Aosta, the debt that he had been forced to incur because of his second imprisonment created problems for him, making it difficult for him to meet expenses on diplomatic missions carried out for the Duke, for example.[125] René's attention to the administration of his lands following his release from prison was thus driven by both financial and political concerns. His secretary Ducrest suggested an investigation of Trolliet, one of his officials at Valangin, who was accused of mismanagement, 'since great ignominy hangs in the balance for him, and repayment for you'.[126] He subsequently farmed the revenues of Valangin

---

122 Fornaseri, 135-36, René to EF, Paris 29-IX-56.
123 In July 1556, as he was still trying to piece together his own ransom payment, René was contacted by Antoine de La Forest, Lord of Feissons, then in prison. 'Estant sy loing de ce peu de bien et parens que j'ay', La Forest asked for help to secure his release (AEN, AS-H16, 7, La Forest to René, 'De la prison de Vallansienne' 3-VII-56). Just a few days earlier, René had made out a promissory note to Bouchet for 140 *écus*, to be transmitted for the balance of La Forest's ransom (ibid., AS-K16, 13, obligation made by René to Bouchet dated 31-VI-56).
124 AHR, FC 25, no. 10, confirmation and augmentation dated 25-II-57.
125 In September, Bonaventure Vaudan delivered 170 *écus* to René from Issogne, Graines, and Challant (AEN, AS-K16, 1, receipt issued to Vaudan, Verrès 15-IX-57). In late 1557, René needed cash to complete his negotiations with the Swiss, and reminded Emanuel Filibert about his long, uncompensated service to the dynasty, dating back to the time of Charles III (Fornaseri, 136-38, René to EF, Valangin 25-XI-57).
126 AEN, AS-F16, 14, Ducrest to René, Aosta 4-XII-57; for a loan of 130 *écus* to René by a saddler from Vercelli, see ibid., AS-G16, 13, René to Loranze, Ducrest, and the Castellan of Aymaville, Vercelli 11-IV-58.

FINANCE AND BROKERAGE   245

to Blaise Junod for four years.[127] Days later, he reached an agreement with Nicolò d'Azeglio over a debt that he had claimed from René, and for which he had filed a lawsuit.[128]

Following the Sabaudian restoration, René continued his efforts to pay outstanding debts. In September 1560, the ducal *Chambre des comptes* appeared to have written on René's behalf to the King of France to request payments of pensions owed to him.[129] In October 1561, René also mortgaged some revenues in the Valle d'Aosta in order to be able to borrow elsewhere so he could repurchase properties near Valangin in a complex operation involving a tenant of his, a *bourgeois* of Neuchâtel named Louis Rossel.[130] The personal crisis provoked by the death of his fourth wife during childbirth in April 1564 was perhaps what prompted René to sell his palace in Casale to the Marquis of Pescara.[131] He then reached out to investors in Milan about investing in his Monferrato property of Guardapasso. In July, the Count's officer Domeyne Lescha began negotiating this sale with Evasio Ardizzone.[132] The deal with Ardizzone fell through, but Ardizzone suggested his nephew Guid'Antonio Grumelli as a potential investor.[133]

The arrival of the Plague in the valley in the late spring of 1564 created more economic, commercial, and financial disruption. René's dispatch of envoys to the Spanish court to seek back pensions 'on the state of Milan' was perhaps a response to the economic downturn caused by the Plague. René claimed that 12-14,000 *écus* were owed. He instructed his envoys,

---

127   AHR, FC 215, no. 20, farm agreement dated 10-III-59.
128   Azeglio and his wife, daughter of the deceased Annibale de Jordani of Montalto, claimed that René had purchased Annibale's property in Montalto and had not paid in full. René promised to provide evidence, by Pentecost, showing that he had satisfied the debt, and, in the meantime, assigned revenues from Verolengo to pay the Azeglio claims. For their part, the Azeglio promised to withdraw the suit filed in the royal *Parlement* of Turin against Michel Gamache (one of René's officers, apparently) in this matter (AEN, AS-F16, 22, agreement dated Issogne 13-III-59).
129   AHR, FC 26, no. 36, CdC to Francis II, 17-IX-60 (although listed in the inventory, this letter, like most of the items in this bundle, has been removed).
130   In October 1561, René mortgaged an annual *censo* of rye for the mills at Pont de Brusson to various local subjects for the price of 225 *scudi*, and, a month later, wrote a promissory note for 2200 *écus* to Louis and Pierre Rossel. This sum was for the purpose of re-acquiring 'nostre bien que les Robins d'Yverdon tiennent de nous, tant a Cronay, Yverdon, Grandson, que aux environs'. René promised repayment in eight years, together with an annual payment of 5 per cent (110 *écus*), in the form of an exemption from the same amount owed annually by the Rossel to René for the rent of property in Yverdon (ibid., FC 151, no. 2, sale with repurchase right dated 8-X-61; ibid., FC 74, no. 21, note dated 9-XI-61).
131   Ibid., FC 260, Hercule Fagnano to Giovanni Federico Madruzzo, Milan 22-V-64.
132   Ibid., FC 131, Domeyne Lescha to René, Châtillon 17-VII-64.
133   Ibid., FC 260, Evasio Ardizzone [?] to Domenico Lescha [Lescho?], Milan 21-VII-64.

Stefano della Rovere di Vinovo and Garcilasco Roero di Ceresole, to address Fernando Rodriguez de Castro, Count of Lemos and Marquis de Sarria (René's former brother-in-law), who was also a 'close relative and ally' of the current Governor of Milan, who apparently had access to cash. They were also to employ Vinovo's consort (Claudia, a well-known poetess, daughter of Filippo Valperga di Villars) as a 'good intercessor' with respect to the Queen.[134] Matters worsened when Jean Mareschal, ducal treasurer at Bourg-en-Bresse (near the castle of Varey, where René was residing), wrote that he was unable to provide the money that René had requested. He had no assignations that were not suspended due to the arrival of Emanuel Filibert in the area – the Duke had crossed the mountains to meet the King of France, then on his *grand tour*.[135] That fall, the Duke of Savoy issued patents assigning René a monthly pension of 370 *lire*, and, five months later, René acknowledged having received 1800 florins in pension payments from Mareschal's agent Bernard Sarpol.[136] Until the eve of his death, René's agents continued to sell property in the Monferrato.[137]

This overview of René de Challant's activities as a broker, borrower, and lender indicates a strong link between such practices and the spatial configuration of René's landed authority. The evidence shows that the proximity of lenders to the lands and fiefs on which loans were secured increased their willingness to extend credit. This gave an advantage to a lord like René, effectively opening up a larger number of credit markets due to the dispersed nature of his lands. His ability to borrow in Lyon, in the Swiss zone, in Lorraine and the Low Countries, and in Milan and Italy was facilitated by his lordship in nearby areas. René's financial use of his property followed a pattern: when he needed to raise money, he tended to mortgage lands that were far removed from his ancestral Challant lands in the Valle d'Aosta (especially Beaufremont and, to a lesser extent Valangin, the latter being especially useful for tapping into the Swiss credit market).

---

134 Vinovo and Ceresole were to make it known that 'combien que le malheur luy soit advenu d'avoir perdu feu Madame sa femme, ce neantmoings il n'a perdu l'affection de l'obligation que pour amour d'elle il avoit aud' S'r marquis' (ibid., FC 290, no. 53, copy of Roussillon 24-VII-64 memoir for Vineufs and Cerisolles). On Claudia, see Cox, 394.

135 Mareschal had not even been able to pay the treasurer of the Duchess, who had come to collect Marguerite's pension. The Plague had delayed matters, but Mareschal promised that René would be first in line after the Duchess (AHR, FC 260, Jean Mareschal to René [at Varey], Bourg 10-VIII-64).

136 Ibid., FC 26, no. 37, patents dated 3-X-64; ibid., FC 290, no. 55, declaration dated 18-III-65.

137 Asclero Cerruto, Paolo Madruzzo, Domenico Lescha, and Nicolas [?] d'Avise all worked on these matters in Casale (ibid., FC 131, Asclero Cerruto to Paolo Madruzzo [in St. Marcel], Casale 13-III-65).

Altenatively, he used lands that had been acquired from his first wife's family (the Monferrato properties) to secure loans. But he then also employed revenues from the valley to pay off mortgages taken out elsewhere. The spatially diversified character of his mortgage portfolio complicated his efforts to collect information about revenues, borrowers, and lenders in different places, and to manage his financial activities. His officials were constantly on the move, and the organization of communications was a challenge in this context. René's ability to master this information and to identify potential lenders and opportunities reinforces the recent scholarly view that, far from being financially inept, many early modern nobles not only attended successfully to the financial dimensions of lordship, but often devised investment and repayment strategies themselves. This was complicated enough in normal circumstances, but even more complex for a transregional lord like René.

René, like great lords elsewhere, was an important financial broker for other princes, and especially for the Duke of Savoy, René's suzerain for the county of Challant. René's experience shows that his ability to act effectively in this capacity depended on his remaining solvent, since his borrowing for the Duke depended on his own ability to provide security. The same could be said of people who brokered for René when the latter needed to raise money. These chains of relationships were crucial elements of early modern state finance, and deserve further elucidation.[138] They call to mind Rabelais's discussion in the *Tiers Livre* about the way in which debts bound society together.[139] Pantagruel's benign view of debts notwithstanding, René did his best to restructure his finances in the 1540s. This derived from a concern for his own dynasty, whose interests seemed to be compromised due to the financial demands of his service to the Sabaudian state. In this setting, the state, far from being a model of financial rationalization, seemed to be pushing René toward insolvency. It was his own 'seigneurial' concerns, and a commitment to proper management of his own house, that prompted him to organize his accounts and reassert his financial independence – at least until he was taken prisoner in 1553.

---

138 Daniel Smail has recently pointed out the degree to which 'city governments in places like Lucca were deeply entangled in the credit market' (Smail, 228). Princely governments likewise acted in ways that had unanticipated (and largely unstudied) knock-on effects.

139 'A completely debt-free world! None of the heavenly bodies, there, will have a predictable orbit. Everything will be in disarray [...]. Faith, Hope, and Charity will be driven out of this world, because men are born to help and take care of other men' (Rabelais, 255-56).

Bibliography

Ernesto Bianco di San Secondo, 'Giovanni Federico Madruzzo ambasciatore di Emanuele Filiberto,' *Studi trentini di scienze storiche* 28, 2 (1928): 103-32

François Boyvin du Villars, *Mémoires*, in *Choix de chroniques et mémoires sur l'histoire de France*, ed. J.A.C. Buchon (Paris: Librairie Charles Delagrave, 1884)

Hans Braun, 'Hans Jakob von Wattenwyl,' *DHS* (2012)

Id., 'Hans Steiger,' in *DHS* (2012)

Thalia Brero, *Les baptêmes princiers. Le cérémonial dans les cours de Savoie et Bourgogne (XV-XVIe s.)* (Lausanne: Université de Lausanne, 2005)

Frederik Buylaert, 'The Late Medieval "Crisis of the Nobility" Reconsidered: The Case of Flanders,' *Journal of Social History* 45, 4 (2012): 1117-34

William P. Caferro, 'Warfare and Economy in Renaissance Italy, 1350-1450,' *JIH* 39, 2 (2008): 167-209

Philippe Contamine, 'Un contrôle étatique croissant. Les usages de la guerre du XIVe au XVIIIe siècle: rançons et butins,' in *Guerre et concurrence entre les États européens du XIVe au XVIIIe siècle*, ed. Philippe Contamine (Paris: Press Universitaires de France, 1998), pp. 199-236

Virginia Cox, *Lyric Poetry by Women of the Italian Renaissance* (Baltimore: The Johns Hopkins University Press, 2013)

Claire Crowston, 'Credit and the Metanarrative of Modernity,' *FHS* 34, 1 (2011): 7-19

Carlo De Antonio, 'La Valle d'Aosta ed Emanuele Filiberto,' in *Lo stato sabaudo al tempo di Emanuele Filiberto*, ed. Carlo Patrucco, vol. 1 (Turin: Miglietta, 1928), pp. 153-237

Benjamin Deruelle, *De papier, de fer et de sang. Chevaliers et chevalerie à l'épreuve de la modernité (ca 1460-ca 1620)* (Paris: Publications de la Sorbonne, 2015)

Jean-Baptiste De Tillier, *Nobiliaire du duché d'Aoste*, ed. André Zanotto (Aoste: Editions de la Tourneuve, 1970 [1733 ms])

Anne-Marie Dubler, 'Geiselschaft,' *DHS* (2009)

Giovanni Fornaseri, *Le lettere di Renato di Challant, governatore della Valle d'Aosta a Carlo II ed a Emanuele Filiberto* (Turin: Deputazione subalpina di storia patria, 1957)

François-Gabriel Frutaz, 'Notes sur René de Challant et sur le passage de Calvin dans la Vallée d'Aoste,' *Musée neuchâtelois* 41 (1904): 242-67

Marta Gravela, 'Comprare il debito della città. Élite politiche e finanze comunali a Torino nel XIV secolo,' *Quaderni storici* 147 (2014): 743-774

Edoardo Grendi, *I Balbi: Una famiglia genovese fra Spagna e Impero* (Turin: Einaudi, 1997)

Elie Haddad, 'Kinship and Transmission within the French Nobility, Seventeenth and Eighteenth Centuries: The Case of the Vassé,' *FHS* 38, 4 (2015): 567-91

Germain Hausmann, 'Jean III d'Aarberg,' *DHS* (2001)

'Henrich Küssenberg's Chronik der Reformation in der Grafschaft Baden, im Klettgau und auf dem Schwarzwalde,' ed. Abbot J. Huber, *Archiv für die Schweizerische Reformations-Geschichte* 3 (1876): 411-74

Reinhard Hildebrandt, 'I "merchant bankers" della Germania meridionale nell'economia e nella politica del XVI e del XVII secolo,' in *La repubblica internazionale del denaro*, pp. 211-42

Martha Howell, 'Movable/Immovable. What's In a Name?' in *Money, Markets and Trade in Late Medieval Europe*, ed. Lawrin Armstrong, Ivana Elbl, and Martin Elbl (Leiden: Brill, 2007), pp. 538-71

Herman Kellenbenz, 'Lo Stato, la società e il denaro,' in *La repubblica internazionale del denaro*, pp. 333-83

Thomas Kuehn, *Heirs, Kin, and Creditors in Renaissance Florence* (New York: Cambridge University Press, 2008)

John Lynn, 'Honourable Surrender in Early Modern European History, 1500-1789,' in *How Fighting Ends: A History of Surrender*, ed. Holger Afflerbach and Hew Strachan (Oxford: Oxford University Press, 2012), pp. 99-110

Charles Marchand, *Charles Ier de Cossé, comte de Brissac et maréchal de France 1507-1563* (Paris: Champion, 1889)

Georges-Auguste Matile, *Histoire de la seigneurie de Valangin jusqu'à sa réunion à la directe en 1592* (Neuchâtel, James Attinger, 1852)

Joanna Milstein, *The Gondi: Family Strategy and Survival in Early Modern France* (Farnham, UK: Ashgate, 2014)

Marco Ostoni, 'Assetti, dinamiche e protagonisti dell'amministrazione finanziaria dello Stato di Milano: la Tesoreria negli anni di Carlo V,' in *Sardegna, Spagna e Stati italiani nell'età di Carlo V*, ed. Bruno Anatra and Francesco Manconi (Rome: Carocci, 2001), pp. 243-64

David Parrott, *The Business of War: Military Enterprise and Military Revolution in Early Modern Europe* (Cambridge: Cambridge University Press, 2012)

François Rabelais, 'The Third Book,' in *Gargantua and Pantagruel*, trans. Burton Raffel (New York and London: Norton, 1990), pp. 237-376

Recueil des traitez de paix, de trêve, de neutralité, et confédération, d'alliance, et de commerce, faits par les rois de France, ed. Frédéric Léonard, vol. 2 (Paris, 1693)

La repubblica internazionale del denaro tra XV e XVII secolo, ed. Aldo De Maddalena and Hermann Kellenbenz (Bologna: Il Mulino, 1986)

Brian Sandberg, *Warrior Pursuits: Noble Culture and Civil Conflict in Early Modern France* (Baltimore: The Johns Hopkins University Press, 2010)

Daniel Smail, *Legal Plunder: Households and Debt Collection in Late Medieval Europe* (Cambridge MA: Harvard University Press, 2016)

Erik Swart, '"The field of finance": War and Taxation in Holland, Flanders, and Brabant, 1572-85,' *SCJ* 42, 4 (2011): 1051-71

Raissa Teodori, 'Cesare Maggi,' *DBI* 67 (2006)

Tomaso Vialardi di Sandigliano, 'Un intruso tra i testamenti di Renato di Challant: Giuseppe Tornielli di Briona, novarese,' *Studi piemontesi* 41, 1 (2012): 23-40

Paul Vo-Ha, *Rendre les armes. Le sort des vaincus XVIe-XVIIe siècles* (Ceyzérieu: Champ Vallon, 2017)

Cornel Zwierlein, 'Deutsche und Italienische Staatsbeschreibungskunst. Die Einkünfte aller Reichsstände, ca. 1547/48 nach einer unbekannten Quelle,' *ZHF* 39, 4 (2012): 593-660

Hillay Zmora, 'The Princely State and the Noble Family: Conflict and Co-operation in the Margraviates Ansbach-Kulmbach in the Early Sixteenth Century,' *HJ* 49, 1 (2006): 1-21

8. Lordship

Abstract
René de Challant was the lord of lands some of which were well over 500 km apart from each other. This required a formidable organization of the practice of lordship, especially in the areas of revenue collection, account keeping, and the administration of justice. Valangin in particular, as a seigniory over which René was committed to demonstrating his sovereignty, demanded significant attention. René left detailed instructions concerning the administration of the barony of Beaufremont. Castellany accounts from Châtillon in the Valle d'Aosta and correspondence from Virieu in Bugey illustrate René's lordship over those places. René sometimes questioned the performance of officials whom he delegated to oversee his fiefs, occasionally interacting directly with his subjects as a way of keeping his officers in check.

Key words: lordship, fief, feudal revenue, seigniorial justice

We have seen how both René's career in the service of the House of Savoy and other rulers and the pursuit of his own transregional interests required of him a life of perpetual motion between Italy and transalpine Europe. The spatial dimension of his rights and responsibilities affected his family relationships, his political networks, and his finances. We now focus more explicitly on how the transregional dimension of René's authority imposed upon him a particular understanding and practice of lordship.

The most recent studies of René as a feudal dynast have situated him in the context of changing structures of domination within the Sabaudian lands without considering the transregional dimension of his lordship. François-Charles Uginet depicted René as the representative of 'an aristocratic class whose continual concern was to maintain its own dominance in government' and to 'affirm its authority'. He was 'one of the last exponents of the old feudal order in the Sabaudian states, who saw a position as the prince's natural counselor as his birthright'. For Uginet, however, René's 'ingrained cowardice and his frequent preoccupation with his own personal interests' prevented him from properly expressing his class consciousness.¹ Alessandro Barbero has likewise situated René in a moment of historical transition, while challenging the idea that the transition automatically led to greater princely power. He first analyzed the Challant family in light of Federico Chabod's model of the historical transformation of the medieval aristocracy into a class of officials who mediated between the Prince and the *'paese'*. He examined whether the Challant underwent a shift in how they understood their own interests, and how those interests related to their dynastic lands and to the process of princely centralization.² Barbero found that, despite their devotion to the House of Savoy, the Challant never abandoned their attachment to 'the traditional liberties of the *patria*'.³ Thus, even from their position at the heart of princely power (c. 1400), the Challant could act against princely policy.⁴ The offices and honors held by the family from the dukes of Savoy had become 'a *de facto* hereditary apanage'⁵ by René's time, when it began changing according to Barbero.⁶ Later, Emanuel Filibert encountered in René 'one of the most disquieting examples of noble domination that could have posed a real obstacle to the effective restoration of ducal authority', and thus appointed an outsider, Giovanni Francesco Costa d'Arignano, as the valley's new governor.⁷ For Barbero, René's example shows the limited reach of Sabaudian princely power between the fifteenth and sixteenth centuries, especially when nobles like the Challant employed 'an ambitious marriage policy'.⁸ But Challant

1 Uginet, 'René de Challant.'
2 Barbero, 'Principe e nobiltà,' 179-80.
3 Ibid., 185.
4 Ibid., 188-89.
5 Ibid., 203-4.
6 Ibid., 205. Barbero claimed that René was not automatically named governor of the valley in 1518 when he inherited his father's other titles, but only in 1536 when he requested it explicitly; Barbero also makes this argument in 'Mediatori,' 154-1555, 302 n. 38. As we have seen, in 1536 and 1537, René requested that the Duchess (in her husband's absence) name him Governor of the valley, but René's justification for this request is worth reiterating. He claimed that, without this office, 'les paisantz et aultres de ce pays' would refuse to obey him 'veu que je ne jouyssoye de la preheminence de mon feu père' (Fornaseri 96-97, René to Beatrice, Issogne 6-IX-37, cited by Barbero, 'Mediatori,' 161-62). Barbero sees this episode as an effort by the center to prevent 'il feudatario più potente' of the valley from trying to 'accrescere la sua base di potere locale' by withholding the governorship. However, René's concern here could have been to counteract those who challenged his jurisdictional claims in the valley, despite his position as Marshal of Savoie. In other words, he might have been responding to challenges from below rather than to top-down efforts to circumscribe his authority.
7 Barbero, 'Principe e nobiltà,' 206.
8 Ibid., 206-7.

kinship strategy had also been crucial in creating a ramified lineage that assigned the comital title to one branch of the family, 'dynasticizing' it, and enabling the head of that line to 'identify the lineage's interests with his personal ones'.[9] Barbero's analysis of the Challant and their strategies is suggestive, and reminds us that state offices such as governorships did not necessarily resolve the power struggle between 'provincial interests and central government' in favor of the latter.[10] But Barbero and Uginet both overlook René's transregional position, which not only linked him to other suzerains, but gave him sovereign claims of his own. Rather than situating René's lordship with respect to narratives about princely centralization and noble decline in a single state, this chapter examines the Count's practical exploitation of territorially dispersed fiefs. It reveals a less structured relationship between noble authority, group interests, and state power than that proposed by Uginet and Barbero.

Some of the most useful recent work on the late-Renaissance and early modern nobility has been produced by scholars investigating the conceptual underpinnings and practices of lordship.[11] These phenomena clearly differed across Europe, including within regions and over time; this was, in part, due to the multiplicity of meanings of 'dominium' during the late medieval and early modern periods and to comparative differences in the importance of Roman or Germanic law.[12] Lordship was a 'shifting field of interaction', according to one scholar.[13] Susan Reynolds has interpreted medieval feudalism as a '"post-medieval construct"' motivated by early modern French desires, for example, to reject Imperial superiority.[14] Christopher Wickham, however, identified an historical link between what he calls the 'feudal revolution' in France and the rise of communes in Italy (*c.* 1100), as both developments profited at the expense of declining Imperial power.[15] Whether one sees early modern lordship in terms of innovation or continuity, scholars have almost unanimously pointed to its importance.[16]

9   Ibid., 207-8.
10 Barbero, 'Mediatori,' 162.
11 For a literature review of recent work on late medieval lordship, see Müsegades, who cites the studies of Oliver Auge on small princes, their territories, and financial resources (Müsegades, 486).
12 Barbier, 'La notion de *dominium*,' 250; Davis.
13 Jerndorff, 215-16. In Italy, 'feudalism' has been completely revised as an historiographic concept since the 1950s (Galasso).
14 Davis; see a discussion of related arguments in Symes.
15 Wickham.
16 Maurice Barbier's argument that, by the sixteenth century, the notion of lordship 'était appelée à décliner et à disparaître au profit de notions modernes, comme celles de pouvoir politique, de souveraineté et de propriété' ('La notion de *dominium*,' 251) is a minority view.

Historians have investigated late medieval and early modern lordship from a variety of perspectives. Some see 'seigniorial lordship' as that which clearly distinguished noble families from other elite families, even while rejecting the image of the feudal lord who blocked market-oriented agricultural practices.[17] One of the reasons why untitled nobles sought to hold feudal lands was in order to ensure property transfers within lineages. Such families also sought service relations with noble grandees,[18] even though relatively little work has been done on the courts of great nobles (as opposed to princely courts).[19] For Nancy Fitch, early modern French feudalism was really about land-tenure relationships and buying and selling rights to land.[20] Few examples have been identified of endemic violence between lords on their estates; rather, disputes tended to be between the subjects and tenants of different lords, over things like rights to woods, water, or transit rights for livestock.[21] The functioning of seigniorial courts and administrations in particular locations has been studied by some.[22] One area of continued debate is whether lord-peasant relations were basically conflictual or cooperative.[23] A number of scholars have focused on the negotiated nature of the lord-subject relationship.[24] In central Germany, lordship implied a 'commonality' between lords and subjects with respect to authority and various social practices. While Alexander Jerndorff claims that the 'processual' character of lordship makes it difficult to theorize

17 Buylaert, 'Lordship, Urbanization and Social Change;' Forclaz.
18 Demade, 622-23.
19 Van Steensel, 'Nobility Identity and Culture.'
20 As the state increased tax rates in areas of the *taille réelle* (where exemptions depended on the status of the land, not the owner), it created an incentive for lords to engage in the capitalistic exploitation of those lands (Fitch). Such practices depended on knowledge of seigniorial rights and who one's tenants were. However, even in eighteenth-century France, 'rarely did the *seigneurs* have adequate knowledge about what they were legally owed', posing challenges to the would-be entrepreneurs among the landed nobility (Friedrich, 54-55).
21 C. Shaw, 76-77.
22 See Hanlon, 'Justice,' for the Tuscan fief of Montefollonico in the seventeenth century.
23 Rafe Blaufarb relates Hilton Root's view of them as conflictual in eighteenth-century Burgundy, to the extent that this conflict helped bring about the abolition of feudalism (Blaufarb). Jeremy Hayhoe challenged this view, and Blaufarb sought to explain the disagreement in terms of the different kinds of problems studied by Root and Hayhoe. For Blaufarb, litigation between communities and lords was a form of negotiation (ibid.)
24 Matthew Clark pointed out the variety of ways in which sixteenth-century English lords exploited common lands, also showing that tenants often cooperated with lords by providing them with information about local customs (Clark). Others have stressed the contractual character of the lord-subject relations, noting that, if subjects were unhappy with their lords, other lords or princes could try to intervene and take advantage (Cengarle, 287; C. Shaw, 20).

about it,[25] historians generally agree that fief-holders were able to carve out spaces of political autonomy for themselves in late-Renaissance Europe. One historian writes that 'the old world of lordship [...] persisted long into the early modern period, when competing jurisdictions jostled for sovereignty', with great families often leading 'provincial resistance' to centralization.[26]

In this light, some historians of lordship have drawn attention to how the spatial distribution of a noble family's lands underscored their political ambitions. Michel Nassiet described the creation of a Chamber of accounts by the Viscount of Rohan in 1421, which enabled the family to create 'patrimonial complexes in several provinces'.[27] Lords of castles along inland communication routes could charge tolls and benefit in ways that compensated for the relative poverty of their lands, in places like the Apennine backcountry in Italy. Franconian nobles sought to raise themselves to grandee status through feudal ties and the creation of 'topo-linearity' based on their fiefs.[28]

Valangin during the war years

The state of surviving records invites one to begin a discussion of René's practice of lordship with Valangin. Despite the history of conflict between the Lord of Valangin and the Counts of Neuchâtel that has been outlined above, officers of these lordships cooperated with other in various ways. For example, in August 1542, they together confronted the matter of a murder

---

25   Jerndorff, 239-40. Domenico Cecere focused attention on the various ways in which rural people exercised agency with respect to their lords. He sees work on lord-peasant relations moving beyond discourses of repression and resistance, instead (following Caroline Castiglione) seeing the ways in which fiefs offered a dialogue (Cecere).

26   H. Scott, '"The Line of Descent",' 231. Noble lords often limited their descendants in order to prevent the dispersion of their property and to 'former le socle de prétentions à la construction d'un État territorial: la revendication d'une qualité princière radicalement différenciée de celle des sujets ne pouvait être tenue que si l'on était soi-même libre de liens de subordination' (Demade, 620). In Bohemia, many wealthy and influential families resolved to 'se maintenir hors de l'orbite aulique, préférant à la faveur fluctuante des souverains et aux risques de déclassement au sein de la cour l'éminence sociale'. This social preeminence was rooted in 'des structures seigneuriales vivaces', which provided significant revenues, and in a lively Bohemian (and Prague-based) sociability (Hassler, 188-89). Maarten Prak's observations about the ongoing significance of citizen militias throughout the early modern period may also apply to rural militias attached to lordships (Prak).

27   Nassiet, *Parenté, noblesse et États dynastiques*, 222.

28   C. Shaw, 35; for representations of the link between family identity and place, see Raggio; Torre; Demade, 619.

and stolen livestock at a Neuchâtel fair.[29] René's officer Martine praised the inhabitants of Neuchâtel who had agreed to underwrite a loan for René from Wendell Sonnenberg of Lucerne, noting that, 'with great fairness they offered a great service to you' and 'never wanted to take a single *écu*, unless for a drink'.[30] Still, relations between René and Neuchâtel authorities were also conflictual, and not just over his claims of sovereignty. They could also involve outsiders.[31] But at least mechanisms existed to resolve such disagreements.

The counts of Neuchâtel appointed governors who were members of the local nobility, such as Georges de Rive, Lord of Prangins, who served until the early 1550s. The Catholic Prangins was married to Isabelle de Vaumarcus, to whom René sometimes referred as 'my grandmother', though there doesn't seem to have been a blood relation between them.[32] He was followed as governor by Jean Jacques de Bonstetten, a Protestant from Berne, who married Anne de Neuchâtel-Vaumarcus.[33] René and Prangins had a particularly close relationship. In some ways, Prangins seemed to be in the service of both René and the Countess of Neuchâtel.[34] During the summer of 1537, after Prangins had returned to Neuchâtel from a trip to Berne, René sent to him for advice concerning a dispatch that he was preparing for the Duchess of Longueville. But, since René was on his way to Berne and thence to the Valle d'Aosta, he asked Prangins to come meet him 'at the lodge where I am staying'.[35] René and Prangins often coordinated their actions, using Bellegarde as an intermediary.[36] In early summer 1542, Bellegarde sent Prangins documentation concerning a certain matter and

29 In Valangin, Bellegarde detained someone who confessed to petty theft. Prangins captured the detainee's cousin, and Bellegarde's prisoner eventually confessed to livestock theft and murder, before recanting again. The two officers coordinated their approach, and the prisoner was executed within a week or so (AEN, AS-R5.10, mmm, Bellegarde to Prangins, Valangin 10-VIII-42; ibid., ggg, same to same, Valangin 12-VIII-42; ibid., bbb, same to same, Valangin 13-VIII-42).
30 Ibid., AS-G16, 20, Martine to René (in Beaufremont), Valangin 19-II-48.
31 In 1548, the Duke of Longueville sent a Monsieur de Pignillion and others to Neuchâtel to address disputes between René, the town, and Collombier; see AEN, AS-K16, 19, Valangin officer to René, s.d. [1-48?].
32 Ibid., AS-R5.10, x, René to Prangins, Virieu 20-IX-39.
33 Quadroni. The Vaumarcus were a cadet branch (itself divided into several lines) of the House of Neuchâtel, whose fief was situated at the southern end of the lake, bordering on the *pays de Vaud*.
34 AEN, AS-R5.10, w, René to Prangins, Beaufremont 5-III-37; ibid., o, René to Prangins, Valangin 19-VI-37.
35 Ibid., ee, René to Prangins, Valangin 3-VIII-37; ibid., gg, same to same, Valangin 9-VIII-37. For a similar example, see ibid., nn, same to same, Valangin 24-XI-?.
36 Ibid., qqq, Bellegarde to Prangins, Valangin 24-III-39.

LORDSHIP

then left on a journey. While away from Valangin, he commended to Prangins 'the business of this place', as he usually does, given that his lord, René, 'trusts you with it'.[37] René and Prangins also seemed to enjoy each other's company. Sometimes, they hunted together or collaborated in venatic activities.[38] Their social activities included noblewomen; in January 1539, René invited Prangins and the Lord of Vallières to come visit him with the ladies, including 'Madame the Governor's wife my grandmother'.[39] It was not unusual for René to invite Prangins to come dine with him and discuss their affairs at Valangin.[40] After shooting a deer one summer day in 1541, René sent Prangins 'a portion for you and the ladies with you', trusting that they would toast him when they ate and drank. René was to leave the next day for Berne and Soleure 'for you know what business', and hoped that, upon his return, they would 'drink some cool wine up there' and have a good conversation.[41] From Issogne, René wrote to Prangins to thank him for his help at Valangin, to send news from Italy, and to commend himself 'without forgetting the ladies'.[42] René's grandmother, Guillemette de Vergy, who lived until July 1543, splitting her time between Valangin and Beaufremont, also enjoyed a cooperative relationship with Prangins. This was important, since she was in Valangin more frequently than her grandson.[43]

One element of the relationship between the seigniory of Valangin and the county of Neuchâtel was cooperation in judicial affairs. At Valangin,

---

37 Ibid., lll, Bellegarde to Prangins, Valangin 25-V-42; ibid., nnn, same to same, Valangin 1-VI-42.

38 In 1537, René had been hunting in the Val de Travers (just outside of his seigniory), and his dogs chased a deer up a mountain where their master shot it with an arquebus. Unable to find it, René informed Prangins, declaring that, 'par le debvoir de la chasse', it was his, and pledged to share it with Prangins and with others 'de la bas' (ibid., hh, René to Prangins, Valangin 15-VII-37). Prangins's men found it and, the next day, the two arranged to butcher and preserve it (ibid., f, same to same, Valangin 16-VII-37).

39 René joked that he would keep the ladies who came 'pour prisonnieres', making it necessary for Prangins and Valieres to come the next day for dinner to 'rachapter' them (ibid., q, same to same, Valangin 19-I-39).

40 Ibid., i, same to same, Valangin 3-V-39.

41 Ibid., ss, same to same, Valangin 7-VI-41.

42 Ibid., ll, same to same, Issogne 26-X-42.

43 Beaufremont was a ten-day trip from Valangin for Guillemette (via Le Locle-Vercel-Bouclans-Besançon-Pin-Gy-Le Froch-Chaniples). She lived frugally and once declared that she would reduce the dues owed by those of her subjects whose lands were located within an area that she could 'parcourir en un jour et à pied. [...] Ce mode symbolique d'affranchissement par la circuition n'est pas rare au moyen-âge et l'on pourrait en citer d'autres exemples' (Matile, 286 n. 2, 287-89). For her interactions with Prangins, see AEN, AS-R5.10, zzzz, Guillemette to Prangins, Valangin, 18-IV-31 [Tuesday after Quasimodo]; ibid., aaaa, Guillemette to Prangins, Valangin 15-X-37; ibid., xxx, Guillemette to Prangins, Valangin 23-IV-42.

justice was rendered at sessions called *audiences generales*, requiring the presence of a certain number of nobles from the area. Claude d'Arberg's *audiences* had included clergy, vassals, officers, and *bourgeois* (three from Neuchâtel and five from Valangin). However, by founding the collegial church in Valangin (completed in 1505), Claude avoided having to include canons from the collegial church in Neuchâtel in the *audiences*.⁴⁴ In early November 1530, René contacted several nobles to attend his *audiences*, stressing his hospitality during the meeting: 'I will see to it that you are well treated.'⁴⁵ He specified to one of them that 'following the good old custom', he also wanted some canons of the chapter of Neuchâtel to be present, and asked this particular canon to come a day early to visit since 'I consider you one of my best friends'.⁴⁶ As in other matters, Prangins was typically René's main interlocutor when it came to arranging for nobles or others to attend each other's *audiences*.⁴⁷ On other occasions, René or his officers wrote to excuse themselves for being unable to return the favor and attend the *audiences* of the county of Neuchâtel.⁴⁸

The *audiences* doubled as an opportunity for nobles of the region to meet and exchange information. Valangin, especially when René was present, was a political center for the local nobility. René was called upon to help resolve conflicts between other lords, to lend them the service of his officers, and to underwrite loans for others.⁴⁹ His lordship of Valangin brought him into contact with other regional powers, too. He sent officers like Castellamonte and Bellegarde on missions to Fribourg and Berne, for example, where they met with city officials and other lords (like the Count of Gruyère and René's cousin Villarsel), discussing financial and diplomatic matters.⁵⁰ A day or

44   Matile, 214-15, 221, 223.
45   Ibid., uuu, René to Castellan of Landeron, s.l. 9-XI-30; also ibid., ttt, René to Castellan of Boudry, s.l. 9-XI-30; and ibid., sss, René to Cortonay, Valangin 10-XI-30 [year penciled in on each letter].
46   Ibid.; a main topic of conversation was undoubtedly the progress of the Reform in the area.
47   Ibid., uu, René to Prangins, Valangin 10-IV-?; ibid., n, same to same, Valangin 10-XI-?; ibid., t, same to same, Valangin 6-VII-41.
48   In 1532, Bellegarde sent his regrets, noting that, given the state of 'les afferes [a reference to the religious situation?] [...] je n'entens poent me trouver aux audiences' (ibid., xx, Bellegarde to Prangins, 7-IV-32 [year penciled in]; see also ibid., gg, René to Prangins, Valangin 9-VIII-37; ibid., AS-H16, 12, René to Bellegarde, Issogne 18-X-37).
49   Ibid., AS-K16, 19, Valangin officer to René, s.d. [I-48?]; ibid., AS-G16, 20, Martine to René [in Beaufremont], Valangin 19-II-48; ibid., AS-F16, 16, Martine to René, Valangin ?-V-49.
50   On one occasion, these envoys discussed René's business in Fribourg with the *avoyer* Praroman and others and then went to Berne, where they met Gruyère and Villarsel. The Bernese were pressing the former to reach a debt agreement, perhaps ceding to them 'des biens quil az aut pays de Vaud comant Daubonne & certeyens auttres villages'. Fribourg was willing to accept

two later, after one such meeting involving these actors, perhaps in 1536, Castellamonte gave René's letters to Watteville (*avoyer* of Berne) and others, but many key figures 'have all gone to the *pays de Vaud*, either on official business or for their own affairs'. Castellamonte spoke with Watteville for an hour, 'in front of the door of his house' and received advice about the next day's council meeting. He learned that the Bernese desired to seize Valangin, since 'you are a leader for their mortal enemy [the Duke of Savoy]', and to force him to submit to their will. Castellamonte had replied that, if Challant did not want to lose all of his lands in the Valle d'Aosta, he could not come earlier 'since enemies surrounded [the valley] on all sides, including in Piedmont and Savoie, and daily tried to enter, and without [René's] presence the danger was obvious'. It seems that René also owned sums to the Bernese, who worried that the war might cause him to default on his loans. Castellamonte insisted that René had 'done his duty as a *bourgeois*'. But Watteville pointed out that that René's envoys, Grandis and Bellegarde, were 'their subjects' (apparently Vaudois), and that he should send 'one of your servants who was not their subject', especially since the Bernese did not like Bellegarde to begin with.[51] At the council meeting the next day, Castellamonte humbly presented letters from René and Guillemette, and René was granted his 'safe-conduct'. Castellamonte urged René to come as soon as possible and reported that the Ammann family of Fribourg was willing to lend money to him.[52]

Castellamonte's response to Watteville about how difficult it was for René to attend to all his lands and responsibilities – both in service to the Duke of Savoy and to his own dynasty – was not an empty excuse. During periods of warfare and strategic uncertainty, the Duke of Savoy naturally expected him to be ready to command or otherwise serve him when necessary, whether in the Valle d'Aosta, in Piedmont, in Flanders, or elsewhere. In an undated letter in response to his request to the Duke that he be permitted to attend to his affairs in Valangin, he received permission to go 'have a visit',

---

the Bernese claims 'pourveu qu'il layssisent mons'r de Gruyere en son entier de saz conté de Gruyere', but they also wanted future counts of Gruyère to recognize them, rather than the Duke of Savoy, as suzerains for certain lands. In general, Fribourg and Berne had deep differences about how to deal with Gruyère and the former were upset that René had negotiated with the Bernese without notifying them. Villarsel was sick and disgusted when he left these talks '& naz poyent voulsu estre present'. Gruyère hoped to see René at Romont soon, 'pour deviser avecqz vous de tout pleyen d'affayeres' (AHR, FC 263, mz. 1, Castellamonte to ?, Berne 18-V-?).

51 Castellamonte's representation of Watteville's comments on Bellegarde might represent competition between these two officers; AHR, FC 263, mz. 1, Castellamonte to ?, Berne 18-V-?.

52 In addition to a pledge of 1000 *écus*, 'moyennant bonnes fiances' from Auche Ludovic Ammann, the innkeeper at 'Laz Corrone' also pledged assistance (ibid).

provided that it was brief and that someone authoritative were left in his place.⁵³ As Castellamonte's letter indicates, being in Valangin tremendously facilitated René's ability to carry out his diplomatic, financial, juridical, and political business with the Swiss cantons.⁵⁴ It also placed René in contact with the French ambassador to the Swiss. Once, after having shot a deer subsequently found by Prangins's men, he resolved to make a present of it to the French ambassador. Given that the deer 'began to spoil', René sent 'my hunter to butcher and dress it so that it will keep for a year in casks that you [Prangins] can send to Monsieur de Boisrigault, to whom I beg you to recommend me'. He also asked Prangins if he would be so kind as to send him 'the deer's right foot and antlers [...] to see how big he was', and to take a letter from him to Boisrigaut at the Swiss Diet in Baden, where he knew Prangins was going.⁵⁵

René's competition with the counts of Neuchâtel over Valangin's sovereignty created opportunities for him to interact with various members of the French court, particularly members of the House of Guise, whose influence with French kings and the governorship of Dauphiné and the occupied Sabaudian lands made them key brokers. René corresponded with them and sent envoys to meet with them and others at court.⁵⁶ Valangin also bordered on Imperial territory (the Franche-Comté), placing René in contact with authorities there as well. In fact, Charles V had granted René the right to import salt for his seigniory from Salins. When the quantity exported was reduced, René contacted authorities in Salins, who blamed 'an ongoing salt shortage', but promised to repay René 'once stocks replenished'.⁵⁷

René only spent a limited amount of time in Valangin, though, in some ways, it seems to be the place that he enjoyed the most. As lord, he dealt with the kinds of administrative, political, judicial, and fiscal issues that any lord confronted. There were 621 hearths in the seigniory in the mid-sixteenth century. The districts were Val de Ruz, where the *bourg* was located (1765 inhabitants), La Sagne (425), Le Locle (725), Les Brenets (155),

---

53 Ibid., FC 264, mz. 1, Bonvalot [?] to René, Nice 10-II-?.
54 He wrote to Mencia about the good welcome that he had received in Berne, where he went for the 'afayrez du pays' (ibid., FC 263, mz. 1, René to Mencia [?], Valangin [?] s.d.).
55 AEN, AS-R5.10, f, René to Prangins, Valangin 16-VII-37.
56 Sometime before July 1543, Claude de Guise promised to write to the Governor of Neuchâtel on René's behalf (AHR, FC 264, mz. 1, Claude de Guise [?] to René, Joinville 5-III-?). For other support from the Guise and in France, see AEN, AS-G16, 12, René to Bellegarde, 12-X-45 [?]; ibid., AS-F16, 16, Martine to René [in Beaufremont], Valangin ?-V-49; Fornaseri, 107-8, René to EF, Vercelli 26-II-51.
57 AEN, AS-F16, 28, Chateau Ruillant [?] and Guillaume Moucher to René, Salins 25-XI-?.

and La Chaux de Fonds (35). About a third of the inhabitants of Le Locle were considered '*bourgeois* of Valangin'. Most of the inhabitants of the mountains were *francs-habergeants* (not *taillables*). About 40 per cent of the Val de Ruz were subject to *taille* payments; others were subject to personal service of other kinds.[58] When many of his subjects refused to pay a *taille* (of one to three *muids* of oats per hearth) in 1529 (due to Claude d'Arberg's promise to eliminate it), René at first threatened to seize their property. They countered by threatening to abandon their lands, and so a compromise was reached, René agreeing to sell them *affranchissements* (freedom from feudal obligations).[59]

In October 1537, René was clearly concerned about the status of Valangin, given the recent Swiss conquest of the *pays de Vaud* and other Sabaudian territories, and his own absence from his lands while attending to the military crisis elsewhere. René had expected Prangins to do certain things for him, which appear not to have been done, so he asked Bellegarde to go there quickly 'to establish order' and address the 'issues that crop up daily' there.[60] Since René was away so often, his letters to Valangin usefully depict the kinds of matters that his officers managed. The Plague had afflicted the area in late summer 1545, when René coordinated with Bellegarde about transporting trunks across the mountains – it is not clear what the *coffrez* contained. René himself was ill at the time, and seemed dejected, writing in code about 'things about which I must be patient for two more years because it won't be necessary if in the meantime something better materializes and it can be dropped' – perhaps a reference to the Valangin sovereignty dispute.[61] René began to recover from his illness but then got sick again and doubted his ability to come to Valangin, also due to the 'bad weather in the mountains'. He was happy to have received news from Beaufremont and Valangin about wine purchases and grape harvests, also giving instructions about making loan payments from Valangin's rents and fiscal receipts. His financial instructions for Bellegarde (which were also sent to Martine and Trolliet) were quite specific and indicated suspicion about the former's abilities or integrity in such matters.[62] The Count's fever continued into December, but his officials transmitted his instructions and

58 Matile, 264-65.
59 Ibid., 256-59.
60 AEN, AS-H16, 12, René to Bellegarde, Issogne 18-X-37.
61 Ibid., AS-H16, 17, 17a, René to Bellegarde, Ivrea 26-IX-45.
62 René wondered how Valangin did not earn him more 'comme font celles de tous mes voysins & autour de moy', especially since 'moy ny ma femme n'y avons fait grant demeure' (AEN, AS-G16, 12, René to Bellegarde, 12-X-45 [?]; see also ibid., 14, same to same, Ivrea 14-XII-45; Matile, 267-68).

his greetings to Prangins and Watteville, and, in January, he planned to send 'the stablemaster [...] to attend to the horses and mares' in Valangin.[63]

René's officers routinely wrote to him about their administration of his fief. They drew up lists of rents and collected feudal dues and old debts; in early 1547, collections were threatened by war rumors from Germany, but Junod and Vulpe managed to send 300 *écus* to the Count. They oversaw village officials and managed land use, such as when the inhabitants of Savagnier protested the enclosure of their common lands at Le Roset, or when André Cugnier requested permission to use wood for building from the Count's lands. They also coordinated the exchange of tools and weapons between Beaufremont and Valangin.[64] When the mills of Les Brenets were ruined by a flood in early 1548 and needed to be rebuilt (along with René's barn at Bussy and the bridge over the Seyon), his officials took matters in hand.[65] They fenced the Count's meadows, kept track of disputes, received officers sent by other lords (such as an envoy from Watteville who sought calves' feet from a villager from Engollon), issued permissions for charcoal-makers, and swore new servants into office.[66] They made suggestions about tax redistricting among villages – in 1551, Junod opined that, if villagers from Villiers were permitted to join their assessment with those of Dombresson, René would collect a bit more and those of Villiers would remember the favor. The villagers of Engollon, however, were criticized by Junod for inadequately preparing René's fields for planting.[67]

Valangin officials also exercised justice in René's absence. The Count was informed when someone broke into the house of Jehan le Meurier at Cernier, when someone was shot and killed between Le Locle and La Saigne (the perpetrator seemed to have fled 'the country'), and in the event of inter-village conflicts, such as those between Dombresson and 'the two Savagniers', and those opposing Cernier to St. Martin and Chesart.[68]

In May 1549, Martine encountered a case from the latter village that he did not want to decide without informing René first. It involved the

---

63   AEN, AS-F16, 29, René to Bellegarde, Issogne 20-XII-45; ibid., AS-G16, 15, René to Bellegarde, Issogne 22-I-46. About a year and a half later, Martine suggested that René move his stables to Beaufremont, where the pastures were less expensive; see ibid., 20, Martine to René (in Beaufremont), Valangin 19-II-48.
64   Ibid., 17, Junod and Vulpe to René, Valangin 7-I-47; ibid., AS-K16, 19, Valangin official to René, s.d. [I-48?].
65   Ibid., AS-G16, 20, Martine to René (in Beaufremont), Valangin 19-II-48.
66   Ibid., AS-F16, 16, Martine to René (in Beaufremont), Valangin ?-V-49.
67   Ibid., AS-G16, 16, Blaise Junod to René, Valangin 16-III-51.
68   Ibid., 17, Junod and Vulpe to René, Valangin 7-I-47; for the community conflicts, see ibid., AS-F16, 16, Martine to René (in Beaufremont), Valangin ?-V-49.

daughter of a valet, Jacques Jehain, who had been 'executed on the wheel in Neuchâtel'. The daughter was about sixteen and worked as a servant for Pernet Tripet in St. Martin, while residing with her brothers and sisters at the home of her uncle in Chesart. Tripet impregnated her, and, in late January, she gave birth to a girl, in a room by herself. She took the baby and threw her in the pig sty behind the house, where the pigs ate her. Rumors eventually spread – people had seen her very pregnant, and she had told them that she would soon give birth – so, in late April, Martine arrested the girl as she was herding cows below Chesart. The girl told the 'wise women' who examined her what had happened, except that she claimed to have buried the baby, and was afraid that the pigs had eaten her. She repeated this story to the judge but added that Tripet had given her roots to eat as abortifacients. Tripet had also ordered her: "'If you have a baby, good God, kill it somewhere where it will never be seen.'" She told Tripet after she had buried the baby, and he replied: "'You did well, God help you and me too.'" But then she disculpated Tripet and assumed sole responsibility. Martine and others went to Chesard with her but could not find the body, and she cried: "'Forgive me, the pigs ate it,'" and started to wail and weep very loudly, as were the women and girls in the house, and it was hideous to see.' Questioned another time back in Valangin, she denied having given birth, claiming to have been mistaken about her pregnancy. But then she returned to her original story. The judge ordered that she be tortured, during which she insisted that she had never had a baby, until she promised to tell the truth. Once on her feet again, she admitted to having given birth to a live baby whom she threw to the pigs in the snow. She alone was guilty, she said. Asked why she had done this, she blamed bad advice and 'the evil spirit' that constrained her. The girl's relatives begged the Count for her life, since they expected a death sentence. Martine promised to intercede on her behalf. The girl 'is devoid of good understanding', and Tripet, who was married to one of the girl's relatives, had also been seized. Tripet had already been convicted of incest, for which René had previously pardoned him, and Martine thought him guilty of having seduced his young servant.[69]

In another case of sexual crime, the suspect, from La Chaux de Fonds, crossed the border into the Franche-Comté when Martine sent men to arrest him. But the men pursued him into the Franche-Comté. Martine stressed the importance of attending to justice in this area, where law-breaking was taking root. Brigands had been spotted on the mountain that winter but had fled when Martine made a show of force. In yet a third incest case,

---

69   Ibid., AS-F16, 16, Martine to René (in Beaufremont), Valangin ?-V-49.

Pierre Perret of Le Locle was engaged to a woman and, when the banns were published, 'the community's oldest man' declared that there was kinship between the two. Others denied this, but the 'minister' declined to celebrate the marriage, and so the couple and their families (the groom was related to the Mayor of Le Locle) asked Martine to intercede with René for them.[70]

René's affection for his subjects of Valangin seemed reciprocated.[71] In August 1550, his subjects swore a loyalty oath to him in front of the gate of the bourg of Valangin, after which René pledged to maintain his subjects' 'privileges and liberties'.[72] He demonstrated his paternalism toward his servants and subjects by finding positions for the capable ones and entertaining requests for extra time to pay their dues.[73] On one occasion, René wrote to Mencia that 'the subjects here' wanted to help him, despite their poverty, and hoped that they could provide a subsidy of 2000 *écus* in two terms. He enjoyed the mild weather 'at this castle', so different from the windy Valle d'Aosta, and was pleased with 'my new building' and with his servants. He only missed her and a certain 'friend and neighbor'.[74] Most of René's officers at Valangin (several of whom also served him elsewhere) were dependable and appreciated. In October 1537, he praised Robin's 'job on the vineyard, and the help of Martine', and planned to assist him in a legal case if the matter 'does not cost me too much [...] because of the goodwill demonstrated toward me by the father and children'.[75] René could count on the help of 'Jehan the muleteer', who made trips from Aymavilles to Valangin for one or two *écus*, and on another servant named André, who had *bastines* made for Jehan's mules at Geneva or Annecy.[76] Martine, Trolliet, and Bellegarde routinely traveled all over Europe on René's business, as did servants like Le Breton and Le Borgne. Likewise, secretaries and other Savoyard and Valdostano officials (Avise, Perruchon, Ducrest, Richard, etc.) went where René needed them.[77]

---

70 The man in the second case had had a child by his wife's sister, and then had the sister marry his brother when she became pregnant (ibid.).

71 But see Matile, 261 for an example of disagreement.

72 Ibid., 265.

73 AEN, AS-R5.10, ii, René to Prangins, Valangin 14-V-?; ibid., AS-G16, 20, Martine to René [in Beaufremont], Valangin 19-II-48.

74 AHR, FC 263, mz. 1, René to Mencia [?], Valangin [?] s.d.

75 AEN, AS-H16, 12, René to Bellegarde, Issogne 18-X-37.

76 Ibid., AS-I16, 2, René to Bellegarde, Aymaville 9-X-?.

77 Ibid., AS-G16, 15, René to Bellegarde, Issogne 22-I-46; ibid., AS-F16, 16, Martine to René (in Beaufremont), Valangin ?-V-49. René's old protégé Claude Collier, subsequently Prevost of Valangin, continued to serve René loyally there, in the Valle d'Aosta, and perhaps elsewhere (AHR, mz. 264, mz. 1, Grat Rolin [?] to René, Aoste 26-XII-?; ibid., François de Riddes to Grandis, Paris 19-VI-?).

The flip side of René's paternalism was his occasional displeasure with his officers' shortcomings. In January 1546, he expressed his particular dissatisfaction with Bellegarde and, to a greater extent, Christophe Trolliet, for the 'lack of care' demonstrated in his affairs.[78] He wrote to Bellegarde that he was reassigning duties from Trolliet to Martine, expecting that the latter would establish 'better order' than had the former. Trolliet had failed to collect the subsidy from the subjects, although he had had four months to do so, and, as a result, René was forced to pay two *écus* per day 'of hostage costs' for sums borrowed. He instructed Bellegarde to sell wheat and oats to cover these expenses, reiterating that he had sent with Martine 'the order and *estat* that I wish to be implemented in my affairs over there'. Despite this, Bellegarde had not responded, which surprised René, who nonetheless continued to trust him as he had when Guillemette was still alive.[79] Trolliet left Valangin after the feast of St. Martin (11 November).[80] By late 1551, if not earlier, a lawsuit had been filed in a dispute between Bellegarde and Trolliet over the latter's demand to have his accounts reviewed – he seemed to claim that money was still owed to him – and the Abbot of St. Maurice intervened with René on his behalf.[81] This was one of the very few cases in the surviving documentation of a dispute between René de Challant and one of his officers or servants.[82]

Beaufremont

Beaufremont was the most geographically remote of René's fiefs and seems to have been René's first choice as he looked for collateral to secure loans. In 1533, he mortgaged it for 2000 *scudi* to repay lenders from Verona who provided sums for his ransom after Pavia.[83] But the barony was still important to René as a communications and transit node on the routes from Valangin to Paris or to Flanders. In the late fifteenth century, an old north-south

---

78 The Trolliet [Trolliouz?] seem to have been a Bressan family whose members served as secretaries in various Sabaudian contexts, such as the Bresse clergy assembly (ADA, G 304, assembly deliberations dated 30/31-XII-68), the ducal secretariate, and *Chambre des comptes* (ASTR, IGTDS, inv. 185, no. 13, document dated 22-IV-73).
79 AEN, AS-G16, 15, René to Bellegarde, 22-I-46.
80 Ibid., AS-K16, 19, Valangin official to René, s.d. [I-48?].
81 AHR, FC 260, Jean Chevallier to René, St. Maurice 27-I-52.
82 Martine defended himself against criticisms by a certain Bastonat; see AEN, AS-G16, 20, Martine to René [in Beaufremont], Valangin 19-II-48.
83 AHR, FC 65, no. 8, mortgage contract with Pietro de Vale and Giovanni Donato dated 16-I-33.

commercial road linking the North Sea to Italy began to be revived. It passed from Bar-le-Duc to Neufchâteau (not far from Beaufremont) to Epinal and to Remiremont, and thence toward Italy. The increase in trade through Lorraine was due to local hemp and glass production and export, and paper production for the Antwerp market. In 1559, Duke Charles III of Lorraine signed an agreement with an Antwerp merchant for glass exports. The area near Beaufremont had seen important cloth, glass, and paper production earlier in the Middle Ages. By the mid-sixteenth century, Antwerpers saw Nancy as a commercial center, with around 50 companies doing business in Lorraine. Pierre Thierry, a Lorraine merchant during the 1550s, carried out commercial activities in Antwerp, Paris, Tours, Lyon, England, Strasbourg, Frankfurt, Basel, Lucerne, Franche-Comté, Milan, Florence, and Bologna.[84]

René's accountants in Beaufremont checked expenses carefully and measured yearly income in wine and grain.[85] In the late 1530s, the Duke of Lorraine requested a census from Beaufremont. By the time René's secretary went to request a delay in submitting this information, 'your seigniories in the bailiwick of Bassoz' had already been seized.[86] An 'Easter tax' was imposed on the inhabitants of Beaufremont, apparently by the Duke, in 1541.[87] Beaufremont officials kept René apprised of the 'price of wine, grain, and other things over there' and, on occasion, assembled sums of cash for him to employ.[88] Once, as he traveled toward Beaufremont, he instructed them to halt their collection and 'pull out their money [from the destination to which the revenues had been assigned?]' if the collection had already been completed.[89] They gave him news about his fish hatchery, the organization of his oat and wheat planting, and the prices and quantities of those grains.[90] His officers kept accounts of revenues collected directly and those farmed out to others.[91] In September 1556, the barony produced 1040 *reseaux* of wheat, 150 of rye, and 400 of oats (not counting the 80 *reseaux* of wheat

---

84 Coornaert, 106-8, 115, 117, 120, 127.
85 In 1535-1536, René's *maître d'hôtel*, 'le curé d'Anthey' (in the Valle d'Aosta), was suspected of submitting bad receipts (AHR, FC 260, cameral officers of Beaufremont to René, 18-VII-37).
86 Ibid.
87 Ibid., FC 290, no. 1, letters dated 22-IV-41.
88 AEN, AS-G16, 12, René to Bellegarde, Issogne 12-X-45 [?].
89 Ibid.
90 Ibid., AS-H16, 18, De Gans to René, Beaufremont 18-II-36 [1537?].
91 AHR, FC 290, no. 25, 1550-1551 general account of the barony of Beaufremont; FC 70, no. 5, 1551-1552 accounts of Beaufremont revenues; FC 290, no. 26, farm agreement dated 9-VI-52; resources farmed included the fish ponds; see AEN, AS-G16, 7, Santhusen to René, Vézelise 12-VII-56.

and 160 of oats that were owed by the treasurer Jean Granier – perhaps as part of his farm payment for the fish pond). There were 27 *muids* of new wine (from which the captain's portion was deducted), and twelve from the previous year, but, of these, another eighteen and a half were reserved for 'the servants'. Grain had been sold to '*messires* of Bergnellvole [Bulgnéville?]' for ten or eleven *gros* per *bichot* and rye for six. *Taille* payments collected in October 1555 from places in the barony amounted to 237 florins:[92]

The *taille* of Beaufremont	40 fl
Lesmecourt	6 fl
Aulnoy	28 fl
Gendreville	51 fl
Morville	37 fl
Mallacourt	33 fl
Hurville	36 fl
Landoville	6 fl

Correspondence with Beaufremont officials thus shows how the spatial distribution of René's fiefs facilitated the distribution of information about European affairs, and how knowledge of harvest sizes and commodity prices (linked to mortgage values) was directly linked to René's financial strategies.

Beaufremont's location, roughly equidistant from Valangin, Paris, and Flanders, increased its importance for René's political activities. In May 1534, René notified Bellegarde that Guillemette de Vergy was about to arrive in Beaufremont, after which René himself was going to travel to the French court.[93] In 1556, René was in the suite of the Imperial court in Flanders and Brabant, which was supposed to be headed to the Diet of Worms as soon as the Emperor convalesced. When this happened, René planned to take a detour to Beaufremont along the way.[94] Santhusen also coordinated communication with the Lorraine court, especially with the Count of Vaudémont, sending letters and memoirs to Vaudémont and forwarding replies.[95] La Fontaine brought him correspondence from René, which he sent along to Paris with various couriers; the letters dealt 'both with grain sales and disputes over measures, and with other matters'. He sent *mulletz* back to

92 Ibid., AS-H16, 13-13a, 'Panthe' [?] to René, Beaufremont 20-IX-56.
93 Ibid., AS-C4.2, d, René to Bellegarde, Beaufremont 15-V-34.
94 Ibid., AS-G16, 1, René to Bellegarde, Brussels 4-II-56.
95 Santhusen also attended to René's hunting dogs, knowledge of which undoubtedly earned him the friendship of other local nobles (ibid., AS-F16, 21, Santhusen to René, Beaufremont 6-VI-56; ibid., AS-G16, 7, Santhusen to René, Vézelise 12-VII-56).

René's other residences and met with local dignitaries (such as the Count Palatine, at Mirecourt) on René's behalf.⁹⁶

Despite not being able to spend as much time in Beaufremont as in his other fiefs, René and his officers did their best to maintain the goodwill of supporters in the area. When Jehan, one of the knights of the Chapel of St. John the Baptist of Beaufremont died, Santhusen farmed out his property. He also supported the request of a monk from Gendreville for charity, since the monk's family 'have always served the house, acting as confessors for Madame and Mesdemoiselles'.⁹⁷ In August 1549, the widow Jehanne Tissotte, who found herself in a state of poverty, asked René for a *muid* each of wheat and oats 'on the salary of my deceased husband André', to whom back wages were still apparently owed.⁹⁸

René and the practice of lordship

Fiefs and fiscality

The chief duties of René's castellans were collecting revenues, dispensing justice, and otherwise governing their fiefs in René's absence. In some fiefs, René treated the castellan as a salaried official and expected any revenues collected to be transferred directly to him. In other fiefs, farm contracts indicated how much the castellan/farmer would pay the Count annually. Eusèbe Gamache paid him 1700 florins each year for the fief of Graines beginning in 1537,⁹⁹ while Jean Verney paid 1100 for Virieu in the 1540s.¹⁰⁰

René's fiefs provide numerous examples of how the fiscal aspect of lordship was flexible and subject to negotiation. In 1519, his subjects of Brusson, in the Valle d'Aosta, were exempted from paying *lods* for sales made between relatives up to the fourth degree, and for sales with repurchases fixed within ten years (that is, ten-year mortgages). Their *cens* payments for cheese, butter, and *séac* were also reduced to 36 *gros* per hundred, and their *franchises* of 1435 and earlier were confirmed. They purchased these

---

96   Ibid., AS-H16, 5, Santhusen to René, Beaufremont 4-XII-56. When one of René's officers lost a falcon while hunting partridges in the snow, the Bailiff of the Count of Vaudémont later found it and returned it (ibid., AS-H16, 18, De Gans to René, Beaufremont 18-II-36 [1537?]).
97   Ibid., AS-F16, 18, Santhusen to René, Beaufremont 4-VII-56.
98   Ibid., 25, Jehanne Tissotte to René, Valangin 4-VIII-49.
99   AHR, FC 140, no. 1, farm contract dated 18-V-37.
100 AEN, AS-I16, 17, farm contract of Jean Verney for Virieu dated 1-X-46.

Fief	Castellan/farmer	Dates	Source
Châtillon	Eusèbe Gamache	1514-16	AHR, FC 107, no. 2
Châtillon	Guillaume Tollen	1523	AST1, PD 188, f 271
Châtillon	Boniface Mistralis	1524-31	AHR, FC 107, no. 5
Châtillon	Domenico Lescha	1559-60	AEN, AS-K16, 22; ibid., AS-I16, 16
St. Marcel and Ussel	Eusèbe Gamache	1520, 1526, 1530-35	AHR, FC 289, nos. 13, 23; ibid., FC 172, nos. 11-12
St. Marcel and Ussel	Grat Rolin	1532, 1538, 1540-41, 1551	AHR, FC 172, nos. 14, 17, 18; ibid., FC 289, no. 48
St. Marcel	Carlo di Loranze di San Martino	Late 1550s	AHR, FC 46, no. 3
St. Marcel	Paolo Madruzzo	1564	AHR, FC 131
Challant	Michel Vercellon	1523	AST1, PD 188, f 271
Challant, Graines, Verres and Issogne	Eusèbe Gamache	1527, 1535	AHR, FC 289, no. 21; ibid., FC 58, no. 1
Challant and Graines	Eusèbe Gamache	1537-38	AHR, FC 140, no. 1; ibid., FC 130, no. 5
Graines	Gamache	1556	AEN, AS-K16, 21
Issogne	Antoine Mothery	1532-38	AHR, FC 172, no. 15; ibid., FC 130, nos. 3-4
Issogne	Antoine de Generys [?]	1560	AEN, AS-I16, 5
Verres and Issogne	Blaise Clerc	1537, 1539, 1542-43	AHR, FC 115, no. 6; ibid., FC 290, no. 4; AEN, AS-G16, 14; 21-IX-43
Aymavilles	Grat Rolin	1523, 1538	AHR, FC 289, no. 48; AST1, PD 188, f 271
Aymavilles	Aymon Vaudan	1549	AHR, FC 182, no. 9
Aymavilles	Amedeo Bonaventure Vaudan (same as above?)	1546-54	AHR, FC 177, no. 20
Coligny	Jean Bolangier	1539	AHR, FC 289, no. 55
Virieu	Jean Verney	1533-49	AEN, AS-I16, 17

Table 2: Some of René's fiefs and their castellans. Table by author.

exemptions for 450 *écus*.¹⁰¹ Sometimes, political circumstances beyond the Lord's control resulted in unexpected windfalls, such as when one of René's castellans in French-occupied Bresse learned that a *taille* payment of 100 *écus* that the French had been expected to collect was not collected due to an exemption. René instructed the castellan to forward the money to him at the Imperial court.¹⁰² In January 1542, Granyer sent the Castellan of Coligny to René to have his accounts reviewed, also noting that the subjects of Conflans (whence he wrote) were seeking exemptions from 'taxes and military levies, as many other towns from this country have secured from the King'.¹⁰³

In the Valle d'Aosta, there were frequent disputes between René's subjects and the valley estates over whether the former should be required to contribute to subsidies voted by the latter. René's subjects (supported by the Count) claimed exemptions from such contributions on the grounds that their payments to René, the valley's governor, already supported valley affairs. Having to contribute to additional *tailles* would amount to being taxed twice.¹⁰⁴ Valley officials pleaded with the Count to have his subjects contribute, thereby creating an example for others in the valley; otherwise, he feared that no one would pay anything.¹⁰⁵ Indeed, it appeared that other valley nobles began to imitate René's practice of seeking exemptions for his subjects from *tailles* voted by the estates.¹⁰⁶

René's fiscal officers typically communicated with him about difficulties in collecting sums owed, or an inability to gather as much as the Count expected.¹⁰⁷ When the subjects of Aymavilles and Jouvençan would not pay, the Castellan Grat Rolin called them to an assembly. After he read a letter from the Count, they replied that they had not promised 'as a group' to pay what was described, and that only those individuals who made particular promises were responsible for payments. At any rate, they said, they were too poor to pay anything, being without wine or wheat, 'because the vines and trellises froze and died [that winter] and the wheat did not produce grain due to the heatwave [that summer]'. Rolin noted that this was 'very true' and confirmed that no grain had been collected for ten months. Desiring that

---

101 AHR, FC 128, no. 2, act dated 2-III-19; see also ibid., FC 150, no. 2.
102 Ibid., FC 263, mz. 1, René [?] to a Castellan of Challant, Aymaville, 3-VIII-?.
103 Ibid., Granyer to René, Conflans 14-I-42.
104 Ibid., FC 260, Roz Favre to the Castellan of Verrès, Aosta 18-IV-43; such examples are frequent.
105 AEN, AS-G16, 29, Lostan to René, Aosta 1-II-39.
106 François Vallesa did this in 1557; see AHR, Fonds Vallesa, 272, mz. 1, Bailiff and Commis to François Vallesa, Aosta 20-VII-57.
107 Ibid., FC 263, mz. 1, Fagnano to René, Casale 21-X-42 [?].

the subjects remain in Rene's good graces, he encouraged them to consult with each other in their parishes.[108]

René and his officials were quite aware of the fact that they often lacked the information that they needed in order to extract what they thought was appropriate from his fiefs. This information was sometimes in the hands of subjects and sometimes in the hands of other officials. In 1540, Louis de Vallesa urged René to require the Castellan Roz Favre to submit his accounts 'so that he will know what happened to his revenues'.[109] In 1552, René appointed Gautier to audit accounts for feudal commissioners in the county of Challant and elsewhere in the valley.[110] One of the key mechanisms by which René collected information about his fiefs was through appointing commissioners who visited particular fiefs to find out what feudal dues were owed by subjects there.[111] Jean Grivonis and his sons collected *reconnaissances* from René's Valdostano lands over the course of several decades. When Bernard de la Fontaine began reviewing the Grivonis accounts in 1561 (along with the accounts of other receivers), he found that they owed a total of 2755 florins, two partridges, and two capons, while their credits amounted to only 2430 florins. More than half of the payments were made during the last six years of a 30-year period, the largest single payment being the 597 florins paid out to Jean Roveryr (Roero?) in 1555 just prior to René's release from prison.[112]

La Fontaine's review had, in fact, been prompted by an investigation into the Grivonis brothers that had begun sometime earlier. An official named Vulliet had been appointed to gather information from the brothers themselves and transfer it to René's secretaries. Vulliet was to retrieve all feudal titles and charters that the Grivonis had taken from the castle of Châtillon (where they would have been 'safer [...] than in a *paisant*'s house'),

---

108 AEN, AS-G16, 3, Rolin to René, Aosta 21-VI-?. See also ibid., AS-H16, 16, Bonaventure Vaudan to René, Aosta 30-XII-?.
109 AHR, FC 260, Louis de Vallesa to Grandis (at court), Ivrea 1-IV-40.
110 AEN, AS-I16, 23a, procuration for Gautier dated Vercelli ?-III-52; this audit perhaps resulted in a rebate for the Castellan of Challant (AHR, FC 290, mz. 1, payment order dated Issogne 14-XII-52).
111 See the report of Louis de Vallesa, Jacques Cachiot, and Grat Rolin from the Monferrato (ibid., FC 290, no. 14, memoir dated Ivrea 20-XI-43).
112 AEN, AS-K16, 25, Grivonis account, Châtillon 4-IX-61. Bernard de La Fontaine was 'juris utriusque doctor [...] auditoris generalis et advocati procurisque generalis in hac patria vallisauguste' and succeeded Ducrest as 'nostre maistre d'hostel qui avoit charge de noz affaires en nous terres et seigneuries qu'avons en la Val d'Aouste' (letter of commission dated Virieu 13-II-61). He had been a counselor in the *parlement* of Dôle, a *maistre aux requestes ordinayres* of the Duchess of Nemours, and Bailiff of Vercel and 'Usye' in the Franche-Comté (ibid.).

in order to facilitate the work of future castellans.¹¹³ The fact that Grivonis *père* had removed these documents from the castle was suspicious. A proper account of the sums collected by these men (including 'a gold or silver plaque that he took from a certain Pierre Magnyatz') was also required. Grivonis had also improperly removed several notarial registers which were to be returned as well, along with 'the interest' for the time when these items had been missing. Finally, the Grivonis were suspected of having collected bribes from subjects in exchange for not requiring them to pay their *reconnaissances* – evidence for which existed in the form of notarized receipts. Vulliet would determine whether a civil or criminal case would be pursued.¹¹⁴ The brothers agreed in October 1561 to turn over their registers of *reconnaissances*, but the record is silent about what happened to them. Vulliet was instructed to 'do the same with respect to the other castellans and commissioners on our lands'.¹¹⁵

Perhaps in response to the Grivonis affair (or to the death of Ducrest), an undated memoir stressed René's need for a procurator general. The author of the text (who seems to have been La Fontaine) argued that René should create this position 'for his utility and profit', for his lands in the valley and elsewhere, where both his officers and his subjects 'usurp, hide, and retain considerable sums' owed to the Count for criminal fines of which the Count is unaware. They need an 'inquisitorial procurator' to punish these crimes, someone who is 'a foreigner and not from the area'. This officer should maintain feudal authority against everyone and should 'secretly' investigate other officers to ensure that they are not extorting from the subjects. Officers are to be prohibited from making 'plea bargains' without the procurator's knowledge, and they must be prepared to display their registers to the procurator. They must not make any *lods, ventes*, etc. without them being counter-registered and sealed 'with *monseigneur*'s seal'. All castellans and judges should seize 'all registers and court papers', so that the procurator could inspect them. Notaries should be informed that the procurator could demand to see their protocols to see any acts relating to René's feudal jurisdiction and should be required to display letters authorizing their constitution as notaries by the Count or the Duke of Savoy. In order to 'chase the wolf from the forest', the procurator needs

---

113 Ibid., AS-I16, 23b, undated memoir to Vulliet about feudal dues in Châtillon, *c.* 1560 [?].
114 Ibid.
115 AHR, FC 93, no. 5, agreement by Grivonis brothers to submit their registers, 25-X-61; see ibid., FC 65, no. 4 for the 1520-1522 protocols of notary Jean Grivonis junior; also see AEN, AS-I16, 23b, undated memoir to Vulliet about feudal dues in Châtillon, *c.* 1560 [?].

to have the *reconnaissances*. These registers were crucial for resolving jurisdictional disputes with other lords in addition to protecting René's income. Without them, heirs of subjects might simply claim not to owe anything. The author advised updating the *reconnaissances* regularly, since 'the *paysans* are clever, don't want to owe anything, and seek only to be *en liberté*'. Finally, the author suggested that, in addition to whatever salary the Count assigned to this person, the procurator should receive a quarter of the fines resulting from his work.[116] That René took at least some of these suggestions to heart is indicated by the appointment of notary Tomaso Vichard to collect *reconnaissances* from the mandement of Châtillon over the course of the 1560s – he apparently took over where the Grivonis had left off.[117]

Castellans thus had to contend with pressures from multiple directions. In early 1541, the Vice-Bailiff of Aosta, Roz Favre, sharply criticized René's Castellan of Verrès, Blaise Clerc. In March, Favre received a payment of 45 *écus* from Clerc, sent back a receipt via the Captain of Verrès, and advised him to submit the criminal case then under his jurisdiction to the Bailiff (Antoine de Leschaux). 'You have Monsieur Cachot', wrote Favre, 'trust his advice and don't take things in such a sour way as in the past'.[118] Favre wrote again about a month later, after having learned from the Bailiff about Clerc's mismanagement of the case. 'It will be more costly than beneficial to you', he wrote, if the witnesses were heard a second time. Another of René's castellans obtained a temporary delay in the case, which seemed to revolve around judicial exemptions enjoyed by Verrès. But Favre argued that 'the privileges' in question did not prevent the Duke or the Bailiff from appointing agents to collect secret information. He also claimed that Clerc had made a serious mistake in refusing to send him testimony collected in the case.[119]

Sample castellany accounts: Châtillon, 1559-1560

Two accounts are available for one of René's fiefs from the period just after the Sabaudian restoration.[120] Domenico Lescha had been appointed

---

116 Ibid., AS-K16, 15, memoir recommending creation of a procurator general, s.l., s.d.
117 AHR, FC 138, no. 1, *reconnaissances* for mandement of Châtillon, acts notarized by Tomaso Vichard, 1560-1570.
118 Ibid., FC 260, no. 11, Roz Favre to the Castellan of Verrès, Aosta 11-III-41.
119 Ibid., same to same, Aosta 8-IV-41.
120 AEN, AS-K16, 22, 1559 accounts rendered by Lescha for Châtillon on 7-X-61; ibid., AS-I16, 16, 1560 accounts rendered by Lescha for Châtillon on 7-X-61.

castellan on 16 April 1559, not by René but by 'the illustrious lords Giovanni Federico Madruzzo and Isabelle de Challant, Count and Countess of Avi, Lieutenant General in the Valle d'Aosta for the very illustrious, high, and powerful Lord the Count of Challant'. The secretary of Giovanni Federico and Isabelle signed the appointment, and the farm agreement was notarized by Antoine Generis of Verrès. The account audits were signed by Bernard de La Fontaine, 'doctor of the laws, counselor and inspector-general of my said Lord the Count of Challant, also commissioner and procurator in the country and duchy of Aosta'. The lease began on 1 February 1559 (prior to Lescha's appointment letter) for a payment of 1775 florins per year. Certain feudal dues (*lods* and *plaictz*) were not included in the account, 'because he is not yet well informed whether the sales made belong to the fief of my said Lord, since the said Castellan is newly appointed and a foreigner and does not yet have complete knowledge of these matters'.[121]

The accounts offer a glimpse at all feudal income received by the Castellan for the castellany of Châtillon for the year in question, from subjects and others. This included specific amounts of of grain, tithes, rye, mill fees, chestnuts, wine, wax, cheese, butter, partridges, capons, hay, straw, cow tongues, fees on slate roofs, taxes from fairs, secretarial fees, and other items. This income was valued at 248 florins in 1560. For the same year, the castellan reported 480 florins in income for 'the harvest of 48 *seisteurs* of meadow', at a rate of ten florins per *seisteur* – rents on meadows belonging to the castellany. The total income in 1560 thus amounted to 873 florins. Lescha then listed payments made on René's behalf, to be deducted from his lease payment. These included: payments and quantities of wine given to the priest of Châtillon 'with those of Vyelly and Brucza for the great Mass of St. Theodule sung every Monday in the church of Châtillon'; payments to the 'hospital of Romeyran'; 25 florins for the castellan's wages; payments made 'upon the death of Monsieur Ducrest'; 318 florins spent 'for the expenses of His Highness [the Duke] and his suite in Châtillon in the month of May', as shown in a list signed by La Fontaine on 8 August 1561; fourteen florins for expenses for him and his servants incurred on a trip to Verolengo on

[121] The appointment letter dated Issogne 16-IV-59 described René as 'tresillustre ault et puissant seigneur monseigneur le conte de Challant seig'r dudit Chastellyon de Sainct Marcel Ussel Grayne Verres Yssogny Montault et baron d'Amaville de ca les montz et de la les montz conte de Varax et de Laz Roche baron de Beauffremont Virieu le Grand Varambon Chastellyon La Pallu Villarssussel Sint Ypolite Chasteau Neufz de Masches seigneur de Sainct Plantin Toussa [?] Malmaux [?] Muczadares [?] Albenaux La Balme et Boullogneux mareschal et chevallier de l'ordre de Savoye lieutenant general pour Son Altesse en ses estatz tant de ca que dela les montz'. Strangely, it did not mention Valangin (ibid.).

René's behalf; and fifteen florins for '*monseigneur*'s tailor who came from Milan'. Lescha also carried over a credit of 767 florins from his 1559 account. Together, between what he collected on behalf of René and what he spent, his credits amounted to 1880 florins. Strangely, although, it looked like he had spent 105 florins more than the farm agreement stipulated, the account indicated that he still owed 50 florins. Even taking into account the fact that he was charged an extra twelve *écus* that Lescha was expected to receive from Panthaleon de Loys de Remond of Ayas, who was currently a prisoner in the castle of Châtillon and had reached an arrangement with Isabelle to pay a judicial fine (a sum paid to the notary George Grivan on 16 October 1560), Lescha should still have been 45 florins in the black. Why he was found to owe money is not clear.[122]

Lescha's account from 1559 was closed on the same day as the 1560 account. In it, he made many more payments on behalf of René, worth a combined amount of 2582 florins. These payments included 258 florins for the expenses of Isabelle and Giovanni Federico at Issogne; 483 florins paid to Ducrest; 151 florins for fabric from Milan and other things purchased in Vercelli and Ivrea for Philiberte, by Ducrest's order; 750 florins paid to Isabelle by René's order; and 445 florins paid on behalf of Isabelle between her arrival from Trento on 4 May 1560 through 17 July of the same year. That year, in addition to his farm payment of 1775 florins, Lescha owed another 30 florins for the protocols of the deceased Martin Grivonis. His credit thus amounted to 777 florins (ten more than indicated in the 1560 account).[123]

Administration of the fiefs

The Count of Challant was routinely obliged to rely on his officers to administer his fiefs, but, on occasion, he felt the need to be physically present to oversee his affairs. In June 1530, for example, he asked Charles III to 'give me leave for a time so that I can go to Bresse where I ordered provisions [...] to order my affairs, which would be costly if I did not resolve them'. He reminded Charles III of the promise that the latter had made on his way to Bologna, that, after the month of April, he could withdraw to his estates and manage his business.[124]

René and his castellans interacted frequently with feudal subjects, at levels of specificity that were sometimes surprising. They discussed how

---

122 Ibid.
123 Ibid., AS-K16, 22, 1559 accounts rendered by Lescha for Châtillon on 7-X-61.
124 Fornaseri, 67-68, René to Ch III, Chambéry 17-VI-30.

seasonal changes following the fall grape harvest affected the counting of subjects, due to labor mobility and to decreasing daylight, and decided to wait until *Chandeleur* (2 February) to carry out this task.[125] In the midst of the French and Imperial invasions in 1536, René asked Captain Jeronimo Mendoza to punish those soldiers of his who had stolen cattle from René's lands in the Monferrato.[126] René's officials approved a marriage between a subject from Aymavilles and the widow of 'Jaques the groom', remarking that 'he has little property but he is young and *du bon gouvernement*, as she wanted'.[127] Subjects occasionally traveled long distances in order to be able to confer with René, such as in the case of the three Valdostano subjects from Ayas who sought out René in Paris.[128]

The subjects of René's fiefs were not afraid of defending their interests and sometimes had to be confronted or otherwise managed. Bernard Boulet, a procurator of René, was empowered by the priest of St. Marcel (his brother, then in Rome) to rent out the benefice. There were two candidates, one of whom had many supporters in the parish, who 'go door to door, day and night, to assemble the people to make a petition' on his behalf. Boulet himself favored another candidate and drew the Count's attention to these unlawful assemblies. Such gatherings constituted 'a monopoly that must not be permitted to subjects, less now than ever', according to Boulet, who asked René to ask a key supporter of the first candidate to withdraw his backing.[129] In 1539, the inhabitants of the Valle d'Aosta, including René's subjects, sent envoys to Charles III to request the observance of certain statutes concerning rents. They timed this delegation to coincide with the arrival in the valley of a French ambassador to discuss the valley's neutrality – perhaps to add weight to their supplication to the Duke.[130] When his subjects of Aymavilles asked René for permission to collect dead wood 'in the forest of your domain' to be used 'to repair their trellises' that had been ruined by the recent heavy snowfall, the Count agreed. He placed his officers in charge of the collection process, though, and declared it a one-time, exceptional event.[131]

125 AHR, FC 263, mz. 1, ? to René [?], s.l., s.d.
126 Ibid., FC 79, no. 4, letter dated 2-IV-36.
127 Ibid., FC 264, mz. 1, Grat Rolin [?] to René, Aosta 26-XII-?.
128 The men from Ayas informed the Count's agent in Paris of the whereabouts of Vallesa and Ducrest, then on their way back to 'le pays d'Oste' (AEN, AS-G16, 26, Chevron to René, Paris 4-XII-?).
129 AHR, FC 263, mz. 1, Bernard Boulet [?] to René, Aosta, 18-VI-?.
130 AEN, AS-G16, 29, Lostan to René, Aosta 11-II-39.
131 Ibid., AS-H16, 27, permission dated Valangin 12-I-58.

Castellans communicated with the Count about making necessary infrastructural improvements. When he was quite young, René ordered Antoine de Jans, Vice-Castellan of Verrès, to 'wall over certain windows and embrasures near the chapel of the Lords of Challant at Verrès'.[132] He received a report from Vallesa about the status of Verolengo. 'Returning [from Milan] I passed by your farm of Verolengo', he wrote, 'which I found quite deserted and almost entirely uncovered [without proper roofing?]'. Vallesa was renting Verolengo from René on the condition that the Count would fund all necessary repairs. Vallesa tried to find workers to undertake the repairs, but this was difficult, and it was even more challenging to keep them there after he left: 'And I did enough to recover the good workers who had departed because I had stayed in Valangin for so long.'[133] Grat Rolin passed along news about the Lord of La Tour, who wanted to establish an iron foundry at Cogne. He worked with the subjects there to identify sources of wood to provide the energy for this project – Rolin was enthusiastic.[134] Rolin also measured the room of the castle and barn at Aymavilles so that he could initiate repairs there (though he warned René that there might be a delay because he was suffering from gout).[135] Indeed, it appears that Bonaventure Vaudan is the one who took up this project, reporting to René that he had two long timbers (each one six *toises* long) placed in the *pallier* of René's castle, because the old ones had been broken.[136]

The Gamache family served René in the valley throughout his life. They administered his lands, helped maintain valley defenses, and kept him informed while he was away. Eusèbe Gamache was his castellan for St. Marcel and Ussel until the 1530s and was succeeded by his son René at some point. In 1525-1526, following René's capture at Pavia, Eusèbe left accounts of payments made by the Count's command, or by that of his grandmother Marguerite. Most of the expenses listed (which dated from 24 October 1525 through 10 April 1526) were for travel, for Eusèbe or other officers and servants, including five payments for messengers sent to Bianca Maria in Pavia between October 1525 and March 1526 (on 14 February, someone brought her 'a hare and two partridges').[137]

Eusèbe kept the Count apprised of relations with the Provost of St. Gilles (over whose convent René held patronage rights). He passed on news gathered

---

132 AHR, FC 289, no. 11, letter dated 22-IX-18.
133 AEN, AS-G16, 21, Vallesa to René, Verrès 17-V-39.
134 Ibid., 3, Rolin to René, Aosta 21-VI-?.
135 AHR, FC 264, mz. 1, Grat Rolin to René, St. Marcel 5-XII-?.
136 AEN, AS-H16, 16, Bonaventure Vaudan to René, Aosta 30-XII-?.
137 AHR, FC 172, no. 11, accounts of Eusèbe Gamache for 1526.

from Ivrea and Rome and managed the accounts of innkeepers in various places who supported Challant couriers.[138] René's confidence in him was expressed through Eusèbe's role as a conduit of instructions for the Count's other officers. He kept René up to date about specific cases, such as the death of a woman in Challant – the husband had been accused of murdering her, but Gamache managed to bring the parties together 'so that the husband and relatives were reconciled'.[139] He identified artisans (such as a 'master mason' from St. Maurice) to carry out repairs; communicated with other nobles (such as Castruczon, Co-Lord of Carema with René) on René's behalf; made payments to various individuals for René; coordinated with René's military officers (like the Captain of Verrès) to oversee and pay for fortification work; and made arrangements with other castellans to do things like 'take a trip to Casale to order affairs there'.[140] He also represented the Count for fiscal purposes in the Val d'Ayas, arranging to meet with people near Brusson who owed René payments (in one case, debtors offered to work for the Count in exchange for food since they had no money to give), and collecting 'limestone' from residents of Ayas. In such circumstances, Gamache was sometimes pressured directly by René's own creditors to make payments to them.[141] He recommended particular individuals to the Count's protection, such as the poor smith Davacz, who was simple.[142] When René failed to respond in a timely way to Eusèbe's queries, he openly wondered whether he still enjoyed the Count's confidence and expressed his fears that the Count's affairs, and especially his castle of Montalto, 'will all go to hell'. In the same letter Eusèbe drew René's attention to the fact that his subjects of Brusson claimed exemption from a subsidy of two florins that had recently been imposed.[143]

During the war years, the Gamache provided regular reports about strategic developments in the region from their vantage point at the castle of Bard. One letter described flies or crickets swarming above Ivrea, headed toward Piedmont and also alerted René to three companies of Spaniards marching toward Turin and four toward Chivasso.[144] They wrote about conversations with other local authorities (on one occasion, the Governor

---

138 AHR, FC 263, mz. 1, Gamache to René, Bard 7-II-?.
139 AEN, AS-G16, 28 Gamache to René, Aosta 3-VII-? [before 1543?].
140 Ibid.
141 AHR, FC 263, mz. 1, Gamache to René, Bard 6-II-?.
142 Ibid., Gamache to René, Bard 6-IX-?.
143 Gamache was especially concerned about the poor upkeep of Montalto by René's castellan there (ibid., Gamache to René, Bard 20-I-?).
144 Ibid., Gamache to René, Bard 6-IX-?.

of Ivrea wanted to place soldiers at the castle of Montalto for reasons that escaped Gamache);[145] about important events (such as the arrival of the Duke of Savoy in the valley);[146] and about judicial matters (a couple, perhaps found guilty of adultery, was executed – 'la Barbre' was thrown off of the bridge of Bard and 'she died well-disposed and devoutly', while her companion 'was condemned to be burned and his property confiscated according to custom').[147] When some *'compagnons'* from Turin and from Castellamonte entered the house of Luigi di Castellamonte's son 'in Champgny' and 'killed him at once', sacking the house and stealing a number valuables, Gamache sought instructions from René about how to proceed.[148] The Gamache also passed along information concerning the popular political climate in the valley and surrounding areas: at one point, René's official Cachot and a Captain Riquarand held a meeting of local communities who complained about being 'always gnawed and eaten up by the soldiers'. Those from the Canavese near French-occupied lands pointed out that their villages were 'full of soldiers who say that they don't care about any government or anyone else'. These residents reportedly sought protection from René and hoped to be placed under his government.[149]

In addition to inheriting many fiefs, René also acquired several during his lifetime. Coligny and Virieu-le-Grand were two such places, acquired in the early 1530s from the Duke of Savoy, who was desperate for cash.[150] Several pieces of correspondence relating to René's lordship of Virieu have survived. Virieu was located in Bugey, near a bend in the Rhône river just downstream from the point where it becomes navigable, on the edge of a pre-Alpine plateau that guards passages through the mountains leading to the plain of Bresse (to the northwest) and to the Franche-Comté (to the north). In late 1533, René was still hammering out the details of the purchase via his Castellan of Aymavilles.[151] Not long thereafter, his agent François de Riddes informed the Count that the Castellan of Virieu had not yet presented himself to the Lord of La Chambre, René's kinsman, as he was apparently supposed to have done.[152] Whether this was Jean

---

145 Ibid., Gamache to René, Bard 7-II-?.
146 Ibid.
147 Ibid., Gamache to René, Bard 9-IV-?.
148 Ibid., Gamache to René, Bard 6-IX-?.
149 Ibid., Gamache to René, Bard 9-IV-?.
150 AST1, PD 170, ff. 187, 150-51, 16 December 1533 acquisition of Coligny-le-Vieux for 6000 *scudi*; ibid., PD 214, ff. 220-24, 1531 acquisition of Virieu-le-Grand.
151 Fornaseri, 90-91, René to Ch III, Valangin 30-XI-33.
152 AHR, FC 264, mz. 1, François de Riddes to René, Chambéry 10-X-?.

Bolongier, who was castellan at the moment of the French invasion in 1536, and subsequently pledged homage to the King for the fief,[153] or a later castellan, is not clear. In subsequent years, Virieu proved to be a difficult fief for René and his officers to administer. For the first ten years of his lordship, there are few records among René's papers relating to Virieu, and it is not clear if he visited the fief on more than one occasion (in fall 1539). There are undated letters that might be from this period, such as a letter to René from Chevron that mentions instructions given to him by René for the Castellan of Virieu; the Count seems to have been trying to govern the fief mainly through intermediaries.[154]

René's officer Granyer described a series of conflicts at Virieu in a letter that seems to date from 1529. The first involved a dispute between the Castellan of Virieu and the Abbot of the Cistercian abbey of St. Sulpice, which was contiguous to the fief. There had long been disputes between the convent and the community, and these continued under René.[155] In fact, they were probably exacerbated by the fact that René intended to obtain the Abbot's resignation in order to replace him with his own illegitimate son François. Granyer's letter first described a new barn that had just been completed, with space for 32 horses.[156] He was having the peasants gather hay and had also stocked the castle with nine *tonneaux* of wine in preparation for an upcoming visit by René.[157]

Granyer then referred to a previous visit by René to Virieu, on which occasion the Count had feigned lack of knowledge about 'how Carrà and the castellan's valet had been *baptiz*'. Thus, 'people think' that René was unconcerned about that event and, as a result, the 'prior' of St. Sulpice and five men on horseback entered René's jurisdiction and went to a house near Ceyzérieu, 'where they were baptizing [or beating] people [*ou se faisoyent des baptiz*]'. There, they found 'a chaplain who was your subject that they *baptirent*'. At this, the Castellan, who was in the house, pulled out his sword and told them that they 'they were wrong to trespass on your jurisdiction'. The Castellan knew that they would not harm him since he was René's officer, and because 'he was commited to spirited self-defense'. Granyer then warned Challant that the situation could seriously damage his subjects and his reputation. 'When you come you will learn the truth and punish

---

153   Callet, 76.
154   AHR, FC 263, mz. 1, Chevron to René, Gye, 3-IX-?.
155   Callet, 76.
156   A stud farm was created at the abbey of St. Sulpice in 1601 (Peugniez, 428).
157   AHR, FC 263, mz. 1, Granyer to René, Chambéry 20-V-59 [?].

LORDSHIP

the evildoers by justice or force, according to where they are.' Granyer and René's other servants were willing to dispense this punishment if René wished. He promised to send more details with the carrier of the letter.[158]

It is not clear whether this letter was referring to associates of the nearby monastery carrying out beatings or adult baptisms. It is worth noting that Philiberte de Nemours, the aunt of Marguerite de Navarre (wife of Giuliano de' Medici, sister of Louise de Savoie), died in 1524 at Virieu-le-Grand; she had been a member of the circle of Meaux, but, having died at 26 years of age, 'she did not live long enough to come out clearly in favor of the Reform'.[159] It is possible that a circle of Reformed converts had implanted itself at St. Sulpice and Virieu, and that René's arrival created religious disruption for them. It is also possible that a jurisdictional and political conflict stemming from René's desire to replace the Abbot resulted in episodes of violence. Either way, these events obviously challenged René's authority in a fief that he rarely visited.

In August 1542, Granyer traveled to Virieu and sent René information about the fief's revenues.[160] A year later, Gautier summoned the Castellan of Virieu, Jean Verney, to a meeting in Chambéry with Martine, who issued Verney a new farm contract.[161] Martine, acting on René's behalf, renewed this contract three years later, for another three-year term and an annual payment of 1100 florins (500 at Easter, and the rest at the feast of St. Michel [29 December]). Verney was empowered to appoint officials to administer justice, but René reserved for himself 'the office of judging [...] and all according to the good pleasure of the King and his *Parlement* of Savoie'. The Count would bear the cost of repairing structures in the fief.[162] Verney was to collect the books of *reconnaissances* of Virieu from Martine, perhaps at Valangin, but, as of January 1548, Verney had not yet complied. Then, since it looked like war might break out, Martine told Verney to hold off.[163]

At some point, the subjects of the fief brought a lawsuit against their Castellan over the question of how a subsidy was to be collected. René's officer Cavet was instructed to take charge of this litigation before 'the court of this country [...] because that concerns your authority'. Cavet wrote that René must preserve his 'rights and pre-eminences', just as the Count

---

158 Ibid.
159 D'Aubigné, 529.
160 AHR, FC 260, Granyer to René, Virieu 29-VIII-42.
161 AEN, AS-F16, 26, Gautier to René, Chambéry 4-VIII-43; AHR, FC 263, mz. 1, Granyer to René, Conflans 14-I-42; AEN, AS-K16, 4, farm of Jean Verney for Virieu, contract dated 1-IX-43.
162 Ibid., AS-I16, 17, farm of Jean Verney for Virieu, contract dated 1-X-46.
163 Ibid., AS-F16, 5, Martine to René, s.l. ?-I-48 [date pencilled in].

of Montrevel (a great lord in nearby Bresse) was doing in a similar case. René's claims were based on 'long-observed custom', according to Cavet, who thought that the suit was driven by the subjects' antipathy toward the Castellan.[164] When René's secretary Richard went to the French court in 1551, his portfolio included the Virieu litigation. René also informed Emanuel Filibert that 'my subjects of Virieu-le-Grand [...] are resisting doing their duty and satisfying what is owed to me, which has serious implications in my said jurisdiction'.[165]

Verrès was another fief that was sometimes difficult to administer due to ecclesiastical claims – in this case, the convent of St. Gilles. By the late fifteenth century, the Challant dynasty had obtained effective control over the prevosture, and, in 1533, René acquired official patronage rights from Rome. Eleven years later, he would appoint his son François as Prevost.[166] In the interim, though, there was a disagreement about how much influence René should exercise over St. Gilles.[167] In May 1539, the Prevost was Augustin Ferraris, who seemed to be doing his best to keep René informed, and cooperated with him in matters involving nearby parish benefices.[168] Ferraris also announced the arrival of 'the teacher Durand [...] whom your lordship required to wear [distinctive] clothing [presumably as penitence]'. Ferraris sought instructions about whether to 'maintain or fire' Durand, 'although it seems to me that the number of Lutherans is increasing'. His concern about the progress of the Reform in the area was not urgent, however; he quickly shifted his discussion to note that he had been in Aosta and Fénis 'to attend to religious matters', and, upon his return, found one of Rene's hounds 'very hot' and bred her with 'a very large *malinois* [...] who hunts very well'.[169]

By 1543, the Castellan of Verrès was Blaise Clerc, who coordinated grain distribution there with Louis de Vallesa, according to an agreement with the Castellan of Challant.[170] Clerc also held a post at St. Gilles, thanks to the intervention of the Prevost-elect (François). He sent 30 *écus* to René with the secretary Grandis, noting that 'we could collect no more from the poor people who are being squeezed hard', though he continued to look for another 50 *écus*. He described his efforts to carry out *reconnaissances* and collect *lods*. He observed, in terms that underscored the situation that La Fontaine

164 AHR, FC 264, mz. 1, Cavet to René, Chambéry 16-V-?.
165 Fornaseri, 107-8, René to EF, Vercelli 26-II-51.
166 C. Passerin d'Entrèves; also De Tillier, *Historique*, 77-82; J.-A. Duc, 5: 261.
167 Castellamonte to René [in Aosta], Turin 23-II-?.
168 AEN, AS-G16, 14, Augustin Ferraris to René, Verrès 24-V-39.
169 Ibid.
170 AHR, FC 260, Vallesa to Castellan of Verrès, Issogne 21-IX-43.

would describe about eighteen years later, that this was a time-consuming matter that required people to 'look through their papers' – especially since many *reconnaissances* had not been renewed in 50 or even 100 years. For this reason, he suggested an extension of the deadline for completing the project (to three years).[171]

This examination of René's fiefs and their management suggests that relations between lords and their officers (who mediated the lords' interactions with their peasant subjects) were characterized by compromise and negotiation. The territorial dispersion of the Challant fiefs contributed to the leverage that officers could bring to bear in this relationship, due to their informational advantage, which increased enforcement costs from the lord's perspective. This leverage was amplified given René's constant movement across Europe, linked both to his diplomatic, military, and administrative service to the House of Savoy, and to his pursuit of his own family's interests. He was obliged to rule through proxies and was placed at a disadvantage in terms of lack of place-specific knowledge necessary for the good government of his fiefs, especially due to their location in border areas. In some ways, this informational problem made it more difficult for him to benefit from his lands financially, creating opportunities for his agents to defraud him or his subjects. On the other hand, this situation also created leverage for the subjects, which, in the long run, may have had the effect of improving René's relations with them, since he had an incentive in maintaining their goodwill as a counterbalance to his agents whose intentions could be difficult to gauge. A close study of René's practice of transregional lordship reveals a complex, spatially inflected dynamic in his relationships with officers and subjects – a dynamic that is obscured when one focuses on macro-narratives related to state centralization and noble power.

Bibliography

Alessandro Barbero, 'Mediatori fra il principe e il paese: i governatori provinciali,' in id., *Il ducato di Savoia. Amministrazione e corte di uno stato franco-italiano (1416-1536)* (Rome: Laterza, 2002), pp. 145-62

Id., 'Principe e nobiltà,' in id., *Valle d'Aosta medievale* (Naples: Liguori, 2000), pp. 179-209

Maurice Barbier, 'La notion de *dominium* chez Vitoria,' *BHR* 68, 2 (2006): 241-51

---

171 Ibid., FC 263, mz. 1, Blase du Cler to René, Verrès 11-V-?; also ibid., FC 264, mz. 1, Grat Rolin to Castellan of Verrès, Villefranche 21-VIII-?.

Rafe Blaufarb, 'Conflict and Compromise: *Communauté* and *Seigneurie* in Early Modern Provence,' *JMH* 82, 3 (2010): 519-45

Frederik Buylaert, 'Lordship, Urbanization and Social Change in Late Medieval Flanders,' *PP* 227, 1 (2015): 31-75

Albert Callet, *Virieu-le-Grand: son château, ses seigneurs* (Bourg and Belley: Veuve Montbarbon & Fils aîné, 1896)

Domenico Cecere, 'Contre les "tyrans". Luttes judiciaires et troubles anti-seigneuriaux en Calabre au XVIIIe siècle,' *RHMC* 60, 3 (2013): 7-30

Federica Cengarle, 'Lordships, Fiefs and "Small States",' in *The Italian Renaissance State*, ed. Andrea Gamberini and Isabella Lazzarini (Cambridge: Cambridge University Press, 2012), pp. 284-303

Matthew Clark, 'The Gentry, the Commons, and the Politics of Common Right in Enfield, c. 1558-c. 1603,' *HJ* 54, 3 (2011): 609-29

Emile Coornaert, 'Le commerce de la Lorraine vu d'Anvers à la fin du XVe et au XVIe siècle,' *Annales de l'Est*, 5th ser., 1 (1950): 105-30

Jean Henri Merle d'Aubigné, *Histoire de la Réformation du seizième siècle*, vol. 3 (Geneva: G. Kaufmann, 1841)

Kathleen Davis, 'Sovereign Subjects, Feudal Law, and the Writing of History,' *The Journal of Medieval and Early Modern Studies* 36, 2 (2006): 223-61

Julien Demade, 'Parenté, noblesse et échec de la genèse de l'état: le cas allemand,' *AHSS* 61, 3 (2006): 609-31

Jean-Baptiste De Tillier, *Historique de la Vallée d'Aoste* (Aosta: ITLA, 1994 [1742])

Joseph-Auguste Duc, *Histoire de l'Église d'Aoste*, vol. 5 (Aoste: Librairie Valdôtaine, 1985 [1901])

Nancy Fitch, '"Entrepreneurial Nobles" or "Aristocratic Serfs"?: Reconsidering Feudalism in Old Regime Central France,' *FHS* 39, 1 (2016): 105-143

Bertrand Forclaz, 'A Careful Management: The Borghese Family and Their Fiefs in Early Modern Lazio,' *Journal of Early Modern History* 12, 2 (2008): 169-93

Giovanni Fornaseri, *Le lettere di Renato di Challant, governatore della Valle d'Aosta a Carlo II ed a Emanuele Filiberto* (Turin: Deputazione subalpina di storia patria, 1957)

Markus Friedrich, 'The Rise of Archival Consciousness in Provincial France: French Feudal Records and Eighteenth-Century Seigneurial Society,' *PP* 230, supplement 11 (2016): 49-70

Giuseppe Galasso, 'La parabola del feudalesimo,' *Rivista storica italiana* 120, 3 (2008): 1130-41

Gregory Hanlon, 'Justice in the Age of Lordship: A Feudal Court in Tuscany during the Medici Era (1619-66),' *SCJ* 35, 4 (2004): 1005-33

Eric Hassler, 'Les Harrach face à la disgrâce. Les stratégies matrimoniales d'un lignage aristocratique autrichien à la fin du XVIIe siècle,' *RHMC* 61, 2 (2014): 176-201

Alexander Jerndorff, 'Gemeinsam herrschen. Das alteuropaische Kondominat und das Herrschaftsverständnis der Moderne,' *ZHF* 34, 2 (2007): 215-42

Georges-Auguste Matile, *Histoire de la seigneurie de Valangin jusqu'à sa réunion à la directe en 1592* (Neuchâtel, James Attinger, 1852)

Benjamin Müsegades, 'Raum – Gruppe – Quelle. Neue Forschungen zu weltlichen Fürsten und Höfen im spätmittelalterlichen Reich (ca. 1250 – 1530),' *ZHF* 43, 3 (2016): 473-500

Michel Nassiet, *Parenté, noblesse et États dynastiques, XVe-XVIe siècles* (Paris: Éditions de l'EHESS, 2000)

Charles Passerin d'Entrèves, 'La Collégiale de St-Gilles de Verrès,' *Bulletin de l'Académie Saint-Anselme* 29 (1951): 91-101

Bernard Peugniez, *Routier cistercien. Abbayes et sites* (Moisenay: Henri Gaud, 2002)

Maarten Prak, 'Citizens, Soldiers and Civic Militias in Late Medieval and Early Modern Europe,' *Past and Present* 228, 1 (2015): 93-123

Dominique Quadroni, 'Jean Jacques de Bonstetten,' *DHS* (2004)

Osvaldo Raggio, *Feuds and State Formation, 1550-1700*, trans. Matthew Vester (Cham, Switzerland: Palgrave Macmillan, 2018)

Hamish Scott, '"The Line of Descent of Nobles is from the Blood of Kings": Reflections on Dynastic Identity,' in *Dynastic Identity in Early Modern Europe*, ed. Liesbeth Geevers and Mirella Marini (Farnham, UK: Ashgate, 2015), pp. 217-41

Christine Shaw, *Barons and Castellans: The Military Nobility of Renaissance Italy* (Leiden: Brill 2015)

Carol Symes, 'The Middle Ages between Nationalism and Colonialism,' *FHS* 34, 1 (2011): 37-46

Angelo Torre, *Luoghi: La produzione di località in età moderna e contemporanea* (Rome: Donzelli, 2011)

François-Charles Uginet, 'René de Challant,' *DBI* 24 (1980)

Arie van Steensel, 'Nobility Identity and Culture: Recent Historiography on the Nobility in the Medieval Low Countries III,' *History Compass* 12, 3 (2014): 287-99

Chris Wickham, 'The "Feudal Revolution" and the Origins of Italian City Communes,' *Transactions of the Royal Historical Society* 24 (2014): 29-55

9. The embodiment of spatial politics

Abstract
The practice of lordship in which René de Challant engaged was determined in large part by the spatial configuration of his lands and activities. In that sense, his case was singular, which offers a reminder that consideration of specific context is important for any discussion of Renaissance political culture. Indeed, the importance of material, spatial context seems to have permeated the very language used by René and his correspondents. Words and expressions denoted an understanding of authority as embodied, personal, and linked to concrete acts of lordship. This view of political culture was perhaps a late medieval one related to the notion of natural law inhering in things, different from a soon-to-emerge early modern one that abstracted individual rights from their spatial contexts.

Key words: spatial history, embodiment, political language

This book has demonstrated that René de Challant was a transregional lord who served not only the House of Savoy, but also the King of France and the Holy Roman Emperor. He also exercised lordship himself, inheriting and defending his own sovereign claims while simultaneously considering himself a *bourgeois* of Berne. Since most of his lands were situated in the Valle d'Aosta, and because of his family's deep ties to the Sabaudian dynasty, he represented a forgotten dimension of the Italian Renaissance – its links with transalpine society and its often lordly and feudal character. The first, narrative part of the book shows how frequently René's political activities, both on behalf of the dukes of Savoy and in his own interest, carried him beyond northern Italy into the French, Habsburg, and Swiss lands. The thematic chapters in Part 2 clarify how the spatial diversification of the Challant fiefs affected René's political influence, in terms of kinship and family relations with other nobles, his political networks, his role as a financial broker, and his activities as a fief-holder.

Vester, M., *Transregional Lordship and the Italian Renaissance: René de Challant, 1504-1565.*
Amsterdam: Amsterdam University Press, 2020.
DOI 10.5117/9789463726726_CH09

Previous scholarly work on René has rarely been rooted in archival sources, the Challant corespondence in Aosta remaining unexploited. It has almost always depicted René in relationship to the dukes of Savoy and the Sabaudian state (especially during the 1860s and the 1920s), rather than considering him in relation to the political and institutional structures of the Valle d'Aosta or the lands of his other domains. Similarly, he has been portrayed as a Sabaudian grandee, but rarely as a European one, and scant attention has been given to how his territorial interests (in Valangin, Beaufremont, the Monferrato, the transalpine Sabaudian lands, and the Valle d'Aosta) informed his actions and his self-conception. Only since 1980 has there been an effort to situate René and his experiences with respect to a non-dynastic or non-nationalist historiographic narrative. Some of the common themes highlighted by studies of René include his formidable authority (especially in the Valle d'Aosta), the temptation that he must have faced to declare himself sovereign of the valley, and Emanuel Filibert's likely wariness toward such a powerful potential competitor. Writers have also stressed the family challenges that he faced and explored the kinds of interior dispositions that enabled him to handle those trials. A key debate has been whether René was a trustworthy servant of the House of Savoy or a devious plotter ready to commit treason at the drop of a hat. The evidence presented here suggests that this is a false dichotomy, and that commitment to the interests of one's own family could express itself through either the continuation or rejection of service ties, depending on circumstances. If René ultimately remained faithful to the dukes of Savoy, his transregional commitments could easily have pushed him into a different direction. By focusing on the territorially diffuse dimension of René's lordship, this book has shed light on problems missing from earlier accounts: his relationships with his extended family, his numerous political networks, his activities as a financial broker, and his experiences as a manager of fiefs.

Throughout his life, René demonstrated a sense of politico-spatial awareness – an understanding of the financial and political implications of location. The geographic reach of his lands and activities, the latter undertaken both in the service of his own dynasty and the House of Savoy – in Italy and across Europe – required an extraordinary level of mobility. It brought him into physical contact with kin and associates from Piedmont and the Monferrato to Flanders, Paris, Lorraine, the Swiss cantons, and elsewhere. The spatial configuration of René's political practices undoubtedly influenced his self-conception as a transregional lord with sovereign status. While the areas of his influence may seem peripheral to an observer of the early 21st century, during the sixteenth century, his landed position enabled him to engage at some of the highest levels of Renaissance political life. His kin relations, friendships with other nobles, political circles, credit networks, and management of his fiefs all connected him, transregionally, to people and places throughout the old 'Middle Kingdom'. These relationships, nurtured by constant movement and repeated physical interactions, sustained René's status not only as a grandee in Sabaudian service, but also a dynastic head ready to assert himself when the opportunity arose.

René de Challant's position in sixteenth-century European politics resembled that of a marcher lord who linked northwestern Italy with transalpine Europe, from the Swiss area through the old Middle Kingdom to Lorraine and Flanders. His connections in Italy flowed through Turin, Vercelli, the Monferrato, and Milan and were linked to his family's tradition of service to the House of Savoy.[1] The landed holdings and political capital that he inherited gave him the role of an intermediary figure, not only geographically, but also in terms of his relationship to social categories such as 'rural nobility', 'state nobility', and 'urban patriciate'. René's experience shows the limits to such categories, since he occupied several of them simultaneously. Recent work by Massimo della Misericordia and other scholars has shown that René was far from the only rural aristocrat whose role in the political world of the northern Italian Renaissance expressed itself from within a culture of feudal chivalry. The Challant case reinforces the argument that, during the sixteenth century, both knightly ideals and lived experiences as a feudal aristocrat continued to serve as an important resource for Italian Renaissance elites seeking to differentiate themselves from other social groups.[2]

It is difficult to disentangle the political role of René de Challant from the situation of the Valle d'Aosta during the first half of the sixteenth century, given his formal leadership role there.[3] Still, it is interesting to note the simultaneity of René's significant political influence and a kind of golden age of political autonomy for the duchy of Aosta. The Franco-Habsburg wars and the occupation of the Sabaudian lands gave the valley political leverage (culminating in its governance by the *Conseil des Commis*) that it had not enjoyed before or subsequently. The accessibility of the Great and Small Saint Bernard passes – and other routes, such as the Théodule

---

1 See *La noblesse des marches*.
2 Della Misericordia, 'Medioevo cavalleresco;' id., 'Gusti cavallereschi.'
3 It may seem surprising that records relating to valley politics offer few biographical details about René – their occasional mentions of him are tangential references to valley defense, fortifications, and subsidy payments voted by the estates. But one must take note of the fact that he spent most of his life away from the valley.

pass, which linked the Valtournenche with Praborno (today Zermatt) in the Valais – gave the valley real geopolitical significance. This eventually changed as the Little Ice Age made transit more difficult and alternate routes developed, depriving marcher lords like René of a valuable strategic resource. But, before that happened, there was a real possibility that, following the Franco-Swiss invasions of 1536, the Valle d'Aosta (together with or separately from the remnant of the Sabaudian lands) could have become another direct Imperial territory (like the Franche-Comté), or even a French-allied one (like the marquisate of Saluzzo), thanks to the local authority of a lord like René de Challant.

If one holds in abeyance knowledge of subsequent events, sets aside modern historiographic categories, and considers the political role of a figure such as René from the perspective of the first half of the sixteenth century, his case and that of his lands seem less peripheral. His experiences illustrate how transregional lords leveraged their territorial situation and related networks in order to achieve political goals. The argument that Charles III and Emanuel Filibert also employed René and his allies to control the Sabaudian periphery relies on a binomial (center-periphery) that needs to be historicized and relativized. In a world of transregional, personal lordship, and especially from the perspective of specific places like the Valle d'Aosta, this way of categorizing significance loses explanatory power. Noble dynasties with dispersed territorial holdings were 'centered' in multiple ways, and, if Issogne or Valangin seemed peripheral from the perspective of many places in Italy, they were not from the point of view of what Kären Wigen might call the 'cultural counter-cores' of the old Middle Kingdom.[4]

Consideration of the Challant fiefs and René's lordship over them offers additional evidence of the variety of political associational forms in late-Renaissance Italy. Many scholars have examined the ways in which political leaders at different levels of society exercised authority through negotiated arrangements with subordinates, often availing common people of the ability to press their own interests. 'Small states' were perhaps more normal than large centralized ones, both in Italy and in the transalpine realm in which René was active. In areas such as these, and perhaps in Europe at large, (proto-)national states were but one element within a broader political field. Scholars have concluded that authority within this field was layered; research has now begun to document what this looked like in practice, and what spatial or territorial form such arrangements assumed.

4 Wigen.

The case of René de Challant helps us to understand the importance of lordship within this discussion of early modern politics, non-state political formations, small states, and the like. Analysis of René's experience shows that lords could never really be politically autonomous, dependent as they were on suzerains, their own vassals, officers, creditors, debtors, and so forth. This raises the possibility that 'political autonomy' itself might be a misleading concept – were even 'large states' or their rulers fully autonomous? If political life expressed itself through overlapping networks of economic, ecclesiastical, institutional, cultural, and kinship-related power, what could 'autonomy' really mean? Perhaps actors were more autonomous in some areas than in others, but the fields that were important for political actors resist representation as clearly defined continua in either spatial or demographic terms. It might be helpful to think about early modern political formations as part of an ecosystem, and as embedded in more extensive sets of social relations. This would make it difficult to abstract such formations from their contexts for purposes of comparison but would invite a more phenomenological approach that enables us to understand political formations, such as the dispersed lands of René de Challant, on their own terms.

In other words, through its discussion of a singular case, this book helps us to understand a larger late-Renaissance political ecosystem. Singularity also draws attention to spatial and physical specificity. James Schall has observed that, while 'the physical sciences are concerned with the repeatability of things', disciplines like history 'deal with those things that pass this way only once'. The human person 'is a "one and only" and cannot be otherwise'. Understanding singular things in the past is more difficult than understanding recurring ones, as is understanding 'the polity, the civic community, [which is] the arena in which the uniqueness of each citizen manifests itself'. Human virtues and faults, taken together – that is, the ways in which they exercise their freedom – are, in Schall's view, what make humans unique. No two human stories are alike. They are also temporally limited, because they are embodied.[5] The uniqueness, limitation, and physical manifestation of the human condition seems to have been more apparent to René and his contemporaries than it became for modern political actors. Patrick Deneen has argued that 'liberalism valorizes placelessness', which involves the abstraction of individuals from their spatial contexts and the elision of their embodiment. What post-Enlightenment observers might see as freedom from bodily constraint results in an undervaluing of

5   Schall.

the uniqueness of the individual, embodied human inhabiting a specific spatiotemporal environment.[6]

Late-Renaissance nobility was a particularly spatially rooted category, tied as it was to fief-holding and the revenues therefrom extracted. We have shown that these were key spatial elements of late-Renaissance financial arrangements, upon which status and political authority were grounded. The practice of lordship and the way in which it was perceived were inseparable from its spatial and physical elements. This was so for the Challant, their noble vassals, and their suzerains, such as the House of Savoy, whose dynastic relics offer a good example of the tight relationship between lordship, physical singularity, and space. In the summer of 1538, René was in Nice, where he saw the Countess of Neuchâtel, who had traveled there 'to see the Holy Shroud'.[7] The Duke of Savoy, then forced into a peripatetic condition due to the occupation of his lands, did not fail to keep close to his family the object whose proximity to Christ both offered protection and guaranteed continued prestige during times of uncertainty.

Sixteenth-century political discourse, as revealed by the correspondence between René de Challant and his interlocutors, was often marked by references to bodily space, displaying noteworthy sensitivity to proxemics and psychomotility (the relationship between bodily movement and mental activity).[8] Constance Classen has pointed out how eating from common bowls, bathing and sleeping together, conserving warmth, etc. contributed to an early modern sense of touch that likely differed from ours. She even suggests that 'corporeal rites of commitment as the kiss and the hand clasp would have been more meaningful and more binding to man than a mere signed document'.[9] René and his correspondents routinely used proxemic language (related to touching, hands, kissing, the bodily aspect of political personhood, neighborliness, spatial control, and geographic features) that expressed a spatialized way of conceptualizing political relationships.

For example, the verb 'to touch' (*toucher*, *toccare*) was frequently employed in a variety of ways. The most frequent meant 'with respect to' or 'as far as concerns' a given thing.[10] A castellan might write '*touchant* the preparations for the large fish pond, it won't be possible until the day of St. Rémy because the ground is too hard' or '*touchant* the two hundred planks of wood that

6   Deneen, 77.
7   AEN, AS-R5.10, René to Prangins, 10-VIII-38.
8   See Hall; for psychomotility, see Honigstein, 142.
9   Classen, 2-5.
10 The fiscal-legal formula *quod omnes tangit ab omnibus approbebatur* is one example of this usage.

you ordered the Castellan of Challant to bring, he gave this task to his assistant'.[11] Correspondents' letters 'touched' topics of importance to those communicating. This use of 'to touch' was extremely common.

Institutions, interests, or persons could also be 'touched' by significant events, such as the military catastrophe of 1536, which *'touche merveilleusement l'estat'*.[12] They could also 'touch' each other, as when René discussed with Charles III 'the jurisdiction which *m'attouche*' in a dispute near the Valle d'Aosta and his desire to avoid 'that my rights [*droit*] not be compromised [*interessé*] but preserved'.[13] Someone most affected by a matter was 'the person who is most touched by the thing',[14] and correspondents were aware of 'the degree to which the thing touches you'.[15] Guillemette de Vergy complained to Prangins about persons being harassed by Reformers in Valangin, noting that 'for the time being, I won't mention that which *m'atoche* – that will be for another time'.[16] In the context of a court dispute with one of René's enemies, Castellamonte referred to the Count as 'the most important man in the whole country, who was most touched by [the rival]'.[17]

One could make someone aware of an issue in political discussions by 'touching on it to them'.[18] René was urged to warn a group of subjects at Settimo Vittone who had taken up arms and declared their political independence that 'he did not wish for them to touch any weapons', and any who did so would have to answer to him. Meanwhile, two criminals executed at Bard had their property confiscated 'since it touches the Duke's jurisdiction'.[19] Documents could also 'touch' people's interests, and thus needed to be carefully guarded. Grat Rolin compiled documentary inventories and then sought out the 'papers and rights that *atouchent* the affairs of Virieu, Coligny, the pond of Chavolley' and other things.[20] People could 'touch', or have access to, their royal pensions – or not, as when Vaudan relayed the information that the 'pensioners [...] still have not *touché* anything' from the Treasurer of Milan. The secretary Cavet was thus told to '*tenir main*' in the matter, while Vaudan delivered 'the amount that I

11   AEN, AS-G16, 7, Santhusen to René, Vézelise 12-VII-56; ibid., 21, Vallesa to René, Verrès 17-V-39.
12   Fornaseri, 95-96, René to Beatrice, Aosta 18-VII-36.
13   Ibid., 102, René to Ch III, Aymavilles 17-X-44.
14   Ibid.., 105-6, René to Ch III, Beaufremont 19-VI-49.
15   AHR, FC 263, mz. 1, ? to ?. s.d.
16   AEN, AS-R5.10, zzzz, Guillemette to Prangins, 18-IV-31 (Tuesday after Quasimodo).
17   Ibid., AS-K16, 20, Castellamonte to René, 8-V-39.
18   Ibid., 16, memoir for René, s.d.
19   AHR, FC 263, mz. 1, Gamache to René, Bard 9-IV-?.
20   AEN, AS-G16, 3, Grat Rolin and Michel Casal to René, Aosta 21-VI-?.

have *entre les mains*.²¹ Another financial connotation of 'touching' meant to be owed something, such as when René's officials tried to collect rents received by the Gaspardone, 'which don't *tocha* them'.²²

Other bodily language that implied touching was also used to describe political relationships, such as when Martine expressed concern about the Bernese calling in a 10,000-*écu* loan by referring to his 'great fear that this horsefly might bite us'.²³ René sought permission from the Duke to 'withdraw to my estates a bit, in order to keep an eye [*avoir l'oeuil*] on my affairs'.²⁴ Subjects who were unable to pay their taxes or dues were referred to as 'poor people who are being squeezed hard [*bien pressés*]'.²⁵

The verb 'to touch' and related bodily language was closely tied to references to 'hands' in political discourse. The hands of political actors were often referred to in ways that related to their authority or control. To have something under one's hand mean to control it. Guillemette de Vergy informed Prangins that 'I had my hand placed' on the revenues of St. Martin parish; according to her grandson's instructions, 'I will gather the revenues under my hand'.²⁶ Lullin wrote to the Duke of Savoy about how important it was to 'remain vigilant over the places that are within your hands, to avoid dangers'.²⁷ Lenders were sought for the mortgage of Beaufremont, 'so that it won't fall into someone's hand, by force'.²⁸

Having one's hand in a matter also meant being involved in it. Sabaudian interests at court could be advanced by having them 'treated in the first instance by the hands of Granvelle', a ducal ally.²⁹ Conversely, the Duke of Lorraine declined to pay back pensions to René, reportedly because the Countess of Vaudémont 'put her hand to the matter'.³⁰ In negotiations with the Bernese, René stressed that 'he would not wish to place his hand in matters unless it were *tresagreable* to you'.³¹

Hands could be both materially and symbolically important. When the Emperor's surgeon, Antonio da Fossano, 'placed a good hand' on the Prince of

---

21 Ibid., 22, Jean François Vaudan to René, Aosta 17-V-39.
22 AHR, FC 290, mz. 1, no. 14, memoir dated Ivrea 20-XI-43.
23 AEN, AS-F16, 16, Martine to René, Valangin ?-V-49.
24 Fornaseri, 67-68, René to Ch III, Chambéry 17-VI-30.
25 AHR, FC 263, mz. 1, Blase du Cler to René, Verrès 11-V-?.
26 AEN, AS-R5.10, yyy, Guillemette to Prangins, Valangin 4-VII-31.
27 Ibid., AS-I16, 30, copy [?] of Lullin to Ch III, Regensburg 24-V-46.
28 AHR, FC 263, mz. 1, Chevron to Mencia, Annecy 25-XII-?.
29 AEN, AS-I16, 30, manuscript newsletter written in Italian.
30 Ibid., AS-G16, 7, Santhusen to René, Vézelise 12-VII-56.
31 Ibid., AS-K16, 10, copy of proposal made by René to Lords of Berne, dated III-56.

Piedmont's bad knee and gout problem, he was restored to health.[32] René made legally binding oaths by 'swearing bodily, his hands on the Holy Scriptures held by me, the undersigned notary'.[33] In 1550, his subjects of Valangin swore a loyalty oath to him as their sovereign in front of the gate of the *bourg*, 'with their hands on their stomachs', according to Matile.[34] Jeanne de Hochberg wrote a thank-you letter to René and promised to send a longer letter 'by my own hand, which you will find *tresbeau*'.[35] Similarly, René regretted being unable to write to Bellegarde 'by my own hand, due to my illness'.[36] René learned that a member of the Duke's *Chambre des comptes* was about to die 'unless God places his sovereign hand on him'.[37] The Count's envoy to court expressed his sorrow about warfare among Christians, 'praying that the Creator will be pleased to place his healing hand on this'.[38]

Attention was called to the hands of actors or their agents who received or transferred something in a way that was unambiguous and definitive. Examples abound of references to things being in someone's hands – financial reparations, places won in battle, soldiers under command of an officer, authority over another's business, revenues from one's fief, important documents, castles or houses, falcons, prisoners (whether commoners or nobles captured in battle), or jurisdiction.[39]

To give attention to and oversee a matter of importance to one or one's master was to '*tenir main*' or '*manier*'. Again, the documentation is rich with examples of this usage; a few illustrations will suffice. Lostan promised '*je tiendray main*' to see justice done with respect to a certain person, according to ducal instructions.[40] René himself wrote to Charles III about his

---

32 AHR, FC 264, mz. 1, Lullin to René, Innsbruck 25-III-?.
33 Ibid., FC 290, no. 38, document notarized in St. Rémy, 6-III-56.
34 Matile, 265.
35 AEN, AS-H16, 11, Jeanne to René, Cave [?] 19-VI-?.
36 Ibid., 17 and 17a, René to Bellegarde, Ivrea 26-IX-45.
37 Fornaseri, 104-5, René to EF, Beaufremont 17-VII-48.
38 AEN, AS-I16, 25, undated copy of draft instructions for René's envoy (the 'baron des Guerres').
39 Ibid., AS-R5.10, iiii, undated draft letter to René; Fornaseri, 87-89, René and 'Jo. Jacobo de Medyo' to Ch III, Crescentino 1-V-33; *Mémoires de Pierre Lambert*, 515-16; AEN, AS-H16, 25, Chevron to René, St. German-en-Laye 14-XI-53 [?]; ibid., AS-G16, 7, Santhusen to René, 12-VII-56; ibid., AS-F16, 14, Ducrest to René, Aosta 4-XII-57; ibid., 26, Gautier to René, Chambéry 4-VIII-43; ibid., AS-I16, 23, memoir to Vulliet about Grivonis; AHR, FC 263, mz. 1, Pierre Bachet to René, Bourg 11-I-?; AEN, AS-F16, 21, Santhusen to René, Beaufremont 6-VI-56; ibid., AS-G16, 7, same to same, Vézelise 12-VII-56; ibid., AS-H16, 18, De Gans [?] to René, Beaufremont 18-II-36 [1537?]; AHR, FC 260, René Gamache to Giovanni Federico, Challant 1-XI-64; ibid., FC 263, mz. 1 Bouchet to Mencia, Meyni [?] 12-X-?; ibid., Gamache to René, Bard 9-IV-?.
40 AEN, AS-G16, 29, Lostan to René, Aosta 11-II-39.

commitment to '*tenir main*' to what was required for the Duke's service.[41] René's envoys to Spain were instructed to '*tenir main* in the count's affairs before their majesties the king and queen',[42] while Blaise Junod declared that '*je tiendray main* that no revenues are lost [in Valangin] pledging to collect them as soon as possible and have them held for René [*les vous feray tenir*]'.[43] Martine wrote of the importance of investing his personal funds in the financial packages that he offered to Swiss lenders, who knew that 'I will pay close attention [to having interest payments made], being invested myself, and that *je tienne main* that they will be promptly paid', also.[44] In 1553, Bressieu was suspected of having stolen 'from all that he had *manyé*' for Charles III, including the Duke's rings, moveable property, and cash – *manyer* here referring both to oversight responsibility and literally having one's hands on valuables.[45] People could be 'handled', as when, during his second imprisonment, René 'so well *mania* the wife of a soldier who cooked for him' that he convinced her to help him try to escape, 'hiding letters in her hair' until she and her husband were caught and hanged at the Valentino castle 'in front of the windows of said Count'.[46]

Hands were political in other ways as well. As was the case with Bressieu, there could be unexpected political consequences of having something in one's hand. After Brissac attacked Vercelli and captured René, the French argued that his imprisonment was legitimate, since he had been taken with weapons in hand.[47] Receiving something from another's hand indicated a political bond. The French were wary of a peace agreement according to which Emanuel Filibert was expected to be neutral, since the Duke, 'from his infancy was nourished by the hand [*de la main*] of the Emperor, born of a cousin of his, and carried arms with him. He would thus never betray an affection that went back so far, almost to his wetnurse [*presque avec le laict*]'.[48] On the other hand, to be 'at hands' also indicated fighting, as when the Bishop of Aosta described how one of his servants and Captain Lostan '*venerò alle mani* [got into a fight with each other]' one night in Aosta 'such that the Captain was a bit injured'.[49]

41 Fornaseri, 74-75, René to Ch III, Virieu 11-VIII-30.
42 AHR, FC 290, no. 53, copy of memoir dated Rossillon 24-VII-64 for Vineufs and Cerisolles.
43 AEN, AS-F16, 23, Blaise Junod to Mencia, Valangin 16-III-51.
44 Ibid., 16, Martine to René, Valangin ?-V-49.
45 Fornaseri, 134, René to EF, coded letter of IX-53.
46 Boyvin, 658.
47 Marchand, 233-37; De Antonio, 176; Segre, 'Il richiamo,' 199; Frutaz, 'Notes,' 251.
48 Boyvin, 686-87.
49 AHR, FC 260, Bishop of Aosta [Ferragatta?] to Giovanni Federico, Aosta 14-X-64.

Thinking about the tactile and spatial implications of '*toucher*' and '*tenir main*' offers a different, proxemic way of understanding the verb '*maintenir*', implying diligence and bodily attentiveness on behalf of a patron or client. René was advised to appoint a procurator general who would 'preserve and *maintenyr* your authority, lordship, fiefs, sub-fiefs, jurisdiction, etc. against anyone and everyone'. Since such an officer would probably be disliked, the Count would 'be obligated to *maintenyr* and defend him so that his person would not be endangered'.[50] René's officers at Valangin were said to be profoundly dedicated to 'the *maintenance* of your authority and property in all of your affairs'.[51] In 1536, when threatened by the Bernese invasion, the inhabitants of Estavayer turned to the lords of Fribourg 'to protect and always *maintenir* us'. The Fribourgeois agreed, not wishing to create conflict with the Duke of Savoy but only 'to avoid that we fall *es mains* [of the Bernese] and also to preserve our Holy Faith'.[52] Challant trusted in Prangins's oversight of his affairs while he was away from Valangin, confident that 'right [...] will be *maintenu* without harm being done to anyone'[53] and that '*maintiendres* the rights of all parties'.[54] Castellamonte prayed that 'God may *maintiennent* [sic] you in good health' after hearing that René was not ill.[55]

Political significance attached to hands, both practically and symbolically, also sheds light on the practice and references to kissing hands (and things handed to one). Again, among the many examples of this language, one finds Emanuel Filibert passing through the Valle d'Aosta in early 1563 and Isabelle unable to go 'kiss the hands [of the Duke] in Aosta', because she was in labor.[56] Isabelle assured her husband about the goodwill of the Lord of Fénis toward him. Fénis 'kisses your hands' and declared that Giovanni Federico 'did not have an enemy in him'.[57] René gave homage for Valangin to Louis, Duke of Longueville in 1535 'by the laying on of hands and kisses of the mouth and all other required solemnities'.[58] In 1548, an Imperial envoy visited Berne to instruct its lords to restore the Sabaudian lands occupied in 1536. This envoy presented his *lettres de créance* to the mayor, who 'took them and

---

50 AEN, AS-K16, 15, memoir recommending creation of a procurator general, s.l., s.d.
51 Ibid., 19, Valangin officer to René, s.l., s.d.
52 AST1, NS, mz. 1 bis, no. 31, 'Diverse lettere al Duca Carlo 3°,' subjects of Estavayer to Ch III, Estavayer 17-II-36.
53 AEN, AS-R5.10, aaa, René to Prangins, Valangin 25-IV-42.
54 Ibid., oo, René to Prangins, Valangin 17-VII-?.
55 Ibid., AS-K16, 20, Castellamonte to René, Issogne 8-V-39 [?].
56 AHR, FC 263, mz. 1, Isabelle to Giovanni Federico, Issogne 12-III-63.
57 Ibid., FC 260, Isabelle to Giovanni Federico, Issogne 9-VIII-61.
58 AEN, AS-B4.9, b, copy of 1535 reception of René's homage to Louis de Longueville.

kissed them and gave them to the secretary of the city, who very reverently took them and kissed them'.⁵⁹ Mouths were not just for kissing – whenever someone was advised of something in person, verbally, it was *'de bouche'*.⁶⁰ Alliances between rulers were 'tightened [*serrées*]', perhaps a term derived from the shaking of hands; likewise, to *déserrer* an alliance was to break it.⁶¹

Many scholars, beginning with Marc Bloch and Ernst Kantorowicz, have written about the political significance of rulers' bodies, but the sources studied for this project indicate that political personhood was conceptualized in bodily ways at other levels of society as well.⁶² René and his correspondents seemed to assume an intimate link between his body (and those of his subjects) and his political authority. In 1558, he issued a receipt to subjects who had contributed to a subsidy and sealed the receipt with 'our blood placed here as a discharge of Ducrest's obligation' (the letter retains its stain – see Fig. 6).⁶³ One of the Count's creditors could not believe that his officers were unable to repay her, and preferred to hear from René *'touchans* the prosperity of your *personne'*.⁶⁴ Granyer warned René about rebellious subjects at Virieu: 'they will rip out the eyes of your subjects and officers, and the shame and mockery will attach to you' if the Count did not make himself feared.⁶⁵ In 1555, René insisted that he would only enter into the Valdostano estates assembly 'alone', rather than 'with the rest of the *paese*', prompting the Bishop of Aosta's remark to Emanuel Filibert that 'you alone are the prince here'.⁶⁶

When Charles III asked René to travel for his service in the 1540s, he expressed his wish that 'your person can bear the burden of the voyage. [...] You are well *incorporé*' in the matter, wrote the Duke, who hoped that René 'would not spare yourself'.⁶⁷ At the Imperial court, René sought to *'tenir main*, through *personnes interposites* with those who attend the council meeting' to advance his affairs.⁶⁸ The Count's advisers described him as *'incorporé'* in the matter of his daughters' ability to inherit, a request René presented

59 AST1, NS, mz. 1 bis, no. 32, '14-IV-48 Ordine dell'Imperatore [...].'
60 AEN, AS-H16, 19, Estienne Perret to René, Antwerp 21-VI-56.
61 Fornaseri, 49-53, René to Ch III, Romont, 4-V-30.
62 For the idea that touching someone in a given way constituted an acknowledgement of their authority claims, see Baert, 24.
63 AEN, AS-K16, 3, René receipt for Ducrest (who collected the subsidy from the subjects) dated 23-IX-58.
64 AHR, FC 262, mz. 1, Marguerite de Fers [?] to René, Montalto 18-V-40.
65 AHR, FC 263, mz. 1, Granyer to René, Chambéry 20-V-?.
66 AST1, LV, Aosta, mz. 20, Gazino to EF, Aosta 30-XI-55.
67 AEN, AS-K16, 2, Ch III to René, Vercelli 10-VI-46 [?].
68 Ibid., 16, memoir for René, s.l., s.d. [c. 1555-1556].

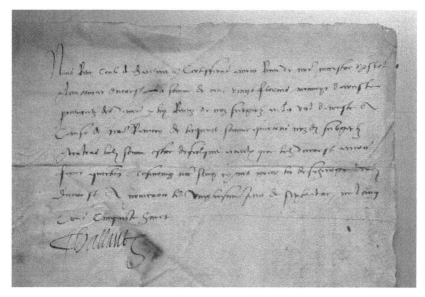

Fig.6: Receipt, sealed with his blood, issued by René to his secretary Ducrêt for 120 florins (1558). Source: Archives de l'État de Neuchâtel, AS-K16.3; used with permission.

to the Duke. This affair was crucial 'both for the *modernes damoyselles* and for others of such sex who might issue from their bodies by legitimate marriage'.[69]

René's political person was thus linked to his dynasty in bodily ways. This was most obviously expressed through his desire to have his heart preserved in the sacristy of the Aosta cathedral. This also pointed to an implicit link between bodily physical presence and dynastic territorial authority. Fabri was joyful in 1555 upon learning that the Count was 'delivered from prison and from the claws of inhumane tyrants, that you were restored to your *maison*, your *patrie*, and to those who have so desired and missed you'.[70] René later sought resources to repay Granvelle, with whose help 'I have satisfied [the debt toward Brissac] and placed my *mayson* in freedom'.[71] Bianca Maria described to the Duke of Mantua a potential marriage into his House of Gonzaga as '*coniugermi* with your very blood'.[72] When Duchess Beatrice named Mencia her Lady of Honor in 1528, she referred to the diligent service

69 Ibid.
70 Ibid., AS-G16, 25, Giovanni Fabri to René, Brussels 20-XI-55.
71 Fornaseri 135-36, René to EF, Paris 29-IX-56.
72 ASMn, Archivio Gonzaga, b. 746, cart. 15, Bianca Maria to Federico II Gonzaga, Casale 25-I-22.

that she had rendered since the Duchess had brought her from Portugal, 'together with the obligations of blood by which she touches us'.[73] In early 1554, Arignano assured Mencia that the Duke of Savoy regarded her with 'the respect owed to a relation of his, of his own blood, and also *Monsieur* the Marshal whom he holds as one of the principal grandees of his state, as he demonstrated by the confidence with which he placed everything in his hands'.[74]

One's political personhood could conversely be limited, or restricted, in spatialized ways due to illness, debt, or, most obviously, imprisonment. Each of these conditions amounted to a kind of bodily entrapment, which could be either literal or metaphorical. On one occasion, when François de Riddes was ill, he wrote of his recovery as being placed 'in liberty, after having been unchained and de-fevered'.[75] René urged his officers to collect revenues carefully, 'to toss me outside of debt'.[76] He wrote to Mencia that 'I let all of my underwriters out [releasing them from their obligations]'.[77] The withdrawal from politics of Charles V manifested itself spatially at court. One observer remarked that the Emperor 'has now retired in a small house at the bottom of the park, where he is separate and does not wish to be spoken to about any [political] affairs'. His physical and bodily distancing effectively disengaged Charles politically, in a location where 'he does not want to hear people speak about anything'.[78] The Duke of Savoy concluded that René's treatment of his daughter Philiberte after her elopement, and, in particular, her detention in a place where she was physically separate from her husband, 'touches our authority and the right of justice'. Emanuel Filibert declared to René that he could not permit this separation, 'which is a proper divorce'.[79] While René saw the matter as a personal offense against his person, the Duke was also offended by these spatialized bodily circumstances.

In other ways as well, René and his correspondents identified links between control of one's body and territorial control.[80] Fiefs, like bodies,

73 Claretta, *Notizie storiche*, 124-25, n. 2.
74 AHR, FC 263, mz. 1, Arignano to Mencia, Brussels 20-V-?.
75 AHR, FC 264, mz. 1, François de Riddes to Grandis, Paris 19-VI-?.
76 AEN, AS-G16, 1, René to Bellegarde, Brussels 14-II-56 ('pour me gecter hors de debtes').
77 AHR, FC 263, mz. 1, René to Mencia [?], s.l. [Valangin?], s.d. ('j'ay mys tous mez fyance hors').
78 AHR, FC 260, Montpon to Mencia, Brussels 21-V-54; see also ibid., FC 26, no. 31, EF to Mencia, Brussels 21-V-54.
79 ASTi, RLC, mz. 9, EF to Bobba [?], Nice 2-III-60.
80 Classen viewed city walls as important in people's mental structures, writing that 'even the human body might be conceptualized as a miniature walled city or castle, inhabited by the soul'. She referred to the religious notion of the soul as a city under attack by vices, citing

were conceptualized organically, with various parts and appendages. One document referred to 'the land and lordship of Beaufremont, its members, dependencies, and components'.[81] In the early 1530s, René's servants were accused by a ducal official of 'violently invading and entering my said house and property and expelling from them, for a time, my servants and workers'. An earlier decision had allegedly prohibited René from 'bothering me or in any way disturbing or impeding me in my property'.[82] Few details are known about this case, other than that René connected his authority as Marshal of Savoie to his ability to secure physical access to any place under his jurisdiction.

After René's capture at Vercelli, Sabaudian officials feared that French pressure would lead him to engineer the capitulation of the Valle d'Aosta to the King. The ducal council thus attempted to garrison Verrès with Sabaudian soldiers, 'so that if the French forced my Lord of Challant to give them Verrès and other castles *nelle mano*, he could reply that they were under the authority of [Emanuel Filibert]'.[83] French control of the Count's body could easily lead to the control of territory under the Count's jurisdiction, through the defection of fortified structures linked to the Count's person. After being released, when René petitioned the Duke of Savoy for reinstatement as lieutenant general, he also sought authority to appoint a lieutenant. He would frequently be unable to reside in Piedmont, he argued, 'since the extent of the country obedient to you is quite small' and thus apparently ill-suited to René's full-time attention.[84] Being freed from captivity implied for René positional restitution; the Duke's failure to reinstitute him would signify a radical demotion. In that case, wrote René (in terms reminiscent of Charles V's action), 'I will be forced to abandon everything and retire to conduct my small affairs', having seen 'my reputation and honor [...] seriously harmed'.[85] As his dispute with Masino continued into the late 1550s, René avoided being physically present in Piedmont, sojourning instead in Pavia, Novara, and Milan.

Territorial control and bodily positioning also overlapped as René oversaw the restitution of the transalpine Sabaudian lands in 1559. This

---

Peter Damian, who urged Christians to '"close then [...] these gates of the senses of the body"', in order to protect one's self against vice (Classen, 12).

81 AEN, AS-S26, 43, copy of a financial arrangement made between Guillemette and René, 1523.
82 Ibid., AS-K16, 26, register of Veillet litigation dated 30-VI-31.
83 AST1, LP, I.8, Dell'Isola to EF, Vercelli 27-XI-53.
84 AEN, AS-K16, 16, memoir for René, s.l., s.d. [*c*. 1555-1556].
85 Fornaseri, 136-38, René to EF, Valangin 25-XI-57.

process was ritualized by a change of seating in the great room of the Chambéry castle. As the representative of the Duke of Savoy, he sat to the left of the President of the French-instituted *Parlement* in one of two velours-covered chairs, and, after receiving the keys of the city, he and the President then changed seats, signifying the Duke's resumption of power. Later that day, officials under his authority received the physical transfer of 'all the titles and papers of the *Chambre [des comptes]*' from the King's officers. Nine days later, an official went to the castle chapel 'to open the tomb of Philiberte de Savoie, Duchess of Nemours, in which many important papers had been hidden'. These were placed with other hidden records, 'which were recovered and reinserted by inventory in the archives'.[86] Here also, we see a link between proximity to dynastic bodies – even deceased ones – and the preservation of territorial political control. The episode at the castle of Nice in 1539, when Sabaudian soldiers feared that the Emperor's residence in the castle would lead to a loss of dynastic control over it, also exemplifies the interplay between physical occupation and dynastic authority.

Living as good neighbors (*voisins*) was a widely recognized political good that emphasized peaceful propinquity between bodies and collectivities. The King of France was happy with the Bernese 'due to the good neighborliness [*la buona vicinita*] that they carry out toward the king'.[87] René wished to avoid conflict with the Longueville sons of Jeanne de Hochberg, desiring instead 'friendship and good neighboring [*voysinance*]'.[88] On behalf of Emanuel Filibert, he transmitted to the Bernese the Duke's wish to 'keep your friendship, neighborliness, and alliance'.[89] In 1529, Bellegarde advised René not to leave Valangin for the time being, as they awaited a response from Berne and Fribourg, since 'your presence and neighboring [*voysinage*] will aid significantly'.[90]

Through René's brokerage, the wife of Prangins had agreed to guarantee a loan for a Valdostano noble. Then she asked to be 'tossed out [*desgectee*] of her underwriting', which created difficulties for the noble in the short term. René asked Prangins that his wife give the noble some time, assuring him that 'neither you nor she can lose anything, and can rest as assured as if he were your own neighbor [*voysin*]. [...] I know that you will be well

86   Capré, 79, 83-84.
87   AEN, AS-I16, 30, Lullin & Stroppiana to Ch III, Regensburg 24-V-46.
88   Ibid. AS-C4.11, b, 7-II-44, response by René's envoys regarding sale of sovereignty and property.
89   Ibid., AS-K16, 10, copy of proposal made by René to Lords of Berne, dated III-56.
90   Ibid., AS-H16, 22, Bellegarde to René, Chambéry 5-X-29.

satisfied', he continued, 'and you can rely on me'.[91] In general, there was a close tie between proximity and financial credit. Sometimes, one's status as a non-local or non-neighbor had another kind of political significance. The author of a financial and administrative advice manual suggested that René appoint a procurator general who was 'a foreigner and not at all from the area'.[92]

An envoy to René's lands in the Monferrato encountered a struggle for control of Calamandrana castle, half of which belonged to René's ally Margherita Gaspardone. This case offers an example of bad '*voisinage*'. Their opponent, Annibale, had locked a room belonging to Margherita and was supported by the subjects of the fief, who occupied the rest of Margherita's portion of the castle. The envoy's servants had to sleep on the ground, and the subjects would not let Margherita's servants enter their rooms. Bandits were already seeking refuge at the castle. The envoy urged Margherita to have the Castellan build a wall between her part of the castle and Annibale's.[93]

The bodily component of sixteenth-century political discourse seems to have expressed itself more generally in other kinds of spatial and proxemic language.[94] Such expressions often referred to controlling spatial access or regulating an immediate geographic or topographical environment. If one sought to block a given initiative, one would 'place a crossbar in the way [*mettergli qualche traversa*]', as the French did to various Sabaudian diplomatic efforts.[95] René and his correspondents frequently discussed the geopolitics of matters at hand. Seeking to have himself appointed Imperial commander in Italy, he would claim that he could not only pacify the lands of Charles III and the Emperor, but could also secure the 'repose of their lands adjacent and contiguous to the places held by the enemy'.[96] On a mission to the Bernese, he noted that the duchy of Aosta was '*circuy* and *environné*' by the French, and wished to avoid being forced to 'place foreign soldiers and nations in their country', who would be impossible to 'expunge'. If Bernese support were secured, the valley could remain 'your good and affectionate neighbor, friend, and ally'.[97] The image here is of the Valle d'Aosta as a collective body being jostled and threatened by contiguous hostile bodies, forced to protect itself by absorbing a kind of parasitic foreign element.

91   Ibid., AS-R5.10, d, René to Prangins, Aosta 25-II-42.
92   Ibid., AS-K16, 15, memoir recommending creation of a procurator general, s.l., s.d.
93   AHR, FC 264, mz. 1, Jo. Baptista Royer [Roero?] to Margarita Gaspardona, Ternavasso 2-VII-?.
94   On the proxemics of seating arrangements at court, see Sternberg, esp. 33, n. 25.
95   AEN, AS-I16, 30, Lullin & Stroppiana to Ch III, Regensburg 24-V-46.
96   Ibid., AS-K16, 15, memoir recommending creation of a procurator general, s.l., s.d.
97   Ibid., 10, copy of proposal made by René to Lords of Berne, dated III-56.

Transit rights were a key element of spatial control for René and his contemporaries. During the 1550s, his envoy to the French court requested a safe-conduct enabling René to travel from Flanders to his lands, 'passing through his houses of Lorraine and Valangin, which he cannot do without touching the *limites* of the country of France'.[98] The Duke of Savoy instructed René that, if the French 'asked for *passaige* [through the Valle d'Aosta] do not permit it to be granted'. However, he was to '*tenir main* that the present neutrality agreement be renewed'.[99] On at least one occasion, unsafe '*passages*' prevented a Savoyard noble from carrying a message to the Duke of Savoy.[100] But a strict control of transit was impossible, even at a fortress like Bard, located in a narrow defile. 'You know well, *monseigneur*', explained the castellan, 'that even if the castle's watchmen do their job well, at night they cannot see or recognize those who pass by, and during the day many kinds of people can pass by since in other places no watch is kept'.[101] Finding ways to force debtors to pay was also described in spatialized terms, such as when Gautier suggested a debt restructuring that would 'seal this passage [*clourre ce passaige*], provided that [the debtor] pay interest in the future and the expenses of having pursued him'.[102]

Access to space was also regulated at more micro-levels, often simply with locks and keys, in ways that demonstrated political control. English envoys visited Chambéry in 1530 and wished to see the Holy Shroud, which was locked up in a place whose key was held by the Duke. René promised Charles III that, after displaying the Shroud, 'I will send the keys back to you by a trustworthy man' if the Duke would 'leave the keys to my wife, so that it could be shown that day'.[103] When Beaufremont was mortgaged to pay for René's second ransom, his procurator 'gave the keys to the gates, bridge, barriers, drawbridge and other places of the castle' to Brissac's procurator, who then returned the keys to René's captain of Beaufremont, who would continue to collect the revenues and transfer them to René.[104] In 1560, Ducrest and Lescha discussed provisioning at Châtillon, where Isabelle would soon 'visit' the wine. Ducrest sent Lescha 'the keys of the cellar', asked him to taste the quality of the wines from the Canavese, instructing him not to

---

98 Ibid., AS-I16, 25, undated copy of draft instructions for René's envoy (the 'baron des Guerres').
99 Ibid., AS-K16, 17, EF to René, Brussels 4-I-56.
100 AHR, FC 263, mz. 1, Charles de La Forest to René, Chambéry [?] 2-VI-?.
101 Ibid., FC 263, mz. 1, Castellan of Bard to ?, s.l. 11-II-?.
102 AEN, AS-H16, 24, Gautier to René, Virieu 23-V-43.
103 Fornaseri 45-46, René to Ch III, Chambéry 9-IV-30.
104 AHR, FC 56B, no. 12, act notarized on 15-XI-55.

store wine in 'the cellar behind the large one'.[105] Controlling access to storage spaces was related to political authority, and physical, bodily controls were linked to cultural capital.

In terms of specific places that were related to the political authority of his own dynasty and the Sabaudian one, mountains occasionally figure in René's discourse, representing alternatively boundaries, hazardous zones, and places of adventure, reinforcement, and delight. Castellamonte described to René the route to take from the Valle d'Aosta to Romont if he left on Saturday and wished to arrive on a Thursday. He should first 'come to the base of the mountain and come by the road that I took toward Châtel-St-Denis', which would take longer than expected 'since I can assure you that it's the worst road in the world'. From Romont, he should go to Fribourg on his way to Berne, since it would be politically useful, and, 'given that it's right on your way, the lords of Berne will not suspect anything'.[106] René sent instructions in 1545 about sending 'the mules to the foot of the mountain to retrieve the trunks', and doing the same on the other side. But, due to the 'bad weather that can be found in the mountains', René doubted his ability to travel.[107] In the early 1540s, a servant from Valangin had sent a raptor across the Alps to René in the valley, but the bird 'died along the way, on this side of the mountain'.[108] An officer in the Valle d'Aosta explained how weather in the mountains could affect commodity prices, as when 'the mountains have been so dry that there has been barely any rain and the animals have not produced as much milk as they usually do'.[109] During a period of illness in 1530, René was advised to 'take some air', and so he decided to go from Virieu up 'into the mountains, to see how I will feel'. While there, 'I will have my men go on a hunt, because I am still too weak for hunting myself.'[110] In 1541, René extended an invitation to young Prince Emanuel Filibert to come and 'visit this area a bit, for some recreation, watching the horses run up the mountains, where you can really wear yourself out before catching up with them'.[111]

The political experiences of René de Challant, together with the language of his correspondence, shows that he and his contemporaries viewed

---

105 AEN, AS-K16, 9, Ducrest to Lescha, Aosta ?-IX-60.
106 AHR, FC 263, mz. 1, Castellamonte to ?, Berne 18-V-?.
107 AEN, AS-H16, 17, 17a, René to Bellegarde, Ivrea 26-IX-45; ibid., AS-G16, 12, same to same, Issogne 12-X-45 [?]; ibid., 14, same to same, Issogne 14-X-45.
108 Ibid., AS-H16, 17 and 17a, René to Bellegarde, Ivrea 26-IX-45.
109 Ibid., FC 264, mz. 1, Lostan to Mencia [?], Aosta 2-X-?.
110 Fornaseri, 74-75, René to Ch III, Virieu 11-VIII-30.
111 Ibid., 100-1, René to EF, Issogne 16-XI-41.

political authority not only as spatialized, but, even more specifically, embodied. Scholars such as Sergio Bertelli have pointed out various facets of the embodiment of political authority during the medieval and early modern periods, suggesting that a shift in this way of conceptualizing power began to take place during the seventeenth century.[112] René's life illustrates the links between spatial specificity and the embodiment of power during the earlier period. Subsequently (and gradually), authority became more depersonalized and abstract, legally defined, separated from moral constraints, more amenable to princely voluntarism, and tied to a notion of territorial sovereignty that was more geometric than singular. René's lordship was embodied and personal, due to accidents of dynastic territorialism and the dispersed authority thereby created. René's sovereignty was muddled, lacking the clarity with which Bodin would invest the concept a couple of decades later. During the seventeenth century, sovereignty was increasingly rationalized, rather than linked to singular places and bodies. One might think of this, to use Richard Tuck's model, as the triumph of a 'humanist' conception of politics over an earlier 'scholastic' way of understanding the law of nature, according to which natural law inhered in the structure of things, rather than in individual rights abstracted from their spatial contexts.[113] Such a shift in conceptualization was likely matched by a change in the practice of lordship, but this remains to be documented.

The lordship exercised by René de Challant was transregional, linking Italy with Alpine and transalpine Europe. It was simultaneously urban and rural, and was constantly preoccupied with practical problems (finance, fief management, family relations) – that were spatially specific. The significance of René's experiences as a great noble operating across a strategically important area of early sixteenth-century Europe has been obscured because of the old problem of historiographic categories derived from nineteenth-century nation-states. The bodily and personalized authority of René and those like him created political spaces linked to the practices in which they engaged: landholding, revenue collection, financial operations, diplomatic activity, hunting, and military engagement. His dynasty's traditional subjection to the House of Savoy had the ironic effect of creating political spaces that he could exploit in Italy and abroad, as he (and his family and officers) crisscrossed Europe, among his fiefs and beyond.

112 Bertelli.
113 Tuck.

Bibliography

Barbara Baert, *Touch with the Gaze: Noli me tangere and the Iconic Space* (Oostakker, Belgium: Sint Joris, 2011)

Sergio Bertelli, *The King's Body: Sacred Rituals of Power in Medieval and Early Modern Europe*, trans. R. Burr Litchfield (University Park, PA: Penn State University Press, 2001 [1990])

François Boyvin du Villars, *Mémoires*, in *Choix de chroniques et mémoires sur l'histoire de France*, ed. J.A.C. Buchon (Paris: Librairie Charles Delagrave, 1884)

François Capré, *Traité historique de la Chambre des comptes de Savoye* (Lyon: Chez Guillaume Barbier, 1652)

Gaudenzio Claretta, *Notizie storiche intorno alla vita ed ai tempi di Beatrice di Portogallo duchessa di Savoia* (Turin: Tipografia Eredi Botta, 1863)

Constance Classen, *Deepest Sense: A Cultural History of Touch* (Champaign-Urbana: University of Illinois Press, 2012)

Carlo De Antonio, 'La Valle d'Aosta ed Emanuele Filiberto,' in *Lo stato sabaudo al tempo di Emanuele Filiberto*, ed. Carlo Patrucco, vol. 1 (Turin: Miglietta, 1928), pp. 153-237

Massimo della Misericordia, 'Gusti cavallereschi, stili residenziali e temi figurativi. Aspetti della cultura aristocratica nella Lombardia alpina alla fine del medioevo,' *Quaderni storici* 51, 3 (2016): 794-96

Id., 'Medioevo cavalleresco nelle memorie familiari dell'aristocrazia alpina lombarda,' *Bollettino della Società Storica Valtellinese* 68 (2015), 7-9

Patrick Deneen, *Why Liberalism Failed* (New Haven: Yale University Press, 2018)

Giovanni Fornaseri, *Le lettere di Renato di Challant, governatore della Valle d'Aosta a Carlo II ed a Emanuele Filiberto* (Turin: Deputazione subalpina di storia patria, 1957)

François-Gabriel Frutaz, 'Notes sur René de Challant et sur le passage de Calvin dans la Vallée d'Aoste,' *Musée neuchâtelois* 41 (1904): 242-67

Edward Hall, 'Proxemics,' *Current Anthropology* 9 (1968): 83-109

Raphael Honigstein, *Bring the Noise: The Jürgen Klopp Story* (New York: Nation Books, 2018)

Pierre Lambert de la Croix, *Mémoires de Pierre Lambert*, in *Monumenta Historiae Patriae edita iussu Regis Caroli Alberti Scriptorum*, vol. 1 (Turin: Regio Tipographeo, 1840)

Charles Marchand, *Charles Ier de Cossé, comte de Brissac et maréchal de France 1507-1563* (Paris: Champion, 1889)

Georges-Auguste Matile, *Histoire de la seigneurie de Valangin jusqu'à sa réunion à la directe en 1592* (Neuchâtel, James Attinger, 1852)

La noblesse des marches, de Bourgogne et d'ailleurs au temps de Marguerite d'Autriche (XVe-XVIe siècle), ed. Sarah Fourcade, Dominique Le Page, and Jacques Paviot, *Annales de Bourgogne* 89, 3-4 (Dijon: Éditions universitaires de Dijon, 2017)

James Schall, 'On Uniqueness,' *The Catholic Thing*, 4 December 2018, https://www.thecatholicthing.org/2018/12/04/on-uniqueness/, 12 November 2019

Arturo Segre, 'Il richiamo di D. Ferrante Gonzaga dal governo di Milano e sue conseguenze (1553-1555),' *Memorie della Reale Accademia delle Scienza di Torino*, 2nd ser., 54 (1904): 185-260

Giora Sternberg, *Status Interaction during the Reign of Louis XIV* (Oxford: Oxford University Press, 2014)

Richard Tuck, *The Rights of War and Peace: Political Thought and the International Order from Grotius to Kant* (Oxford: Oxford University Press, 2001)

Kären Wigen, 'Introduction' to 'AHR Forum: Oceans of History,' *AHR* 111, 3 (2006): 717-21

About the author

Matthew Vester is a Professor of History at West Virginia University and the author of *Renaissance Dynasticism and Apanage Politics: Jacques de Savoie-Nemours, 1531-1585* (Truman State, 2012). He is the editor of *Sabaudian Studies: Political Culture, Dynasty, and Territory (1400-1700)* (Truman State, 2013) and coeditor of *Tra Francia e Spagna: Reti diplomatiche, territori e culture nei domini sabaudi fra Tre e Settecento* (Carocci, 2018).

Index

Aarau 93, 93n106, 230n48
abortion 263
absolutism 25, 29n84, 31, 82, 134, 212
Achey, Jean d' (Baron de Thoraise) 96n131
Adda family 110n6
Adriani, Giovanni Battista 34, 140-41
Africa 77
agency 16-17, 255n25
Agneres, Baron of 195
Aiguebelle 197
Aigues Mortes 92
Aikin, Judith 201
Alardet (son-in-law of Baron of Vallesa) 155n91
Alardet, Claude-Louis (Abbot of Filly) 97n133, 187, 209
Albon de Saint-André, Jacques d' 237
Alciato, Andrea 170n177
Alençon, Anne d' (dowager Marquise of Monferrato) 56, 59, 148n51, 149, 226
Algiers 210n175
Alicante 140n3
alienation of property 89, 116, 205
Alps 11, 13-15, 18-23, 26, 27n71, 40-41, 56, 68, 95-96, 105, 127, 130, 156, 158, 173, 194, 230n53, 305, 306
Alps
  as boundary 20-21, 20n28, 21n30, 194
  cultural traditions 20-21, 21n31, 22, 22n38, 24n57
  economic developments 21n33
  military passage across 21-22, 54n3, 55, 81
  political consolidation 21-22, 21n34
  religion 22n39
Alsace 36, 194
Amadeus IX of Savoy 68
Amadeus VIII of Savoy 21
Amadis de Gaule 160
Ambronay 61, 129, 132
Amiens 118
Ammann family (from Fribourg) 259
Ammann, Auche Ludovic 259n52
Ammann, Barbe (Lady) 236
Ammann, Bartholomey 229
André (servant at Valangin) 264
Andrion, Michicl 183n23
Angiolini, Franco 26, 26n62, 26n64
Anne of Saxony 140
Annecy 3, 210n175, 264
Annibal (captured by corsairs) 151
Annibale (opponent of René at Calamandrana) 303
Annonciade, order of 54, 117n44, 120, 195, 274n121
Anthey, Curé of 266n85
Antoine, Duke of Lorraine 95n119, 139
Antoine, Marc 172

Antwerp 140n3, 198, 243n119, 266
Aosta 11, 54, 78, 82, 90, 95, 97, 119n51, 125, 154, 166, 190, 197n105, 199, 211, 213, 215, 240n106, 282, 288, 296
Aosta, Bailiff of 94, 115, 154, 173n196, 184, 186
Aosta, Bishop of (see also Gazino) 63n43, 91, 94n113, 112, 116, 151, 166, 172, 198, 200, 240, 240n106, 241n107, 296, 298
Aosta, cathedral see Notre Dame
Aosta, cathedral chapter of 130
Aosta, diocese of 150, 173
Aosta, duchy of 91, 117n40, 182, 274, 289, 303
Aosta, Franciscan convent 159
Aosta, governor of 90, 97
Aosta, hospital of 159
Aosta, Vice-bailiff of 273
Aosta, viscount of 143
Apennines 255
Arberg, Claude d' 71, 144, 225, 258, 261
Arberg, county of 122
Arberg, Jean d' 224n21
Arberg, Louise d' 144, 162
Arbois 195
Archives 15, 37n128, 90n84, 100, 111, 119, 119n51, 121, 125n88, 133, 160n124, 207, 211, 288, 302
Ardizzone, Evasio 245, 245n133
Arnay-le-Duc 229n44
Arras, Bishop of see Perrenot de Granvelle, Antoine de
Arscot see Cröy, Philippe III de, Duke of Aarschot
astrologers 190-91
Attalens 144n24
Aubonne 258n50
Aubonne, Lord of 87
Auge, Oliver 253n11
Aulnoy 267
Aumale, Claude d' see Guise, Claude de and Guise, Claude II de
Austria 20, 22
Autun 155
Avi, Count of see Madruzzo, Giovanni Federico
Avignon 21
Avise, Jean Boniface d' 183n25
Avise, Jean d' 91n92, 264
Avise, Lord of 156
Avise, Nicolas d' 200, 246n137
Ayas 275-76, 276n128, 278
Aymavilles 95, 127n97, 143-44, 146, 159, 162n140, 198, 200, 206, 244n126, 264, 269-70, 276-77, 279
Azeglio 189
Azeglio, Manfredo d' 93n104, 190n60
Azeglio, Nicolò d' 245, 245n128

Bachet, Pierre   211, 211n178, 295n39
Baden   61, 98, 188, 260
Balbi family   15, 140n3, 201, 223
Balbo, Niccolò   170, 170n177
Bamberg   84n39
Bandello, Matteo   56-57, 56nn12-13, 59, 60n26, 131, 140
bandits/brigands   71, 158, 263, 303
bankers   19, 63-64, 93n106, 110n6, 208, 210, 222-24, 222n8
banners   115
Baptendier (ducal secretary)   186
baptism   61, 146, 146n38, 281
Baptiste (servant of René)   208
Bar, duchy of   37n128, 147
Barberis, Walter   26-27, 27n71, 27n74
Barbero, Alessandro   27, 144n25, 252-53, 252n6
Barbier, Maurice   85, 253n16
Barbre   279
Barcelona   91
Bard   53, 72-73, 82, 90, 94n113, 115, 118, 154, 155n91, 159, 169, 169n172, 205, 209n168, 225, 225n27, 226, 229n40, 278, 279, 293, 304
Bar-le-Duc   266
Bartolus   160
Basel   40, 65n61, 70, 81, 83, 84n39, 224n21, 229, 235, 235n79, 266
Basel, bishop of   69, 70n85, 72n93, 86n60, 94n112, 102
Bassoz   266
bastards   33n105, 54n3, 57, 99, 122, 151, 152n72, 154, 196, 197, 241, 280
Bastonat   265n82
Baugé, Sébastien de see Luxembourg, Sébastien de
Bavaria   21n34
Beatrice of Portugal (Duchess of Savoy)   55, 60, 90, 91n95, 146, 151, 161, 185, 204, 228, 299
Beatrix (baker)   164
Beaufort de Rolle, Jean-Amédée de   127n93
Beaufort, Gauvin de   188n50, 188n52
Beaufremont   13, 40-41, 61, 87, 91, 94, 97, 97n134, 97n136, 98, 103, 122, 147, 150, 155, 165-66, 182, 194-95, 198, 202, 211, 225, 230, 235, 236n81, 241n108, 243, 256n30, 257, 257n43, 258n49, 260n56, 261-62, 262n63, 262nn65-66, 262n68, 263n69, 264n73, 264n77, 265-68, 288, 301
   fishpond   266
   household ordinance   164-65
   mortgage   55, 230n48, 238-42, 241n110, 246, 294, 304
   taxes, dues   266-67
Beaugency   57
Beaumont-Carrà, Nicolas de see Carrà, Niccolò
Belleforest, François de   56n12, 131
Bellegarde, Claude de   63, 70, 70n85, 85, 88, 99-101, 102n167, 146, 154, 157-58, 165, 170, 191-92, 198, 203, 210, 229, 229n43, 230, 232-34, 242, 256, 256n29, 258-59, 258n48, 259n51, 261, 264-65, 267, 295, 302
Bellegarde, Nicolas de   154
Belmond   200n121
Berne   19, 30, 40, 54-55, 55n5, 61-64, 64n56, 65n60, 66-67, 69, 73, 73n99, 77-83, 78n2, 78n5, 85, 85n50, 87n61, 88, 95-97, 97n134, 97n137, 100, 102-5, 103n169, 116-19, 116n30, 117n40, 118n47, 128, 129n109, 134, 134n137, 144, 191-92, 197, 199, 224n21, 225, 230n53, 232-33, 235, 235n76, 235n79, 236n81, 241, 241n110, 256-59, 258-59n50, 260n54, 287, 294, 297, 302-3, 305
   almshouse   230n48
Bertelli, Sergio   306
Bertolin, Roberto   130
Besançon   70, 70n85, 170, 206, 257n43
Besançon, Archbishop of see Vergy, Antoine de and La Baume, Pierre de
Bezzina, Edwin   84
Bichereit, Heinrich   237n85
Biel, Arnold   134n137
Biella   112
Bienne   85-86
Billens   144n24
biography   15-17, 34, 212
   transnational   16-17
birds (for hunting)   157-58, 158n115, 161, 190n60, 268n96, 295, 305
Blakeley, James   83
Blaufarb, Rafe   167, 254n23
Bloch, Marc   16n13, 298
Blois   57, 194
Bodin, Jean   85, 104, 306
Bogiis, Antoine de   150
Bogiis, Laurent de   150
Bohemia   255n26
Boisrigaut see Daugerant de Boisrigaut, Louis
Bolangier, Jean   269
Boldù, Andrea   14, 128, 131, 131n117, 179n2
Bologna   195, 266, 275
Bonaventure (friar)   157
Bonini, Loys   163-64
Bonivard, François   65
Bonnivet (Guillaume Gouffier, Lord of)   55n9
Bonstetten, Johann Jakob von   102-3, 103n169, 256
Bonvillars-Mezieres, Louis de   82n32
border zones   16, 19, 21, 25, 27, 28n78, 33-34, 36-38, 37nn130-31, 40, 72, 92n103, 104, 180, 194, 256n33, 260, 263, 283
Borre (cameral official)   187
Borromeo family   153
Bouchet see Maillard du Bouchet, Pierre
Bouclans   257n43
Boudevilliers   85, 88, 88n77, 89, 99, 101
Boudry   68n68, 258n45
Bouillon, Duke of see La Marck, Robert IV de

INDEX

Boulet (priest of St. Marcel, brother of Bernard)   276
Boullet/Boulet, Bernard (servant of René)   173, 211, 166, 176
Boulogne   210
Bourbon dynasty   33n105, 195
Bourbon, Antoinette de (Duchess of Guise)   100, 193, 201, 206n154
Bourbon, François II de   195
Bourbon, Henri de   69
Bourbon, Marie de   69
Bourg-en-Bresse   81, 130, 246
Bourjod   205
Boyvin du Villars, François   131-33, 240n104
Brabant   267
Braganza dynasty   33n105
Braganza, Teodosio I, Duke of (Mencia's cousin and brother-in-law)   238n95
Braudel, Fernand   16n13, 20n23, 23
Breen, Michael   168
Brenner pass   20n28, 98
Bresse   79-81, 121, 121n69, 128, 130, 211, 265n78, 270, 275, 279, 282
Bressieu, Louis de Gallier de   111-13, 111n9, 115, 215, 296
Bretagne, Odet de   122n75
Breton Gros   240
bribery/corruption   109-12, 135, 172, 212, 272
Brion, Gilles de   171n185
Brissac *see* Cossé de Brissac, Charles de
Broissure, Mlle de   117n42
Brucza   274
Bruno, Ludovico   183n25
Brussels   96, 103, 117, 125, 187, 195, 202, 208, 236, 239-41, 243n119
Brusson   245n130, 268, 278
Bruzzo, Luigi   135-36, 141
Buda   209
Bugey   56, 61, 79, 94, 128, 171, 213, 279
Buonconsiglio castle (Trento)   22n38
Burgundy   22, 31n94, 32n100, 32n102, 33, 36, 38, 64n56, 96n131, 105, 154-55, 167, 180, 192, 194, 254n23
Bussy   262
Busto Arsizio   158
Buylaert, Frederik   30

Cachiot/Cachot, Jacques   170, 200, 233, 273, 279
Caferro, William   223
Calais   119
Calamandrana   149n56, 150, 303
Calderini, Gian Angelo   84n39
Cambiano, Luca   190
Canavese   57, 63, 189, 279, 304
Candelo   158
Candia   158
Caplan, Jay   207
Capris, Gaspare (Bishop of Asti)   112, 123n77, 197, 229

Capua, Isabella di   98
Cardona, Pietro (bastard son of the count of Golisano)   57
Carema   226, 241, 278
Carinthia   21n34
Carniola   21n34
Carrà, Giovanni/Jean (cameral official)   110n2, 112, 115, 121, 187
Carrà, Niccolò (ducal treasurer)   110n2, 112-14, 116n33, 119, 154, 228, 280
Carutti, Domenico   133, 180, 212
Casale Monferrato   30, 54, 56, 59-60, 128n105, 149-50, 149n56, 155-58, 155n96, 157n108, 170, 190, 200, 214, 226, 231, 241, 245, 246n137, 278
Casale, Bishop of   169
Casella, Laura   34, 37
Castellamonte, Luigi di   63, 72, 91n92, 93-94, 93n109, 93n111, 94n112, 154, 156-57, 159, 170, 184, 189, 197-98, 213-15, 226, 228, 258-60, 259n51, 279, 293, 297, 305
castellany accounts   163-64, 166, 172-73, 266-67, 270-75, 277
Castiglione, Caroline   168, 255n25
castles (palaces)   14, 22n38, 24n57, 38, 38n134, 40, 57, 61, 68-69, 81, 83, 85-86, 92, 92n97, 95, 99, 110n6, 113n16, 114-15, 121, 133, 150, 161-64, 170, 180, 197, 205, 227, 230, 241-42, 245-46, 255, 264, 271-72, 275, 277-80, 295-96, 300n80, 301-4
Castro Lemos, Pedro de, Bishop of Salamanca (Mencia's brother)   238n95
Castro-Osorio, Brites de   60
Castruczon, Co-Lord of Carema   278
Cateau-Cambrésis, treaty of   120
Cattaneo, Geronimo   154
Cauda, Antoine   229n40
Cavalli, Sigismondo   179n2
Cavallo, Sandra   161
Cavallo, Venetiano   170n174
Cavet, Etienne   81, 154, 281-82, 293
Cecere, Domenico   255n25
center-periphery   18-19, 23, 23n45, 288-90
ceremony   61, 69, 71, 73, 97n137, 110, 120-21, 126-27, 126n92, 130, 146, 146n38, 151, 161, 167, 199, 210n175, 280, 295, 297-98, 301-2
Cernier   262
Cerruto, Asclero   246n137
Ceyzérieu   280
Chablais   65, 134n137, 170
Chabod, Federico   24n55, 252
Chakrabarty, Dipesh   18
Challant, Charles de (René's uncle, apostolic notary, prior of St. Gilles and St. Ours)   54, 145
Challant, Claude de (illegitimate son of René?)   152n72
Challant, Claudine de (half-sister of René?)   183n26
Challant, county of   40, 54, 198, 244n125, 247, 269, 271, 278, 282, 293

Challant, Emanuel René de 183n25
Challant, François de (husband of Bonne de Gingins) 144
Challant, François de (René's bastard) 122, 151-52, 152n71, 154, 196, 198, 280, 282
Challant, Françoise de (René's aunt) 143, 150
Challant, House of 13, 26, 36, 53, 59, 134-35, 141-43, 144n25, 145, 153, 156, 170, 180, 183-84, 197-98, 201, 207, 224-25, 246, 252-53, 278, 282, 287-88, 292
Challant, Isabelle de 61, 97, 115n27, 118, 122-27, 125n86, 126n90, 129-30, 146, 152, 157, 159, 161, 163-64, 163n144, 179, 274-75, 297, 304
Challant, Jacques de (René's uncle) 143-44
Challant, Jeanne de (René's aunt) 143
Challant, Louis de (René's grandfather) 53, 143, 151, 224n21
Challant, Louise de (René's aunt) 143
Challant, Philibert de (René's father) 53, 143-45, 170, 225
Challant, Philiberte de 61, 97, 115n27, 122-27, 122n75, 125n88, 126n90, 127n97, 132, 140, 146, 152, 156-57, 159, 163, 275, 300
Challant, Pierre de (son of Yblet) 144n22
Challant, René de
 administration of fiefs 164-65, 203-4, 206, 234, 242-44, 260-73, 275-77, 280-83, 297
 as ducal adviser 61, 63-66, 68, 80, 90, 97-98, 109-11, 116-17, 128, 134, 185, 204-5, 251-52, 259
 blood 141, 151, 298-99
 Church networks 196-98
 combourgeois of Berne 9, 54, 55n5, 259, 287
 commercial activity 117, 195, 199, 236, 243, 243n119
 death and funeral 129-30, 299
 debts 116n30, 124, 130, 171, 224-26, 229-30, 232-47, 262, 299-300
 diplomatic activity 61-68, 72-73, 78-80, 91-92, 95-96, 98, 102-3, 117-19, 128-29, 132-34, 185-86, 196, 208, 227-28, 230, 244, 260, 298
 fiefs in the Valle d'Aosta *see* Châtillon, Challant, Fénis, Issogne, Verrès, St. Marcel; also Valle d'Aosta – Challant fiefs in
 finance and brokerage 41, 55, 61-67, 89, 93-95, 101, 116n30, 145, 221-50, 258-59, 265, 296
 fiscal contributions of subjects *see* taxation
 French pressure on 82, 114-15, 240, 301
 genealogyM142-47
 heart 130, 130n114, 299
 historiography, biographers 17, 130-36, 140-41, 179-81, 211-12, 251-53, 288
 household management 122-27, 140-41, 150, 152, 161-65, 247
 imprisonment 55, 127-28, 141, 146, 152, 170-71, 179, 211

 information resources and challenges 87, 94, 98, 110, 112, 118, 153-54, 189, 191, 193-94, 196-97, 199, 206-11, 247, 258-59, 267, 271-73, 277-79, 283
 inheritance 13, 55, 117, 122, 126-28, 141, 146, 152, 160, 170-71, 179, 211, 252n6, 279, 287, 289, 298-99
 kin network 14, 134, 140-53, 167, 170, 185, 189, 196, 237n85, 252-53, 279, 287-89
 legal disputes 167-73, 293
 library 159-60
 lieutenant general 41, 90, 98, 109-14, 117-22, 117n44, 128, 162, 172, 180, 274n121, 301
 liminality 18, 91, 288-90
 marriages for him and his daughters 14, 41, 54-55, 54n3, 59-61, 118, 122-23, 125-26n88, 126-27, 126n92, 135, 140-42, 149-51, 226, 228, 252
 Marshal of Savoie 13, 41, 61, 63, 82, 90, 115n27, 117n44, 120-21, 128-29, 134, 161, 186, 189, 192, 213, 215, 239, 252n6, 274n121, 300-1
 pensions 54-55, 57, 94, 116, 187-88, 192-93, 213, 225, 228-29, 229n44, 230-31, 233-35, 233n68, 239, 242-46
 political networking, as patron and client 104, 110n5, 111-12, 116, 145, 171, 182-200, 238, 260
 potential competitor to House of Savoy 82, 98, 115, 118-19, 130, 133, 135-36, 179-81, 252
 relations with officers/servants 165-66, 172-73, 198-200, 203-5, 234, 244, 247, 264-65, 283
 relations with state officials 110-13, 171-72, 186-87, 189, 211-16, 232, 246
 religious devotion 73, 85-86, 135, 151, 159, 186
 reputation 59, 70n83, 72, 88, 88n70, 90, 95n124, 111, 118n48, 119-20, 126, 131-32, 141, 162, 172, 187-88, 231, 252n6, 281-82
 revenues 14, 57, 86, 116, 118, 205-6, 230, 238, 240, 242-43, 261-62, 264, 266-68, 270-71, 274-75, 280-81, 294, 296, 300
 taking possession of transalpine lands for Duke 120-22, 301-2
 testaments 56, 122, 126, 126n90, 146
 threatening behavior 118n48, 119-20, 135n143, 231
 transregional lord 13, 22, 25, 29-30, 40, 55, 68, 77, 83, 98, 104-5, 109, 112, 129, 173, 200, 216, 244, 251, 253, 287-89, 306
Challant, Yblet de 144n22
Challant-Aymavilles, Jacques de 13, 143
Challant-Fénis, Boniface II de 143
Challant-Fenis, Charles de (Lord of Villarsel) 63, 102n167, 103n169, 110, 144-46, 145n35, 150, 185, 191, 191n71, 229, 237n85, 258, 258-59n50

INDEX 315

Challant-Fénis, Claude de (son of Charles)   116n30, 144, 146
Challant-Fénis, François de (son of Charles)   144, 146
Challant-Fénis, Gaspard de (brother of Charles)   144, 150
Challant-Fénis, Georges de   144
Challant-Fénis, Georges de (son of Charles)   144, 146, 297
Challant-Fénis, Humbert de   144
Challant-Fénis, Jean de (son of Charles)   144, 146
Challant-Varey, Amédée   185
Challant-Varey, Anne Françoise de (daughter of Pierre)   145
Challant-Varey, Etienne-Philibert de (son of Pierre)   145, 171
Challant-Varey, Georges de   143, 145, 170
Challant-Varey, Jean de (son of Pierre)   151
Challant-Varey, Marguerite de   185
Challant-Varey, Pierre de   143, 145, 189
Challant-Verrès, François de (first count of Challant)   13, 143
Chambéry   60-61, 63, 65-66, 72-73, 79-82, 112n14, 120-21, 127, 129, 161-62, 168, 171-72, 182, 186, 189, 199, 215-16, 228, 232, 233n66, 281, 304
Chambéry, castle of   61, 121, 227, 302
    Sainte-Chapelle   121, 161
Chambéry, *Parlement* of   95, 121, 172, 199, 205
Chambrier, Pierre   99n147
Champdepraz   166
Champgny   279
Chandeleur, feast of (2 February)   279
Chandiou (Castellan)   157
Chaniples   257n43
Charlemagne   36
Charles II of Valois (Duke of Orléans)   102
Charles III   14, 27n72, 41, 53, 54n3, 55, 57, 60-66, 67n68, 68, 68n68, 71-73, 78-83, 87-88, 90-95, 91n90, 92n97, 96n132, 97, 109, 110n6, 111n9, 122-23, 123n77, 132, 134, 145, 151, 157, 166, 168-69, 172, 184-86, 192, 208, 210, 212, 214, 223n18, 225-27, 229-31, 233-34, 244n125, 275-76, 290, 293, 295-96, 298, 303-4
    death and funeral   109-10
    debts to Swiss   63-67, 72, 94, 226-27, 236n82
    relations with Swiss/Geneva   61-68, 73, 77-82, 90, 96
    treasury   109-13
Charles IX of France   128, 245-46
Charles V (Holy Roman Emperor)   32n100, 32n102, 55, 59, 62, 72, 77-78, 79n11, 82, 91-93, 92n97, 92n101, 92n103, 93n110, 94n112, 95nn118-19, 96-97, 96n131, 105, 110n6, 116, 123, 125n85, 126, 133, 191, 209-10, 210n175, 212, 230, 237n84, 238n95, 239-40, 239n101, 242, 244, 260, 267, 294, 296, 300-3

Châtelard, Lord of *see* Châtillon, Louis de
Châtel-St-Denis   144n24, 305
Châtillon   127, 127n97, 143, 150, 157, 159, 163-64, 199, 269, 271, 272n113, 273-75, 304
Châtillon, Louis de (Lord of Châtelard)   110, 112-14, 215n195
Chaumousey, monastery of   198
Chavoley/Chavelley, marsh of   211
cheese   21n33, 164, 206, 268, 274
Chesart   262-63
Chevallier, Jean   265n81
Chevron *see* Villette, Michel de
Chillon   65
Chittolini, Giorgio   24n55, 27
Chivasso   208, 278
Christine of Denmark   95n119
Christopher I, Margrave of Baden   89n83
Cicero   160
Claretta, Gaudenzio   134-35, 140, 180, 212
Clark, Matthew   254n24
Classen, Constance   292, 300n80
Claudine de Brosse (Duchess of Savoy)   227
Clauser, Conrad   233n69, 237n85
Clement VII, Pope (Giulio de' Medici)   196
Clerc *dit* Vulpe, Jean   86n59, 101, 234, 262
Clerc, Blaise   269, 273, 282
Clerc, Hugues   98n143
Clermont-Tallard, Louise de, (Countess of Tonnere, Countess of Valence, Lady of Crussol)   193
clothing   146n38, 149-50, 155-56, 193, 202, 232, 275
Cly   143, 152, 231
coats of arms   32n99, 123
Cocconato, Annibale di   128-29, 129n106
Coffranes   86
Cogne   277
coins (minting)   94n112, 104, 149, 230
Cole, Janie   181
Coligny d'Andelot, François de   117, 202, 239, 242
Coligny-le-Neuf   101, 211, 229-31, 269-70, 279, 293
Coligny-le-Vieux   279n150
Collier, Claude   88, 99-100, 104, 171, 171n188, 264n77
Collini (servant of Mencia)   155
Collot, Honoré *see* Lespal
Cologne   94
Colombier, Lord of *see* Watteville, Jean-Jacques de
Colonna, House of   125n85
combourgeoisie   62
commons   35, 254, 254n24, 262, 276
conciliarism   21
Conflans   270
Conseil des Commis   89, 98, 115, 119n51, 120, 135, 180, 184-85, 204, 215, 289
Contamine, Philippe   238, 238n90

Coolidge, Grace 160
Corbières 192
Cornellio (creditor of René) 232
Correr, Giovanni 179n2
Cortonay, Jehan de 68n68
Cortonay, Lord of 258
Cossé de Brissac, Charles de (marshal) 98, 113-14, 120, 131, 194, 238n94, 240-41, 240n104, 240n105, 241n108, 241n110, 243-44, 296, 299, 304
Costa d'Arignano, Giovanni Francesco 113-14, 118, 202, 204, 239, 252, 300
Cotta, Giovanni Battista 242n115
Counts Palatine of the Rhine 209, 243n118, 268
court of France 19, 64, 70-71, 78, 87-89, 94, 105, 117, 122, 188, 190-94, 209n167, 230n53, 233, 260, 267, 282, 303n94, 304
court of Savoy 14, 22, 27nn71-72, 40, 54, 60, 91n95, 93-94, 94n112, 97, 122, 129, 131, 154, 156, 185-86, 189, 197, 214-15, 235n76
courts (including Imperial court) 22, 24, 26, 28-29, 29n84, 33n105, 38, 38n137, 38n140, 94, 96, 96n128, 98, 116, 134, 147, 195-96, 200-1, 204, 209-10, 212, 223, 232, 234, 245, 254, 267, 270, 294-95, 298, 300
Crans 63
Cravotto, Martino 128n105
Crémieu 128
Crescentino 72, 228
Crescentino, Count of 229
Crete 30n90
Cronay 245n130
Crowston, Claire 222n5
Croÿ, Guillaume de (Marquis of Renty) 33, 37, 239
Croÿ, Nicolas de 195
Croÿ, Philippe III de (Duke of Aarschot) 239
cuckoldry 60, 132
Cudrefin 78, 80
Cugnier, André 262
Cuneo 110n5, 155, 189
Curbis, Gio Giacomo 187
Cusinens, Antoine de 202
Cypierre *see* Marcilly, Philibert de

DaCosta Kaufmann, Thomas 21-22
Dal Pozzo, Cassiano 93-94n111, 131n116
Damian, Peter 300-1n80
Damours, Henrys 200
Daugerant de Boisrigaut, Louis (French envoy to Swiss) 90-91, 260
Dauphiné 21n34, 36, 144, 260
Dauverd, Celine 26, 27n67
Davacz (smith) 278
Davalle, Ludovico 155
D'Avalos d'Aquino d'Aragona, Antonia (daughter of Alfonso) 123n78
D'Avalos d'Aquino, Francesco Ferdinando (Marquis of Pescara) 245

D'Avalos, Alfonso (Marquis Del Vasto) 92n103, 94n113, 95n122, 123n78
D'Avalos, House of 125n85
David, Jacques 236n83
De Antonio, Carlo 133, 180-81
De Clercq, Wim 30
De Gans 266n90, 268n96, 295n39
De Laudes (captain of Bard) 115, 186
De Riddes, Claudine 199
De Riddes, François 94, 193, 193n83, 198-99, 202, 209n167, 279, 300
De Sales, François 198
De Tillier, Jean-Baptiste 180, 183n26
debt (in general) 247
Del Vasto *see* Alfonso d'Avalos
Della Misericordia, Massimo 24n57, 289
Della Porta di Castellamonte, Fernando 198
Della Rovere di Vinovo, Stefano 246
Dell'Isola, Franco 186
Dell'Isola, Giovanni Battista 113-15, 119, 119n51, 133, 186, 204-5
Dell'Isola, Stefano 118
Delompnes (secretary) 214
Demade, Julien 39
Demolendino/De Molendino 79n8, 80n18
Deneen, Patrick 291
Denmark, Christine of (Duchess of Lorraine) 195, 243
Derouet, Bernard 152
Desportes, Guillaume 121
Di Negro, Negron 128n101
Diesbach family 116n30, 236n82
Diesbach, Felix de 236
Diesbach, Louis de 236
Dijon 192, 235n76
dining (meals, banquets) 57, 72n97, 89, 97n137, 154, 156-58, 257, 257n39, 162-64
diplomacy 60
dogs 147, 157, 165, 190, 232, 257n38, 267n95, 282
Dôle 271n112
Dombresson 85-86, 262
Donati, Claudio 26, 26nn63-64, 26n66, 27n71, 60n26
Donato, Giovanni 238
doors (thresholds) 35n121, 81, 113, 259, 276, 303-5, 300-1n80
Doria, House of 125n85
dowry 37n132, 54, 60-61, 123, 123n77, 143-45, 148-51, 153, 159, 201, 206, 221-22, 225-26, 234
drinking 87, 160, 190, 256-57
Du Bellay, Guillaume 95n119
Du Bois, Pierre 132
Du Val, Jacques 240n105
Duc, César 93, 93n109, 93n111
Ducrest, Pierre (secretary) 118n50, 126n92, 159, 163, 163nn144-45, 166, 198, 204-5, 215, 239, 244, 264, 271n112, 272, 274-75, 276n128, 298, 304

Dugnano, Raphael de   150
Dumolyn, Jan   30, 32n100
Dupuis (captain)   110n2
Durand (teacher at Verrès)   282
dynastic identity   18, 28-29, 39n144, 228, 252-53, 305
dynasticism, bodily aspects of   292, 299-300, 302, 306
dynasty/dynasticism   13-15, 22-23, 25, 25n59, 27, 27n67, 27n72, 29n84, 31, 33n105, 34, 37, 54, 62, 68, 90, 109, 111, 111n9, 133-35, 140, 153n80, 160, 167, 179, 201, 212, 224, 247, 251, 259, 282, 287-90, 306

Emanuel Filibert of Savoy   14, 25n59, 41, 61, 86, 97, 110, 110n6, 112, 114, 116-18, 120-21, 123, 125, 125n86, 127-31, 133n130, 134, 141, 159, 166-67, 171-72, 181, 185, 187-89, 187n43, 195, 202, 204-5, 209, 212, 238-42, 238n95, 241n107, 244, 244n125, 246, 252, 282, 288, 290, 296, 298, 300-2, 304
    accession   109, 168-69
    and Philiberte de Challant   126n90, 127, 300
    baptism   61
    conflict over lieutenant-generalship   118-20, 118n48, 162, 301
    Governor-General of the Netherlands   27, 103, 243-44, 243n121
    Imperial commander   27, 103, 237
    irritation with Imperial leaders   114n20, 116
    Prince of Piedmont   92, 96-98, 96n128, 215, 231, 305
    visit to the Valle d'Aosta   127, 157, 164, 297
England/English   30n90, 33, 35, 35n121, 36, 36n126, 38n137, 93n110, 113n16, 131, 161, 207, 207n162, 209-10, 238n95, 242, 254n24, 266, 304
Engollon   85, 262
Épinal   266
Erlach family   191
Erlach, Hans von   66, 225
Erlach, Rudolf von   82n32
Escott/Estott, Lady of   206, 206n154
estates assemblies   37n132
    of Neuchâtel   71, 88, 99n146, 103
    Sabaudian   64
    of the Valle d'Aosta   89-91, 96n130, 116, 118, 135, 180, 182-83, 215, 215n198, 270, 289n3, 298
Estavayer   297
Estavayer, Jean d'   78, 80
Este di San Martino family   26, 26n66
Este di San Martino, Carlo Emanuele di   26n66
Estouteville, Adrienne d'   206n154
Excofferi, Claude   173n196
execution   57, 93n109, 115, 226, 256n29, 263, 279, 293

Fabri, Giovanni   241, 299
fabric   121, 149, 155-56, 166, 266, 275, 302
Fagnano, Jeronimo   154-56, 196-97, 199, 232
Farel, Guillaume   85, 85n47
Farnese, House of   125n85
Fasano Guarini, Elena   24n55
Faucigny   90
Fauzone, Giovanni   183n25
Favre, Nicoline   184
Favre, Roz   94, 154, 183-84, 183n26, 199, 212-14, 226, 230n50, 271, 273
Federico II, Duke of Mantua   148, 148n51, 190
Felga, Guillaume   225
Felice (Friar)   199
Felix V, Pope (Amadeus VIII of Savoy)   21
Fénis (fief)   282
Fernandez de Cordoba, Gonzalo (Duke of Sessa)   166
Ferrara   125, 125n88
Ferraris, Augustin   196, 282
Ferrero di Candelo, Andrea   143, 150
Ferrero Fieschi, Filiberto (Marquis of Masserano)   150, 190
Ferrero, Bonifacio (Cardinal)   197
Ferrero, Filiberto (Bishop of Ivrea and Cardinal)   197
Ferrero, Sebastien (Bishop of Ivrea)   54n3, 155
Fers, Marguerite de   230n50, 298n64
Feste, Francoys   198
feudalism   14-15, 19, 23n49, 24-27, 26nn63-64, 26n66, 27n67, 31-32, 34, 37-38, 39n143, 40, 72-73, 123-24, 135, 182, 188, 194, 200-1, 206-7, 212, 229n43, 235, 251-55, 253n13, 254n23, 261-62, 271-72, 274-75, 287, 289
Fieschi family   26
Fillion, Jean   113
finance (*see also* Challant, René de – finance and brokerage)
    military   202, 223, 238, 278
    mortgages *see* Beaufremont – mortgage, Valangin – mortgage
Fitch, Nancy   254
Flanders   30-31, 34n94, 32n100, 81, 89, 94, 96-98, 105, 110, 116, 119, 152, 195, 202, 210, 230, 233, 244, 259, 265, 267, 288-89, 304
Florence   23, 266
Foldon, Pierre   157, 240n105
Fontaneto   158
Fontavel (treasurer)   157
food   72n97, 89, 97n137, 157, 162-66, 257, 257n38, 274
Fornari family   95n122
Fornaro (Spanish treasurer)   204
Fornaseri, Giovanni   40, 133-35, 134n137
Fossano, Antonio da   294-95
Frainel, Jean de (Abbot of Chaumousey)   198
France, Italian influence in   19-20
France, king of   32nn104-5, 33n108, 92n103, 131, 260, 287

Francesca (Portuguese Lady) 202n132
Franche-Comté 34, 64, 94, 94n112, 99, 105, 117, 194-95, 230, 235n76, 260, 263, 266, 271n112, 279, 290
Francis I of France 19, 29n84, 55-56, 60, 62, 78-80, 82, 89, 91, 93, 93n110, 95n119, 133-34, 139, 150, 181, 191-93, 202, 213, 229n44, 302
Franciscan convent in Aosta 159
Franconia 221, 255
Frankfurt 266
Frankish custom *see* law – customs
Franquemont, barony of 94, 94n112
Frassineto 149
Frederick II (Elector Palatine) 209
Fribourg 40, 55, 62-63, 64n56, 65-66, 65n91, 72n97, 78n5, 79, 81, 88, 97, 97n134, 99-100, 105, 117-19, 118n50, , 134n137, 144, 190-92, 224n21, 225, 227, 227n35, 229, 233, 235n76, 236n81, 258-59, 258-59n50, 297, 302, 305
Friedrich, Markus 207
Friuli 21n34, 37
Frutaz, François-Gabriel 96n128, 133, 141, 180, 223
Fugger family 210
furniture 121, 150, 166

gaigements 88-89
Galeanus de Grecia 160
Gamache, Eusèbe 150, 155, 197-98, 206, 226, 230n50, 268-69, 277-79
Gamache, Michel 245n128
Gamache, René 277, 295n39
Gamberini, Andrea 24n55
gambling 157, 157n107
Gaspardone family 59, 61, 141, 148, 148n51, 169-70, 226, 294
Gaspardone, Bianca Maria 54, 56-60, 131, 140-41, 146, 146n38, 148-50, 199, 277, 299
  inheritance 59-60, 131, 141, 150, 169-70, 170n174, 226-27
  wardrobe 149-50
Gaspardone, Giacomo/Jacobi 149
Gaspardone, Margarita 303
Gaul 180
Gautier d'Hostel, Pierre 102, 103n169, 123, 129, 129n108, 187, 198-99, 202, 232, 271, 281, 304
Gayanin 158
Gazino, Pietro 112, 166, 172, 240, 240n104
Geevers, Liesbeth 28
Gendreville 267-68
Generiis/Generys, Antoine de 157n109, 163n144, 269
Geneva 55, 62-68, 78-80, 103n172, 105, 128n102, 134, 191, 195, 264
Geneva, Bishop of 62, 73, 195, 198, 208
Geneva, cathedral canons of 62
Geneva, Lake of 61, 65, 129n109, 144, 191
Geneva, Sabaudian blockade of 77
Geneva, town council of 62, 66, 77
Genève-Lullin, Aymon de (Governor of Vaud) 63, 72, 78, 80, 82n32, 96n130, 96n132, 97, 134, 191, 210, 294
Genève-Lullin, François-Prosper de 202
Genevois 103, 198, 227
Genoa 15, 28, 30n90, 98, 113, 140n3
Gex 82n32, 131, 134n137
Ghignonis, Jehan Baptiste 240n105
Gichar/Guichard (René's servant) 154, 156, 156n100, 161-62, 210n175
gifts 64, 72-73, 72n97, 97n137, 151, 157, 190, 198-99, 202, 204, 232-33, 260
Gilley, Jean III de 94n112
Gilley, Nicolas de (Baron of Franquemont and Marnoz) 93-94, 94n112
Gingins 86
Gingins, Antoine de (Lord of Divonne) 144, 144n23
Gingins, Bonne de 144, 144n22
glass 84n39, 266
Glauser, Fritz 207-8
godparentage 161
Golye, Jaques 191
Gomez, Ruy 239
Gondi family 223
Gonzaga di Vescovato, Sigismondo 148
Gonzaga dynasty (Dukes of Mantua, Marquises of Monferrato) 14, 72, 148-49, 148n51, 299
Gonzaga, Federico II (Duke of Mantua) 72, 148, 148n51, 154, 190, 299
Gonzaga, Ferrante 96n132, 98, 112n13, 114, 114n20, 116, 203, 238n94, 239
Gonzaga, Guglielmo (Duke of Mantua and Marquis of Monferrato) 154, 241
Gorizia 7nn131-32
Goumoëns 83
grain, granary 67, 78-79, 86, 164-65, 232, 234, 243, 243n119, 265-68, 270, 274, 282
Graines 143, 197, 206, 244n125, 268-69
Grandis 96n130, 154, 157, 198-99, 259, 282
Grandson 245n130
Grand-St-Bernard pass 90, 196
Granier (Granyer), Bernardin de 63, 103, 155, 157, 193-94, 198, 210n175, 270, 280-81, 298
Granier, Claude de (Bishop of Geneva) 198
Granier, Jean 267
Grendi, Edoardo 15, 30n90, 39, 201, 223
Grenoble 115, 172
Grimaldi, Onorato I (Lord of Monaco) 211
Grivan, George 275
Grivonis, Jean (father and son) 271-73
Grivonis, Martin 275
Grotius, Hugo 85
Gruffydd, James ap 33
Grumelli, Guid'Antonio 245
Grumello, Antonio 56-57, 56n12, 57n16, 59
Gruyère 97n104, 144, 157, 206, 235
Gruyère, Françoise de 144
Gruyère, Jean II (Count of) 63, 64n54, 92n101, 191

Gruyère, Michel (Count of)   97n134, 147, 191-92, 191-92n71, 205, 258, 258-59n50
Guardapasso   149, 228, 231-32, 245
Guasco, Antonio   91n89
Guichenon, Samuel   134
Guillet, Jean   63-64, 63n43, 213-14
Guillet, Michel, co-Lord of Monthoux   62-63
Guise, Charles de (Cardinal of Lorraine)   101, 194
Guise, Claude de (Duke, also Duke of Aumale, died in 1550)   69, 89, 139, 181, 193, 195, 202, 260n56
Guise, Claude II de (Duke of Aumale in 1550)   101-2
Guise, François de   103
Guise, House of   34, 98, 181-82, 260, 260n56
Guise, Louis de (Cardinal)   117n42, 194
Guise, Marie de   71

Habsburg dynasty   25, 29n84, 31n94, 32, 32n102, 38, 131, 133n130, 158, 194, 196, 287, 289
hands   294-98, 301
harvests   67, 70n81, 235, 242, 261, 267, 274, 276
hay   163, 166, 274, 280
Hayhoe, Jeremy   167, 254n23
hemp   86, 266
Henry II of France   19, 29n84, 97, 97n134, 120, 115-17, 120, 235, 240
Henry IV of France   131
Henry VIII of England   33, 93n110
Hermont, Count   161
Hesdin, battle of (1553)   239
historical sources   40, 100, 104, 119n51, 133-34, 288
history
    comparative   15, 17, 28n78, 34, 41, 135, 201, 291
    global and transnational   14-17, 21, 28, 37, 201
Hobbes, Thomas   85
Hochberg, Jeanne de   68-71, 82, 85, 87, 91n93, 95, 99, 256, 292, 295, 302
Holdermeyer, Jost   55
Holland   31-32n99
Holy Roman Empire   24n52, 25n59, 26n66, 28n77, 29n84, 32, 37, 39n144, 94n112, 195
Holy Shroud   98, 114, 161, 292, 304
homogamy   39, 148
honor/dishonor   29n84, 38, 59-60, 65, 81, 88, 90, 93, 109, 110n6, 111-12, 114, 118-20, 119n54, 125n85, 128, 130, 132, 146, 150-51, 160-62, 172-73, 199, 209, 214, 223, 227, 229n43, 237-38, 242n112, 252, 301
horses   114, 156-58, 163, 165, 181-82, 184, 190, 191-92n71, 202, 262, 280, 305
hostage-taking (*Geiselschaft*)   65, 229n43, 236, 240, 265
Hoteman   206
Houston, R.A.   35

Howell, Martha   167
Hubodi   162
Huizinga, Johan   37n128
Humbert (cook)   163
Hungary   14
hunting   87, 147, 154, 157-58, 158n115, 161, 181, 190, 257, 257n38, 260, 267n95, 268n96, 282, 305-6
Hurville   267
hypogamy   147-48

Iberia   21n31, 196, 238
illness   94, 96, 129, 151, 158-59, 166, 189, 199, 203, 209n167, 233-34, 261, 277, 295, 300, 305
Imperial treasury   242
incest   263-64
infanticide   262-63
information   18, 41, 67, 87, 110, 129n108, 154, 189, 198-99, 200, 202, 206-11, 224, 247, 254n24, 258, 266-67, 271, 273, 279, 281, 283, 293
historiography   206-8
inheritance *see* kinship – inheritance
inns   72n97, 158, 211, 223, 259n52, 278
Innsbruck   208
invasion (of Italy by French in 1556)   117
invasion (of Sabaudian lands in 1536)   29n84, 41, 77-82, 90, 134, 144-45, 229, 276, 280, 290, 297
Inviziati, Margherita degli   150n60
Ireland/Irish   32n105, 35, 35n121, 38
iron   277
Isabella of Portugal   60
Isonzo valley   37n131
Issogne   115, 125, 150, 157, 159n109, 157n123, 160, 163-64, 163n144, 165n156, 166, 185, 234, 240, 255n125, 257, 269, 275, 290
Italian wars   15, 21, 28n77, 29, 55
Italy   14-15, 18-21, 21n31, 23-29, 23n45, 23n49, 24n52, 28n77, 31, 32-33n105, 33-34, 36n126, 37, 39-41, 61, 91, 93n110, 95, 95n119, 96n130, 96n132, 97-98, 103n170, 114, 116-19, 132, 136, 153, 173, 180, 189-90, 199, 203, 206, 209, 212, 224, 230, 239, 244, 246, 251
    political system   24-25, 24n55, 253, 253n13, 255, 257, 266, 287-90, 303, 306
Ivrea   57, 90-91, 93n111, 96-97, 146, 149, 163-64, 182, 213, 215, 239, 240n104, 275, 278-79
Ivrea, bishop of   54n3, 151, 155, 197

Jacques (muleteer)   199
Jacques, Guyot   199
Jacquier, Claude   113, 190, 226n30
James I of England   38n137
Jans, Antoine de   277
Jaques, Guyot (groom)   199
Jaquete (debtor of René)   226
Jehain, Jacques   263
Jehan (muleteer)   165

Jehan Jacques (servant of René) 189
Jerndorff, Alexander 254
jewelry 56, 59n21, 111-14, 111n9, 123n77, 125, 149-50, 167, 232
Joinville 195
Jordani, Annibale de 245n128
Jory (stable hand) 166
Jouvençan 270
Junod, Blaise 86n59, 203-5, 234, 245, 262, 296

Kantorowicz, Ernst 298
Kappel, second war of 84
Kellenbenz, Hermann 222n8
Kettering, Sharon 158n115, 161, 200
King of England *see* Philip of Spain
kinship 16-17, 33, 37n131, 39, 139-40, 153n80, 153n82, 181, 195, 222, 264, 291
    inheritance 36, 55, 79, 148n49, 152-53
    inheritance by females 153
kissing 292, 297-98

La Baume de Montfalconet, Philibert de 230
La Baume, Pierre de (Bishop of Geneva, Cardinal, and Archbishop of Besançon) 62, 195
La Chambre family 146, 211, 279
La Chambre, Aymon de 143
La Chambre, Jean de (Count) 146, 211
La Chambre, Marguerite de 54, 60, 143, 146, 155n94, 170
La Chambre, Mlle de 117n42
La Chambre, Péronne de 128
La Chambre-Sermoyé, Charles de 146, 211
La Chaulx, Lord of 202
La Chaux de Fonds 68, 87n61, 127n95, 261, 263
    preacher 236
La Creste, Nicolas 82, 91n92
La Croix (castle) 81
La Croix, Madame de 199
La Croix, Mlle de 154
La Cuiller 62, 66
La Doye (baker) 164
La Fontaine, Bernard de (secretary of René) 103n169, 163n144, 196, 206, 240, 267, 271-72, 271n112, 274, 282
La Forest de Feissons, Antoine de 244n123
La Forest, Benoît de 197
La Forest, Charles de 189
La Forest, Philibert de 197
La Manta castle (Saluzzo) 22n38
La Marck, Robert III de 237
La Marck, Robert IV de (Duke of Bouillon) 242n112
La Môle, Boniface de 129n106
La Palud, Françoise de 127m93
La Palud, Jean de (Count of Varax) 127, 127n93
La Palud, Marie de 126-28, 127n93, 159, 171
La Sagne/Saigne 72n93, 89n81, 260, 262
La Sarraz, Baron of *see* Mangerod, Michel
La Tour, Gabriel de 154, 157, 277

La Vulliermina, Marie de (daughter of Peronnette Mistralis) 183
Lalaing de Bugnicourt, Ponthus de 243n121
L'Aliod, Bartod 157
Lambert de La Croix, Pierre (President of the *Chambre des comptes* of Savoy) 68n68, 132, 189, 212-13
Lancelot of the Lake 160
Landeron 67-68n68, 258n45
Landoville 267
language, bodily *see* spatiality – language
Lannoy, Fernand de 127n93
L'Aubespine, Claude de 145, 194
L'Aubespine, François de 240n105
Lausanne 62, 64, 67-68, 81
Lausanne, bishop of *see* Montfalcon, Sébastien de
Lausanne, episcopal chapter 63
Lausanne, Treaty of (1564) 129n109, 134n137
law
    customs 31, 59, 70, 141, 144, 152-53, 152n75, 167-68, 222, 254n24, 258, 279, 282
    judicial institutions 63, 70, 95, 99n146, 101-3, 115, 121, 167-71, 169n173, 240n105, 254-58, 271n112, 281
    jurisdictional disputes 64n51, 68, 70-71, 88-89, 101-3
    legal books 160
    legal historiography 35-36, 35n121, 167-68
    property and patrimony 167
    religious conflict 84-85
Lazzarini, Isabella 24n55
Le Borgne (servant) 264
Le Bretton 158
Le Châtelard (near Montreux) 144n24
Le Froch 257n43
Le Galier 215
Le Locle 68, 71-72n93, 86, 86n59, 87n61, 89n81, 257n43, 260-62, 264
Le Meurier, Jehan 262
Le Roset 262
Lehfeldt, Elizabeth 160
Les Brenets 86, 260, 262
Lescha, Domenico/Domeyne 127n94, 159, 163, 245, 269, 273-75, 304
Leschaulx/Leschaux, Antoine de (Bailiff of Aosta) 115, 173n196, 273
Leschiel, Pierre de 143n18
Lesmecourt 267
Lespal (Philiberte's lover, perhaps the same as Honoré Collot) 125, 125n88
letters, blank and credential 117n44, 205-6, 208
Leynì *see* Provana di Leynì, Andrea
Leyva, Antonio de 82
Lhuillier, Odette 147
Liguria 27
Livy 160
Locarno (ducal treasurer) 110n2, 113-14, 213

INDEX 321

Locke, John 85
locks and keys 35n121, 303-5
lodging 55, 92, 97n137, 113, 154, 166, 194, 256
Lombardy 21n34, 22, 24n57, 27, 56, 59, 60n26, 78, 110n6, 119, 126, 153, 158, 180
Loranzè di San Martino, Carlo di 173n196, 269
lordship
    and local political, financial credit 38n140, 66-67, 81, 116, 222, 224, 228-33, 235, 240-43, 245, 302-3
    historiography 253-55
    rural 31n99, 87
    spatial significance (*see also* spatiality – politics) 28-29, 38-40, 60, 66, 68, 83, 87, 99-100, 124-25, 167, 211, 224, 241, 246-47, 255, 255n26, 257n43, 259, 267, 279, 283, 290, 292, 306
Lorraine, Antoine de (Duke) 95n119, 103, 139, 241, 243
Lorraine, Charles III (Duke) 266, 294
Lorraine, court of 19n20, 195, 234, 267
Lorraine, duchy of 13, 29n84, 30n90, 36, 37n128, 39, 61, 68, 84n39, 91, 97, 125, 136, 182, 194-95, 200-1, 216, 240, 246, 266, 288-89, 304
Lorraine, House of 33n108, 84n39, 95n119, 98, 195
Lorraine, Jean de (Cardinal) 95n119, 139, 181, 194
Lorraine, Nicolas de, Count of Vaudémont) 33n108, 84n39, 195, 239, 243, 243n117, 267, 268n96
Lorraine, treaty of 105
Lostan, Mathieu 93, 93n111, 154, 157, 190-91, 295
Lostan, René 154, 157, 163, 296
Louis XIII of France 84, 161
Louis XIV of France 36n127
Low Countries 20, 27-28, 30-31, 31n94, 33-34, 33n108, 36-38, 36n126, 37n132, 41, 91, 103, 182, 194, 198, 207, 237, 243n121, 244, 246
Loyse (baker) 164
Lucas (fiscal official) 157
Lucca 247n138
Lucerne 65n61, 80n22, 93, 93n106, 100, 225, 230n48, 233n69, 235, 235n79, 237n85, 239, 256, 266
Lucernolo, Geronime de 229n40
Lugnano, Rafaello da 200
Lullin *see* Genève-Lullin, Aymon de
Luxembourg, François II de 237n88
Luxembourg-Martigues, Sébastien de 237n88
Luynes, Duke of 161
Lynn, John 237n86
Lyon 91, 121n69, 128, 170, 192, 193n83, 210n175, 227-28, 239, 246, 266

Machiavelli 105
Madrid 140n3
Madruzzo, Charles Emanuel (Prince-Bishop of Trent) 125n88, 132
Madruzzo, Cristoforo (Cardinal Prince-Bishop of Trent) 124-26, 125n86, 126n90, 126n92, 179, 209
Madruzzo, Giovanni Federico 118, 124, 126-27, 126n92, 129-30, 129n107, 129n109, 166, 274-75, 297
Madruzzo, House of 125, 125n85, 127, 141, 179
Madruzzo, Ludovico (Cardinal Prince-Bishop of Trent) 126n92
Madruzzo, Niccolò 126, 126n92, 190n65
Madruzzo, Paolo 163, 241, 246n137, 269
Maggi, Cesare *see* Napoli, Cesare di
Magnyatz, Pierre 272
Mahuet family 29
Mahuet, Jean-François de 140
Maillard du Bouchet, Pierre 187, 202, 206, 238-39, 244n123
Maissen, Thomas 104
majority (adulthood) 144
Maleo, county of 123
Malines 208
Mallacourt 267
Malopera, Carlo 110n5, 190, 190n65
Malopera, Claudio 126n90, 126n92, 190
Malopera, Giorgio 190
Mandallaz, François de 65-66, 66n63
manganese mines 236, 236n83
Mangerod, Michel (Baron de La Sarraz) 65n58, 66, 71, 82n32
Mantua 154
Manuel I of Portugal 60, 151
marcher lords *see* nobility – marcher lords
Marcilly, Philibert de (Lord of Cypierre) 202
Mareschal, Jean 246, 246n135
Margaret of Austria (Duchess of Savoy) 94n112, 197n105, 227
Margaret of France (Duchess of Savoy) 97, 120, 133n130, 240, 246n135
Marie de Marc (baker) 164
Marini, Lino 214n194
Marini, Mirella 28
Marnix, Jean de 97n105
Marnoz *see* Gilley
marriage 25n59, 30-32, 32-33n105, 37, 37nn131-32, 38-39, 57, 60-61, 69, 71, 93n110, 95n119, 96n136, 120, 127n93, 133n130, 140, 143-45, 144n22, 147-48, 148n51, 151-54, 183-84, 202, 211, 222, 235n76, 239-40, 256, 263-64, 264n70, 276, 299
    clandestine 59-60, 140
    negotiations 60, 122-25, 148-49, 152
    spousal relationships 59, 131, 140-41, 147-51, 185-86
Marston, John 56n12
Martigues, Lord of *see* Luxembourg-Martigues, Sébastien de
Martine, François 87n61, 99, 101-3, 103n172, 186, 192, 195, 198, 203, 233n66, 234-36, 235n79, 236nn81-82, 256, 261-65, 262n63, 265n82, 281, 294, 296

Mary of Hungary   239
Masino *see* Valperga di Masino, Amedeo
masons   22, 278
Masserano   158, 190n64
Matafelon   213
Matile, George-Auguste   69, 71n92, 100n153, 104, 122n73, 223, 238, 241n110, 295
Maure/Mauro, Jehan/Giovanni Antonio   240, 242
Maurix (stable hand)   166
Maville, Jehan   192, 210n173
Meaux, circle of   281
Medici dynasty   27n72, 125n85, 201
Medici, Catherine de'   129n106, 193
Medici, Giuliano de'   238
medicine   159, 201
Mediterranean   14-15, 20n28, 21n31, 41, 105, 222
Medyo, Jo. Jacobo de   72nn94-95, 295n39
melancholy   132, 147
Meltinger family   65n61
Memoriale (anonymous author)   14
Mencia of Portugal-Braganza (Countess of Challant)   41, 60-61, 95, 97, 114, 119, 122-24, 126, 135, 141, 146n38, 151-52, 155-59, 163, 166, 186, 191, 191n71, 199, 206, 227, 231, 234, 236, 238-39, 260n54, 264, 300
   dowry   60, 151, 226, 228, 234
   political network   140, 154, 185, 189, 196, 198, 200-6, 238, 238n95, 299-300
   proxy for René   114-16, 116n30, 204-5, 239, 241
Mendoza, Jeronimo   276
Menthon de Rochefort, François de   185
Metz   105, 117, 147, 240
Michaud, Hugues (cameral official)   121, 187
microanalysis/singularity   15-18, 41, 291-92
Middle Kingdom   36, 41, 194, 289-90
Milan   22, 25n59, 30, 54, 56-58, 57n16, 79, 81, 92n103, 94-95, 94n113, 95n118, 95n122, 96n130, 98, 116-18, 125, 126n92, 140n3, 150, 154-56, 156n100, 161, 166, 190, 190n65, 200, 202, 206, 226, 226n30, 239-40, 242, 245-46, 266, 275, 277, 289, 301
Milan, dukes of   153, 153n80
Milan, Treasurer of   162, 204, 242, 293
Miles, Jean   170
Miolans   54n3, 170
Miolans, Claudine de   54n3
Miolans, Louis de   54n3
Mirecourt   268
Mistralis, Boniface   269
Mistralis, François   183n25
Mistralis, Panthaleon   183n25
Mistralis, Peronnette   183
Mistralis/Mistral, Philibert   155
mobility/transit   35, 37-38, 40, 61, 72, 88, 90-91, 94-98, 100, 117-19, 130, 157, 166-67, 233, 236, 247, 255, 264-66, 276, 287, 289-90, 304
Mombello, Carlo di (Count of Frossasco)   190

Monaco   92n97
Monaco, Lord of *see* Grimaldi, Onorato
Monahan, Greg   84
Moncalieri   158
Mondovì   214
Monferrato   13, 15, 40, 54, 56, 60-61, 68, 72, 72n94, 72n96, 95, 113, 123n77, 148-50, 154, 158, 169-70, 182, 189, 208-9, 214, 216, 226-28, 230n48, 231-33, 233n67, 245-47, 271n111, 276, 288-89, 303
Monferrato, Blanche of (Duchess of Savoy)   227
Monferrato, Senate of   169-70, 170n174
Monferrato, wars of   26n66
Montalto   241, 245n128, 278-79, 278n143
Montalto, Magherita   155
Montbasin (French Governor of Ivrea)   240n104, 278-79
Montbreton   144
Montchenu, Marin de   189
Monterminod, Lord of   121
Montfalcon, Sébastien de (Bishop of Lausanne)   64, 78, 80, 197
Monthey   191
Montjean de Beaupreau, René de (French governor of Turin)   93
Montjovet   90, 90n84, 94n113, 95, 118, 118n45, 163, 183, 214
Montmélian   128, 211
Montmorency, Anne de (Constable of France)   93, 95n119, 117n42, 193-94, 237, 242n112, 243n121
Montmorency, Louise de (Maréchalle of Châtillon)   101n159
Montpon *see* Richard de Montpon, Hugues
Montréal   213
Montrevel, Count of   281-82
Morges   62
Morgex   211
Morsel, Joseph   15
Morville   267
Moselle River   243n119
Moucher, Guillaume   260n57
Moudon   64
Mozzarelli, Cesare   26
Mudry   215
Mughal Empire   32n104
mules/muleteers   165-66, 199-200, 211, 226, 264, 305
Mülinen, Kaspar von   65n60
Munich   22
Munn, Nancy   38
murder/assassination   57, 70-71, 93, 96n130, 131, 158, 255-56, 256n29, 262-63, 278-79
Musinens, Lord of   184
mutiny   92, 235n80

Naegli, Hans Franz   78
Naegli/Nägeli, Sebastian   236

Nancy 195, 266
Naples 24n53, 26n64, 27, 33, 153
Napoli, Cesare di (Cesare Maggi/Mayo) 236-37, 237n84
Narbonne 91
Nassau dynasty 32
Nassiet, Michel 16n8, 39, 255
natural prince 117n40, 121
Navarre, Marguerite de 281
Navarrin, Baptiste 171
neighborliness 63, 71n91, 73, 89, 96, 101-2, 117, 169, 180, 261n62, 264, 292, 302-3
Neuchâtel 69-71, 78, 85, 88-89, 99-102, 103n169, 105, 193, 243, 245, 256-58, 256n31, 263
   castle of 69
   collegial church 258
   estates *see* estates – Neuchâtel
   governor of 69, 87, 101-3, 103n169, 184, 228, 260
   mayor of 70
   town council 100, 235n79, 236
Neuchâtel, canton of 69, 104
Neuchatel, counts of 41, 68-70, 83, 87, 101-4, 255-56, 260
Neuchâtel, lake of 61
Neuchâtel-Vaumarcus, Anne de 256
Neuchâtel-Vaumarcus, house of 256n33
Neuchâtel-Vaumarcus, Isabelle de (wife of Prangins) 147, 184-85, 256, 302
Neuchâtel-Vaumarcus, Jean III de 89n81
Neuchâtel-Vaumarcus, Lancelot de (bishop of Basel?) 89n81, 102
Neufchâteau 266
neutrality 55, 80, 91, 98, 114-15, 115n25, 117, 120, 133n130, 205, 215, 241, 276, 304
Nice 87-88, 90-93, 91n90, 91nn95-96, 93n110, 93-94n111, 95n122, 113, 115, 121, 121n69, 127, 133, 139, 143, 154-55, 210-11, 213, 292
Nice, castle of 92, 92n97, 110n6, 133, 302
Nice, truce of 92
Nicollet de Lensigne, Jacques 73n99
Nizza Monferrato 150
nobility
   levels of 30, 34
   as a spatially rooted category 292
   chivalry 24-25n57, 29, 29n84, 238, 289
   correspondence 148, 148n49
   European 15, 27-31, 238n94
   family history 29-30, 125n88, 132
   female networks 28, 152n73, 200-1, 156, 160, 189, 200-6, 257, 257n39
   finance 154-56, 221-23
   historiography 16, 18, 25-34
   Italian 26-28, 60n26, 189-90, 238n94
   legal resources 167-68, 170, 170n177, 207, 262-64, 281
   marcher lords 18, 29, 31-34, 36-37, 37n128, 37nn130-132, 60, 87, 94, 94n112, 136, 251, 283, 290

masculinity 27, 57, 60, 160-61
military activity 29nn83-84, 32-33n105, 90, 92, 132, 134, 160-61
patron-client relations 30, 181-82
political autonomy 18-19, 31-34, 31-32n100, 41, 122, 135-36, 255, 291
relations with bourgeois elites 24, 29-31, 29n84, 34, 148-49, 169-72, 184, 223, 266, 289
response to invasion 80-81, 82n32, 91n96, 117, 144, 261
rural 26, 27n67, 152
Sabaudian 27, 57, 61-62, 82n32, 91n96, 92, 128, 184, 288-89
social interactions among 128-29, 153-67, 256-57
transregional 33
urban *see* urban patricians
North Sea 266
Notre Dame (cathedral of, Aosta) 130, 159, 170, 299
Notre Dame (church of, Bourg-en-Bresse) 130
Novara 119, 127, 166, 186, 244, 301
Nus family 184

oaths 69, 71, 71n92, 79, 81, 87, 103-4, 110n5, 117n44, 121, 184, 264, 295
Occimiano 149
Oddinet de Montfort, Louis 129
Olgiato, Alessandro 156
Orléans 57
Orléans, duke of *see* Charles II of Valois
Orléans-Longueville dynasty 68-70, 98, 100n153, 101n158, 102-4, 191, 302
Orléans-Longueville, François (marquis of Rothelin) 69, 85, 101-2
Orléans-Longueville, François III d' 69, 101-2, 256
Orléans-Longueville, Leonor d' 69
Orléans-Longueville, Louis d' 68-69
Orléans-Longueville, Louis II d' 69, 71, 83, 297
Orvieto 95n118
Ottoman Empire 14, 95n123

Pacher, Michael 20
Pagnano (Madruzzo agent) 125nn86-87
Painter, William 56n12, 131
Palazzo Canavese 163
Paleologue dynasty 72, 148n51
Paleologue, Guglielmo IX (Marquis of Monferrato) 148n51
Paleologue, Maria 148n51
Pallavicino family 26
paper 163, 192, 266
Paré, Ambroise 237n88
Paris 33n108, 120, 132, 153, 192-94, 198-99, 208, 210, 239-40, 265-67, 276, 276n128, 288
Passerin d'Entrèves, Giulio Romero 160n124
Pattoulles (banker in Paris) 210

Paul III, Pope (Alessandro Farnese)   91-92, 93n110, 133, 190n64
Pavia   55-57, 93n108, 95n119, 120, 128n105, 150, 190, 190n65, 192, 196, 210n175, 223, 225-26, 235n76, 237-38, 237n87, 265, 277, 301
Pavillard, Christophe   63
Payerne   61, 63
Payerne, conference of   67, 67-68n68, 132-33, 134n137
Perrenot de Granvelle, Antoine   34, 114n20, 126n92, 239
Perrenot de Granvelle, Marguerite   96n131
Perrenot de Granvelle, Nicolas   95, 196
Perrenot, Thomas   196
Perret, Étienne   156, 243n119, 243n121
Perret, Pierre   264
Perruchon   211, 264
Pescara, Marquis of *see* D'Avalos d'Aquino, Francesco Ferdinando
Petit Jehan (servant of René and Mencia)   166
Petit-St-Bernard pass   54n3, 90
Petrarch   160
Pfandschaften   221
Pfyffer family   93n106
Philip II of Spain (and King of England)   32n102, 98, 120, 206, 238n95, 242, 244
Picardy   237
Piedmont   27, 36, 41, 53, 68, 72, 78, 82, 86, 91, 95, 95n122, 97-98, 110, 118-22, 121n69, 128, 134, 156, 158, 162, 182, 189-90, 194, 204, 212, 214, 216, 228, 230, 236, 237n84, 238, 259, 278, 288, 301
    historians from   179, 212
    Senate   168, 168n168
Pierre (servant of Mencia)   166
Pigniere, Bonne   171
Pignillion, Lord of   256n31
Pin   257n43
Pinerolo   150
Piobesi, Ayme de   80n21
Pisseleu, Anne de (Duchess of Étampes)   202
Plague   245, 246n135, 261
Plancy (French secretary)   133
Po River   26, 72, 113
poisoning   188n171
political formations
    composite polities   32n102, 38n140
    ecosystemic perspective   24-25, 290-91
    small states   16, 24, 29n84, 38
political networks   179-206
    multiple service   29-30, 32-34, 33n108, 33n110, 37-38, 37nn130-32, 55
political personhood
    and territorial control   300-2
    bodily aspects   298-300, 305-6
    debt   247n139, 299-300
Poncet (debtor of René)   226
Pontbriand, Antoinette de   189
Porporato, Giovanni Francesco   170n177

Portugal   206, 243n119, 300
Portugal-Braganza, Diniz of (Count of Lemos)   60
Portugal-Braganza, Fernando Ruiz (Count of Lemos and Marquis of Sarria, Mencia's brother)   202n132, 238n95
postal service   191, 207-8
Praborno   290
Prak, Maarten   36n126, 255n26
Prangins *see* Rive, Georges de; for his wife see Neuchatel-Vaumarcus, Isabelle de
Praroman (*avoyer* of Fribourg)   258n50
Prat, Antoine   92n103
prisoner exchange   116-17, 204, 237-39, 239n101, 242n113
procurator general, office of   272-73
Provana di Leynì, Andrea   114, 115n27, 120
Provence   36, 82
proxemics   292, 297, 303, 303n94
psychomotility   292

Quart   183, 213
Quincinetto/Quincenay   95, 226, 241
Quintilian   160
Quisard, Urbain (Lord of Crans)   191

Rabelais, François   247
ransoms   41, 55-56, 113-14, 116-17, 132, 141, 150-51, 156, 194, 226, 237-44, 265, 304
    historiography   237-38
Raphaello (correspondent of Castellan of Bard)   169, 225n27
Ray, Claude de   195
Réal, Jean   117n41
reconnaissances   182, 197, 206, 271-73, 281-83
Reformation   22n39, 40, 62-65, 70
    bi-confessionalism   83-85, 87
    nobility   84-87, 84n39
    pastors   86-87, 236, 264
    rural   65, 83-86
Regard (secretary)   216
Regensburg   210
Regis, Vincent   183
Reiffemberg, Colonel   243n118
relics (*see also* Holy Shroud)   292
Remiremont   266
Remond, Panthaleon de (son of Loys)   275
Renaissance
    Alpine   19-23, 40
    historiography   14-15, 18-28, 32, 34
    northern   18-21, 25, 27
    periodization   21-22
    political culture   21, 23-26, 291-92
    René as emblematic of forgotten dimension   28, 34, 39-40, 224, 287, 289
    urban vs. rural   14, 19-20, 23, 26nn63-64, 27n67, 34, 40
Renard, Simon   117, 194
Renty, battle of   (1554) 238

republicanism/republics   14, 22-24, 26, 32-33n105, 128n102, 194, 222
revenues, ecclesiastical   63n43, 70, 86-87, 99, 188, 195-96, 191, 233, 274, 276, 282, 294
revolt, civil unrest (*see also* mutiny)   85, 90n84, 120, 235n80, 276
Reymond, Jehan de (stable hand)   166
Reynods, Susan   253
Rhineland   194, 243n118
Rhône River   36n126, 121, 191, 279
Ricarand family   182-93
Ricarand, Bernard   83
Ricarand, Bernardin   183
Ricarand, François   183
Ricarand, Giovanni Giacomo   183n25
Ricarand, Jean   182
Ricarand, Pierre   183
Ricarand/Riquering, Jean Bartholomé   182
Richard de Montpon, Hugues   186-87, 187n43, 203-4
Ricotti, Ercole   133, 212
Risorgimento   212, 288
Rive, Georges de (Lord of Prangins)   69, 70n85, 71n91, 87-89, 91, 99, 101-2, 103n169, 147, 185, 228, 256-58, 256n29, 257nn38-39, 257n43, 260-62, 293-94, 297, 302
Robertello da Udine, Francesco   125n85
Robin, Jehan   116, 236, 205, 234, 245n130, 264
Roero di Ceresole, Garcilasco   246
Roero/Royer, Elena   150
Roero/Royer, Giovanni Battista   150
Rohan, Alan VIII (Viscount)   255
Rohan-Gié, Jacqueline de   102
Rolin, Grat   170, 198-200, 211, 233, 269-70, 271n111, 277, 293
Romanov dynasty   32-33n105
Rome   20n28, 21, 27n71, 95n118, 180-81, 186, 190, 197, 276, 278, 282
Romeyran, hospital of   274
Romont   64, 82n32, 144, 197, 200, 258-59n50, 305
  collegial church   197
Root, Hilton   254n23
Rosey, Aymé du   191
Rossel, Louis   245
Rossel, Pierre   245, 245n130
Roussillon   245n130
Roveryr, Jean   271
Rua, Bassan   118n45
Rua, Jchan de   155
Ruggiero, Guido   20n24, 20n28, 21
Rumilly   80
Rundig, Ludwig   229n40
Rye, Claude de (Countess of Varax)   127, 127n93, 171

Sabaudian lands   13, 15, 17, 19, 21, 21n31, 21n34, 36, 40-41, 55, 61, 66, 77, 79, 81-82, 90, 95-98, 105, 109, 112, 118-20, 128-29, 128n102, 131, 157, 171, 179-80, 182, 188, 196, 214n194, 229, 240, 251, 260-61, 288-90, 297, 301
  uniqueness in Italy   27, 27n71, 27n74, 34

Chambre des comptes   68n68, 81, 110n5, 111, 186, 189, 210, 212, 215, 245, 265n78, 295
chancery   111
ducal council   110, 110n2, 112, 115, 121, 144n23, 168, 172, 187, 200, 215-16, 301
judicial system   168, 168n168, 281
transalpine   13, 97, 120, 121 n. 69, 127, 182, 188-89, 211, 288, 301
Sabaudian state finance   223-24
Sabaudian Studies   20
saddler   244n126
safe-conducts/passports   35, 80, 112n13, 243n119, 259, 304
Sagisser, Baltasar   93n106
Salins   260
Salm, Jean VII (Count of)   147, 202, 234n71
salt   149, 163, 190, 260
Saluzzo   22n38, 290
Saluzzo, Gian Gabriele (Marquis of)   72n94, 202
Saluzzo, Pietro di (Apostolic Notary)   169n173
Salzburg   21n34
San Giorgio, Benvenuto (Count of)   169n173
San Salvatore   149, 170, 241
San Stefano (farm near Pinerolo)   150
Sandberg, Brian   29n83, 84n40, 181
Sanseverino di Caiazzo, Roberto   57
Sanseverino, Archbishop of   190
Santa Croce of Casale, convent of   149n56
Santhià   112, 230-31, 233, 240, 242
Santhusen, Jean Guillaume (Captain of Beaufremont)   234, 240n105, 243, 243nn117-18, 267-68, 267n95, 304
Sappin, Aynard   155, 198
Sariod de la Tour family   184
Sariod d'Introd family   184
Sarpol, Bernard   246
Saugey/Sougey, Pierre   199, 228, 232, 232n63
Savagnier   70, 86, 262
Savoia-Racconigi, Bernardino I of   146n38
Savoie   13-14, 40-41, 54n3, 61, 72, 79-80, 117n44, 120-21, 128, 170, 185-86, 189, 215-16, 227, 252n6, 259, 301
  Senate of   121, 171, 216
Savoie, Jeanne de (Countess of Vaudémont)   239, 243, 243n117, 294
Savoie, Louise de   55, 79, 201, 237n87, 281
Savoie, Madeleine de   162
Savoie, Marie de   68
Savoie, Philiberte de (Duchess of Nemours)   121, 206, 281, 302
Savoie, René de   54n3
Savoie-Nemours, Jacques de   198, 210n175, 239, 243n117
Savoie-Nemours, Philippe de   55, 63, 73, 151
Savoie-Villars, Honorat II de   194
Savona   197
Savoy, Adriano Giovanni Amedeo of   146
Savoy, Duke of   19, 26-27, 53, 61-62, 68, 128, 130, 132, 135, 143, 180, 183, 186-87, 189-91, 208, 210, 224, 247, 252, 259, 259n50, 272, 287-88

Savoy, House of   13, 15, 19, 25n59, 27n72, 53-55, 62, 65, 72, 77, 103, 133n130, 134-36, 141, 149, 180-81, 189, 212, 224-25, 232, 244n125, 251-52, 283, 287-89, 292, 305-6
Savoyards   66, 78, 80, 86, 128, 162, 185, 189, 202, 214, 214n194, 264, 304
Savyoz, Francoys   200n119
scale of analysis   16-17, 35n121
Schall, James   291
Schetz, Gaspard   195, 243n119, 243n121
Schleiff, Hentzman   93n106
Schmalkaldic War   96
Schmitziger, Jeronimus   93n106
Schwarzburg-Rudolstadt, Aemilia Juliana of   201
Schwyz   80n22
Scotland/Scots   35, 35n121, 38n137
Scott, Hamish   36
Scott, Tom   194
Segre, Arturo   113n16, 120n59, 126n90, 135, 180
Seisenegger, Jakob   124
Sessa, Duke of (see also Fernandez de Cordoba)   166
Setours, Lord of   230n53
Settimalier/Santimachre, Hans   227
Settimo Vittone   94-95, 182-83, 241, 293
Sevilla-Buitrago, Alvaro   35
Seyon (creek)   85, 262
Sforza, House of   125n85
Shaw, Christine   27-28, 28n77
Sheehan, James   35
Sicily   23, 140n3
Silly de La Roche Guyon, Louis de   238
Simplon pass   118
Sion   118
Sion – episcopal court   173
Sion, Bishop of   89
Slack, Paul   207n162
Smail, Daniel   247n138
Soen, Violet   34, 37, 37n130
soldiers, depredations by   55, 66, 78-79, 90, 90n84, 114, 226, 276, 279
Soleure/Solothurn   192, 210, 229n40, 235n79, 257
Sonnenmeyer, Wendell   225, 225n26
Sovereignty   16, 18-19, 25n59, 31, 32n100, 32-33n105, 34-35, 40, 68-69, 99, 101-5, 101n158, 109, 121, 130, 180, 184, 188, 207, 212, 223, 253, 255-56, 260-61, 287-88, 295, 306
   signs of   71, 101-2, 104, 295
Spain   20n27, 26n66, 27-28, 28n77, 57, 88, 98, 195, 206, 230
Spain, court of   196, 296
spatial history, historiography   35-36
spatiality   17, 35-40, 35n119
   and liberalism   291-92
   financial aspects   64-65, 73, 213, 224-25, 237, 239, 244, 246-47
   historical geography   36, 36n126
   language   292-305
   noble identity   29, 37-40, 288, 292, 301-2
   politics (see also lordship – spatial significance)   14, 18, 35, 54n3, 55, 64, 91, 97, 97n134, 105, 135-36, 194-95, 253, 259, 283, 287-88, 304-6
   the body and political personhood (see also political personhood – bodily aspects)   38-39, 130, 290-303, 298n62, 300-1n80, 305-6
Speciano, Giovanni Battista   95n122, 161-62
Speyer   94, 209
Spinola Carretto, Benedetta   197
Spinola, Agostino (Cardinal)   197
St. André de Bellentre, priory of   145
St. Bernard de Montjoux, hospice of   118n50, 196-97, 203
St. Catherine, monastery of (Aosta)   143
St. Gilles, priory of   143, 152n71, 196, 198, 282
St. Gilles, Provost of   143, 145, 151, 157, 159, 180, 277, 282
St. John the Baptist, knights of (Beaufremont)   268
St. Julien   79
St. Julien, peace of   66-67
St. Marcel   143-44, 146, 150, 172, 173n196, 236, 236n83, 241, 269, 276-77
St. Martin de Graines   197
St. Martin, feast of (11 November)   265
St. Martin, parish of   70, 262-63, 294
St. Maurice d'Agaune, Abbot of   170, 197, 265
St. Maurice d'Agaune, monastery of   197
St. Maurizio   149
St. Michel, feast of (29 December)   281
St. Miguel, Sebastiano   110n2
St. Ours   143, 170
St. Pierre family   184
St. Pierre, Guilliermine   184
St. Pierre, Jacques de   184
St. Pol, Lords of   195
St. Quentin   118, 237
St. Rémy, feast of   292
St. Sulpice, abbey of   280-81
St. Theodule, Mass of   274
St. Vincent   183
Stainville family   33n108, 147n46
Stainville, Louis de (Seneschal of Barrois)   147
Steiger, Hans (treasurer)   192, 236, 236n82
stoicism   29n84, 73, 141, 151, 234
Strasbourg   195, 266
strategy (as an object of historical inquiry)   16n8, 36n124, 148n49, 222, 252-53
Stroppiana, Giovanni Francesco   96n132, 209-10
Styria   21n34
subjects
   political action   38, 82, 85-86, 88, 90, 90n84, 92-93, 255n25, 270, 276, 280-82, 293, 298, 303

INDEX 327

poverty 110, 159, 165, 203, 255, 264, 268, 270, 282, 294
public opinion 80n17, 89-90, 96, 112, 114-15, 235, 235n80, 252n6, 262, 264, 270-71, 279
Swiss cantons 19, 21n34, 22, 28, 36, 41, 55, 61-69, 71, 72n97, 77-80, 82-84, 86, 89-91, 95, 97n137, 98-99, 102, 102n168, 105, 114-15, 117-19, 128-29, 128n102, 132-34, 145, 170, 179, 182, 186, 189-92, 194, 208, 216, 229n43, 260-61, 287-90
   financial interactions with René 19, 40-41, 55, 72, 94, 224-28, 230-33, 235-36, 236n82, 237n85, 244n125, 246, 296
   support for René at French court 187-88
Swiss Diet 97n134, 98, 188, 260
Swiss Germans 104-5

Taieb, Paulette 160n124
Tarentaise 82, 90, 145
taxation 88, 98-99, 112, 213, 222, 254n20, 261-62, 266, 270, 274, 294
Ternavasso 150
Ternier 134n137, 227n36
Théodule Pass 289-90
Thérouanne 237n88
Thierry, Pierre 266
Thonon 73, 203
Ticino 22
Tissotte, André 268
Tissotte, Jehanne 268
Toledo 196
Tollein, Guillaume 198
Tollein/Tolleni (officer in Savoie) 157n106
Tornielli, Giuseppe 127
Torny-le-Grand 144n24
touching 292-94, 297-98, 298n62, 300, 304
Toul 125n88
Toul, diocese of 105, 240
Toulouse 232
Tournon, François de (cardinal) 91n92, 193
transregional patronage *see* political networks
   – multiple service
transregionality/transregional approach 12-15, 17, 19, 24-28, 34, 41, 61, 100, 143, 182
Trent/Trentino 22n38, 96, 132, 275
Trent, Council of 84-85
Trino 72
Tripet, Pernet 263
Trivulzio family 123, 153
Trivulzio, Gian Giacomo 123, 123n78
Trivulzio, Gianfrancesco (Marquis of Vigevano) 123n76
Trivulzio, Giovanni Niccolò (Marquis of Vigevano) 123n76
Trolliet, Christophe 99, 101, 166, 203, 242, 244, 261, 264-65, 265n78
Tuck, Richard 306
Turin 22, 27n71, 81, 91-93, 93n109, 114-15, 128n105, 131, 134, 168, 189, 223n18, 226, 239, 240n105, 278-79, 289

Turin, *Parlement* of 115, 245n128
Turrillia 163
Tyrol 20, 21n34

Uginet, François-Charles 134, 251-53
unicorn horn 111, 114
United Provinces 84n42
Unterwald 80n22
urban patricians (*see also* bankers; nobility
   – relations with bourgeois elites) 19, 24, 28, 30-31, 31n94, 34, 40, 54-55, 77, 88, 100, 105, 148-49, 195, 222-25, 227, 229, 229n40, 230n48, 233, 235-36, 235n79, 236nn81-82, 237n85, 243n121, 245, 247, 256, 258-59, 259n52
Uri 80n22
Ussel 143, 146, 150, 241, 269, 274n121, 277

Vaccarone, Luigi 141
Vagnone, Paolo 93-94n111
Val d'Ayas 278
Val de Ruz/Valderuz 71-72n93, 101, 260-61
Val de Travers 257n38
Val de Travers, Castellan of 89n80
Valais 79, 89, 97, 105, 115, 117, 196-97, 290
Valangin 13, 19, 40-41, 55, 55n5, 61, 63, 65, 67-73, 89, 91-92, 94-105, 118, 122, 127, 134, 147, 150, 158, 162n138, 190-92, 199, 205, 210, 216, 238, 245, 265, 267, 274n121, 277, 281, 288, 290, 297, 302, 304-5
   administration of lordship 203, 225, 233-35, 244-45, 261-64
   boundaries 71-72n93
   building projects 203
   collegial church 86, 159, 171n188, 258
   conflicts with Boudevilliers 85, 88, 99
   conflicts with Neuchâtelois and their counts 70, 88-89, 103-4, 170, 191, 193, 260
   districts 260-61
   judicial system 71, 101-2, 255-58, 262-64
   mortgage of 116, 225, 228, 230n48, 232-33, 235, 235n79, 236n82, 241-42, 241n110, 246, 255-65
   officers of 63, 86-88, 101, 103n169, 154, 158, 166, 171n188, 203, 234-35, 244, 256, 261-62, 264-65, 296-97
   Reformation 73, 78, 83, 85-87, 85n46, 135, 293
   sale of rights 99-101, 295
Valangin, Claude de (bastard) 197
Valenciennes 244n123
Valentino, castle of 114, 296
Valle d'Aosta 13-14, 17, 19, 40-41, 53, 54n3, 56, 61, 68, 72, 82, 88, 91-92, 94-98, 100, 112, 112n13, 114-18, 120, 122, 127, 130, 132, 135, 141, 145, 151-52, 159, 160n124, 164, 179-85, 189-90, 196-97, 204-5, 213, 215-16, 215n196, 233n66, 236, 245, 256, 259, 264, 264n77, 266, 276, 287-90, 293, 297-98, 301, 303-5

Challant fiefs in   13, 40, 54-55, 61, 122, 135,
    144-45, 172, 203, 205, 226, 235, 243-46,
    259, 268, 271-72, 274, 276-77
  defense of   72, 79, 81-82, 87, 89-90, 94,
    94n113, 114-15, 115n25, 118, 133, 141, 204,
    212, 239, 259, 289n3
  Governor   90, 252, 252n6, 270
  nobles   143, 153-58, 160n124, 162, 182-85,
    270, 302
  public finance   89, 116, 118, 179, 215, 270
  regional identity   135, 180
Valle, Pietro de   238
Vallesa, Antoine de   156
Vallesa, François de   270n106
Vallesa, Ludovico/Louis de   154, 170, 233, 271,
  276-77, 282
Vallesa, Marguerite de   156
Vallesa/Vallaise family   184, 226
Valois, Elisabeth de (Queen of Spain)   120
Valperga di Masino, Amedeo   91, 91n95, 114,
  118-20, 120n59, 121n69, 122, 127, 162, 180,
  187n43, 212, 301
Valperga di Masino, Ardizzino   56-57, 131
Valperga di Masino, Tommaso   113n16
Valperga di Villars, Claudia   246
Valperga di Villars, Filippo   246
Valromey   213
Valtournenche   290
Van Brederode, Reinoud   31-32n100
Van Schoonbeke, Gilbert   243n119
Van Steensel, Arie   31, 39n143
Varallo (Sacro Monte of)   22n38
Varax, county of   274n121
Varey   61, 143, 145, 171, 246
Vasa dynasty   33n105
Vaucelles, treaty of (1555)   237, 241
Vaud   61-64, 64n56, 66-67, 78-83, 78n5, 104, 117,
  133-34, 134n137, 144, 170, 190, 197, 202, 205,
  256n33, 258n50, 259, 261
Vaudagne, Jean de   163
Vaudan, Aymon   269
Vaudan, Bonaventure   244n125, 269, 277
Vaudan, Jean François   96n130, 154, 184, 293
Vaudan, Nycoline/Nicoline (née Favre)   154, 184
Vaudan, Panthaleon   156
Vaudémont, Count of see Lorraine, Nicolas de
Vaumarcus, Lord of   103, 103n172, 147
Veigie, Claude de   95n120
Veillet, Aubert   110n2, 112, 112n14, 171-73, 182, 187
Venice/Venetian   14, 23, 30n90, 37, 37n132,
  113n16, 125, 126n90, 126n92, 128, 131, 140n3,
  190
Vercel   257n43, 271n112
Vercelli   41, 82n32, 90n84, 91, 95-96, 95n122,
  98, 100, 109-10, 110n2, 110n6, 112-13, 117-20,
  126-27, 156-57, 166, 187, 202, 210, 213, 215, 226,
  226n30, 232, 236, 238, 240, 244n126, 275,
  289, 296
  French attack on   111n8, 113-14, 132, 204, 301

Vercellon, Michel   198, 269
Verdun   105
Vergy, Antoine de (Archbishop of
  Besançon)   147n43
Vergy, Elene/Eqeme de   147n43
Vergy, François de (Count of Champlitte)   147
Vergy, Guillemette de   54, 69-70, 85, 94, 144,
  146-47, 150, 191, 200, 225, 257, 257n43, 259,
  265, 267, 293-94
Vergy, Marguerite de   191
Vergy, Pauline de   147n43
Vergy, Rose de   147
Verney, Jean   268-69, 281
Verolengo   149, 227n32, 241, 245n128, 274, 277
Verona   265
Verrès   90, 115, 143, 157, 159, 196, 211, 214, 269,
  273-74, 274n121, 277, 282, 301
Verrès, Captain of   157, 273, 278, 282
Verrua   113
Vescovi, Vigilio   125n88, 132, 132n121, 140,
  152n72
Vespolate   244
Vialardi di Sandigliano, Tomaso   125n88,
  126n90, 241n110
Vichard, Tomaso   273
Vieilleville (François de Scépeaux, Marshal
  of)   117n39
Vienna   38n140
Villargiroud   144n24
Villarsel (fief; otherwise see Challant-Fenis,
  Charles de)   144, 144n24
Villersexel   127n93
Villette, Michel de, Baron of Chevron   88n70,
  154, 157, 185, 194, 198, 216, 280
Villiers   262
Viret, Jérôme-Luther   152
Virieu   66, 94, 122, 127-29, 152, 158, 166, 211, 228,
  232, 274, 305
  administration of fief   268-69, 279-82,
    293, 298
Viry, Michel de, Baron of Coppet   80-81,
  147n43
Visconti di Somma, Battista   148
Visconti, Ermes   148
Visconti, Filippo Maria   158
Visconti, Francesco   151, 169
Visconti, House of   32, 153
Viseu, Isabella of   151
Vo-Ha, Paul   238
Vosges   198
Vuillet de St. Pierre, Jean   93n107, 184-85
Vulliet (official ca. 1560)   271-72
Vulliet de St. Pierre, Pierre-Hercule   186-87
Vulpe, Jehan see Clerc dit Vulpe, Jehan
Vulpin, Guillaume   155
Vyelly   274

Waldensians   86
Wales/Welsh   33, 35, 35n121, 207n162

Watteville, Jean-Jacques de, Lord of Colombier   65n60, 87n61, 235-36, 235n76, 235n79, 236n81, 259, 259n51, 262
Weapons   97, 113, 115, 157, 190, 200, 257n38, 296
Wickham, Christopher   253
Wigen, Kären   290
William of Orange   32n102, 140
Williams, Megan   32n100, 35
wine   162, 163-64, 163n145, 170, 190, 195, 257, 261, 266-67, 270, 274, 280, 304-5
Wingarten, Wolfgang von   66, 66n64, 67n68, 82n32, 236, 236n82

Worms   96
Worms, Diet of   267

Yverdon   64, 78, 205, 245n130

Zahringen dynasty   89n83
Zanolli, Orphée   126n90
Zeeland   31, 31n99, 198
Zermatt   290
Zug   80n22
Zwierlein, Cornel   222n9
Zwincker (doctor from Basel)   229n40